# Latinos in American Society

## Families and Communities in Transition

RUTH ENID ZAMBRANA

*Cornell University Press*

Ithaca and London

First published 2011 by Cornell University Press
First printing, Cornell Paperbacks, 2011
Printed in the United States of America

Library of Congress Cataloging-in-Publication Data
Zambrana, Ruth E.
  Latinos in American society : families and communities in transition / Ruth Enid Zambrana.
       p. cm.
  Includes bibliographical references and index.
  ISBN 978-0-8014-4938-3 (cloth : alk. paper)
  ISBN 978-0-8014-7657-0 (pbk. : alk. paper)
    1. Hispanic Americans—Social conditions.   2. Hispanic American families.   3. Hispanic Americans—Study and teaching (Higher)
  I. Title.
   E184.S75Z37 2011
   973'.0468—dc22                        2011000870

*I dedicate this book to past and contemporary academics and practitioners who have provided incisive and powerful scholarship to make visible the impact of social inequality on the lives of historically underrepresented Latino subgroups. Su trabajo initiated an emerging oppositional discourse in mainstream social science research. I also dedicate this book to Latino families and communities, who continue to strive, thrive, resist, overcome, and triumph in spite of exclusionary practices. Their victories offer daily inspiration.*

# Contents

# Figures and Tables

# Preface

Writing this book has allowed me to ask—and I hope answer—many questions that have been on my mind since I began my educational journey in the early 1970s. Throughout my days as a student, I was struck by the fact that the lives of Latinos in the United States and their contributions to American society were largely missing from what I learned; they were never mentioned in either my undergraduate or graduate study. Once I left school in the late 1970s, I began to conduct my own research on the experiences of Latinos, but I discovered early on that there was very little scholarship available that went beyond treating Latinos as social "others," people whose cultural ways were considered to be different from and alien to U.S. mainstream culture. So, in addition to documenting Latino experiences, I also faced the difficult task of trying to insert into the scientific and scholarly discourse a different theorizing orientation, one that better reflected what I personally knew about the experiences of Latinos in American society.

My own experience as a volunteer in mentoring programs for Latino youth, in juvenile detention centers, and in national advocacy organizations (where I often served as the facilitator for parent groups and visited community-based Latino organizations) acquainted me with proactive and knowledgeable Latino consumers and leaders. I valued the opportunity to meet with and listen to Latino parents and youth in communities from coast to coast. I participated as they discussed their dreams and frustrations with teachers, administrators, police officials, and social service workers who often made erroneous assumptions about them. I witnessed the material conditions in their communities and their lives and heard far too many stories of mistreatment, exclusion, and poor-quality services.

My personal experiences in both community and education settings provided the initial impetus to journey into the world of academic research in sociology. In 1999 when I joined the faculty at the University of Maryland,

I was asked to develop a course on U.S. Latino families that incorporated gender, race, class, and nation. I had never taught a course specifically on Latinos, although I always tried to incorporate the Latino experience into the courses I taught—bringing in whatever data were available and assigning a few articles in this area. I also had the privilege of mentoring Latino and non-Latino students who had intellectual and personal interests in exploring varying areas of Latino life in the United States. I thought I knew a lot about the area and also assumed that an overview course would not be that difficult to prepare as emerging scholarship was gaining some prominence in the scientific and scholarly social science world.

In truth I was not prepared intellectually or emotionally for the journey into the scholarship of and about Latinos. My first step was to conduct systematic literature reviews on Latino families, changing gender roles for women and men, health, education, and media representations. I was surprised and dismayed by the outcome of this search. Where, I asked, is the information about the material conditions of Latino families and how these conditions are shaped by structural barriers and institutional practices, and the ways in which these conditions influence families' hopes and dreams? Where was the Latino middle and professional class? Where were the narratives of institutional racism and mistreatment? In almost every scientific and academic discipline, discussion of Latinos was shrouded by a veil of culture, acculturation, and proposed solutions that masked the ways structural racism, discrimination, and inequity maintain Latinos as a marginalized group. I felt sad, angry, and frustrated at the persistent public scientific and scholarly presentation of Latinos as a group of foreign, marginalized, and poor people.

Unfortunately, the scholarly emphasis on the plight of Latino immigrants overshadows the reality that the majority of Latinos are U.S.–born citizens who over many generations have helped to build and inform what we now think of as American culture. Yet who was documenting these struggles and contributions? There are a number of distinguished scholars whose work focused on U.S. Latinos, but too often, I discovered, their research was hidden in book chapters, in small and sometimes obscure journals, and in reports that gathered dust on shelves. For example, a modest but important body of historical, ethnic, Chicana feminist, and LatCrit scholarship was generated in the 1970s through the 1990s that addressed racial, ethnic, and class inequality and structural inequity. Yet I observed that these theorists were rarely if ever referenced in mainstream scholarship. Absent were the Chicano/Mexican American and Puerto Rican historians and social scientists who had chronicled the "lived experiences" of Latinos and who had heralded U.S. Latino (Mexican American/Chicano/a, Puerto Rican) ethnic studies in the civil rights and post–Civil Rights era. Notably, neither historical nor contemporary (post 2000) scholars whose work challenges existing cultural deterministic paradigms are generally referenced in major policy or scholarly publications. Consequently, the critique of marginalization and racialization that pervades this scholarship has remained virtually hidden until recently. Fortunately, in the ten years that it has taken to write this book, I have seen a remarkable outpouring of scholarship that challenges the invisibility of the Latino experience and their racialized treatment. This book is meant to both draw attention and contribute to this outpouring of scholarship.

Another realization came to me when I began to teach the U.S. Latina/o courses. Students who signed up for the course came from all disciplines on campus and from various racial/ethnic and nonminority groups, and repeatedly they told me that they had not been taught anything about Latinos and wanted to know more. Who are Latinos? What is their history, their culture? Why were they missing from the curriculum, and why the negative stereotypes? Many of the Latinos who took the class were eager to learn about their heritage in a systematic way that had been absent throughout their educational careers. African Americans often said that their main reason for taking the class was that someone in their family had married a Latino/a or they had new Latino friends and wanted to know more. I was struck by these questions and even more so by the confusion and the stereotypes. It made me think that my faculty colleagues were not including Latinos as part of their disciplinary course content in such fields as business, education, sociology, political science, and public health. For a large majority of students, this class was their first encounter with academic content on Latinos. We all came away with new perspectives on Latinos, and I saw firsthand how higher education can participate in perpetuating the lack of informed knowledge about a racial or ethnic group.

Thus the writing of this book culminates a long personal and intellectual journey. In it, I build extensively on the work of other scholars, those who came before me as well as my contemporaries. In interpreting the scholarship of my predecessors and contemporaries I take full responsibility for any errors or omissions. One amazing gift of this journey has been learning that I am not alone. Many of these scholars have already made observations and drawn conclusions about racialization, stratification, and hyperculturalization and its relationship to the social location of U.S. Latinos. I made every effort to give credit to those scholars who had already provided a critique of science and scholarship that had failed to adequately include the lived experiences and material conditions of Latinos by gender, race, ethnicity, class, and nation in the continuum of human experience. I delved into areas that I was not familiar with and learned far more than I could ever have imagined.

One of my primary goals in this book is to apply the analytic lens of intersectionality to the study of ethnicity, gender, race, class (socioeconomic status), and nation. I hope to draw attention to a new discourse that takes into account how mutually constituted identities, representations, and community context implicitly and explicitly shape the lived experiences and context of inequality in which a disproportionate number of Latino families are represented. On the other hand, the book also seeks to make visible the milestones of Latino integration in U.S. society in spite of the obstacles, to deconstruct Latinidad as a negative cultural identity marker, and to reveal the heterogeneity of Latinos, especially by ethnic origin, socioeconomic status, and place. My hope is that other scholars will build on this work as I have built on the work of my predecessors to provide depth to each of the areas included and to explore other areas not included here. For example, there are areas of tremendous importance in U.S. Latino studies that represent new frontiers of inquiry such as sexual identity and LGBT studies, disability, racialization, racism, and race or color privilege (Whiteness) of Latinos that require focus and inquiry in the future.

～

As in all intellectual projects, many individuals contributed to the development of this one: to its framing and its focus. I begin with my questioning students who, throughout my career and especially in my recent classes on U.S. Latino Families, were hungry for knowledge and appreciative of what I had to offer. They motivated, encouraged, and inspired me to delve into this field even deeper and to produce scholarship that would give them an accurate and more comprehensive view of Latinos in the United States.

Another tier of inspiring and hard-working students are those who have served as graduate research assistants in the Interdisciplinary Scholars Program of the Consortium on Race, Gender and Ethnicity (CRGE) at the University of Maryland since 2000. These students identified and annotated articles for inclusion in this book as well as in our intersectional database. I acknowledge the commitment, enthusiasm, and contribution of the following graduate students: Bianca Laureano, Clare Jen, Ana M. Perez, Cristina Perez, Vanessa Lopes, Angel Love Miles, Manouchka Poinson, Anaya McMurray, Crystal Espinosa, Lynette Boswell, Sylvette Touche-Howard, Tamyka Morant, and Maria Velasquez. I am grateful for their thorough search, location, printing, and annotation of articles about U.S. Latinos that contributed to the completion of this book.

So important in this endeavor were the anonymous reviewers who challenged some of the tenets of the work and pushed me to rethink, rework, and investigate more and to explain better my theorizing. I am grateful for their encouragement, kindness, and their challenges. I also acknowledge and thank Dr. Doris Capello, who read the entire manuscript in its draft form, raising invaluable questions and providing points of clarification, direction, and feedback and Dr. Linda Burton, who guided the final development of the theorizing on Latino families in chapter 3. Reviewers, named and unnamed, helped to significantly improve this book, and I am grateful for their critique and support.

There are few words that can capture the debt of gratitude felt for the staff at CRGE. Dr. Laura Ann Logie, a graduate of the Department of Women's Studies at the University of Maryland, assisted during her graduate study and later as assistant director of CRGE. Her mastery of information gathering, including quick searches and data compilation, and her review of chapters are deeply appreciated. Her knowledge and commitment to the field of U.S. Latino Studies was repeatedly demonstrated as she skillfully managed the contents of the book. Ms. Wendy Hall has become a master in handling logistics, publication requirements, and large and small requests. Wendy has been a steady-hand, behind-the-scenes producer. Beth Douthirt-Cohen, a graduate student in the College of Education and CRGE communications coordinator, has caringly contributed to producing models and figures and to editing the manuscript. She labored through the 2010 snowstorms and did an outstanding job in editing, questioning, and discussing sections that she did not understand or that needed clarification. I thank them all sincerely for their unwavering support and commitment to the production of the final manuscript.

I am equally grateful to my initial editor, Peter Wissoker, who shepherded the book idea in its initial stages and passed it on to Peter Potter at Cornell University Press. Peter Potter has been responsive, clear yet diplomatic and supportive in his feedback as there was no time to dawdle. He wanted the book finished, but he also demanded rigor and excellence. His patience and kindness along with a firm hand and sense of humor consistently pushed the project forward, and with his thoughtful editing, he helped insert my voice. Thank you, Peter. I want to express my utmost gratitude to Susan Specter, manuscript editor, who has brought this book process to its conclusion. Susan has provided meticulous attention to the final editing process, a supportive and caring approach to unexpected hurdles and details, and a mastery of her art that has been extremely helpful and reassuring in these final stages. I also acknowledge the support of the University of Maryland Department of Women's Studies; Dr. Claire Moses (former chair), who started me on this journey by asking me to teach a U.S. Latino Families course; and current chair Dr. Bonnie Thornton Dill, who supported the intellectual project and assisted in the final editing of the preface.

Last, on the domestic front, my adult children Amad and Jahan, patient, kind, and supportive, always accommodated our time together but would continue to ask: "Are you still working on that book?" It is finally over, and I thank them for their unwavering love and support throughout all these years.

∿

Throughout this project, I became aware that an immense amount of knowledge, experience, commitment, and passion is present in the scholarly community that studies structural inequity, racialization, and marginalization among racial/ethnic groups including U.S. Latinos. This interdisciplinary scholarship and human capital must be brought together to ensure that these new findings, insights, and perspectives become fundamental building blocks in future knowledge production to create a shift in the public discourse and the American imagination so as to truly uphold our democratic values and social justice for U.S. Latinos. My scholarly goal in this book has been to make the invisible visible and to challenge the persistent and sometimes subtle claim that culture is a predictor of social inequality and determines social location. The image on the cover of this book represents the Intellectual as Worker; indeed, for many Latino and some non-Latino scholars, intellectual pursuits of U.S. Latina/o scholarship has also included the scholar as a worker for social justice and social change. In the end, it is my sincere hope that this book will shift how we think about U.S. Latinos, how we study them, and how a new discourse is imagined so that we can more fully appreciate and accurately incorporate into science and scholarship the heterogeneity and contributions of U.S. Latinos and their historical and contemporary place in the U.S. social fabric.

# Latinos in
# American Society

# 1

# Introduction

## *Why Study Latino Families?*

> Hispanics need to become an integral part of the
> movement to uncover the complex forces intensifying
> inequality, poverty, political passivity, exploitation, and
> social isolation, not only within their own ranks but in
> the United States as a whole
> —Camarillo and Bonilla 2001, 131

A ll social scientists must be prepared to explain, when asked, why their
chosen area of inquiry merits attention and research. When it comes to
the study of Latino families in the United States, this "So what?" question
looms large because Latinos are the largest racial/ethnic minority group in the
United States, and yet as a group they remain virtually invisible in the national
political agenda as citizens in the United States.[1] At the same time, the reality

---

1. For the purpose of this book, and consistent with the federal standards for racial and ethnic
data, I use the terms *Hispanic* and *Latino* interchangeably. Though often used interchangeably in
American English, Hispanic and Latino are not identical terms, and in certain contexts the choice
between them can be significant. This book uses the terms interchangeably, especially by staying
true to direct quotes and/or data in which Hispanic is almost always used in the collection of
empirical data. *Hispanic,* from the Latin word for "Spain," has the broader reference, potentially
encompassing all Spanish-speaking peoples in both hemispheres and emphasizing the common
denominator of language among communities that sometimes have little else in common. *Latino*
is a political construct that challenges hegemonic notions of a singular European Spanish ancestry.
(Rangel 1977, 3–5; Skidmore and Smith 2005, 1–10). Of the two, only *Hispanic* can be used in
referring to Spain and its history and culture; a native of Spain residing in the United States is a
Hispanic, not a Latino. Yet one cannot substitute *Latino* in the phrase "the Hispanic influence
on native Mexican cultures" without garbling the meaning (see the *American Heritage Dictionary of the English Language,* 4th ed., 2006). In the United States, survey after survey of Latinos
have found that their preferred form of identification is through their specific national origin; that
is, as Mexicans, Mexican Americans, Puerto Ricans, Hondurans, and the like (De la Garza et al.
1992; Rodriguez 2000). The basis of Latino/Hispanic identification as "others" in U.S. society
is through a nationalism and/or ethnicity grounded in their country of origin, whether born
there or not. This creates the constant potential for transnational identities fed by very active international circular migrations, supporting such broad and (to many) obscure notions as cultural

is that Latino families are seriously affected by federal and state policy because they are deeply embedded in the structures of inequality and subordination.

Undertaking the study of families within this ethnic group presents special challenges for a few reasons. First and foremost, data collection in all states and the District of Columbia did not occur for Latinos until 1997, and we still face many difficulties interpreting the data due to limited analyses by subgroup, gender, and socioeconomic status (Rodriguez 2000; Zambrana and Carter-Pokras 2001). In addition, research on Latinos has traditionally suffered from an inherently Eurocentric perspective that has resulted in fundamental misunderstandings of how Latino families are structured and operate from within. Moreover, researchers have often ignored the powerful impact of historical and structural factors that shape the lives of the Latino community. One must also account for the factors that contribute to a distinct heterogeneity of Latino family processes. These factors include differences associated with national origin, socioeconomic status in country of birth, racial phenotype, educational attainment of family of origin, and the access to or denial of social capital due to parental education attainment. Among U.S. born and immigrant Latino populations one must also consider historical modes of incorporation and discriminatory immigration policies and practices, which contribute to a very different life experience. For these groups, family formation, intergenerational differences, and options and opportunities available to members of Latino families differ by socioeconomic status, nativity and subgroup (Hernandez 2009; Lansford et al. 2007; Telles and Ortiz 2008).

Mexican Americans and Puerto Ricans constitute the majority of the Latino population. Emerging Latino subgroups from the 1960s to the present include Cubans (1960s) and Central Americans and South Americans, who have steadily increased in numbers since the 1970s (Dorrington et al. 1989; Gonzalez 2000; Organista 2007). The influx of Spanish-speaking ethnic subgroups over the last three decades has yielded a number of interesting debates regarding differences and similarities among the groups. In the intellectual and political discourse, I have seen attempts to broaden the empirical lens to better explain how Latinos fit within the existing social structure and class hierarchy of the United States, but until recently little attention has been devoted to examining the sociopolitical and structural factors that keep poverty, racial discrimination, and limited opportunity firmly in place among Latino groups (Almaguer 1994; Oboler 2006; Telles and Ortiz 2008). Because the

---

citizenship (Flores and Benmayor 1997; Oboler 2006) and other postcolonialist perspectives (Soja 1996). Last, an effort to use nonsexist language has included the use of *Latina/o* to acknowledge both female and male groups. *Latina* usually refers to feminine, while *Latino* is usually a masculine form. For the sake of simplicity, *Latino* will be used throughout when referring to the total population and is inclusive of both male and female.

data are not commonly situated in the political context of resource allocation (as it affects employment and educational opportunities, for instance), the reasons for disparities in educational, income, and employment opportunities and their relationship to family processes and well-being remain misunderstood and misrepresented.

Fortunately, we have seen a growing body of scholarly research in recent years that has begun to fill the void in our understanding of the lives and daily experiences of the Latino population. This research is emerging predominantly from interdisciplinary fields such as Chicano studies, U.S. Latino studies, family studies, and women's studies. Taken as a whole these scholarly orientations are enabling us to see the true heterogeneity that exists within and across subgroups of Latinos by citizenship, mode of historical incorporation, and socioeconomic status. The purpose of this book is to synthesize this growing body of scholarship conducted on Latinos by national origin, age, gender, and socioeconomic status or position (SES or SEP)[2] (education and income), focusing specifically on how these factors have shaped family processes and family well-being. I analyze the multicausal factors that contribute to the disproportionate burden of low educational attainment, high residential segregation, and high morbidity and mortality among Latinos through the life course. I also examine how these factors come together and result in economic disadvantage while contributing to the widespread perception of Latinos as poor and unsuccessful.

An important feature of the book is the nuanced approach it takes to the relationship between ethnicity and culture. Cultures transform as ethnic groups are shaped by factors including immigrant status on arrival, length of time in the United States, increased education and dominant perceptions and ideology of the racial and ethnic group by the host culture. Culture is also interpreted and informed by racial phenotype and educational and economic resources. In assessing the study of Latino families, the unmeasured factors or the assumptions inherent in interpreting cultural behaviors require interrogation. Thus culture is only one of the multiple dimensions that shape family outcomes, and

---

2. I use socioeconomic position (SEP) and socioeconomic status (SES) interchangeably throughout this book. Socioeconomic position (SEP) is a commonly used concept and is usually measured by completed years of schooling. Galobardes et al. (2006) state, "Although researchers have an intuitive sense of what SEP means, the numerous ways of measurement indicate the complexity of the construct. 'Socioeconomic position' refers to the social and economic factors that influence what positions individuals or groups hold within the structure of a society and encompasses concepts with different historical and disciplinary origins. A variety of other terms, such as social class, social stratification, social or socioeconomic status (SES), are often used interchangeably despite their different theoretical bases and, therefore, interpretations." These issues have been discussed in detail by Krieger et al. 1997. See also Galobardes et al. 2006; Lynch and Kaplan 2000; Liberatos et al. 1988; Williams 1990; Williams and Collins 1995.

it is important to consider its influence in the context of historical, economic, political, structural, and representational factors.

### Intersectional Lens: Theoretical Assumptions

Any study of minority groups in the United States must consider multiple dimensions of inequality. Focusing solely on race/ethnicity, class, gender, or nationality (nation of origin) is insufficient. It must also explore relations of domination and subordination in the structural arrangements that determine the distribution of resources and the availability of services. For this reason, I have adopted in this book an intersectional approach to examine the experiences of Latino families, women, children, and youth. As an analytic tool, intersectionality has proved to be extremely useful for studying the experiences of minority groups because it acknowledges the many dimensions of inequality and seeks to understand how they are interrelated and how they shape and influence one another. It also requires us to think in complex and nuanced ways about identity and challenges us to look at the points of cohesion and fracture *within* ethnic groups as well as those *between* ethnic groups and the dominant group culture (Dill and Zambrana 2009).

Intersectionality has a set of foundational claims and organizing principles for understanding social inequality and particularly the social location of subordinate groups. Drawing on Critical Race Theory (CRT),[3] it begins with the basic premise that race is a social construction and that racism is widespread, systematic, and institutionalized. Moreover, traditional laws and values are seen as "vessels of racial subordination." Therefore, the lived experiences of racial/ethnic groups can be understood only in the context of institutionalized patterns of unequal control over the distribution of a society's valued goods and resources (such as land, property, money, employment, education, health care, and housing).

An intersectional approach challenges traditional modes of knowledge production in the United States by taking into account the full range of historical and social experiences of individuals within minority groups with respect to class, gender, sexuality, and race. For example, the generalized social problem of Latino girls having high pregnancy rates belies differences by SES and intragroup and intergroup differences. Since most data are collected on individuals of Mexican origin and most studies are conducted in low-income Mexican-origin communities, Latino girls as a whole become maligned as socially irresponsible.

---

3. Critical Race Theory (CRT) draws from critical legal studies, feminist or gender studies, the American civil rights tradition, and nationalist movements that began in 1989. CRT can be considered a progressive movement in the law and legal education that seeks to secure the rights of people of color. For a history and discussion of this legal theory, see Bell 1980; Crenshaw 2002; Delgado and Stefancic 2001. Its basic theoretical organizing tenets have been infused into intersectional theory, Latina/Latino Critical Theory (LatCrit), and Asian Pacific American critical race theory.

The intersectional lens contextualizes the experiences of low-income, young Mexican-origin girls within a community context where schooling resources limit their options; for example, by not providing sex education and restricting access to such opportunities as after-school academic programs.

An intersectional approach also recognizes the role played by economic and social positioning of groups within society along with racialized institutional practices that are strongly linked with family and child well-being. For example, the location of educational and health services with respect to low-income Latino communities determines access to quality education and health care and is a major factor affecting the well-being of Latino women, children, and families. An intersectional approach takes into account the distribution of public educational and health resources in terms of historical patterns and political considerations, which in turn makes it possible to see that the concentration of wealth and public resources in middle- and upper-income communities and the prioritization of public policies such as tax cuts and college-level financial aid are more likely to benefit those communities.

Intersectional analysis, therefore, enables us to see the direct impact of the unequal distribution of society's goods and resources on the development of low-income Latino communities. Examining the interaction of poverty with race/ethnicity and gender demonstrates that these factors, taken together, have a disproportionately negative effect on Latino women (Latinas) and result in detrimental health consequences. Low-income Mexican American and Puerto Rican women, historically underserved groups, experience poorer physical and mental health status, suffer with undetected medical conditions longer, are less likely to have health insurance coverage, and have less access to preventive and curative services than the majority population (Aquirre-Molina et al. 2003; National Research Council, 2002; see chap. 7). Structural inequities are important dimensions when examining questions of social and economic justice, both to reveal the sources of the social and economic inequality among Latino groups and to identify ways to redress them (see, e.g., Cammarota 2007).

Race, ethnicity, class, and community context matter; they are all determinants of access to *social capital*—that is, resources that improve educational, economic, and social position in society. For instance, one measure of social capital within a community is the quality of its neighborhood schools (do they have strong libraries, computer resources, and advance placement courses?), which has a direct bearing on entry into higher education and future economic and employment opportunities. Studies have found that when Latinos are concentrated in segregated or hypersegregated communities, their access to such resources declines dramatically relative to other communities (Acevedo-Garcia 2000; Kumashiro 2008; Noguera 2003).

In addition to structural, political, historical, and locational factors, intersectional analysis emphasizes the importance of representation—the ways social groups and individuals are viewed and depicted in the society at large and the expectations associated with these depictions (Chin and Humikowskie 2002; Davila 2001; Zambrana et al. 1987). Stereotypes that all Latinos are immigrants, do not speak English, have too many children, and have come to the United States to get government handouts affect the discriminatory way in which public policies are designed and implemented to decrease their access to public resources (Silliman et al. 2004, 216). We have seen the effects of this dynamic in the early twenty-first century with the resurgence of xenophobia directed especially at Mexican immigrants, and this is despite the fact that diversity and color-blindness are heralded as markers of a democratic society.

The role that non–English-language proficiency plays in the formation of a negative portrayal of Latinos and not for other language minority groups is worthy of exploration for it can tell us much about a host society's receptivity, perceptions, and the integration of immigrant groups into the host society. For example, English-language proficiency and citizenship status data reveal that 70 percent of Latinos speak English "well" to "very well" and that only 39 percent of Latinos are immigrants, with about half of those residing in the country for more than ten years (see chapter 2). Understanding the origins of these portrayals, as well as the multiple and simultaneous factors that contribute to negative perceptions of Latinos as a group, is a vital step toward reducing inequality.

Individual and group identity are complex—influenced and shaped not simply by race, class, ethnicity, gender, sexual orientation and identity, physical dis/abilities, or national origin but by the confluence of all of those characteristics. Nevertheless, in a hierarchically organized society, some statuses become more important than others at any given historical moment and in specific geographic locations. Within groups there is far greater diversity than appears when, for analytic purposes (e.g., censuses), people are classified with a single term. For instance, the meaning of the term *Latina*—as a gendered, ethnic, and racial construct—varies depending on the social context in which it is employed and the political meanings associated with its usage. The term *Latino/Latina* emerged as a direct counterpoint to the term *Hispanic*. It challenged the privileging of Spanish or Hispano lineage over the other indigenous and African lineages of Spanish-speaking individuals in the United States. The renaming was important in that it drew attention to the roots of Latino/a ethnic/cultural identity, raising awareness of the multiple lineages and histories of Spanish-speaking people in the United States, particularly historically underrepresented groups and more recent Caribbean immigrants. As Lourdes Echazabal-Martinez (1998, 21) has noted, "Mestizaje, the process of interracial and/or intercultural mixing, is a foundational theme in the Americas, particularly those areas colonized by the Spanish and Portuguese. Mestizaje underscored the affirmation of cultural identity as constituted by national character."

In the United States Latinos have historically been classified as White, although they resist simple racial categorization (Rodriguez 2000). Since the 1980s Latinos have been provided the opportunity to identify both ethnic and racial categories in census reporting, but this has not solved the problem.[4] In the 2000 Census 48 percent of Latinos described themselves as White, 2 percent as Blacks, 6 percent as mixed, and 42 percent as "other." The resistance to racial categorization obscures the fact that Latinos have been classified as White but historically perceived as people of color and thus they have been economically and socially marginalized. The situation faced by certain Latino groups is even more complicated. Caribbean immigrants and migrants confront a two-tiered division of racialized identity in the United States between Whites and non-Whites derived from the rule of *hypodescent*—the assignment of the offspring of mixed races to the subordinate group. According to Jorge Duany (1998), "Caribbean societies tend to be stratified in terms of both class status and color gradations. Phenotype and social status rather than biological descent define a person's racial identity, especially in the Spanish-speaking countries" (148). Therefore the reconstruction of one's racial and social status and cultural identity by the host society can generate significant social and psychological tensions within and across these groups.

All of this points to the fact that the term *Latino* needs to be further examined and discussed because its underlying political discourse is not largely understood. Homogenizing all Latinos/as into one category forecloses the discourse on national identity and overlooks the effects of the intersection of gender, race, ethnic subgroup, and SES on Latino social location. Identity for foreign-born Latinos is complicated by differences in national origin, citizenship status, and class (in both the sending and host countries), as well as race and ethnicity. In other words, it is important to look beyond how the public discourse represents negative differences in certain ethnic groups, such as Mexican-origin people, and understand why this group gets the most attention in the social science literature and the media. An intersectional approach forces

---

4. The 2010 questionnaire lists fifteen racial categories, as well as places to write in specific races not listed on the form. The 2010 Census continues the option first introduced in the 2000 Census for respondents to choose more than one race. Since the 1970 Census, the questionnaire has asked U.S. residents whether they are of Hispanic origin and, if so, which broad Hispanic group they identify with. Hispanic origin is considered separately from race in the Census—and Hispanics may identify with any race. In this book, *White* may be used interchangeably with *non-Hispanic White* (NHW) who self report within these two categories. *Black* will be used to refer to individuals who self-report as *non-Hispanic Black* (NHB) or African American or Negro and specific designations such as Black Caribbean are used when appropriate as part of original research. For further information on racial and ethnic categories, see U.S. Census Bureau, *The 2010 Census Questionnaire: Informational Copy* (January 2009), http://2010.census.gov/2010census/pdf/2010_Questionnaire_Info_Copy.pdf.

us to acknowledge these differences, which in turn enables us to examine and understand these differences.

Any discussion of Latino groups in the United States must confront the issue of naming and categorization: Hispanic or Latino? The very question often draws an impassioned response, which in turn can lead to unproductive debates over how Hispanics/Latinos got here in the first place. The historical incorporation of Latinos into the American society has been one of granting citizenship but not granting equal access to citizenship rights (Obler 2006). The struggles of Mexican American people in the United States are well documented, albeit not necessarily taught with great depth or profundity in our educational system. The history of Puerto Ricans as a conquered colonial people is even less spoken about, even though it is well documented. Citizenship for U.S.-born Latinos, namely Mexican Americans and Puerto Ricans, has not provided equal protection under the law (for example see Johnson 1995). In effect citizenship rights have been implemented as an earned privilege rather than a right. Using the term *Latino* as a political category impedes the accurate measurement of structural and political factors such as institutional racism, and the data serve only a limited purpose in advancing knowledge on family processes and gender within and across Latino subgroups.

In summary, an intersectional lens is a critical, interdisciplinary tool used by social scientists to interrogate racial, ethnic, and gender disparities and to contest the ways those disparities are often explained as linear rather than multifaceted. Equally important, an intersectional lens envisions knowledge production as a tool to improve the lives of the people we study and to unveil those structures that require change and remediation. This information can inform advocacy efforts and public policy; for example, in school systems. Furthermore, the production of knowledge cannot occur in a vacuum. A central tenet of intersectionality is the comparative approach both within and across U.S. racial and ethnic groups as a way of providing a fuller understanding of the nature of dominance, subordination, and inequality (Dill and Zambrana 2009, 2). For example, new survey data from different sources permit intragroup comparison of Latinos by national origin and foreign-born versus U.S.–born that helps to disrupt the generalized notion that all Latinos fit the stereotype of poor, non–English-speaking aliens. Using an intersectional lens we can identify these differences and dispel stereotypes so as to produce knowledge and promote public policy solutions to decrease inequality in American society.

## Organization of the Book

My goal in this book is to explore the multiple intersecting social factors that influence Latino family processes and social location. To do this I survey and synthesize the wealth of work on Latinos by subgroup, citizenship status, gender, and developmental life course within the last two decades. In the process, I bring multiple disciplinary voices into conversation with each other and systematically examine the research as part of a larger set of issues that include racialization, inequality versus inequity, and neutrality versus bias. I include examples of studies from the major social science disciplines including sociology, psychology, media and communication, and education as well as interdisciplinary fields including women's studies, racial/ethnic studies, public health, family studies, and social work. Analyses of major thematic approaches to Latino ethnicity employing systematic techniques are used to assess use of definitions and characteristics of Latino population under study, methods used, results and interpretation of data, and gaps in information and implications.

Chapter 2 presents the basic demographic data, showing that Latinos are a diverse and growing population. I integrate and elaborate on the major demographic social, educational, and occupational indicators by national origin to illustrate the disadvantage incurred by Latino subgroups as a result of the intersection of race, ethnicity, and national origin. I present the sociodemographic data by national origin, gender, geographic distribution, citizenship status, and language use, including trend data when available. I describe specific immigration patterns by country of origin as well as information in states of Latino concentration. Projections are included as Latinos represent the largest racial/ethnic minority group in the United States, and, when available, data are comparative with non-Hispanic Black (NHB), non-Hispanic White (NHW), Asian, and by Latino subgroup. Ultimately, chapter 2 reveals, through data, that Latinos are not a homogeneous racial and ethnic group. For example, significant differences exist in levels of socioeconomic status; namely, educational achievement by national origin. As a group, those individuals who self-report as Latino constitute a mixture of European, indigenous, American Indian, and African backgrounds. Despite the growth in and the diversity of this significant minority group, Latinos are socially, economically, and educationally underrepresented in all major levels of the U.S. infrastructure. I also argue that there are racial and ethnic distinctions in the perception of Latino subgroups and these distinctions shape the material conditions of their lives. These data serve to contest the representativeness of empirical works that have ignored key historical, demographic, and socioeconomic indicators while claiming to advance our knowledge of Latino subgroups in the United States.

Chapter 3 synthesizes the major paradigms used in the social sciences including examples of family studies to understand variation in patterns of family structure and functioning. I describe selected empirical studies conducted in the multiple domains of family processes, such as parent-child communication, mothering and parenting, and gender-role socialization in Latino families. I focus on the themes and the context used or omitted to explore knowledge production on the dynamics of Latino family processes in the United States.

The studies are critically reviewed to assess their contributions to furthering our knowledge of Latino family processes by subgroup and the multiple factors that are associated with particular family patterns in the United States. The scholarship and voices of Latino critical legal theorists, gender theorists, and racial and ethnic theorists are also included to assess different perspectives on the factors associated with the material conditions and social location of Latino families in American society.

Little has been written about the heterogeneity of Latino families by socioeconomic status (SES), subgroup, family structure, and gender role attitudes and behaviors. I review the research to determine if there are themes and differences that distinguish Latino family processes from non-Latino families by SES and to identify similarities with non-Latino families. I critique culturally driven models and seek to disrupt conventional, traditional models that produce knowledge on essentialized Latino families. My intent is to deconstruct culture as a negative Latino identity marker and reframe culture as an ethnic asset that contributes to the group strengths but does not contribute to the production of inequality. I propose an intersectional model in the study of Latino families and communities that can provide different ways of thinking and theorizing on the multiple social locations of Latina/os and explore ways to more profoundly understand why negative perceptions of Latinos in the American public imagination persist.

Chapter 4 presents data on the impact of parental involvement, SES, and school structure on Latino educational achievement. A significant amount of work has been conducted in the field of education and much of it has excluded historical, social, and economic factors in their analyses. I challenge existing frameworks that continue to perceive parents and culture as the primary reasons for educational failure often excluding factors such as institutional racism and low SES that hinder active parental participation in a child's education. Studies that examine the role of parents in education are reviewed as well as factors that contribute to the engagement or disengagement of students in the educational pipeline from prekindergarten through twelfth grade. The experiences of boys and girls reveal different outcomes particularly in the areas of education, health, and juvenile and criminal justice. Therefore, chapters 5 and 6 are dedicated to examining the lived experiences of Latino girls and boys.

Chapter 5 focuses on Latina adolescents from a developmental life course perspective with analyses of gender roles, schooling, and motherhood at an early age. Specific demographic and educational profiles are included, and comparisons are made with other racial and ethnic girls and Latino boys. Examples of studies on school leaving, gender role performance, motherhood, and gender identity are examined using an intersectional perspective. New emerging scholarship expands the understanding of the factors such as neighborhood context that shape the material conditions and life options of predominantly low-income Mexican American girls and women. Not unexpectedly barriers to upward mobility are shaped by the lived experiences and material conditions of adolescence, and barriers to the opportunity structure in their youth limit women's strategies for success and enhanced life options.

Chapter 6 discusses males from a developmental life course perspective. Significant research has been conducted in the last ten years on behavioral risk factors among young adolescent males. I review studies on changing gender roles, schooling, employment, fathering, family roles and relationships, and the social construction of masculinity. I interrogate the traditional cultural scripts that have framed the study of Latino boys and men, predominantly Mexican American, absent of the context of SEP, negative representations, and marginalization of Latino males. Emerging scholarship is presented that contextualizes the lives and life options of Latino males within the context of a racialized and inequitable opportunity structure.

Chapter 7 provides an overview of physical and mental well-being indicators among Latino children, adolescents, women, and men. A critique of the Hispanic epidemiologic paradox is proffered based on new data by Latino subgroup, gender, and SES. Extensive health data has been generated that masks differences by Latino subgroups or reports only on Mexican-origin groups. Health data like other empirical areas of inquiry are embedded in a culturally driven framework of acculturation. Powerful critiques have surfaced regarding the scientific rigor of health findings, since most studies generalize findings of low-income Mexican—immigrant samples to *all* Latinos. Factors associated with health conditions and the potential impact on family health are discussed. I draw conclusions from consensual findings on social and economic determinants of health that move beyond culture-driven explanations.

Chapter 8 examines public systems as sites of the reproduction of inequality. The major argument is that public systems act as gatekeepers rather than safety nets for historically underrepresented racial and ethnic minority groups. Data are presented on poverty rates by race and ethnicity and access to and use of public benefits intended to enhance opportunity for economic self-sufficiency. Findings show that public systems experience a continuous lack of resources to help vulnerable populations who need it most. These systems differentially allocate resources based on race and ethnicity—and are not designed to provide the skills and resources needed to escape poverty. Persistent documentation of discriminatory patterns within public systems, such as child welfare, public assistance, education, housing, health, and juvenile justice and correctional systems that privilege Whites over Blacks and Latinos exists. I argue that poor, racialized groups are more likely to interface with multiple public service systems through the life course. Social science research that omits measures of neighborhood conditions and institutional practices, such as zero tolerance policies in schools, produce distorted information on Latinos as a "culturally deviant" group.

Chapter 9 provides an overview of the media and social science representations and their role in maintaining and promoting the discourse on Latino identity as a homogeneous, foreign group. Brief analyses of the images and representations of Latinos in mainstream channels of communication in the United States illuminate the underlying dynamic that has persisted in dismissing the contributions of U.S. Latinos, presenting negative images, and a persistent cultural production of Latinos as an inferior, singular ethnic entity. Interrogating these stereotypic representations challenges the essentializing of U.S. Latino groups in terms of intergenerational differences in values and behaviors, wealth and rates of home ownership, diasporic movements, and voting participation rates. These trends refute the discourse on Latinos as a static, unacculturated citizen group.

The last chapter, "Capturing the Lives of Latinos in the United States: Advancing the Production of Critical Social Science Knowledge" summarizes major findings and draws on existing work to propose a set of theorizing conclusions for future use in studies on Latinos. I also present areas of intellectual gaps that require more research. Research precautions are proffered for better inclusion of critical factors that differentially affect family processes and the dynamic changes in normative family patterns and gender role performance that are taking place. I also encourage the conduct of both intergenerational family research and within group research by SEP and type of family structure to extend the boundaries of knowledge production.

In summary, the predominant conceptual model embraced for understanding Latinos (U.S.–born or recent immigrant) has been a culturally driven explanatory framework that more often than not omits differences by nation, history, SES, ethnicity, and race. I aim to interrogate the narrow frameworks that have yielded the hyperculturalization of the Latino experience in the United States in order to propose a more comprehensive and critical perspective for the study of predominantly U.S.–born Latinos.[5]

The mutually constituted identity markers of race, SES, gender, and nativity, associated with structural inequality matter in the lived experiences of Latinos, and these assumptions must be explicit and not ignored. Notably,

---

5. Immigration studies are prolific in the study of immigrants as a homogeneous category and the study of the impact of Mexican immigration on the social order in the United States. The current obsession with Mexican immigration is not a new phenomenon but reflects the cyclical xenophobia in the United States regarding the influx of Mexican nationals and the racialized and targeted policies against this Latino subgroup. In this book, I include foreign-born Latino data in comparison to native-born groups to assess differences and similarities and to identify racialized and discriminatory institutional practices; however, I do not address processes of adaptation. For additional information on immigrants and Mexican immigration, see Chavez 2001, 2008; Eckstein 2009; Foner 2005; Hondagneu-Sotelo, 1994, 2003; Suro 1998; Portes 2000, 2007; Portes and Rumbaut 2006).

I cover a selected body of work as research on U.S. Latinos and immigrant Latinos has proliferated in the last two decades. The included works drawing predominantly from the social sciences illustrate how a narrow lens can produce knowledge that can be interpreted as a particular ethnic group or culture having inherent deficits. Yet I recognize that scientific conventional models represent the thinking of the dominant culture within the scientific community. These models have served to shape research, and thus determine who is published in mainstream science and who is not. In effect the critique is of the research, including my own, and the goal is to challenge the conventionality of these research approaches to promote a different way of thinking that captures the multilevel set of historical and social factors that are associated with Latino social location, family processes, gender roles, and community context.

# 2

# Demographic Trends

*Past, Present, and Future*

> Latinos are constructing their vision of society,
> claiming their rights and entitlements based on their
> daily cultural practices and in the process, recreating
> America.
> —Flores and Benmayor 1997, xi

L atinos currently number 41.3 million people, or 15 percent of the total
U.S. population, and are the largest racial/ethnic group in the country.
The Hispanic population of the United States is projected to grow to 132.8
million by July 1, 2050, and will constitute 30 percent of the nation's population. Latinos may be of any race and have diversity even within their own
ethnic identity and heritage.

Despite their growing numbers and influence within American society, Latinos have not received extensive national attention until recently, most notably
during the 2008 presidential campaign. Historical accounts and descriptions of
Latinos abound in the literature and in government reports as well as in social
science research.[1] Yet few high schools, colleges, or universities have stand-alone
courses devoted to Latinos nor do they typically include Latinos as a comparative group to understand demographic trends. Thus in many ways Latinos as
a national, heterogeneous demographic, and predominantly citizen group are
not a visible part of the American public imagination. In this chapter, therefore,
I review the data on Latinos, drawing attention to the sociodemographic indicators by national origin and gender, geographic distribution, immigration patterns and status, nativity (foreign-born vs. U.S.–born), citizenship status, and
language use.[2] As much as is possible I describe specific immigration patterns by

1. For recent government reports and empirical social science research, see Tienda and Mitchell 2006; Organista 2007; Gonzalez 2000.
2. A cautionary note regarding data sources and potential data inconsistencies: Many sources
are used to present data, including U.S. Census Bureau data conducted by the federal government,

country of origin as well as state information by Latino concentration. Data are comparative with non-Hispanic Black (NHB), non-Hispanic White (NHW), and Asian[3] and by Latino subgroup when available to ensure insertion of Latino groups as part of the American social and political landscape.

"Hispanics," as Latinos are most commonly known, are foundational to the fabric of American society. They were not an officially recognized population until 1976 as a result of the passage of Public Law 94–311 and the federal standards for the collection of racial and ethnic data by the Office of Management and Budget (OMB) Directive No. 15 in 1978[4] (del Pinal 1996; Zambrana and Carter-Pokras 2001). In 1980 Hispanics were officially counted for the first time not as an aggregate White category but as a distinct racial/ethnic group. The push to disaggregate the data by Hispanic subgroups was led by Latino leaders who believed that specific information on each subgroup could provide some legitimacy for claims to public resources and new avenues of economic opportunity. They argued that the development of a political voice by historically underrepresented groups, especially Mexican Americans and Puerto Ricans, who had similar patterns of experiences based on their racial and ethnic ancestry, was important since limited representation of their concerns at the national level kept them largely invisible. Moreover, they saw it as important to reaffirm these groups as separate American racial/ethnic citizen groups distinct

---

studies conducted by researchers, and studies conducted by nonprofit organizations such as the Pew Hispanic Center. These studies may represent different cohorts and different years and may not be consistent. Other limitations of data sources: Data may still be reported only for Latino/Hispanics as an aggregate, and other studies may report data only for Latino immigrants without indicating country of origin.

3. An excellent source on demographic information for Asians can be found at U.S. Census Bureau 2007. The American Community Survey (ACS) estimated the number of Asians to be 13.5 million, or 4.7 percent of the U.S. household population. The number of individuals who reported Asian as their only race was 12.1 million, or 4.2 percent of the population. About another 1.4 million reported their race as Asian and one or more other races, including 882,000 people who reported their race as Asian *and* White. The Asian-alone-or-in combination population included 328,000 Hispanics, and the Asian-alone population included 142,000 Hispanics. People who reported one or more Asian groups on the ACS question on race, such as Asian Indian or Japanese are included as Asians. Among Asians, Chinese (excluding those of Taiwanese origin) were the largest group in the United States, with a population of 2.8 million, or 23 percent of the Asian-alone population. Asian Indians were the second-largest group, with a population of 2.2 million, or 19 percent of the Asian-alone population. Filipinos were the third-largest group, with a population of 2.1 million, or 18 percent of the population. These three groups—Chinese, Asian Indians, and Filipinos—accounted for about 60 percent of the Asian population. Other sizable populations included 1.3 million Vietnamese and 1.3 million Koreans. More than two-thirds of Asians were U.S. citizens, either through birth (about 33 percent) or naturalization (about 37 percent).

4. See *Joint resolution relating to the publication of economic and social statistics for Americans of Spanish origin or descent,* Public law 94-311, 94th Cong. (June 16, 1976); Office of Management and Budget, Directive 15: Race and Ethnic standards for federal statistics and administrative reporting, in *Statistical Policy Handbook* (Washington, DC: U.S. Department of Commerce, 1978).

from European and Anglo Americans to underscore their historical treatment and yet invisible contributions to U.S. society.

As of 2000 the terms *Latino* and *Hispanic* have been used together or interchangeably in many data-collection forms to refer to persons who lived in, became part of through conquest, or came to the United States from regions and countries that share a cultural heritage with the Spanish conquerors.[5] The term Hispanic was devised by the Census Bureau to identify "a person of Mexican, Puerto Rican, Cuban, Central or South American or other Spanish culture or origin, regardless of race." The definition has major flaws. One is that Mexican-origin peoples were in North America prior to its founding by Europeans and its naming as the United States of America. Second, the emphasis on Spanish culture erases the influences of indigenous, African, and other European cultures in defining the current "Latino culture" in the United States. Thus preference for a particular identity label, Hispanic or Latino, reflects a political and social consciousness of the meaning and implications of each term. Identity as Latino or Hispanic is left to the individual to self-report and therefore it can change with generations, historical moments in time, and political identity. Some argue that the term Latino has become a negative identity marker that contributes to the social location and persistent negative perceptions of Latinos in the United States.

Contemporary Latino communities are a complex mix of native-born and immigrant families. The specific social and cultural influences found in a particular community reflect the dominant historical settlement patterns of the area as well as more recent demographic shifts by geographic region. For example, the Southwest is home to a predominantly Mexican-origin population that is dominated by people of mixed Indian and Spanish heritage. Many of these communities predate the earliest European settlements in the eastern United States. The New York/New Jersey area is home to people who migrated to the Eastern seaboard from the Caribbean basin more than a century ago (around the same time as the great Irish, Italian, and Jewish immigration from Europe), including people who came from the Dominican Republic, Cuba, and the U.S. territory of Puerto Rico. As Edna Acosta-Belén and Carlos Santiago (1998) noted, a *colonia hispana* of intellectuals was a vital

---

5. Latin America is made up of around twenty nations that have different histories, traditions, constitutions, backgrounds, and culture. Latin America can be subdivided into several subregions based on geography, politics, demographics, and culture; some subregions are North America, Central America, the Caribbean, the Southern Cone, and Andean states. In one sense, *Latin America* refers to those territories in the Americas where the Spanish or Portuguese languages prevail: Mexico, most of Central and South America, and the Caribbean (Cuba, the Dominican Republic, and Puerto Rico). *Latin America,* therefore, is defined as all those parts of the Americas that were once part of the Spanish and Portuguese Empires.Rangel 1977, 3–5; Skidmore and Smith 2005, 1–10.

part of Latino life in New York and other major U.S. cities as early as the late nineteenth century. Their work more generally has uncovered many of the important contributions that Latinos have made to American history, offering invaluable "glimpses into the everyday life of the diverse Latino communities at different historical periods" (34).

The long and varied history of Latino groups in American society has been well documented by historians and social scientists. There are accounts of conquest, subjugation, and marginalization as well as accounts of the long and continuing struggle for incorporation (see, e.g., Almaguer 1994; Acuña 2007; Barrera 1979). Kurt Organista (2007) provides an in-depth historical account of Latino citizens and the more recent waves of Latino immigrants, and work such as that by Victoria-Maria MacDonald (2001) on Mexican Americans in Texas shows historical patterns of subordination and unequal treatment faced by specific cultural citizenship communities.

These latter works exemplify an important approach used by social scientists for theorizing about Latino families called Critical Race Theory that proposes a method of analysis that incorporates a legal and historical dimension into the interpretation of social science data. Such an approach is important for revealing persistent patterns of low socioeconomic status of Latino subgroups in comparison to other European groups or other Latino groups. For instance, it can bring to the fore distinct differences between Mexican Americans and Puerto Ricans and other immigrant groups associated with mode of incorporation into the United States; for example, citizenship by conquest in contrast to voluntary immigration or political refugees, visas for professionals, and surplus low-skilled labor force needs such as Mexican-origin workers.[6]

Latinos represent over twenty Spanish-speaking countries, with significant populations in over twenty other countries. Latinos represent multiple cultural formations that are a result of a blend of European, indigenous, American Indian, and African backgrounds and many religious sects. Further significant differences exist in educational attainment, race, and national origin. These differences have powerfully shaped how historically the dominant culture has perceived who Latinos are. In turn these perceptions have shaped the legal and institutional practices that are significant determinants of the material conditions of Latino families and communities. It is only in the last decade that differences between and among Latinos have been truly acknowledged and recognized. However, most of the mainstream research has looked at Latinos as one cultural group with a focus on low-income Mexican-origin and Puerto Rican families and communities.

---

6. For an excellent study on intergenerational Mexican-origin groups, see Telles and Ortiz 2008.

## Latino Immigration and Incorporation

Mexican Americans have been in the United States for multiple generations as U.S. citizens. Puerto Ricans have been citizens since 1917, and Cubans were granted refugee status and citizenship under the 1966 Cuban Adjustment Act.[7] In this section I provide a brief account of the historical incorporation of these three major Latino subgroups in the United States.

### Mexicans

Americans of Mexican descent resided in the Southwest long before the founding of the United States. As the United States expanded westward in the nineteenth century, Mexican Americans found work on the railroads, mines, and farms as well as in other industries. By 1900 their number had reached about 500,000 (Sáenz 2005). As each wave of Mexican immigrants arrived, they faced widespread discrimination, which affected their attempts to establish stable communities and labor and religious organizations (Acuña 2003). During the early 1990s a recession in California severely diminished the need for a surplus labor force, which adversely affected Mexican Americans and the immigrant labor force. Resulting anti-immigrant sentiments served to racialize public policies such as the passage of Proposition 187 in California, which denied undocumented immigrants public social services and fueled witch hunts as undocumented immigrants were reported to the Immigration and Naturalization Service (INS) (Johnson 1995; Vásquez et al. 2008).

### Puerto Ricans

Puerto Rico became a possession of the United States at the conclusion of the Spanish-American War in 1898, beginning years of military rule by the United States with its officials, including the governor, appointed by the U.S. President. In 1917, the Jones Act granted Puerto Ricans American citizenship. New York became the primary state that Puerto Rican immigrants settled in, and by 1920 approximately 41,000 Puerto Ricans resided there (Acuña 2003; Laó-Montes and Dávila 2001). Today the political status of Puerto Rico is that of a commonwealth, and though there remains some autonomy, most Puerto Rican affairs have been controlled by U.S. federal agencies since 1952 (Vélez 2008), with most colonial policies based on paternalistic and prejudiced views of the Puerto Rican people, aimed at "Americanizing" the island (Acosta-Belén and Santiago

---

7. See Fact Sheet on the Cuban Adjustment Act (Public Law 89-732), http://www.state.gov/www/regions/wha/cuba/cuba_adjustment_act.html. Subsequent waves of Cubans who were not all of White race and/or of similar educational background may have had different experiences and not experienced the same integration into U.S. society as first wave Cubans did in 1959. This very brief history does not adequately address all waves of Cuban settlement in U.S.

2006). Puerto Ricans are a racialized mix of indigenous, European, and African heritage and thus racial identity is an important factor in understanding their social location. Race has been relatively invisible in the discourse of Latino ethnic identity but recent scholarship is inserting race as an important construct in understanding Latino social location (Bonilla-Silva 2006; Rodriguez 2000).

## Cubans

We most often think of Cubans coming to the United States as political refugees in the wake of the Cuban Revolution in 1959. However, the Cuban presence in the United States dates back to the first half of the nineteenth century when Cubans migrated to U.S. cities including New Orleans, Philadelphia, and New York (Acuña 2003; Vélez 2008). From 1959 to 1963 the revolution led hundreds of thousands of Cubans to leave the island and enter the United States, mostly settling in Miami. In 1966, the Cuban Adjustment Act gave Cubans political asylum and made them eligible for government-subsidized programs. Between 1960 and 1980 the number of Cuban immigrants grew from 50,000 to 580,000 (Acuña 2003). Their more privileged status is connected with their predominantly White racial identity and higher levels of education compared to other Latinos. Twenty-five percent of Cubans ages twenty-five and older—compared with 12.6 percent of all U.S. Latinos—have obtained at least a bachelor's degree (Pew Hispanic Center 2009a).

Specifically in the following sections, I present immigration trend data and social and economic demographic indicators by gender and national origin to illustrate diversity within these subgroups and the connection between different indicators associated with social inequality. I draw on the extensive sociodemographic data on the ten largest Latino subgroups residing in the United States as recently made available from the Pew Hispanic Center at www.pewhispanic. org.[8] For a more detailed historical account of the incorporation of all three groups, see Juan Gonzalez 2000.

## New Latino Immigrant Populations

Since 1970 waves of Latino immigrants have entered and settled in the United States, in the process transforming the makeup of the Latino population. Whereas in the pre–Civil Rights era Mexican American and Puerto Ricans were the majority, the influx of new groups from Central and South America meant an increasingly diverse and heterogeneous mix of peoples from multiple

---

8. The Pew Hispanic Center is a nonpartisan "fact tank" that provides information on the issues, attitudes, and trends shaping America and the world. It does so by conducting public opinion polling and social science research, by reporting news and analyzing news coverage, and by holding forums and briefings. It does not take positions on policy issues.

national origins, different races, and socioeconomic positions (Horowitz and Miller 1998; Portes 2007). Many of the immigrants from Central America arrived as a result of civil wars and government repression in the region (Dorrington et al. 1989; Sabagh and Bozorgmehr 1996). South Americans make up a small proportion of the overall foreign-born Latino population but their numbers have grown rapidly over the past thirty years (Dixon and Gelatt 2006). Countries with relatively stable governments, such as Costa Rica, Honduras, Belize, and most South American countries, still experience economic crises that prompt immigration to the United States in search of economic opportunities.

As of March 2007 all immigrants account for 12.6 percent of the total U.S. population, or one in every eight U.S. residents, the highest percentage in eight decades (Camarota 2007). Immigration flows are tied to such factors as proximity to the United States (as in the case of Mexico), civil unrest in foreign countries (as in El Salvador, Iran and Bosnia), and economic opportunity (associated for instance with the need for unskilled labor as has been the historic case for Mexican peoples). Among foreign-born immigrants, Latinos (of any race) constitute 54.6 percent and Asian/Pacific Islander, 23.0 percent. White (15.4 percent) and Black (7.6 percent) immigrant groups represent smaller percentages of the total foreign-born population (Camarota 2007).

Over the last forty years the steady flow of immigrants from Mexico and the increased flow from Central and South America and the Caribbean have been vital factors in diversifying the nationality and citizenship of Latinos in the United States. From 1970 to 2000, the percentage of foreign-born Latinos has more than doubled from 7.9 percent to 20 percent. Puerto Ricans and Cubans were the largest foreign-born Latino subgroups to enter the United States prior to the 1970s. The 1990s saw a significant shift in national origin of immigrants with Mexicans, Dominicans, Central Americans, and South Americans representing the largest foreign-born groups in the United States (Portes 2007). Overall, immigrants from Mexico, Central and South America, and the Caribbean account for the majority of immigrants (Camarota 2007, 7). Mexico accounts for 31.3 percent of all immigrants, with 11.7 million immigrants living in the United States. Table 2.1 shows trends in immigration of Latino subgroups since 1970 by national origin and by decade.

Illegal or undocumented Latino immigrants have become a key public policy issue in the United States.[9] According to the March 2007 Current

9. Public concern and fear in response to media hypersensationalism about undocumented immigrants have contributed to a hegemonic response. For example, in November 2009, U.S. Census stakeholder organizations stepped up their opposition to a proposal by Senators David Vitter (R-LA) and Robert Bennett (R-UT) to add new questions to the 2010 census on citizenship and immigration status. However Senate action on the Fiscal Year 2010 Commerce, Justice, and Science (CJS) appropriations bill (H.R. 2847) that focused on citizenship was defeated

**Table 2.1.** Foreign-Born Population by Year of Entry and Nation of Origin (%)

| Year of entry | Total Hispanic | Mexican | Puerto Rican | Cuban | Central American | South American |
|---|---|---|---|---|---|---|
| 2000 or later | 20 | 21.2 | 11.3 | 10.8 | 20 | 25.8 |
| 1990–1999 | 36.5 | 37.9 | 21 | 23.7 | 38.1 | 32.9 |
| 1980–1989 | 24 | 23.5 | 17.6 | 20.3 | 27.7 | 21.3 |
| 1970–1979 | 11.6 | 11.4 | 19 | 12.6 | 9.6 | 12.5 |
| Before 1970 | 7.9 | 6 | 31.1 | 32.6 | 4.6 | 7.5 |

*Source:* U.S. Census Bureau 2004d.

Population Survey "illegal aliens" or undocumented workers are estimated to compose 5.6 million of the 10.3 million immigrants who arrived in 2000 or later. The best estimates are that 57 percent of undocumented immigrants come from Mexico, 11 percent from Central America, 9 percent from East Asia, 8 percent from South America, and 4 percent from the Caribbean (Camarota 2007). In 1990, for the first time, immigration from Latin America exceeded the combined flows from Asia and Europe, making Latinos the largest foreign-born population in the United States. By 2000, Mexican immigrants constituted the largest immigrant group, accounting for 57 percent of the 3.3 percent of the entire undocumented U.S. population (Acuña 2003; Camarota 2004). Illegal immigrants are more likely to have limited formal education, to have no health insurance, and to live in poverty (Camarota 2007). Undocumented workers are less likely to be in the formal or official labor force (62 percent) than U.S. citizens, and they generally earn considerably less than working U.S. citizens (Passel et al. 2004). Table 2.2 presents national-origin groups by percent of total Hispanic population. The majority of all Latinos in the United States, 64.3 percent, are Mexican American; 9.1 percent are Puerto Rican; 7.8 percent are Central American (Costa Rica, El Salvador, Guatemala, Honduras, Nicaragua, and Panama); 5.5 percent are South American (Argentina, Bolivia, Chile, Colombia, Ecuador, Paraguay, Peru, Uruguay, and Venezuela); 3.5 percent are Cuban American; 2.6 percent are Dominican; and 7.5 percent are other self-identified subgroups.

---

(http://www.ombwatch.org/node/10507). Most recently, Arizona enacted a stringent immigration law that proponents and critics alike said was the broadest and strictest immigration measure in generations and would make the failure to carry immigration documents a crime and give the police broad power to detain anyone suspected of being in the country illegally (http://www.azleg.gov/legtext/49leg/2r/bills/sb1070s.pdf). This state law is currently being challenged by the U.S. Department of Justice.

Table 2.2. U.S. Hispanic Population by Nation of Origin, 2007

| Nation of origin | Number | Percentage of U.S. Hispanic population |
|---|---|---|
| Mexican | 29,189,334 | 64.3 |
| Puerto Rican | 4,114,701 | 9.1 |
| All Other Latino | 2,880,536 | 6.3 |
| Cuban | 1,608,835 | 3.5 |
| Salvadoran | 1,473,482 | 3.2 |
| Dominican | 1,198,849 | 2.6 |
| Guatemalan | 859,815 | 1.9 |
| Colombian | 797,195 | 1.8 |
| Honduran | 527,154 | 1.2 |
| Ecuadorian | 523,108 | 1.2 |
| Peruvian | 470,519 | 1.0 |
| Spaniard | 353,008 | 0.8 |
| Nicaraguan | 306,438 | 0.7 |
| Argentinean | 194,511 | 0.4 |
| Venezuelan | 174,976 | 0.4 |
| Panamanian | 138,203 | 0.3 |
| Costa Rican | 115,960 | 0.3 |
| Other Central American | 111,513 | 0.2 |
| Chilean | 111,361 | 0.2 |
| Bolivian | 82,434 | 0.2 |
| Other South American | 77,898 | 0.2 |
| Uruguayan | 48,234 | 0.1 |
| Paraguayan | 20,432 | 0.0 |
| *Total* | 45,378,596 | 100 |

*Source:* Pew Hispanic Center 2009f.

## Emerging Latino Community Settlements: Geographic Concentration and Diasporic Movements

Latinos make up 37 percent of the population in California and Texas. New Mexico's Latino population in 2008 was 45 percent, the highest of any state. Nevada (26 percent), Florida (21 percent), and Colorado (20 percent) all account for large proportions of the overall U.S. Latino population. While still highly concentrated in the Southwest, Southern California, New York, and Florida, Latinos can no longer be thought of as being confined to these areas. From 1980 to 2000 we have seen diasporic settlements of Latinos in almost all states, metropolitan areas, smaller cities, and suburbs. New Latino destinations include diverse metropolitan areas scattered across thirty-five states in every region of the country (table 2.3). Within these metropolitan areas the Latino population grew at rates ranging from 303 percent (Tulsa) to 1,180 percent (Raleigh-Durham) during the years 1980 to 2000 (Suro and Singer 2002). Most recently, South Carolina and North Carolina have seen the highest percentage increases in the Hispanic population—7.7 percent and 7.4 percent

**Table 2.3.** The New Latino Destinations, 2000

| Metropolitan area | Percentage of total Latino population | Latino growth, 1980–2000 (%) |
|---|---|---|
| Raleigh-Durham, NC | 6 | 1,180 |
| Atlanta, GA | 7 | 995 |
| Greensboro, NC | 5 | 962 |
| Charlotte, NC | 5 | 932 |
| Orlando, FL | 17 | 859 |
| Las Vegas, NV | 21 | 753 |
| Nashville, TN | 3 | 630 |
| Fort Lauderdale, FL | 17 | 578 |
| Portland, OR | 7 | 437 |
| West Palm Beach, FL | 12 | 397 |
| Washington, DC | 9 | 346 |
| Indianapolis, IN | 3 | 338 |
| Providence, RI | 8 | 325 |
| Tulsa, OK | 5 | 303 |

*Source:* Suro and Singer 2002.

respectively between July 1, 2007, and July 1, 2008 (U.S. Census Bureau 2009). No doubt, metropolitan areas will continue to have large Latino communities, but new ones are emerging throughout the United States.

## Social and Economic Indicators

When comparing Latino native-born subgroups with the non-Hispanic White (NHW) population, some generalizations can be made. On average Latinos tend to be younger, less educated, and more likely to have low-income, low-skilled jobs. The Latino population is a young population, with 25 percent of children younger than age five, and 22 percent of all Latinos younger than age eighteen. The median age of Latinos is twenty-seven for both sexes compared to forty for NHWs (thirty-nine for males and forty-two for females) and thirty-one years for non-Hispanic Blacks (twenty-nine for males and thirty-three for females) (see table 2.4). Within Latino subgroups, however, there is considerable variation in age. The median age of Cubans is forty, making them older than other Latino groups and older than the U.S. population overall. By comparison, the median age of the U.S. population is thirty-six, and for all Hispanics it is twenty-seven. Puerto Ricans, Salvadorans, and Dominicans all have median ages of twenty-nine years, with Mexican Americans younger (twenty-five years) than the U.S. population and Hispanics overall (Pew Hispanic Center 2009b).

In the year 2000, 69.1 percent of all Latinos participated in the labor force. Overall, Latinos age sixteen and over represented 12.7 percent of the total

**Table 2.4.** Social and Economic Indicators by Hispanic Subgroup, 2007

| Indicators | Median age (male/female) | Educational attainment (%) | | | Median personal earnings ($) | Unemployment rate (%) |
|---|---|---|---|---|---|---|
| | | High school graduate | Some college | College graduate | | |
| All Latinos | 27/27 | 28.2 | 19.9 | 12.6 | 21,048 | 7.3 |
| U.S. born | 17/18 | 31.5 | 29.0 | 16.0 | 23,274 | 7.6 |
| Foreign born | 35/38 | 25.8 | 13.4 | 10.1 | 20,238 | 7.5 |
| Non-Hispanic White | 39/42 | 30.7 | 28.3 | 30.5 | 30,357 | 5.2 |
| Non-Hispanic Black | 29/33 | 34.7 | 28.6 | 17.3 | 24,286 | 10.1 |
| Asian | 34/36 | 17.7 | 18.4 | 49.8 | 32,786 | 3.2 |
| Mexican American | 25/25 | 52.4 | | 9 | 25,298 | 7.2 |
| Puerto Rican | 29/29 | 71.4 | | 16.2 | 34,405 | 10 |
| Cubans | 40/40 | 74.2 | | 25 | 34,405 | 5.1 |
| Salvadorans | 29/29 | 41.3 | | 6.2 | 25,298 | 6.0 |
| Dominicans | 29/29 | 61.6 | | 15 | 26,310 | 8.8 |

*Source:* Pew Hispanic Center 2009f.

civilian workforce in 2000 compared to 10.4 percent in 1998. In 2008 Latinos comprised 13.0 percent of the total labor force, and by 2010 the Latino labor force is expected to be larger than the NHB labor force (U.S. Bureau of Labor Statistics 2008).

Among the Latino subgroups, there are significant differences across groups by level of education, occupation, and income, all of which intersect to determine one's socioeconomic position in society. In the remainder of this section I briefly present an overview of education, occupation, and income and make observations on how these factors are linked to labor force participation and poverty. Table 2.4 shows economic and social indicators by race/ethnicity and Hispanic subgroup.

Education, especially the completed level of schooling, is a major indicator of current and future socioeconomic position. For instance, Cubans and Puerto Ricans are more likely to be high school graduates than Salvadorans and Mexican Americans. Looking at the Latino population as a whole, 12.6 percent of all Latinos have obtained at least a college degree. U.S.–born Latinos are more likely to have a college degree than foreign-born Latinos. If we look across foreign-born groups, on average South Americans and those from the Caribbean such as Cubans (25 percent), Puerto Ricans (16.2 percent), and Dominicans (15 percent) have higher rates of college completion than Mexican Americans (9 percent). Education is also an important benchmark for determining English language proficiency and marketable skills in the labor force. Higher levels of education generally translate into access to the social and economic opportunity structure. Maternal education has been shown to correlate with academic achievement of children and youth (see chapter 4).

Another indicator of socioeconomic position is occupational status. About 24 percent of civilian-employed Latinos ages sixteen and older work in service occupations. Latinos are more likely than NHWs to work in service, construction, and production jobs. Disparities in occupational positions held and median earnings between Latinos and NHWs and Blacks are evident. Latino men and women are less likely to hold managerial and professional positions in comparison to NHWs and NHBs (U.S. Bureau of Labor Statistics 2008). Non-Hispanic Whites comprise 83 percent of officials/managers, 77.4 percent of professionals, 72.4 percent of technicians, whereas NHBs comprise 6.7 percent of officials/managers, 7.4 percent of professionals, and 12.7 percent of technicians. Latinos comprise 5.6 percent of officials/managers (3.6 percent males and 2.0 percent females), 4.5 percent of professionals (2.1 percent males and 2.4 percent females), and 7.9 percent of technicians (4.6 percent males and 3.3 percent females) (U.S. Equal Employment Opportunity Commission 2006). Latino and Black men and women are underrepresented in the highest paid occupational categories.

Within the labor force 92 percent of Latinas sixteen years of age and older are employed compared to 97 percent of White women. Latinas in the workforce are disproportionately concentrated in low-paying, part-time, or seasonal jobs and experience twice the rate of unemployment compared to White women. In comparing Latino women with other racial/ethnic women, the disparities are striking. In 2006, Latinas comprised 2.0 percent of official/manager positions, compared to 28.7 percent of White women and 3.2 percent of Black women; 2.4 percent of professionals, compared to 40.4 percent of White women and 5.0 percent of Black women; and 3.3 percent of technicians, compared to 33.9 percent of White women and 7.7 percent of Black women (U.S. Equal Employment Opportunity Commission 2006).

Disparities in median earnings between Latinos and non-Latinos are evident at all levels of educational attainment. This earning gap is lower for those Latinos (male and female) with at least a bachelor's degree. In 2000 the annual earnings of Latino males between twenty-five and thirty-four years of age with a bachelor's degree or higher was $39,389, which compared to $23,566 for their female counterparts. These variations in earnings overlap at different educational levels. In 2000 the median earnings of Latino men twenty-five years of age and older were about $13,000 less than for White men. Overall, Latino males earned the lowest income ($23,425), whereas White males ($36,668) and Black males ($28,167) received higher earnings. At each educational benchmark (high school diploma, some college but no degree, or an associate degree) the median earnings gap between non-Hispanic White and

Black and Hispanic was between $6,000–10,000 and the gap between Blacks and Latinos was about $400–600 with Blacks earning a slightly higher salary. For a bachelor's degree or higher, the median earnings for Whites ($55,906) were considerably higher than for Blacks ($42,591) or Latinos ($42,518). Latino men earned less than their White and Black counterparts at comparable educational levels.

In 2000, the median earnings of Latino women twenty-five years of age and older were about $6,500 less than their White counterparts. Overall, Latino women earned the lowest income ($16,601), whereas White ($23,887) and Black ($22,028) women received higher earnings. Although these median earnings are lower for women than for men, Latino females at each educational level had lower median earnings than their White and Black counterparts. However White women earned more than Black or Latino women at all levels except for college graduates. With an associate degree, the median earnings for Whites ($25,480) and Blacks ($25,411) were higher than for Latinas ($22,347). For a bachelor's degree or higher, the median earnings for Whites ($35,472) and Blacks ($37,898) were higher than for Latinas ($32,035) (NCES 2003a). Similar to Latino men, Latinas earned less than White and Black counterparts at comparable educational levels. Differences in median personal earning are shown by U.S.–born Latinos and foreign-born. Accordingly U.S.–born Latinos had higher median personal earnings ($23,274) than foreign-born Latinos ($20,238), and Cuban and Puerto Ricans had higher median personal earnings ($34,405) than Dominican ($26,310) and Mexican American ($25,298) groups (Pew Hispanic Center 2008a, 2009b).

Income is an important marker that is associated with educational level and occupational status. Income gaps may represent discriminatory institutional practices that contribute to Hispanic households remaining in lower socioeconomic positions. Higher income provides access to the goods and benefits of society such as employment-based health insurance and residence in safe neighborhoods. The total median income of Hispanic households in 2004 was approximately $36,000. This was less than three-quarters of the median income of non-Hispanic White households, which was about $48,000 (U.S. Census Bureau 2004d). The lowest median household income was reported for Dominicans and Hondurans ($31,256) followed by Salvadorians ($36,789), and Guatemalans ($37,912) (U.S. Census Bureau 2004d). These lower incomes may also be associated with underemployment and unemployment among Latino subgroups.

Puerto Ricans have the highest unemployment rate (10 percent) compared to the total U.S.–born rate (7.6 percent). Cubans have the lowest (5.1 percent). Mexican Americans (7.2 percent) are comparable to the total Latino population (7.3 percent) (see table 2.4). Job losses for both Hispanics and non-Hispanic Whites emerged primarily in the manufacturing, transportation, communications, and wholesale trade industries. Both groups gained jobs in entertainment and recreation, hospitals and medical services, and educational services. Job losses for non-Hispanic Blacks, however, were more widespread because they also lost jobs in service-sector industries, such as finance, insurance, real estate, and other professional services (Kochhar 2003).

The spike in Hispanic unemployment has hit immigrants especially hard. Over half (52.5 percent) of working-age Latinos (sixteen years of age and older) are immigrants (Kochhar 2008). Their unemployment rate was 7.5 percent in the first quarter of 2008, marking the first time since 2003 that a higher percentage of foreign-born Latinos was unemployed compared to native-born Latinos. Labor market outcomes for Latino women appear to be worse than for men during 2007. They left the labor force in a greater proportion and experienced greater increases in unemployment than did Latino men. Some 130,000 more Latino women became unemployed in 2007, and their unemployment rate increased from 5.6 percent to 7.0 percent (Kochar 2008).

These indicators (education level, occupation, income, and unemployment) are highly associated with rates of poverty.[10] In 2007, close to one-quarter of both U.S.–and foreign-born Latinos lived in poverty. The poverty rate of Latinos in 2000 matches the record lows reached in the 1970s. In 2000, a total of 7.2 million Latinos were poor, and approximately 33.6 percent of Latino children were living in poverty compared to 10 percent of White children. Mexican American and Mexican-origin children and Puerto Rican children have the lowest household income and highest rates of poverty. In 2001, the number of poor Latinos rose to 8 million, an increase from 7.8 million in 2000. Table 2.5 displays 2007 poverty rates by age, race, and ethnicity, and Latino nativity (U.S.–born vs. foreign-born). About one in five (20 percent) of Latinos is poor, and while Hispanic children represent 17.7 percent of all children, they constitute 27 percent of all children living in poverty. Foreign-born children are more likely to be poor than U.S.–born children, and about 10 percent of Asian and White children are poor. Children under eighteen are the most likely age group to be poor among all groups (Pew Hispanic Center 2009f).

Researchers who study the effects of social stratification have increasingly viewed wealth as the key to understanding socioeconomic inequality in the

---

10. Research suggests that, on average, families need an income equal to about two times the federal poverty guidelines to meet their most basic needs (http://aspe.hhs.gov/poverty/10poverty.shtml). Families with incomes below this level are referred to as *low income:* $44,100 for a family of four, $36,620 for a family of three, $29,140 for a family of two. These dollar amounts approximate the average minimum income families need to make ends meet, but actual expenses vary greatly by locality. For a family of four, the cost of basic living expenses is about $37,000 per year in El Paso, TX; $42,000 in Spokane, WA; $45,000 in Detroit, MI; and $49,000 in Buffalo, NY. See Wight and Chau 2009.

**Table 2.5.** Poverty Rates by Age, Race, and Latino Nativity, 2007

| 2006 household population | Age (years) Less than 18 (%) | 18–64 (%) | 65 and older (%) | All (%) |
|---|---|---|---|---|
| All Latinos | 27.0 | 16.3 | 17.9 | 20.0 |
| Native-born | 26.2 | 14.5 | 16.0 | 20.5 |
| Foreign-born | 34.1 | 17.8 | 19.6 | 19.3 |
| Non-Hispanic White | 10.5 | 8.2 | 7.0 | 8.5 |
| Non-Hispanic Black | 33.5 | 19.1 | 19.8 | 23.4 |
| Asian | 10.9 | 8.8 | 11.2 | 9.4 |
| Other | 20.9 | 16.3 | 14.9 | 18.1 |

*Source:* Pew Hispanic Center 2009f.
*Note:* Due to the way in which the IPUMS assigns poverty values, these data will differ from those that might be provided by the U.S. Census Bureau.

United States (Oliver and Shapiro 1997). *Wealth* is defined as both savings and assets over your lifetime and has been identified as important in understanding intergenerational upward mobility. Hispanic households have less than ten cents for every dollar in wealth owned by NHW households. In 2004 the poverty rate declined for Asians (9.8 percent in 2004, down from 11.8 percent in 2003), remained unchanged for Hispanics (21.9 percent) and Blacks (24.7 percent), and increased for NHWs (8.6 percent in 2004, up from 8.2 percent in 2003) (DeNavas-Walt et al. 2007). Wealth is related to the accumulation of assets over multiple generations, which is transferred to children and heirs in the form of not only money but also social capital such as access to professional networks for job placement, "legacy students," (children of alumni) or trust funds for education. These invisible resources play an important role in the lives and social location of middle-class dominant culture individuals and for those foreign-born immigrants who come to the United States with human capital such as high social status of family of origin, prior formal college education, and/or marketable skills. In contrast many Puerto Ricans and Mexican Americans who have historically been excluded from access to the educational and economic structure have not had the opportunity to acquire possessions and savings to transmit to their children and heirs. Thus, the accumulation of wealth in the form of savings or real estate is the buffer that can help individuals' weather economic crises such as unemployment or illness and avoid downward mobility and poverty. Middle-class NHW professionals are more likely to have these wealth buffers than middle-class Black and Latino groups. The persistence of the income gap between NHWs and Latinos, limited accumulation of wealth, and limited access to social capital have strongly contributed to the modest intergenerational social mobility of historically underrepresented groups in the United States and their social location.

## English Language Proficiency, National Origin, Citizenship Status, and Identity

When addressing the problem of socioeconomic inequality with respect to Latinos, scholars and policy makers often propose solutions that are tied to factors such as English language proficiency (ELP) and citizenship. Of course, these solutions overlook the fact that some Latino groups—such as Puerto Ricans and Mexican Americans—already are U.S. citizens and typically have ELP. Many of the common misconceptions about Latinos can be traced back to basic misunderstandings regarding such issues as limited ELP and citizenship status. Approximately 358 million people speak Spanish, making Spanish the fourth (behind Mandarin Chinese, English, and Hindi) most frequently spoken language worldwide. Further, Latinos may speak a variety of dialects, which are derived from Spanish, as well as regional dialects, indigenous languages, and English. About 31 million U.S. residents speak Spanish at home— easily making it the second-most spoken language in the country (Kent and Lalasz 2006). This growth has motivated concerns about the adoption of English by immigrants from Spanish-speaking nations. But a majority of those who speak languages other than English at home report themselves already proficient in English (U.S. Census Bureau 2004a; Pew Hispanic Center/Kaiser Family Foundation 2004a).

Almost 70 percent of American adults ages eighteen to sixty-four who spoke Spanish in the home said they also spoke English either "well" or "very well" (U.S. Census Bureau 2004b). Young immigrants (those ages five to seventeen) typically speak English over their native tongues by adulthood. According to Rúben Rumbaut (2005), "Those who arrive by age 12 or 13 make a quick transition to English—that's the dividing line. It's a piece of cake for those who arrive much earlier on, because of the dominance of English in every medium in the United States, from video to the Internet, English wins." English language proficiency varies by Latino subgroup. Table 2.6 shows that Mexican groups have the third highest citizenship rates after Puerto Ricans and Cubans and second highest rates of English language proficiency (ELP) after Puerto Ricans. Colombians and Dominicans have high rates of citizenship and ELP. Evidence suggests that Spanish-speaking immigrants acquire English fluency during their time in the United States.

Immigrants now account for a large share of the increase in the size of the U.S. population. This is different than in the past when most of the increase in population was from within. Perhaps not surprisingly, therefore, many Americans see the growing Latino immigrant population as a threat to the traditional U.S. way of life. Among foreign-born, the length of residence and citizenship status differs by race and ethnicity. The median length of residence of foreign-born was 14.4 years, and 37.4 percent were naturalized citizens. Of the

**Table 2.6.** English Language Proficiency and U.S. Citizenship by Latino Subgroup, 2007

| Country of origin | Speak English proficiently (%) | U.S. Citizen (%) |
|---|---|---|
| Mexican | 59.1 | 68.9 |
| Puerto Rican | 79.5 | 99.4 |
| Cuban | 56.7 | 74.1 |
| Colombian | 55.0 | 61.9 |
| Dominican | 52.2 | 67.7 |
| Peruvian | 51.3 | 54.3 |
| Ecuadorian | 47.4 | 59.7 |
| Salvadoran | 43.8 | 52.9 |
| Guatemalan | 40.3 | 46.8 |
| Honduran | 37.2 | 43.5 |

*Source:* Pew Hispanic Center 2009b.

foreign-born with residency and citizenship, NHWs had the highest number of years of residency in the United States and the highest rates of naturalized citizenship status (21.2 median years of residency, and 50.3 percent naturalized), followed by Asian/Pacific Islanders with the second highest rates (13.6 years, and 45.7 percent naturalization). Foreign-born Latinos with residency and citizenship had the lowest rates (13.2 years, and 25.7 percent naturalization).

Further, about 60 percent of Latinos are U.S.–born citizens, 10 percent are naturalized citizens, and 30 percent are immigrants or children of immigrants (28 percent) (del Pinal 2008). Among Mexicans, Cubans, and Salvadorans, there is a high degree of variation in citizenship status. Cubans and Dominicans have the highest rates of citizenship acquisition (57.4 and 46.3 percent respectively), while Salvadoran (28.8 percent) and Mexican immigrants (21.9 percent) have the lowest rates of citizenship acquisition (Aguirre and Sáenz 2002).

Several studies have examined issues of American identity of long-time foreign-born residents and naturalized citizens. Key findings from the 2006 Latino National Survey (LNS) report how Latinos identify themselves: as Americans? As Latinos? As members of a particular national group? Approximately two-thirds of the survey's respondents identified themselves as Americans. According to John Garcia (2006),

The respondents reported multiple identities, with Latino being only one of them. When forced to choose only one identity, the number of first generation immigrants who answered "American" was low but it increased greatly for U.S.-born Latinos. High percentages thought of themselves in a pan-ethnic context, and the doubling of such identification since 1989 holds implications for the possibility of Latinos as a political force. Interestingly, a higher sense of pan-ethnicity was found among women, among Latinos/Latinas who identified themselves as

Democrats and moderates rather than as liberals, and among those with more years of education, more involvement in community activities, and more regular media use.

Within the small body of literature concerning citizenship attitudes among Latinos in the United States, Sarah Gershon and Adrian Pantoja (2008) report that the subjective feelings that Latino immigrants have toward the American political system significantly impact their acquisition of U.S. citizenship.[11] Just over half of all Hispanic adults in the United States worry that they, a family member, or a close friend could be deported. Nearly two-thirds say the failure of Congress to enact an immigration reform bill has made life more difficult for all Latinos. Smaller numbers (ranging from about one-in-eight to one-in-four) say the heightened attention to immigration issues has had a specific negative effect on them personally. These effects include more difficulty finding work or housing, less likelihood of using government services or traveling abroad, and more likelihood of being asked to produce documents to prove their immigration status (Pew Hispanic Center 2007).

A more simple measure of attachment may be considering how long an immigrant plans on remaining in the United States. Roger Waldinger (2007), in his analyses of the 2006 National Survey of Latinos, reports that while immigrants who gain citizenship are more likely than noncitizens to plan to stay, the difference is slight. Indeed, the great majority of noncitizens plan to live permanently in the United States. Significant differences by country of origin are observed, with Colombians and Dominicans maintaining more active connections with their home country, and Mexicans and Cubans having the least contact. Whether Latino immigrants maintain active, moderate, or limited connections with their country of origin is an important marker of their attitudes toward the United States, their nation, and their own lives as migrants. Those with the highest levels of engagement with their country of origin as a result of children or other family members who have remained have deeper attachments than immigrants whose connections are less robust. They also have more favorable views of their native country in comparison with the United States. These attachments are perhaps strongest for first-generation immigrants and decrease with each generation. Nonetheless, a clear majority of immigrants envision their future in the United States rather than in their countries of origin (Pew Hispanic Center 2007).

11. The final sample used in Gershon and Pantoja's analysis consisted of 1,042 Latino immigrants: 47.6 percent U.S. citizens, 16.0 percent applying for citizenship, 25.7 percent planning on applying, and 8.8 percent who had no plans to apply for citizenship. Mexicans, Cubans, and Salvadorans were the largest groups in the sample.

## Globalization and Transnationalism

Globalization and transnationalism have become major topics of intellectual interest in the last few decades. In the most basic terms, *globalization* refers to the economic transformation of the nation-state. In short, the nation-state has changed to meet the needs of transnational corporations and to invest heavily in the transport of capital, goods, and labor across national lines (Brecher 1998). The role of Mexican immigrants in particular as a surplus labor force and the opportunities available in the future economy of the United States in light of reindustrialization and privatization or outsourcing to global entities may have a detrimental effect, as observed by Victor Valle and Rodolfo Torres (2000), "to render the population that occupies Central Los Angeles invisible politically and economically" (9). The concern of the deleterious effects of globalization on Latino men and women is that it will spread to other Latino residential areas of concentration especially urban spaces, increasing economic and social inequality.

Feminist scholars have also studied the relationship between globalization and the gendered division of labor (Toro-Morn 2008). Several domains have grave consequences for the Latino community. Recent studies have identified the following issues: (1) the exploitation of Mexican *maquiladora* workers, (2) the rise of sex and tourist work in Cuba and the Dominican Republic, and (3) the impact of the North American Free Trade Agreement (NAFTA) and Central American Free Trade Agreement (CAFTA) on lives of Latino nations. Valle and Torres (2000) discuss the impact of globalization in Los Angeles, stating that "the convergence of these new systems of production and social formations demands a reconsideration of the meaning of so called ethnic workers and their role in the new global economy" (17). Other scholars interested in the cultural and political implications of globalization use the term *transnationalism* to highlight human agency and the multidirectional flows of power, capital, and culture across the globe (Grewal 2005; Ong 1999).

The term *transnationalism* when used in the context of migration and immigration refers to the processes by which immigrants "forge and sustain multi-stranded social relations that link together their societies of origin and settlement" (Basch et al. 1994, 7; Lee 2007). The concept of transnationalism is used in the more defined way that has been accepted by those researchers and policy makers who attempt to capture distinctive characteristics of contemporary immigrants whose lives cut across national borders while living in other countries (Portes et al. 1999). Transnationalism is important because it has changed over time and with each generation. Most Latino immigrants maintain some kind of connection to their native country by (1) sending remittances, (2) traveling back, or (3) telephoning relatives, but the extent of their attachment varies considerably (Waldinger 2007). Roughly one in ten

(9 percent) Latino immigrants engage in all three of these transnational activities. Sixty-three percent engage in one or two of these activities, while 28 percent do none (Waldinger 2007).

Michael Jones-Correa (2006), speaking about "the decline of transnationalism," noted that immigrants to the United States generally loosen connections with their home countries over time. Contact with family and friends, remittances to home countries, plans to return to the country of origin, and use of Spanish language decline markedly the longer Latinos stay in the United States as well as across generations. For example, seventy-five percent of Latino immigrants report Spanish as the primary language of media use during their first year in the United States. From that point on, the use of English increases dramatically, with a large majority emphasizing the importance of speaking English (as well as looking White and being Christian) as part of being American. What Jones-Correa (2006) speculates is that this is a result of Latinos eventually becoming socialized and integrated in the United States.

Although globalization and transnationalism potentially represent a serious burden that can promote social inequality among U.S. Latinos, exploring the impact of globalization and transnationalism on U.S. Latino families and communities is a much larger subject that goes beyond the scope of this book.[12]

~

From these demographic data, it is clear that the socially constructed category of Latino/Hispanic is not monolithic but comprises distinct ethnic formations that differ significantly by such factors as size, racial mix, historical incorporation, immigration patterns, and socioeconomic status. Of the twenty distinct Latino subgroups, Mexican-origin, Puerto Rican, Cuban, Salvadoran, and Dominican are the largest groups (see table 2.2). The aggregation of all Central and South Americans into one group comprises a complex mix of people who do not share a common heritage but have distinct historical experiences in their country of origin as well as in the United States. Language, which is often used as the major marker of social integration without accounting for education, appears to be an unreliable measure. For instance, Cubans are the most likely among Latino groups to speak Spanish and yet they have experienced the most upward mobility in the United States.

Mexican-origin and Puerto Ricans continue to be the most disadvantaged economic groups and have the highest levels of segregation in major urban areas. Although the United States has experienced significant immigration from all Latin American countries over the last three decades, Mexicans are still

---

12. An extensive literature has developed in the last two decades on the demography, economics, and political processes of immigration and globalization. See, e.g., Saenz 2002; Suárez-Orozco 2001; Korzeniewicz and Smith 2000; Portes and Rumbaut 2001, 2006.

associated with immigration and all the negative connotations of that term. A consensus exists that "Immigration has always been transformative—no different now than from the past. Those that push to restrict it simply worry that today's (im)migrants are transforming the society into something they find alien. It is a reflection of the ignorance of alternative cultures more than an objection to (im)migration itself" (Acosta-Belen and Santiago 1998, 40; Bender 2003; Chavez 2008; Valle and Torres 2000).

In light of the demographic data, it is safe to say that the social context of the Latino families and communities are in transition. Language acquisition, fluctuating economic conditions, acquisition of resident status and citizenship, and continued immigration of Latinos—including family reunification—ensure that Latino families will continue to be subject to fundamental transformations. Given the relative national invisibility of the Latino political agenda, the projected population growth, structural inequalities, and inadequate material conditions of over one-fifth of the Latino population, the ability of these families to provide a healthy environment to raise their families and meet their own needs will do much to determine the social course of the nation in the next generation. Researchers who study Latino families must be prepared to move beyond traditional assumptions and stereotypes of Latino homogeneity and take into account historical, economic, and structural barriers that will continue to play a role in the social trajectory of Latino families in the next generation.

# 3

# How Have Latinos
# Been Studied?

The challenge is to recognize that we cannot continue
to waste human talent because of outdated racial/
ethnic conceptualizations. The competence and
productivity of minority populations are crucial to our
collective well-being.
—García-Coll et al. 1996, 1908

Latinos have been the subject of social science research in the United States
since at least the 1960s, but this research has traditionally not been as extensive as is needed nor has it covered all Latino subgroups equally, particularly
socioeconomic status (SES) differences. Moreover, in some cases the research
methods were flawed. As a result, we have an incomplete, insufficiently nuanced, and at times inaccurate picture of Latinos in the United States. This is
especially the case with Latino families. Mexican families are not the same as
Cuban families, and Cuban families are not the same as Puerto Rican families. Between the late 1960s and 1990s studies of Latino families focused
predominantly on low-income families while giving only limited attention to
social, economic, and political context. The major themes of study were family structure, marriage, childbearing, fertility, and feminization of poverty and
single-parent households. A second line of inquiry focused on important family relationships and processes including gender role socialization, parent-child
relationships, mother-daughter communication, marital relationships, gender
role performance, and the role of family in educational achievement. Researchers conducted these empirical studies from multiple perspectives in the major
social science disciplines including sociology, psychology, communication/
media, and education as well as in the interdisciplines of ethnic studies, social
work, and public health.

The goal of this chapter, therefore, is to provide an overview of the scholarly
landscape of research on Latino families since the 1960s to show how we got

to where we are today and where we need to go in the future.[1] In the process, I will question the assumptions that have guided much of the traditional research on Latinos and, I hope, help us rethink the models we use to guide the production of knowledge on Latino families. We need to be aware of, and correct for, the implicit cultural lens that has guided much of the research in years past. To achieve a more accurate and more complete picture we need to take into account not only culture but also the historical and structural factors that have powerfully affected the real-life experiences of Latino families in the United States.

## Family Formation

Latino families of differing national origins have different histories, structural and cultural integration, regional residence, and family formation and structure. Family structure is one of many factors that influence life course processes and family and child well-being. The majority of Latino households in 2007 were composed of families; that is, individuals related by bloodlines or marriage. Table 3.1 shows that about half of all Latinos are now married, with foreign-born more likely to be married than U.S.–born. Among household types, about 60 percent of U.S.–born and foreign-born Latino households are married-couple families, which is slightly lower than the rate for non-Hispanic White (NHW) households (Guzmán and McConnell 2002; McConnell 2008). Foreign-born children are more likely than U.S.–born children to live in a home with both parents (Hernandez 2004). Asians are the most likely to be married, followed by NHWs. Female-headed households are highest for non-Hispanic Blacks (NHB) and lowest for Asians and NHWs. About one-fifth of Latino family households are headed by a female, and U.S.–born Latinos have higher rates of single female households than foreign-born Latinos.

Latinos live in family households that tend to be larger than households of NHW and NHBs (Brindis et al. 2002; Ramirez and de la Cruz 2002). As table 3.1 shows, over one-quarter of Latino family households consisted of five or more people.[2] Other data (not shown) provide information on family structure and family size by Latino subgroup and nativity in comparison to European and Asian households. Close to one-third of foreign-born Latinos live in households of five or more persons. When disaggregated by country

---

1. The work on Latino families is extensive and broad across many specialized disciplinary subfields and areas of interest including substance use, domestic violence, child rearing, elderly care, caretaking and many others. These areas are not covered in this book due to limited scope of my work.

2. Family households consist of two or more people, at least one of whom is related to the householder (the person who owns or rents the housing unit). Latino family households have a Latino householder.

**Table 3.1.** Median Age, Marital Status, Household Type, and Family Size by Nativity, Race, and Ethnicity, 2007

| Indicator | Latino | | | Non-Hispanic White | Non-Hispanic Black | Asian |
| | Total | U.S. born | Foreign born | | | |
|---|---|---|---|---|---|---|
| Median age | | | | | | |
| Male | 27 | 17 | 35 | 39 | 29 | 34 |
| Female | 27 | 18 | 38 | 42 | 33 | 36 |
| Marital status (%) | | | | | | |
| Now married | 50.8 | 41.6 | 58.4 | 56.6 | 32.8 | 62.6 |
| Separated | 4.1 | 3.5 | 4.5 | 1.6 | 4.9 | 1.4 |
| Divorced | 8.4 | 10.5 | 6.8 | 11.7 | 12.4 | 5.0 |
| Widowed | 3.6 | 3.7 | 3.6 | 7.3 | 6.9 | 4.9 |
| Never married | 33.1 | 40.8 | 26.7 | 22.7 | 42.9 | 26.2 |
| Persons, by household type (%) | | | | | | |
| Married couple | 59.5 | 58.9 | 60.5 | 66.5 | 37.5 | 72.3 |
| Female householder | 20.9 | 24.5 | 15.4 | 10.8 | 38.9 | 10.0 |
| Male householder | 10.3 | 8.4 | 13.1 | 4.7 | 7.3 | 5.9 |
| Nonfamily household | 9.3 | 8.2 | 11.0 | 18.0 | 16.2 | 11.8 |
| Family size (%) | | | | | | |
| Two-person families | 26.7 | 33.7 | 21.6 | 50.4 | 40.1 | 31.2 |
| Three- or four-person families | 46.9 | 47.1 | 46.7 | 39.2 | 45.1 | 50.5 |
| Five+ person families | 26.4 | 19.2 | 31.7 | 10.4 | 14.8 | 18.3 |

*Source:* Pew Hispanic Center 2009f.

of origin, U.S.–born Mexican children are over twice as likely to live with a single parent (36 percent) than foreign-born Mexican children (15.1 percent) (Hernandez 2004).

Overall, foreign-born children are twice as likely to live in a household with five or more people (29.3 percent) than U.S.–born children (11.5 percent). Foreign-born Mexican households are almost three times more likely to have five or more people (37.8 percent) compared to NHW (10.4 percent) and Cuban households (10.6 percent). Cubans (43.1 percent) were as likely as NHW households (48.7) and almost twice as likely as all Latino households (25.9 percent) to have a two-person household. European (9.8 percent) and Asian (19.2 percent) immigrant households have family size households more consistent with United States households while immigrant Mexican (37.8 percent) and Central American (39.3 percent) had close to 40 percent of families or households with five or more people compared to 22 percent for South American households (Fry and Gonzales, 2008; Pew Hispanic Center 2008c). The patterns of family formation and family size have not changed considerably in the last decade. The reason Latino families have larger household size is associated with economic factors, educational level, and generational status.

Latinos who live in extended families tend to do so because of their stage in the life course or to facilitate sharing of caretaking responsibilities for children and older family members (Blank and Torrecilha 1998). Living arrangements vary with generational status, with first-generation Mexican and Cuban immigrants more likely to live in extended family households than second- or third-generation families (Landale et al. 2006). Family income or median household earnings are also associated with large household size and extended family arrangements. Arriving in a new country requires time to learn a language and find employment and thus extended family and nonfamily households provide social and economic support while the individual seeks self-sufficiency.

Here it is worth making a few observations about the importance of family size, income, and educational attainment of mothers. It is well known that family size and socioeconomic position (SEP) influence family functioning and processes that critically shape a child's access to early learning activities and future academic achievement (Lee and Burkam 2002). Although having a two-parent family is considered most favorable for providing positive learning and schooling experiences, this axiom holds most true when both parents have a decent standard of living, have knowledge of their role as advocates in the school system, and have the emotional energy and economic means to provide extracurricular opportunities for their children. For example, children in low-income families with a large household size tend to demonstrate lower cognitive and academic abilities than children from small household sizes (Lee and Burkam 2002). I argue along with other scholars that we cannot study Latino family processes, childhood socialization, and development without recognition of the basic associations of family structure, family size, family income, maternal education as an indicator of SEP, and neighborhood effects or community context (García-Coll et al. 1996; Baca Zinn 1995; McLoyd et al. 2000; Lareau 2003).

## Theoretical Assumptions in the Study of Families

Scholarship on family processes has historically used middle-class Euro-dominant culture groups as a baseline for assessing the values, norms, and behaviors of all families, whether White or non-White. This predominantly normative approach assumes that well-educated, middle-class groups are the cultural standard against which all other groups can be judged. Such research, however, serves in many respects to maintain the unequal treatment of ethnic group families based on a superior-versus-inferior binary (Bonilla-Silva 2006). Even within the field of family studies, researchers reinforce this false binary by generalizing research findings about low-income Latino families to the entire Latino population.

Arland Thornton (2005) has provided valuable insight into this problem by analyzing the assumptions that informed the foundations of family sociology.

In the most basic terms, he argues that a developmental idealism perspective has permeated family studies research since the beginning. Developmental idealism is based principally on four concepts: (1) modern society is good and attainable, (2) the modern family is good and attainable, (3) the modern family is a cause and effect of a modern society, and (4) individuals have the right to be free and equal (8–10). These concepts are the bedrock of highly industrialized societies such as the United States and the United Kingdom (England), where modern is systematically pitted against tradition, rural against suburban, and developed against underdeveloped. Moreover, the developmental paradigm assumes a social and political trajectory whereby non-European societies move in the social organization continuum toward values, preferences, and behaviors similar to what are deemed "more developed, more civil, and more advanced" (245). From its inception, the study of new societies (which evolved from privileged Western Europeans maintaining travel logs of "unknown family practices" in places such as India and Africa) the study of families has been conducted in comparison to invisible cultural referents; namely, White, privileged, middle-class families. Central to early family studies scholarship, as noted by Thornton, was the view that families would naturally progress, develop, and embrace Western European cultural norms (107). These developmental assumptions, not unexpectedly, served as normative guides to social science theorizing about racial and ethnic groups in the United States.

An undeniable feature of the social sciences is that fields of inquiry systematically build on prior ways of thinking and theoretical paradigms. It is essential, therefore, that we interrogate the epistemological roots of the intellectual traditions (family theory and assimilation/acculturation theory) that have been used to capture the lived experiences of Latino subgroups in the United States. One barrier to understanding the heterogeneity of Latino families is the lack of substantive research on Latino subgroups, and much of the research conducted has focused primarily on low-income Mexican and Mexican American families, treating them as representative of all Latino families (Vega 1995; Weaver 2005). In the process, a set of values has been ascribed to all Latino families regardless of national origin and SEP. Researchers and the media typically portray Latino families with strength, solidarity, and unity derived from their "*familism*"—a form of family values in which the needs of the family as a group are more important than the needs of any individual family member (Hurtado 1995; Sabogal et al. 1987). In reality, "family values" are important in all cultures, and the role of family is integral in maintaining sources of social support such as child care, family tradition, and cultural expression. Yet cultural values also change through cultural encounter with other groups, and family members develop new forms of expression and attachment over time. In Latino families, attachment varies within and across groups and differs by national origin and generational status (Landale et al. 2006; Organista 2007).

The body of literature on Latinos persists in defining its values as a static entity with limited recognition of the structural barriers to integration in a new social context and differences in adaptation associated with SEP. Since the 1990s, scholars have increasingly questioned the use of a theoretical approach that viewed Latino families as monolithic and invariably governed by traditional, patriarchal values and behaviors.

Over time, certain researchers began to challenge paradigms that viewed Latinos as a culture-bound group, yet often they failed to incorporate important factors such as the intersection of race, ethnicity, SEP, intragroup variability, community context, and racism (García-Coll et al. 1996; Baca Zinn 1994, 1995; Baca Zinn and Wells 2000; McLoyd et al. 2000; Perez 2004). Even today the culture-bound perspective continues to permeate our perceptions and the theoretical lenses through which we explore Latino families. Thus it is as important as ever to heed the warning given by Cynthia García-Coll et al. (1996) regarding the role of family in child development: "There is no theoretical or empirical reason to assume that individual primary developmental processes operate differently for children of color than for Caucasian children in Western society" (1893).

## Culture-Driven Family Perspectives: Latino Families as "Other"

All too often, to understand the present we need to return to the past. Two aspects of family research prior to around 2000 are striking: (1) narrow conceptual models were used to understand family structure and formation and (2) a limited inclusion of families in data sets that reflected the changing demographics of U.S. society (McLoyd et al. 2000, 1071). Social science research on Hispanic/Latino (Puerto Rican and Mexican American) families in America began as early as the 1920s but was relatively rare prior to 1960. This changed during the 1960s and 1970s. In those decades, two research methods were most common: (1) ethnographic approaches to describe culturally based practices and behaviors and (2) secondary analyses of census data to describe high rates of fertility, poverty, and educational attainment. While some of this research was extremely important and no doubt seminal, much of it was also deeply flawed, and unfortunately it has shaped the scholarly inquiry on Latino families ever since. Take, for instance, the anthropologist Oscar Lewis, best known for his work on the lives of poor people and for his theory that there is a "culture of poverty" among the poor that transcends national boundaries. He published a number of books including *Five Families: Mexican Case Studies in the Culture of Poverty* (1959), which was intended, he said, "to give the reader some glimpses of daily life in five families on five perfectly ordinary days." Another book, *La Vida* (1965), focused on a single Puerto Rican family living in the "culture of poverty." Lewis's work gained tremendous public attention at the time, and while he was undoubtedly motivated by a belief in the need to ameliorate poverty, his work unwittingly contributed to a stereotype of all Mexican Americans and Puerto Rican Americans as culturally different and as "social problems" for American society—a stereotype that lives on today.

## From Culture to Acculturation

Culture and assimilation have been central themes in the study of Latinos in all disciplines in the forty-plus years since the publication of Oscar Lewis's influential books. Early models of assimilation were designed to assess progress toward "Americanization" or normative cultural standards. Over time, however, many researchers questioned the applicability of the assimilation construct in view of the perceived resistance of Latino groups to completely abandon their culture. Consequently, the concept of acculturation emerged to replace assimilation. Underlying the concept of acculturation remained the assumptions that racial/ethnic/cultural groups would progress toward normative dominant culture behaviors. The epistemology of the construct of culture and acculturation provides insights into origins and meaning.

*Culture* as a concept has multiple disciplinary definitions, and its meanings have evolved over time (Finkelstein et al. 1998). Culture is etymologically derived from the Latin word *cultura*, which means cultivation. In anthropology, culture is defined as concepts, beliefs, and principles of action and organization (Trueba 1991). In sociology, culture is defined as "[t]he accumulated store of symbols, ideas and material products associated with a social system, whether it is an entire society or a family. It does not refer to what people actually do, but to the ideas they share about what they do and the material objects that they use" (A. Johnson 2000). In psychology, culture is defined by "shared attitudes and habits, called schemas, adaptive to one's family, ethnic community, and occupation" (Rudmin 2003, 10). The cultural systems of societies differ from one another (e.g., American society is different than Chinese society, and Greek society is different than Iranian society) and differ within groups, making them unique in the way knowledge or cognition is stored, formed, and transmitted (Spradley 1972). While there is no single, consistent definition of culture within the social sciences, one recurring problem common to much social science literature is the failure to account for the varying effects of social inequality on cultural expression, enactment, and adaptation of ethnic groups to dominant hegemonic groups. Culture has become a negative identity marker for U.S. Latinos. Latinos are and have been perceived by dominant culture as a subordinate culture, resistant to embracing normative cultural standards, leading to diminished social and economic opportunities. In trying to understand the perceived resistance to normative hegemonic standards, social scientists developed acculturation measures.

The acculturation construct was developed by sociologists in the early twentieth century out of the idea of the "melting pot" theory (Persons 1987). The theory of the melting pot viewed acculturation as an irreversible, three-stage process consisting of contact, accommodation, and assimilation. Multiple revisions of this construct have expanded the notion of acculturation, but the underlying assumptions and focus on culture have not changed considerably (Social Science Research Council 1954; Teske and Nelson 1974; Berry 1980; Cuellar et al. 1980; Padilla and Perez 2003). The origins of the acculturation construct are rooted in the study of immigrants who recently arrived in the United States, with the goal of measuring the effects of the interaction of new immigrant groups with the host culture (Carter-Pokras and Bethunc 2009; Zambrana and Carter-Pokras 2010). There are various disciplinary definitions of *acculturation,* as shown in table 3.2. For each the foundational root of the definition lies in the notion of change or integration as each social group interacts with another culture. What these definitions fail to account for are difficult-to-quantify forces such as the effects of the dominant culture's view of subordinated groups by conquest, and for immigrant racialized Latino groups such as Mexicans, the historical roots of the relationship between the two cultures, and the legal treatment of that ethnic group. All these factors represent barriers to the integration and acceptance of racialized Latinos in U.S. culture. The real issue is whether the forces at play were (or are) resistance or exclusion.

In short, a basic problem with much of the theorizing on acculturation is that it is often marred by flawed assumptions. The first assumption is that an individual born outside the United States must abandon his or her culture of origin to be acculturated. A second assumption is that an individual is free to choose to become an integral part of American society. Yet Mexican Americans who are an integral part of American society are not perceived or accepted as

**Table 3.2.** Examples of Definitions of the Term *Acculturation*

| Academic discipline | Definition |
| --- | --- |
| Anthropology | "Culture change under conditions of direct contact between the members of two societies" (Winthrop 1991, 3) |
| Psychology | "The process by which groups or individuals integrate the social and cultural values, ideas, beliefs and behavioral patterns of their culture of origin with those of a different culture" (VandenBos 2007, 3) |
| Public health | "Adoption and assimilation by a person or social group of the cultural customs, traditions, practices and behavior of what previously had been for them an alien culture" (Last 2007, 306) |
| Sociology | "Two or more cultures come in contact with one another through images in the mass media, trade, immigration, or conquest so that they affect one another. With acculturation, a dominant group imposes its culture on subordinate groups so effectively that these become virtually indistinguishable from the dominant culture" (Johnson 2000, 70) |

*Source:* Zambrana and Carter-Pokras 2010, 19.

full citizens. An unexplained use of the acculturation scale is its administration to U.S.–born Mexican Americans and the comparison of scores between Mexican immigrants and Mexican Americans. (The overwhelming majority of Mexican Americans speak English as their primary language and have been in the United States for multiple generations, in many cases long before Europeans settled in North America.) In reflecting on this conundrum, it seems to me that it reveals the belief that U.S.–born Mexican Americans are perceived to be perpetual non-Americans or forever foreigners.

The third flawed assumption is that most scales use proxy measures that rely mostly on language-based questions, an indirect measure of the cultural process (Perez and Padilla 2000). Often multiple factors that are associated with the process of acculturation including educational level, family structure, power relationships between the majority and minority groups, and social stigma are left unmeasured. Common to social science definitions of acculturation is that they are based on the initial assumptions of culture-driven models derived from earlier work and are either operationalized using individual proxy indicators of a unidirectional process such as English-language proficiency, self-reported ethnic identity, or a composite of these indicators (Giddens 1993; Johnson A. 2000; Schaefer 2002; VandenBos 2007). Noteworthy, limited English-language proficiency in and of itself is not a major barrier to integration or acceptance in U.S. society if one has high professional status. Thus, use of English language proficiency and ethnic identity do not measure the deleterious perceptions of Latinos by dominant culture or structural barriers such as geographic segregation and other exclusionary discriminatory institutional practices that have contributed to a portrayal of Latino families as resistant to progress or modernization.

In other words, the portrayals of Latinos continue to focus on low-income Latinos and immigrants who do not measure up to White middle-class normative standards; those Latinos who possess the class and race privilege of middle-class normative standards of mainstream society remain invisible. One can argue that the epistemological roots of the acculturation construct are based on some cultures being viewed as inferior to White dominant culture. A central question, then, is why do some ethnic groups remain in subordinate social locations while others achieve upward mobility and economic success?[3]

3. Historically many White ethnic cultures were excluded from full participation in American society. However these ethnic groups such as the Irish, Italian, and Jewish communities were voluntary immigrants; did not have a history of conquest in the United States; many arrived with human capital (e.g., education or a crafts skill) similar to many Cubans and South Americans; and racially were eventually able to claim their whiteness. As Bonilla-Silva (2006) observes, different ethnic groups who are closer phenotypically to dominant culture are more likely to access the economic opportunity structure in the United States. Those groups who fit the criteria of "honorary white" based on skin color, class, and immigration status can be bicultural (segmented assimilation) and experience more equitable access to the social and economic opportunity structure (179–180).

Latinos are the most studied group under the rubric of culture or ethnic group, acculturation, and immigrant status, especially Mexican-origin groups (Chun et al. 2003). While acculturation research may acknowledge the role of socioeconomic factors (see, e.g., Organista 2007), culture as implicit in the acculturation measure is foregrounded as a determinant of disparities. Acculturation studies as a whole produce a panethnic view of the Latino population as a foreign, homogeneous cultural group, ignore differences by Latino subgroup, SES and nativity, and omit the impact of structural and institutional forces on an ethnic group's ability to integrate; that is, have access to the opportunity structure to sustain family well-being and upward mobility. In a review of family scholarship on racial and ethnic families, Shannon Weaver et al. (2001) focus on the challenges family scholars confront in the study of Latino families. The authors encourage studies on Latinos by SEP, educational attainment, subgroup, geographic location and other contextual factors. They emphasize the need to be "clear about which Latinos they are sampling" and "to be cautious about generalizing from one subgroup to another" (925). Further, they state, "regardless of which racial and ethnic group family scholars are studying, they will have to consider the contexts in which relationships and families are embedded" (927), and they astutely acknowledge that "the ability to adapt our work to trends in family diversity may be impeded by the social and political climate. The current political climate suggests that some people are threatened by changes and are clinging to the status quo or their perceptions of it" (936).

This body of work on acculturation and Latino families has been plagued by multiple conceptual and methodological issues. As a result, acculturation findings reveal conflicting and inconclusive results with respect to the domains of marriage, parental socialization, child-rearing, and developmental child outcomes. Culture-driven models as exemplified by acculturation have contributed to a stagnant theorizing regarding Latino families and the factors that have played a role in family formation and development, particularly the political, economic, and social processes associated with family life course processes.

## Latino Families and Culture

In understanding the social construction of the concept of the Latino family as theorized in U.S social science, a selected review of the literature provides a map of the study of the Latino family. Cultural values have framed the entire discourse of familism as a form of social structure in which the needs of the family as a group are more important than the needs of the individual family member. Latino and non-Latino social scientists alike proffer multiple ways of defining family. The vast majority of studies, predominantly on low-income

Mexican American and Puerto Rican families, have theorized a broad set of attributes about Latino family cultural enactment that include a strong sense of commitment, dedication, and service to family (Hurtado 1995); extrafamilial responsibilities as part of cultural norms; and personal aspirations and self-sacrifice driven by familial factors (García 2001; Massey et al. 1995; Rodriguez 2000). Latino families have also been characterized as having a strong sense of caring for each other, rely on each other for support (e.g., economically, psychologically) (Brice 2001); and seek to have close geographic proximity to family and extended family members (Trueba 2002).

Investigators also extend the attributes of Latino families and argue that self-esteem and self-identity are byproducts of strong Latino family ties (Pérez et al. 1997). *Familia* is synonymous with security, nurturance, love, and comfort; the concept of family is idealized as something sacred (Baca Zinn and Eitzen 2002; Rodriguez 1999); and *compadrazgo* or co-parenting represents a value on extended family. Family and extended families are viewed as centers for survival and nurturing (Massey et al. 1995), family support, transmission of Latino culture that provides stability, and coping mechanisms (Abalos 1998; Farkas 1996). Scholars have reported that regardless of their national origin or individual group membership, Latinos hold a strong sense of family unity and preference for extended family networks (Hidalgo 1998; Hurtado 1995; Trueba 1999). These *familia* characteristics are representative of the values of Latino families but are also representative of many other cultural groups' family values globally and in the United States. In American culture these family values may be similar but are culturally enacted and expressed in different forms depending on SEP, race, nativity, language, and religion.[4]

---

4. Religion as an important factor in family processes has received limited attention, and its role in family life is beyond the scope of this book. However, several informational points are in order because religion is often cited as important among Latinos. In a commissioned paper, Joseph Palacios (2003) describes the importance of access to Catholic schools as vehicles of educational achievement and upward mobility. Yet he argues that actual programs to enrich or assist the Latino family are virtually nonexistent (258). He also points out that a large sector of the Latino community does not regularly attend religious services and is the "unchurched" (263). Interestingly, researchers often identify religious affiliations and tradition, particularly Catholicism, as an integral part of Latino culture as connected to childbearing and passive gender roles. For example long-standing explanations for why Latino women have more children include their being opposed to birth control and abortion and being passive recipients of their destiny as "good" Catholic women, wives, and mothers. Although Latinas may hold pro-life and anti-contraception attitudes based on religious attitudes, for many Latinas limited education, lack of sex education, and economic access to contraception are also important factors in higher fertility patterns and a presumed lack of agency. The association between Latin Americans and Catholicism is so strong that it belies a surprising fact: Almost one quarter of all Latinos in the United States are Protestants (Murray 2006). Of the 41.3 million Latinos in the United States in 2004, about 23 percent (9.5 million) identify themselves as Protestants or other Christians (including Jehovah's Witnesses and Mormons). Moreover, 37 percent (14.2 million) of all Latino Protestants and Catholics say they have been born again or are evangelical. One percent of Latinos identify with another world religion,

The major explicit argument by a substantial number of scholars, particularly Latino scholars, has been that Latinos/Hispanics share many commonalities. For example, language is claimed to be a cultural marker and a principal means through which socialization processes occur. Language has been described as one of the most powerful and pervasive purveyors of culture that holds a fundamental role in the transmission of beliefs, values, and customs and "is at the heart of Latino cultures" (Brice 2001; Hidalgo 1998, 113). For many Latinos, the Spanish language represents a common bond that promotes solidarity within a diverse population, a cultural link, despite its many dialects and transmutations (Massey et al. 1995), and a bridge between nationalistic/individual and collective identities that provide a unifying force for ethnic identity (Larraín 2000; Darder et al. 1997). These claims are challenged by data that show that by the third generation, few individuals of Latino heritage speak Spanish yet many of these third-generation Latinos may self-identify as Latino. The point is that language per se does not always offer the bridge between individual and collective identities. Thus language, religious, and cultural commonalities are relevant perhaps for specific national subgroups but have shifted in meaning with the expansion of Latino national groups and resettlement communities in the United States.

In effect, these "cultural asset approaches" in the social sciences by Latino scholars have sought to counteract existing cultural-deficit model approaches in investigations of Latinos by identifying unique strengths, cultural assets, and language. Inadvertently, this scholarship in many ways has reinforced negative formulations of Latino families as "foreign and inassimilable," essentialized the category of Latino, and contributed to reinforcing Latinos as "other" by emphasizing difference. Although acknowledging difference is important, simultaneously challenging the social and racialized construction of Latino culture as both different and deviant is imperative within the ethnocentricity of U.S. social science.

Unquestionably culture is an important identity marker. However the major argument here is for a theoretical intervention that deconstructs culture and its measurement by acculturation as a negative identity marker in social science theorizing and reconstructs it as an attribute that captures ways of knowing and being that may strengthen individual ethnic identity and family processes. Latino culture in the United States intersects with race, SEP, nation, gender, and other ascribed statuses, all of which influence how an individual performs his/her role and their own self-construction of cultural or ethnic identity. An

---

such as Buddhism, Islam, or Judaism. Another 37 percent of all Latinos report being atheist or agnostic (Espinosa et al. 2005). Although 70 percent of Latinos in the United States—the majority of whom are Mexican American, Puerto Rican, or Cuban—identify as Catholic, adherence to religious beliefs, values, practice, and affiliations differ by national origin and SEP.

explicit assumption inherent in this process of identity is that *culture* is a fluid and dynamic process that evolves over time; adapts in different geographic locations and in particular historical time periods; and is shaped by history, contemporary events, and reception by host society (Portes 2000). Thus I argue that culture is not a principal predictor of social inequality. However ethnic/cultural groups such as Mexican-origin, American Indians/Native Americans, have historically experienced social inequality in the form of exclusionary institutional practices that contribute to low SES and economic and social marginalization. By decentering cultural/ethnic group as a predictor of social inequality and centering SEP, social scientists can disrupt the subordinate–dominant cultural binary (Zuberi 2001). Inserting SEP (poverty) and its correlates as important factors that contribute to differences can shift our conventional theorizing lens regarding individual and group attributes as responsible for their own marginalization and provide powerful insight into how the historical and contemporary power relationships between Latino ethnic subgroups and the dominant culture group have shaped social location and perceptions of Latinos in the American public imagination. García-Coll et al. (1996) argue in discussing family socialization processes and child development processes that for existing theoretical models to address critical aspects of the environment such as the influences of social position, racism and its derivatives, and segregation, these factors need to be at the core—not the periphery—of the model (1908).

In conclusion, building on an invisible comparative marker of White, educated, and middle-class European society; American sociology developed its frameworks of assimilation and acculturation theory to assess the progress of immigrant groups and then of racial and ethnic groups in the United States. A preeminent focus on culture as the lens to understand differences between Latinos and NHWs, the normative point of reference, has yielded a set of results that marginalize Latino families as "deviant," as aptly observed by William Vega (1995):

> Latino family literature is framed by discussions of *familism,* the behavioral manifestations of Latinos that reflect strong emotional and value commitments to family life. Although other family groups are also family-centered, the style of Latino *familism* presumably makes it distinct from the behavior of non-Hispanic Whites. However the empirical evidence is sparse and inconsistent and the traditional family archetype is controversial because the social science literature has attributed negative social outcomes to it. (7)

## Family Socialization Processes

*Family* is a social arrangement that contributes to economic stability and support and advocacy systems for children and adults and is a central institution in shaping gender socialization and establishing parameters of control

(Hunt et al. 2000). Scholars in the field of family studies and generally social science have conducted research on Latino families with sparse attention to key variables such as access to social and economic resources to support family functioning and well-being. Although parental support, in the form of information, economic and emotional, can be effective in promoting a child's developmental growth, a significant relationship exists between low family economic resources, parent-child communication, and early educational leaving (Davalos et al. 2005). The association between these factors is almost self-evident. Yet in the study of Mexican American youth and family processes, the body of knowledge often does not take into account the consequences of structural inequality in the neighborhood, community, and schools on family processes especially family relationships and gender role expectations. Andrew Fuligni (2007) edited a groundbreaking volume that addresses how institutional expectations based on cultural/ethnic stereotypes are perpetuated and hinder the academic achievement of racial/ethnic students. The authors also cogently illustrate how students themselves in spite of the institutional expectations create agency for themselves by challenging stereotypes and fully participating in the educational pipeline. For example, in a 2009 interview study with Latinas, a current college student reported that she had experienced very low expectations from her teachers in high school (National Woman's Law Center and Mexican American Legal Defense and Education Fund 2009). She stated:

> Generally, academic expectations are lower. You are supposed to get married and have kids and not set high academic goals for yourself. For example, at one point when I told a teacher I was heading away to college, he said he gave me two years before I was married and pregnant. (20)

This example cogently captures the expectation by a school official of stereotypic gender role performance of marriage and pregnancy by a Latina adolescent. These stereotypic representations discourage alternative avenues of opportunity; yet, they also capture the material reality of many young Latinas in the community.

Among low-income Latino families, socialization of children is deeply embedded in the material conditions of their parents' lives. Several observations are representative of the gender-specific scholarly findings on low-income Mexican and Puerto Rican families:

- Specific family responsibilities, such as sibling care and economic contributions, in low-income Latino families have been linked to less time and emphasis on educational goals (Gándara 1995, 1999; Zambrana et al. 1997).

- Closely related are more traditional gender role attitudes and behaviors among low-income families that hinder independence in pursuing one's individual goals, such as education (Gonzalez-Ramos et al. 1998).
- Latino mothers are viewed as passive yet respected and honored as the heart of the family (Rodriguez 1999). Fathers are described as the head of the household, seat of authority, and provider for the family (Mirande 1997).

In the study of Latinos, traditional gender roles that are associated with SEP have been subverted into deviant cultural characteristics of male dominance and female submissiveness characterizing familial processes, especially in regard to value on education and gender role socialization. Historically, low-income families have experienced the necessity of having their children contribute in instrumental ways such as child care so that parents could earn a living to support the family. For Latino girls and boys, traditional gender role expectations are more likely to exist in low-income Latino families than in middle-class Latino families. Parent's material conditions (poverty) generate a necessity of support from both daughters and sons—often in terms of household chores and child care responsibilities—that may limit their acquisition of the skills required to negotiate the larger social world to succeed academically and socially (Rivera and Gallimore 2006). Family roles and processes are further complicated yet reinforced by societal racialized perceptions and stereotypes of the class, ethnic, and gender expressions of Latino girls and boys in public locations. As a result, these youth often experience serious barriers in both school and work settings that hinder their access to the educational and economic opportunity structure (Marlino and Wilson 2006; Bettie 2003).

The scientific discourse on Latino family socialization processes requires shifting the lens to account for an understanding that the transmission of values are filtered through racial/ethnic origins, class background, multiple prisms of poverty, lived experiences, and treatment in the host society. However, parents are only one influence on their children's lives; today's youth are also strongly influenced by secondary socialization agents such as schools and media. These three socializing agents intersect and shape the nuances of the values transmitted, how youth interpret the messages, and their ability to use values and skills to negotiate their place in U.S. society. To more deeply understand how families and youth successfully negotiate their role in the larger society, we need to look more closely at how cultural identity markers—ethnic subgroup, SEP, and race—serve as yardsticks for assessing behaviors and performance in the larger society and act as facilitators of integration or exclusion from U.S. society. Thus the study of Latino families and youth can best be understood by examining the social forces including neighborhood effects and perceptions of school representatives on the developmental processes and life course of family members. Familial patterns and processes in low-income families are significantly linked to material conditions as they are in middle-class families. As observed by Crouter et al.(2006):

> The literature on the implications of parents' employment for families and children has focused almost exclusively on European-American, middle-class and professional families; much less is known about the implications of parents' work for minority families and children. This lacuna is problematic because members of minority groups are more likely to experience negative occupational conditions, such as low-wages, discrimination and underemployment, which may pose challenges for them and their families. (843)

However, the cultural-driven theoretical perspectives on Latino families have rarely captured the importance of these aforementioned factors. In the latter part of the twentieth and early twenty-first century, multiple critiques have been proffered on the theoretical and methodological flaws inherent in these perspectives.

### Critiques of Cultural-Driven Models

A critical review of the literature of Latino family studies yields four major themes in the study of family life. First, a primary and persistent theme is that Latino ethnicity, as a cultural marker, holds primacy as a major analytic category. A second central theme is that the body of knowledge on Latino families does not take into account historical modes of incorporation, treatment, and representations of Latino subgroups. Third, few studies incorporate adequate recognition of the material conditions associated with poverty and its consequences for family processes. Fourth, studies conducted on low-income Latino subgroups are not generalizable to all subgroups and are not representative of high-income Latino groups.

Clara Rodríguez (2004) provides an assessment of the subthemes of the literature on Puerto Ricans prior to the 1970s. These subthemes included a lack of historical context on the relationship between Puerto Rico and the United States; the dominance of an assimilationist, immigrant framework; a tendency to overgeneralize to an entire population from small numbers or extreme cases; a single-group focus with no comparative and equivalent population groups; and the application of paradigms, categories, and contexts on Puerto Rico that were informed only by U.S. experiences (289). Maxine Baca Zinn (1995) challenges the dominant assimilationist and modernization paradigms that have ruled the social science literature on Latino families by decentering the set of assumptions that underlie traditional social science frameworks that have falsely universalized family forms. She argues that:

- Families are socially constructed, shaped by specific historical, social, and material conditions.
- Family development and processes are closely linked with other social structures and institutions.
- Gender is a basic organizing principle of society that shapes families in historically specific ways.
- Race shapes family life and is an integral organizing principle in the United States.

In a subsequent thoughtful and rigorous review article, Maxine Baca Zinn and Barbara Wells (2000) cogently address the limitations of family studies as based on a problem-oriented framework for the study of Latino families. The authors describe several flaws in the analytic categories used to study Latinos families.

- Diversity and heterogeneity within Latino families have been ignored.
- The findings for Mexican-origin families have been generalized to all Latinos.
- Hispanics are officially defined as an ethnic group, and are also defined as a separate racialized group.
- Native-born and immigrant Latinos are subordinated in similar ways.
- Definitional and measurement flaws include inconsistent definitions of the concepts of familism and extended family systems.

Because of inadequate conceptualization of structural factors such as SEP, segmented labor markets, and institutional discrimination and racism associated with differences in family development and processes, knowledge production has been limited in advancing our understanding of Latino families in the United States (Baca Zinn and Pok 2002).

Critique of the empirical work on Latino groups in general and of Latino family studies, in particular, has been growing. Dominant or mainstream social scientists who have a privileged voice in the academic world (with few exceptions) often conduct research on Latino groups and families without theorizing about the development of these groups within the larger United States context (Rodriguez 2008, 5). Additionally, these social scientists frequently explain family processes outside the structural and contextual arena such as unemployment, economic development, and globalization, all of which effect low-income Latino families (Baca Zinn and Pok 2002; Perez 2004).

Edna Viruell-Fuentes (2007) presents cogent arguments regarding the assumptions of acculturation research: (1) culture is located within an individual, and cultural traits are inherent to members of a particular group (instead of envisioning culture as a system that is socially constructed); and (2) the onus of culture is placed on the individual and is likely to lead to individual-centered interventions at the expense of addressing the structural contexts that reproduce social and economic inequities. Thus attention is diverted from examining the historical, political, and economic contexts of migration. Linda Hunt et al. (2004) similarly provide a cogent critique of acculturation research in the field of public health and conclude that "in the absence of a clear definition and an appropriate historical and socio-economic context, the concept of acculturation has come to function as an ideologically convenient black box, wherein problems of unequal access to health posed by more material barriers, such as insurance, transportation, education, and language, are pushed from the foreground, and ethnic culture is made culpable for health inequalities" (982). These critiques highlight the major flaw of prior research that does not include the intersection of ethnicity and SEP to better explain disparities in wealth, education, and family processes between and across Latino subgroups and NHWs. Observed disparities, however, have more to do with access to social capital and variables such as SEP and racism than to cultural capital. In other words, if low-income Latino families were compared with low-income NHWs, the results would most likely generate similar family patterns (Newman and Massengill 2006, 429).

More recent work embraces a more complex perspective on family development and acknowledges the role of nation, SEP, and other nonfamily factors in the ability of families to fulfill their roles. For example, a study of Central and South American families provides some insight on family structure and functioning. Jennifer Glick and Jennifer Van Hook (2002) report that Central and South American parents are more likely to live in households in which their adult children provide most of the household income and this dependency decreases with duration in the United States. Another study on family processes found that 96 percent of the Central Americans had experienced a disruption in their family unit because of separation during immigration; that is, remaining in their home country until parents could bring them to United States. The authors caution that the data apply to low-income families and may not be representative of higher SEP Central and South Americans (Suarez-Orozco et al. 2002). In contrast, a study conducted in Canada on groups from El Salvador, Guatemala, and Nicaragua found few differences between family life in homeland and in resettlement. The authors report that values on the family unit were strong and gender roles were traditionally defined. Glick and Van Hook (2002) discuss that differences in family structure are, "in part, attributable to the recent immigration of many from Central and South America." (72). The important message in these studies is that family structures and practices brought from the country of origin change as immigrants adapt to the new living arrangement and social norms in the United States. The authors conclude: "Yet there is great variation in the family behavior patterns of Latinos in the United States and it is difficult to conclude that these differences are solely based on cultural preferences from the origin community" (72).

These studies break new ground by underscoring variation in family processes and patterns. Emerging scholarship on Latino families examines family and gender role changes embedded in an understanding of ethnicity/culture as a fluid and dynamic construct and family processes that represent variability by SEP. The emerging scholarly discourse contests prior frameworks that argue that commitment to *familia,* as a culturally bound ideology of rigid patriarchy, maintains low-income Latinos in conditions of inequality. Empirical work on Latino families has consistently demonstrated variability in gender role attitudes and family processes (Baca Zinn 1995; Cofresi, 1999; Toro-Morn 2008).

## Emergent Scholarship on Family SEP, Gender Socialization, and Roles

The twenty-first century is witnessing an emerging body of work that is decentering culture as a predictor of Latino family structure and processes and focusing on the role of SEP and social inequality. Emerging scholarship is also contesting family science and sociological paradigms that have not fully incorporated conceptualizations and measurement indicators of the role of racialized systems and the effects of class on social location of families (Newman and Massengill 2006; Burton et al. 2010). In a recent review of a decade of research on qualitative studies conducted on poverty, Katherine Newman and Rebekah Massengill make two important observations that are relevant to Latino family scholarship: (1) the hardship of poverty, its neighborhood effects, and its impact on family formation are not new observations although the economic context has changed; and (2) "disconnects between parenting and marriage hold across race lines and therefore appear to be more of a question of class and poverty than of race and culture"(429). A most compelling observation by the authors that perhaps denotes new theorizing guidance is:

> The reintroduction for the language of class has been a hallmark of the past decade, drawing it closer to some of the original concerns of sociologists in the 1940's, contrasted with a nearly universal emphasis on race and ethnicity characteristic of more recent decades (423).

Several studies are presented as illustrative of an emerging lens that centers SEP rather than culture as a critical marker of a family's ability to serve its role of protector, teacher, and advocate for the offspring. As noted by sociologist Annette Lareau (2003), "conceptualizations of the social processes through which families differ are underdeveloped and little is known about how families transmit advantages to their children" (249). Lareau conducted an in-depth, comparative ethnographic study of African American and White families to assess different child-oriented educational practices. Detailed descriptions of what any observer of family life would readily find include the following: middle-income parents have more economic resources to provide multiple access points to the economic opportunity structure for the development and growth of their children in their specific talents, or in activities such as sports, which will serve them well in accomplishing future goals; Middle-income families who are more educated tend to engage in parenting practices that stress communication, negotiation, and logic and reasoning; and values of assertiveness and competitiveness are associated with high parental education level in all cultures. In general, parents with higher education and marketable skills tend to be more economically and psychologically prepared to engage in early learning activities and skill building with their children and to be actively involved in their child's education across racial/ethnic groups. In contrast, low-income Latino and immigrant parents require skills and knowledge to effectively engage in their child's early learning. Low-income Latino immigrant parents face a lack of access to information, challenges in adjusting to a new environment, and fear of current immigration policy as barriers to their full participation in their child's education (Murguia 2008). Other studies are briefly discussed to illustrate the role of SES (as measured by education level) in family processes and gender role attitudes.

In a study of ethnic differences in family integration among Mexican Americans, Puerto Ricans, and Whites, the authors found that social class position matters more than culture. Higher SEP was found to be associated with less proximity to family members, less coresidence, and greater likelihood of financial support. The authors conclude that family integration varies among Latino families and "that familial practices and cultural beliefs should be differentiated to avoid collapsing differences to simply culture" (Sarkisian et al. 2006). These findings are confirmed in a recent study of the Current Population Survey (CPS) pooled data for 2000–2005 to document living arrangements of Latino children ages zero through seventeen among Mexican-, Puerto Rican-, and Cuban-origin children. The authors found that national origin and generational status are associated with different family structures, and within-group differences were observed by family income and parent's education. The data strongly suggest that the structural position of the child's family is of continued importance in academic achievement over time and explains some of the difference across ethnic and generation status groups. These findings are confirmed by Nancy Landale et al. (2006) in the trend analyses of family formation and structure with several indicators of social change. Similar to national patterns, the data show a marked decline in early marriage across Latino subgroups, decreased fertility rates, increase in female householders, and increased cohabitation. Consistent with differences in their histories and social locations, there are specific differences across and between Hispanic subgroups and Whites (145).

In another study on gender role attitudes, college students' perception of parents' gender role ideologies, values, and behaviors concerning work and family intersections was conducted (Franco et al. 2004). A survey was administered to forty-seven Latina and sixty European American/White females with a mean age of 19.4 at a public university in Northern California. Although Latino family of origin background in terms of education and job status was significantly different from White families, respondents did not differ in terms of the correspondence between gender role ideologies and subsequent behavior. The authors found that Latino and White mothers and fathers largely resembled each other in gender role ideologies, showing "gender differences were not more exaggerated in one group than in the other" (763).

Recent work on socialization practices of Latino families, using interviews with twenty-two Latino faculty and staff at a large Midwestern university who were raised in Spanish-speaking families, examined gender role socialization, differential treatment of girls and boys, and stereotypic feminine behaviors and curtailment of girl's activities (Raffaelli and Ontai 2004). Building on an initial study, a second study was conducted with ninety-seven women and sixty-nine men (median age twenty-one) with almost 50 percent of the participants of Mexican origin. The study measured gender role socialization, differential treatment of girls and boys, parental gender role attitudes, family language use, and background characteristics. Although families expected both girls and boys to contribute to household chores (girls indoors, boys outdoors) and sibling care, boys reported more freedom and more interaction outside the home with members of the opposite sex. Sex-typing is observed whereby girls are expected to be more appropriately feminine and boys masculine. Parents encourage male or female behaviors in the child of their same gender.

However, parents with less traditional gender role attitudes were more likely to speak English at home and with their spouse and to have higher levels of education. Fathers who encouraged their sons to do chores and limited their son's freedom regarding social activities tended to have higher levels of education and to hold more egalitarian gender role attitudes. Similar patterns of results were found for mothers; that is, higher education and use of English were positively associated with more egalitarian gender role attitudes. Of interest, fathers who encouraged *manliness* (masculine gender expression) also encouraged their sons to do chores. Not surprisingly, activity restrictions for girls are associated with traditional and religion-oriented values that are linked with fears of early sexuality. The author concludes that these findings are consistent with those reported in studies of non-Latino families and that "the current body of literature suggests that the process of gender-typing is similar across different ethnic groups" at similar levels of education (Raffaelli and Ontai 2004, 11).

Another study of 140 Mexican American female and male undergraduates at a midsize Southwestern university measured attitudes toward the role of the female in the workplace and child care responsibility of working parents. Results showed that males and females generally disagreed with traditional attitudes regarding the role of females in the workplace and child care responsibility. Although there was a trend toward more traditional attitudes on the part of males, the differences were minor. The authors conclude: "Our subjects had retained an important part of their heritage by retaining their Spanish language, but their attitude toward the female's role in the workplace and parental responsibility for child care reflected a more Euro-American orientation" (Gowan and Trevino 1998, 1091).

Norma Cofresi (1999) conducted an in-depth study of the gender role expectations of thirty professional Puerto Rican women with an average age of 38.6 residing in Puerto Rico. The study explored the domains of mothering, marital relationships, sexuality, domestic responsibility, and reputation (or community image). All but one of the participants defined their sex-role ideals in terms of their professional identities and/or in terms of their capacity to combine a professional life with a family life. Three analytic gender role categories emerged from the data: traditional, transitional, and egalitarian. The study concluded the following: traditional patterns of behavior, particularly with respect to mothering coexist alongside more egalitarian attitudes; women expected companionship and cooperation from their mates but were willing to be flexible to preserve their marriages; in their sexuality, they were active and expressive; and women wanted to have a good reputation but also valued their own standards.

Based on this current body of work, I draw two conclusions: Latino family socialization practices and gender role norms and expectations are in transition, and gender role socialization is highly associated with higher education levels in Latino men and women.

### Intersectional Perspective on Family Development and Processes

Social science theorizing using an intersectional perspective allows the analyses of the social location of racial/ethnic groups within the larger social, economic, and political context and the exclusionary racial hierarchy (Bonilla-Silva 2006; Burton et al. 2010; Dill and Zambrana 2009; Portes 2000). The illustrative examples included in the previous section provide new ways of thinking to improve our understanding of the variability of Latino family development and processes. These studies have yielded a more in-depth understanding of variations in family processes and gender role socialization by SEP and contest the generalizability of studies on low-income families. The majority of studies on low-income Mexican-origin families do not represent the rich heterogeneity of family processes within either Mexican-origin groups or other Latino subgroups. Further the majority of studies do not take into account the construct of *colorism* as a stratification variable (Burton et al. 2010). In a 2010 review, Linda Burton and colleagues examine the intersection of race, ethnicity, and colorism (defined as granting privilege to lighter skin vs. darker skin; that is, skin color closest to White) in the scholarly family science literature on racial/ethnic and immigrant families in the last decade. The authors focus on three substantive research areas that have been most frequently studied: inequality and socioeconomic mobility within and across families, interracial romantic pairings, and the racial socialization of children. The authors found that while social scientists have incorporated elements of critical race theory and colorism in family relevant research, there is a need for more attention to these perspectives. They state:

> The use of elements equates with some progress, but we argue that in a multicultural society that is shifting in numbers and potentially in the distribution of power, researchers must be mindful of the roles that racialized systems and differentiations based on skin color play in families' lives. The use of critical race theories and perspectives on colorism in research fosters that mindfulness. (454)

Thus, new critiques of conventional paradigms used in family relevant research and emerging studies disrupt the formulation of Latino families as social problems. These new paradigms contribute to new ways of thinking about Latino families and gender role performance, and in that process emerging scholarly production extends the boundaries of knowledge.

To advance our understanding of U.S. Latino families, research may be improved by operating with critical explicit assumptions that contest conventional explanatory paradigms about inequality and social location. I am proposing the use of an intersectional lens that includes three foundational critical theorizing assumptions:

1. Racial/ethnic characteristics are mutually constituted and are embedded in power relations. *Power-based relations* are defined as "hierarchical, stratified (ranked), centered in power-benefiting and providing options and resources for some by harming and restricting options and resources for others" (Weber 2010, 23). One aspect of power-based relations is to make invisible the structural factors that contribute to restricted resources and options and to uphold a paradigm that attributes success or upward mobility to the myth of an individual's "pulling themselves up by their bootstraps," meritocracy, or color-blind society (Bonilla-Silva 2006).

2. History shapes lived experiences that in turn are reflected in dominant–subordinate group relations that shape access to resources and policies and practices that maintain subordination of groups, and hinder social mobility.
3. Gendered and racialized social constructions are made visible and filtered to the American public imagination through primary mechanisms of socialization such as schools, media, and science. The major argument is that the marking of Latinos as a *racialized other* has consequences that limit access to the economic opportunity structure. The consequent power relations and the racialized social constructions of targeted Latino subgroups as poor and culturally stagnant—a negative identity marker—are inserted in social science research, reinforced in public service systems, and centered in the public American imagination by the media.

Figure 3.1 illustrates a set of intersectional relationships that make central the multiplicity of factors associated with low social location of Latinos and shows pathways to understand why negative perceptions of Latinos in the American public imagination persist. The intersectional lens is used to understand why some but not all Latino families have remained disproportionately in low socioeconomic position and why the implicit attributions associated with cultural values, acculturation, and Latinidad (an essentialist characterization of the social construction of all Latino groups sharing a common heritage that is based on food and language) shape and reinforce this social location (Caminero-Santangelo, 2007).

In the study of Latinos, intersectionality provides an alternative analytic lens that seeks to inform theorizing around Latino families. The use of this lens provides an opportunity to deconstruct culture in explanatory paradigms as a reason for difference and inequality. In addition, it aims to insert "mindfulness" of factors such as historical incorporation (conquest vs. voluntary immigration) its connection with historical and contemporary policies and laws, and institutionalized practices such as housing segregation to extend understanding of variation in family development by SEP and race among Latino subgroups. The pathways in the paradigm show links among nation/geographic origins or ethnicity, historical mode of incorporation, and political and legal initiatives that have resulted in denial of historic access to basic citizenship rights such as education and voting rights (Johnson 1995). These interconnected factors in turn influence SEP (as measured by low educational attainment and income) and shape the community context in which Latinos live, and impact their knowledge, beliefs, and attitudes of options and resources. The resulting material conditions fuel representational negative cultural identity markers that contribute to differential access to the

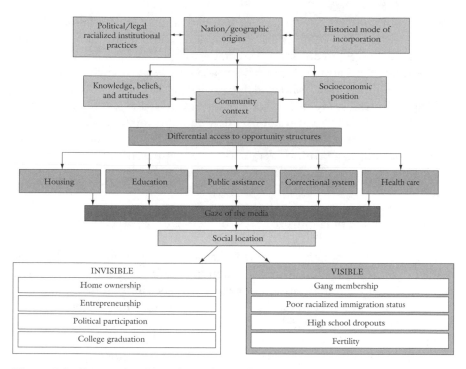

**Figure 3.1.** Intersectional lens for understanding the patterns of social inequality and social location of Latinos. *Source:* Modified from Zambrana and Carter-Pokras 2004b.

source and economic opportunity structure and disproportional interaction with public services systems. Media gaze more often than not serves as the basis for racialized public policies and institutionalized practices that reinforce the social location of Latinos, particularly racialized Mexican Americans and Puerto Ricans.

This paradigm foregrounds the importance of theorizing knowledge to disrupt conventional cultural cognitive maps or schemata in social science and disciplinary knowledge production and mass media communication channels. To advance new ways of thinking, we must look beyond culture to examine the variation of family processes and structure by SEP, historical incorporation, and race and how these factors contribute to (or hinder) optimal functioning, social integration, and social mobility of U.S. Latino families.

Multiple factors in the twenty-first century, such as demographic changes, educational and professional mobility within and across subgroups, immigration status, and public policy, have significantly altered the social location, family development, and family processes of Latinos. Studies to date have included predominantly low-income Mexican American and Puerto Rican samples. These studies are assuredly not representative of the U.S.–lived experiences of groups studied or Latino subgroup heterogeneity. Most disciplinary scientists who study culture, race, ethnicity, and society have tended to be outsiders looking in. In the study of Latinos who are perceived as "different," physically, emotionally and socially, an overarching implicit social construction of a culturally, racialized, and gendered group has become embedded over time in the American imagination. Yet, I have demonstrated in this chapter examples of a contemporary and emerging body of scholarship that has initiated important new approaches in the study of Latino families. The new scholarship takes into account SEP and its impact on family development to inform our understanding of family processes and gender role socialization in Latino families.

What emerging research is showing is that higher education (SEP) is a major marker of more egalitarian attitudes and more fluidity in family gender roles, and that the parental transmission of gender role socialization messages varies by SEP. Transmission of these egalitarian gender roles may be enacted differently than in dominant culture families, but what matters is the material conditions (SEP) of the family and how these conditions shape gender role performance, family formation decisions, and family functioning. Thus, what these data explicitly confirm is that culture is not the major predictor of material conditions but that material conditions regardless of culture can positively or negatively impact family processes and structure. To reiterate, the future study of Latino families must include the varying forms of structural inequality to better understand the multiple and varied ways that Latino families enact their roles to negotiate their place in U.S. society.

In the following chapters, I build on this paradigm to discuss more specifically the role of education in Latino children's lives, including parental involvement, academic indicators, and college pathways.

# 4

# The Importance of Education

> Unless concerted action is taken to alleviate the
> hardship and suffering related to poverty and to spur
> development that can lead to economic and social
> stability for communities and families, little change
> in the character and quality of urban education in the
> U.S. will change.
> —Noguera 2003, 142

E ducation is a critical asset for Latinos, yet it has been an elusive reality. Structural inequality in public schools has generated a plethora of research that has generally been ignored by education and social science researchers. For example, works such as *Savage Inequalities* (Kozol 1991) and in particular the report of the White House Initiative for Hispanic Educational Excellence (WHIHEE) (2003) produced extensive documentation of inadequate school settings, inferior curriculum, and low-quality schools that offer clear evidence as to why Latino students underperform. Most important, WHIHEE produced thousands of transcribed pages on the lived experiences of students and parents who understood the importance of education for their children's social mobility and wanted change. Although most research continues to focus on individual characteristics of students and test scores, structural inequality in access to quality of schooling and historic and persistent patterns of discriminatory institutional practices shed light on long-standing disparate academic performance indicators (Carter and Segura 1979; Kumashiro 2008; MacDonald 2004; Noguera 2003; Valenzuela 1999).

To answer some of the questions on why low-income Latino youth are not doing as well as other racial/ethnic youth, I provide an overview of selected studies conducted on parental attitudes and involvement in Latino children and youth's educational experiences, a statistical portrait of Latino children and youth in the educational pipeline,[1] and the institutional practices that serve

---

1. Data on educational pipeline from KewalRamani et al. 2007; National Center for Education Statistics 2003a. Data from the U.S. Department of Education, National Center for Education Statistics are used in this chapter.

as a context for understanding their social location in U.S. society. Five main Latino groups comprise the Latino student population in U.S. schools, colleges, and universities. The largest Latino group is of Mexican origin, followed by Central and South American, Puerto Rican, Cuban American, and other Latino/Hispanic groups (Ramirez 2004). Each Latino subgroup varies by socioeconomic position (SEP), education level, and immigration status (e.g., U.S. citizenship/permanent residency/naturalization). New data for specific Latino groups on educational indicators permit the ability to assess differences by nativity and citizenship. Combining naturalized and Latino immigrants' together makes invisible differences such as parental education that is highly associated with academic performance in schools. Comparisons are included when data are available.

Schools that low-income and poor immigrant children attend are usually low-resourced and under surveillance (e.g., video cameras and police on or near premises) as noted in chapter 6. All too often teachers are not well-prepared in their educational training programs, nor are they aware of the underfunding of the school systems in which they will teach. Thus, the data presented are not representative of the dedication of many teachers in these systems and the struggles they confront with policies, for example, of school boards, local boards of education, and the state. As for most professionals in the United States, teachers are socialized into official roles that may not be consistent with the understanding of the inadequate material conditions of Latino families and language barriers.

### Parental Involvement in Schools by Race and Ethnicity

Many racial and ethnic parents experience barriers in navigating the school system and in translating their cultural assets and beliefs about education into social capital for their children in the schools. A number of factors contribute to the translation of a family's social capital to school capital, including parental income and educational attainment, English language proficiency (ELP), parental beliefs and educational aspirations for their children, and parental involvement in schools. A commonly held stereotype is that Latino parents do not value education; however, the empirical data suggest otherwise (Lareau and Horvat 1999; McDermott and Rothenberg 2000; Quiocho and Daoud 2006; Van Velsor and Orozco 2007).

Assumptions regarding low-income families are prevalent in educational institutions from prekindergarten (pre-K) to the university level. A primary assumption is that for families living in poverty their children's education is not one of their main priorities. Understanding the structural constraints of families due to poverty is essential to understanding the impact of these constraints on parental involvement. Specifically, the parents are often working

**Table 4.1.** Parental Perceptions of Education and Involvement in Children's School and Literacy-Related Activities, 2002–2003

| Item responded to | Non-Hispanic White (%) | Non-Hispanic Black (%) | Latino (%) |
|---|---|---|---|
| "Had at least some influence over their children's education" | 88 | 91 | 94 |
| "It was very important for their children to attend college" | 78 | 94 | 95 |
| "Participated in school-based parental involvement activities" | 63 | 51 | 45 |
| "Attended parent-teacher conference or general school meeting" | 91 | 87 | 86 |
| "Children had someone help them with their homework daily" | 82 | 93 | 92 |
| "Children having been read to (during the week)" | 89 | 76 | 63 |
| "Children visiting a library (during the week)" | 43 | 34 | 26 |

*Source:* Adapted from Vaden-Kiernan and McManus 2005, 11–26.

multiple jobs to meet their basic needs such as food, shelter, and clothing, and although participating in the educational development of their children may be very important, it is not always feasible. Specific structural barriers associated with social class location rather than culture often limit parents from fully and regularly participating in the different levels of school involvement.

Latinos across social class groups report interest in having their children fully participate and integrate within the public school system. Because Latinos are disproportionately affected by poverty, they are also overwhelmingly affected by the barriers to parental involvement resulting from poverty. Table 4.1 shows percent of parental perceptions of influence and aspirations for their child's education and involvement in children's school and literacy-related activities by race and ethnicity. Latino parents (94 percent) were more likely to report that they had "some influence" over their children's education than White and Black parents. When asked if it was important for their children to attend college, almost all the Latino and Black parents reported that it was very important compared to 78 percent of Whites. Latino parents do value education, perceive that they have a significant role in positively influencing their children's education, and are involved in their child's education (Vaden-Kiernan and McManus 2005; Fry and Gonzales 2008).

Parents were asked about overall school-based involvement and engagement, for example, if they had attended a general school meeting or a regularly scheduled parent-teacher conference. Parents were also asked if they had attended a school or a class event, acted as a class volunteer, or served on a school committee or participated in a school fundraiser.[2] Interestingly, few differences were reported in the rates of parental participation in attending teacher-parent meetings or school meetings, although White parents had slightly higher participation rates (Vaden-Kiernan and McManus 2005). Differences in school-based parental level activities were observed by race and ethnicity. Latino families (45 percent) participated in these activities almost 20 percent less than White families (63 percent). For Latino households where neither parent spoke English, that rate declined to 35 percent, while 51 percent of the Black families reported participating in these school-related activities.

Additional parental involvement included what the parents did in the homes to help their children; that is, reading to the students and providing help with homework. Ninety percent of all parents, regardless of race or ethnicity, reported that they or someone in the home read to the child during the week. Further, 37 percent of Whites, 32 percent of Blacks, and 35 percent of Latinos reported that they or someone in the home read to their children at least five days a week. Trend data reveal that daily family reading to young children (3–5 years of age) significantly increased for non-Hispanic Whites (NHWs; 59.1 to 67.4 percent) and Asians (45.7 percent to 60.4 percent) from 1993–2007. Among Latino children the trend shows that close to 40 percent engage in this parental activity, and it has remained stable. For Black (NHB) children there has been a slight decrease (38.7 percent to 34.6 percent in 1993 and 2007 respectively). Several parental characteristics are associated with daily reading to children, such as family structure (married couple), bachelor's degree or higher (73.7 percent vs. 30.8 percent for less than high school but increases for each level of education completed), and mothers who work less than thirty-five hours per week (Federal Interagency Forum on Child and Family Statistics [FIFCFS] 2009, 151). These factors are most likely associated with all other early learning activities.

In terms of someone helping with the students' homework at least five times a week, only 9 percent of White parents answered in the affirmative compared to 17 percent of Black and 15 percent of Hispanic parents, with only 5 percent of Whites, 4 percent of Blacks, and 6 percent of Hispanics reporting that no homework help was given at all. Finally, of parents who checked to be sure homework was completed, 82 percent of Whites reported someone in the

2. The National Parent-Teachers Association (2010), *National Standards for Parent/Family Involvement,* categorizes six levels of parent involvement, ranging from the simplest level of comfort with the school to the most complex level of parents as codecision makers. Parental involvement can include receiving and responding to school communication by e-mail, telephone, newsletters, memos, or notices; attending parent-teacher conferences; serving on a school committee; and doing home-based activities, such as homework supervision and reading with the student. See National Parent-Teachers Association at www.pta.org and the National Coalition for Parent Involvement in Education at www.ncpie.org.

home checked the homework, while significantly more Blacks (93 percent) and Hispanics (92 percent), reported the same (see table 4.1). Not unexpectedly, only about one-quarter of Latino children visited a library during the week, while one-third of Blacks and over 40 percent of White children did so (Vaden-Kiernan and McManus 2005). These parental involvement indicators show that Latino parents are interested and concerned about their children doing well in school, and they check their homework and read to them with frequency; yet, they are the least likely to use the library. Availability of libraries in their community as well as scheduled hours may be a barrier to this important resource, particularly if parents cannot afford to buy books or educational videos. Although these data challenge commonly held perceptions that Latino parents are not active participants in school-related activities, individual as well as institutional factors delimit the participation of low-income parents in school-related activities.

### Factors Associated with School Involvement

High levels of parental school involvement are positively associated with higher levels of parental education, English language proficiency, and welcoming and responsive school systems. Educational level of parents reveals a significant gap between Latino and White parents who have a high school education or a bachelor's degree. Between 1974 and 1999, although Latino maternal education level slightly increased, it was not significantly related to students' achievements and remained well below White and Black parents' educational level (National Center for Education Statistics [NCES], 2003a). English language use shows that an increasing number of Latino children and youth speak mostly English at home. For example, 55 percent of Latino students grade K–5 spoke mostly English at home, 68 percent in grades 6–8, and 62 percent in grades 9–12 (NCES 2003a). In 2007, 68 percent of Latino children and 64 percent of Asian children spoke a language other than English at home, although less than 20 percent of Asian (16 percent) and Latino (18 percent) children had difficulty with English. The percentage of school-aged children who have difficulty with English varies by region, from a low of 3 percent in the Midwest to a high of 9 percent in the West (9). For example in 2006, 74 percent of Latino children said they spoke English, "well" or "very well" (Fry and Gonzales 2008). Patterns of another language spoken at home for both Asian and Latino children have remained stable from 2000 to 2007 (FIFCFS 2009, 108). These data suggest that speaking a language other than English at home is not in and of itself a major risk factor. It becomes a risk factor when it is linked with low maternal and paternal education and poverty. Though language and citizenship have been attributed to Latinos' underachievement in schools, the majority of Latino school-aged children and youth

(77 percent) are U.S. citizens who, although they speak Spanish, do not report difficulty speaking English.

Poverty affects Latino families' involvement in schools in multiple ways, such as computer access, available and flexible time, work demands, personal safety concerns, transportation costs, and English language proficiency to meet the demands for parental involvement by the schools. As noted above, parental involvement was high for all parents regardless of race/ethnicity. Yet, low-income Latino parents are at a disadvantage also in participating in Internet-based school-related activities due to lack of access to/or knowledge of Internet forms of communication.

Parental education is strongly linked with increased use of the Internet and greater likelihood of having a home Internet connection and a broadband connection among Latinos. Those with less than a high school degree are much less likely than those with a college degree to have and use the Internet and to have a broadband connection.[3]

Other employment, economic, and community factors may impede parental participation in school-related activities. Low-income Latino families often have jobs that are more inflexible and include an hourly salary that does not include paid leave, which means that taking time off from work would result in a loss of income for the family. Poor Latino families may also have multiple jobs that cause them to be unavailable to attend school meetings, participate in school functions, or attend other parental involvement activities (even if meetings are held in the evening, an accommodation by schools to meet the needs of working parents). For example, additional trips to the school in the evening or on a Saturday are an additional expense that may compromise spending allocations (McDermott and Rothenberg 2000). Transportation cost and safety issues may represent a significant barrier for high-level parental participation (Van Velsor and Orozco 2007). Neighborhood safety is an additional consideration for many parents when deciding to attend school-related evening activities.

In terms of availability for supervising homework, multiple jobs and household responsibilities may not allow the time to help with school-related work.

---

3. Since 2006, Latino Internet use has risen more rapidly among those with less education and lower income, while it leveled off for other groups. In 2006, 31 percent of those who never graduated from high school used the Internet, but the share increased to 41 percent in 2008. At the same time, for high school graduates, there was a four percentage point increase in Internet use, and for college graduates, there was a three percentage point increase. Some 41 percent of Latinos lacking a high school degree went online in 2008; almost three-fourths (74 percent) of Latinos with a high school degree went online, and 92 percent of Latino college graduates went online. Among Internet users, 64 percent of Latinos lacking a high school degree had a home Internet connection in 2008, as compared with 84 percent of Latino high school graduates, and 94 percent of Latino college graduates. Some 62 percent of Latino home Internet users who lacked a high school degree had a broadband connection in 2008; this share was 78 percent for Latino high school graduates, and 86 percent for Latino college graduates (Livingston et al. 2009).

This dilemma that low-income parents face coupled with the lack of resources to afford Internet and broadband, tutoring or assistance outside of the home for their children seriously affects both academic success for the child and active parental involvement. School-related committee service or classroom volunteering that can immensely assist parents in understanding school systems, knowing the teachers, and meeting fellow parents—all of which can promote the child's academic achievement—are difficult if not impossible for low-income families.

In addition, parents own level of educational attainment may significantly affect decisions to be involved in their children's educational activities and their confidence to contribute to their child's learning in a positive manner (Hoover-Dempsey and Sandler 1997; Quiocho and Daoud 2006). Limited academic skills are not always self-imposed but rather may be the result of lack of access to schooling in their country of origin or prior attendance in poor-quality U.S. public educational systems often found in low-income Black and Latino neighborhoods (Kumashiro 2008; Valenzuela 1999; Noguera 2003,). For example, parents may have been placed into special classes, such as English as a Second Language (ESL), based on language spoken at home versus language ability and thus were excluded from general education classes or the academic track. Parents excluded from the general education academic experience may lack the basic academic skill set necessary to help their children and knowledge on how to navigate this system, and thus are less likely to know how to advocate for their children in schools.

Latinos tend to be more affected by lack of formal education because low-income Latino families are most likely to have a head of household that has not graduated from high school (with the second largest population being high school graduates). Latino immigrant parents may not be English language proficient and may also have low literacy levels in Spanish, which impede their ability to understand the translated information communicated to them from the schools. On the other hand, this is not to say that immigration status and English language proficiency predict low socioeconomic status. Latinos or any foreign-born immigrant who arrive in the United States with a strong educational background (who were often middle class in their countries of origin) are more likely to understand their role as educational advocates for their children and to be aware of options and resources to help their children, such as scholarships, after-school academic programs, and summer camps. Thus, it is not language alone but rather the intersection of language ability and educational attainment of parents combined with attitudes of school personnel toward low-income Latino immigrants or U.S–born racialized Latinos that often result in exclusionary institutional practices. These practices adversely affect educational progress of these children in the K–12 educational pipeline. For low-income Latino parents, lack of school involvement is often not representative of individual beliefs concerning the value of education but rather of social and structural barriers that impede equitable access to school resources, after-school enrichment programs, and knowledge regarding the importance of their active and assertive role in school systems.

## Institutional Barriers to Active Parental Involvement

A significant barrier to parental involvement of low-income Latino parents is the trust and authority invested in teachers. Parents may trust that teachers have the best interest of the child in mind, and parents need not be interfering in the educational life of their children. Parents reported that in their native countries they were not expected to be involved with the school and/or challenge the teacher's authority. Thus parents need to be informed that instructional personnel have a specific set of expectations regarding the role of parents in terms of attending school functions and the importance of contacting teachers with child concerns. Patricia Van Velsor and Graciela Orozco (2007) summarize the position of the public school personnel on parental engagement that involves the parents meeting the needs of the school as they relate to the children's education. Specifically, the authors state: "parents are invited to support school activities in the classroom, on field trips, and in the library or school office" (17), activities that Latino families participated in the least. Although the lack of Latino parental participation is a long-held belief, other studies show that schools themselves are discouraging parental participation.

Latino families whose children attend Title I schools are often either intentionally or unintentionally excluded from school activities.[4] Teachers, who believe that parents do not have much to offer in the way of educational value and social capital, end up judging the presence of parents in the classroom as a challenge to their authority as well as a distraction. Low-income immigrant parents who speak languages other than English may not be invited to participate or volunteer in classrooms. Teachers report being burdened with having to plan special activities for parents to participate in once they enter the classroom (Van Velsor and Orozco 2007).

The most limited interaction between homes and schools occurs in decision-making–level activities where parental involvement may play a significant role, which is widely reported as central in a child's academic performance. For example, parents can serve as part of the selection of curriculum, part of the team that assigns their children to certain tracks and placements, and on advisory committees and boards to select teachers with whom their children are placed. However, schools are often perceived as having an uninviting climate for the

4. A federally funded school designation that provides resources to allow for additional basic skills instruction for low-achieving students in eligible schools.

parents who are interested in being actively involved at this level (DeGaetano 2007). True partnership is at the heart of parental involvement that engages parents as active participants in the processes that affect their children's education, which is the model in schools in middle-class communities. However, this is not a form of parental involvement that is widely practiced or encouraged by school personnel in low-income racial/ethnic communities.

Latino parents express great interest in participation when they are informed about the benefits of active involvement, and when they are engaged in these processes, they respond positively (Hoover-Dempsey and Sandler 1997; Mc-Dermott and Rothenberg 2000; Quiocho and Daoud 2006). When parents are not actively included in the decision-making processes for their children, school decisions that result in adverse effects for their children may contribute to conflict. Further, when differing expectations between teachers and families are irreconcilable due to different communication styles or conflict resolution practices of school officials, parents often feel that their voices are not being heard or respected, and they feel silenced (Lareau and Horvat 1999; Lawson 2003). Most low-income Latinos do not have the mainstream, middle-class, social and cultural capital that is generally valued by school personnel. Thus low-income Latino parents in contrast to middle-class parents regardless of race or ethnicity often do not voice their concerns because teachers have not welcomed their participation. As a result they may often not be aware of decisions to place their children in nonacademic tracks, nor are they informed of options and consequences of those decisions for their children's educational future. (Teachers' perceptions and attitudes and institutional practices that adversely affect Latino student performance are presented in chapters 5 and 6).

These data begin to provide some insight as to the reasons why the educational underperformance of Latino students has persisted. It broadens the framework in understanding the "clash" of low-income parental expectations and constraints and school culture expectations, which can be termed institutional exclusionary practices. In a 2009 report, the question of whether efforts at involving parents have helped poor children concluded a resounding no. Although since the 1960s the federal government has provided funds and required schools serving poor children from early childhood through twelfth grade to involve parents with such practices as remedial education for parents and skills in using the Internet, there is no oversight on accountability for how schools spend the funds. Thus, a central question remains: How do we translate what we know works into active institutional practice in school systems? (Foundation for Child Development 2009, 7).

Active parents are associated with more active children and youth. Few studies if any have documented Latino youth activism and advocacy in the schools. Julio Cammarota (2008) investigates educational practices at public schools in Arizona. The researcher assigns the students (stakeholders) the task of documenting unfair institutional practices in the school they attend. Thus the students become an integral part of the knowledge process as they become knowers and interpreters of data and agents of change (through application of findings). The author uses an integrative theoretical frame that brilliantly captures the forces of structural inequality that contribute to low educational achievement among Latinos. The ethnographic data narrates the process of students presenting their findings to school boards and advocating for institutional change so as to improve their educational options. Further, the students initiated a new culture for themselves whereby they embraced their right to guide and direct their educational experience.

The unique theoretical contribution of this work is that it challenges existing epistemological assumptions regarding causality of academic underachievement by redefining culture as a dynamic and fluid group characteristic that interacts with structures of inequality. These intersectional findings have implications for how research can be used as a form of critical consciousness raising among Latino youth and serve as praxis for social justice and change of educational structural inequality.

## Risk Factors Affecting Latino Student Performance in Educational Pipeline

In the following sections, data are discussed regarding risk factors and academic performance indicators. The risk factors associated with student academic performance are linked to family structure, poverty, community context, and school structure. A 2009 report states:

> The data for 2008 are in and the numbers tell a troubling story: 44 percent of American children grow up in families that face serious struggles to make ends meet. Parental employment, parental education, family structure and other variables each play an important role in predicting the likelihood that a child will endure economic hardship. (Wight and Chau 2009, 1)

Students' academic progress and success are inversely correlated with four family background factors: (1) having foreign-born parents whose primary language is a language other than English, (2) living in a single-parent family, (3) having a mother with less than a high school education, and (4) living in a family on welfare or receiving food stamps. Table 4.2 compares demographic, family structure, education indicators such as low rates of participation in early schooling, emotional difficulties, and school dropout rates, and health access risk factors for children zero to seventeen years of age by race and ethnicity.

In 2000, about 62 percent of Latinos were born in the United States, and by 2006 U.S.–born Latinos increased to about 84 percent (Fry and Gonzales 2008). Among U.S.–born Latino children, 32 percent had both parents who were U.S. native-born and about 58 percent had non-native born Latino or mixed parentage (FIFCFS 2009). Most Latino families are composed of married couples (65 percent) with 25 percent of the Latino children living with their mothers and 4 percent living with only the father. Latino children are more likely than any other racial/ethnic group to have a mother with less than a high school education (49 percent). About 72 percent of Latino families with school-aged children, compared with 82 percent of NHW families and 64 percent of NHB families, have secure employment all year round but NHB and Latino children are still more likely to experience food insecurity defined as limited or uncertain availability of nutritionally adequate and safe foods. Thus, the percentage of Latino children with two or more risk factors (low

**Table 4.2.** Demographic, Family Structure, and Other Risk Factors among Children by Race and Ethnicity

|  | Non-Hispanic Whites (%) | Non-Hispanic Blacks (%) | Latino (%) |
|---|---|---|---|
| 1. Demographics |  |  |  |
| Percentage of U.S. children (0–17) | 56.2 | 15.2 | 21.8 |
| U.S.–born/foreign-born parent | 21.0 | 9.0 | 55.0 |
| 2. Family structure |  |  |  |
| Two married parents | 75.4 | 34.5 | 64.2 |
| Mother only | 15.5 | 51.1 | 24.1 |
| 3. Risk factors |  |  |  |
| a. Children whose mother had not completed high school[a] | 7.0 | 20.0 | 49.0 |
| b. Food-insecure households | 11.9 | 26.1 | 26.7 |
| c. Children (3–5) who attend early childhood care and education programs[b] | 59.0 | 66.0 | 43.0 |
| d. Children (grades 1–3) who repeated a grade[b] | 3.6 | 9.9 | 5.5 |
| e. School dropout rates[c] | 6.0 | 10.4 | 22.4 |
| f. Emotional and behavioral difficulties (ages 4-17) |  |  |  |
| Serious difficulties | 5.6 | 5.9 | 3.7 |
| Minor difficulties | 15.2 | 16.5 | 12.1 |
| 4. Health insurance coverage[d] |  |  |  |
| Private insurance | 71.8 | 40.6 | 35.6 |
| Medicaid/public insurance | 19.7 | 46.1 | 45.4 |
| No insurance | 7.1 | 11.2 | 17.9 |

*Source:* Unless otherwise noted: Federal Interagency Forum on Child and Family Statistics 2009.
[a] *Source:* National Center for Education Statistics 2001, table 4–1.
[b] While this indicator does not provide information on aspects of quality, it represents the percentage of three- to five-year-old children (not yet enrolled in kindergarten) in early childhood care and education programs. Such programs include day care centers, Head Start programs, preschools, nursery schools, and prekindergarten. *Source:* National Center for Education Statistics 2006.
[c] *Source:* National Center for Health Statistics 2006.
[d] *Source:* Kaiser Family Foundation 2009.

maternal education and food insecurity, a proxy indicator for poverty) is higher than other racial and ethnic groups (FIFCFS 2009). A single-parent household in which a parent has less than a high school education exacerbates risk for poverty for Latino children. These trends have remained relatively stable over the last decade (FIFCFS 2009).

Economic risk factors are usually connected with a host of other issues that affect family processes and physical and mental health. Latino children are most likely to have no health insurance coverage or sporadic public insurance coverage and least likely to have private insurance coverage, which deters early prevention, screening, and detection of health conditions associated with school performance. Untreated acute and chronic health and emotional conditions complicate the profile of risk factors among Latino children and youth (Flores et al. 2002). These youth may not be receiving dental care, screening tests for vision and hearing, or diagnosis for attention deficit hyperactivity disorder (ADHD) (Diaz and Zambrana, forthcoming).

Mexico-born children and adolescents who speak Spanish have a higher rate of decayed teeth (higher mean number of decayed and missing teeth) and higher rates of gingivitis and periodontal pocketing, and they are less likely to have dental insurance and to have visited a dentist (than those who were born in the United States and Mexico-born children who spoke English). Higher education level and dental insurance are the most important factors in determining use of dental care and dental cleaning services among Mexican Americans (Scott and Simile 2005; Stewart et al. 2002; FIFCFS 2009, 25).

Hispanic children are likely at risk for inaccurately discriminating between consonant sounds, which are vital for English language acquisition and general intelligibility of the language. Screening tests for hearing are important in academic achievement. The National Health and Nutrition Examination Survey (NHANES) II survey provides data regarding hearing loss in several groups of children including Puerto Ricans, Cuban Americans, and Mexican Americans (Lee et al. 1997). In a breakdown of unilateral hearing loss in six- to nineteen-year-old children, Lee and colleagues found that the highest incidence of this type of impairment was among Cuban American children, where the occurrence was 12.3 per 1,000. The highest incidence of moderate to profound unilateral loss was among the Puerto Rican children, with a reported rate of 5.2 per 1,000.

Although unilateral hearing loss may not pose significant communication impairment in a quiet environment, even moderate background noise renders the child nearly deaf. Language acquisition is notably delayed in children with unilateral hearing loss, and children learning a second language would be significantly impaired in this process. These same groups were more likely to reside in economically disadvantaged families and to be below their expected school grade level (Lee et al. 1997). In younger Hispanic children, hearing loss might be more devastating. Early identification of hearing loss in the United States remains unacceptably low. However, Hispanic and Black children are identified as having a hearing loss significantly later than NHW children regardless of socioeconomic status (Flores et al. 2002). Undiagnosed and untreated hearing loss places Hispanic children at a significant disadvantage and can impede speech and language acquisition during critical periods of learning and contribute to academic underperformance.

Untreated physical and mental health conditions may also be associated with special education services. In the 2005–2006 academic year, 14 percent of children between zero and seventeen years had a special health care need (such as allergies, and asthma), and between 2001 and 2007 about 5 percent of all children were reported to have emotional or behavioral difficulties (such as ADHD). The prevalence of special health care needs was highest for mixed race (18 percent), NHW (15 percent) and NHB (15 percent) youth and lowest for Hispanic (8 percent) and Asian (6 percent) children (FIFCFS 2009). Latino students (ages three to twenty-one years of age) are about as likely as Whites to receive special education services, but less likely than Blacks and Native Americans/Alaskan Natives to receive special education services. Latinos receiving services under the Individuals with Disabilities Education Act[5] accounted for 11 percent, Asians/Pacific Islanders were 6 percent; Blacks were 15 percent; Native Americans/Alaskan Natives were 14 percent; and Whites were 11 percent (NCES 2003a). Recent data show that about 16 percent of Latino students experience minor to serious emotional difficulties (see table 4.2). Children living below the poverty level are more likely to experience emotional and behavioral difficulties than children in families who live at or above the poverty line (FIFCFS 2009, 61).

Latino children with special needs experience disparities even in special education services. Overall, 36 percent of Latino students classified as having learning disabilities spend the majority of their day in separate settings such as restricted classrooms or schools compared to only 20 percent of White students with such special needs (Buysse et al. 2004; Harvard Civil Rights Project 2002). A connection among health indicators, special needs, and English

---

5. The Individuals with Disabilities Education Act (IDEA) helps children with disabilities receive special education. The precursor to IDEA—the Education for All Handicapped Children Act (EAHCA)—was first passed in 1975 to provide federal funding for the education of individuals with disabilities. This act was amended in 1990 to become IDEA. IDEA aims "to ensure that all children with disabilities have available to them a free, appropriate public education that emphasizes special education and related services designed to meet their particular needs; to ensure that the rights of children with disabilities and their parents or guardians are protected; to assist States and localities to provide for the education of all children with disabilities; and to assess and ensure the effectiveness of efforts to educate children with disabilities" (U.S. Department of Education, *Twenty-Second Annual Report to Congress on the Implementation of the Individuals with Disabilities Education Act,* 2000; National Center for Education Statistics, 2003a, 32).

language proficiency suggest that Latino children confront exceptionally difficult barriers in the school system. Thus in speaking of Latino child readiness for school, poverty (28.9 percent are poor) and access to preventive health care services (screening and detection of health, special needs, and behavioral and emotional conditions) are important. Since Latino children are less likely to have health insurance coverage, less likely to have access to treatment for physical and emotional or behavioral conditions, more likely to experience food insecurity, and more likely to have undiagnosed health and behavioral conditions, their ability to learn and succeed academically is compromised.

The understanding of low-income Latino children's academic performance cannot be examined without contextualizing the school structures and resources in which they learn. Several assessments of educational environments have been conducted that permit us to better understand the role of structural inequality in academic success and failure for low-income children. These include:

1. A disproportionate number of failing schools, across grade levels, are predominantly composed of poor, racial and ethnic minority students. These segregated schools tend to have fewer financial, human, and material resources than schools in more affluent areas. By the time these students reach high school, the academic challenges they face have been compounded by years of substandard education (Alliance for Excellent Education 2007, 1).

2. In public preschool programs, out of ten quality benchmarks related to teacher quality, including class size, support and wraparound services, and student–teacher ratio (for each area, states receive a checkmark on a scale from 1–10 when their policy meets or exceeds the related benchmark standard) only seven states received a score of 9 or 10 for meeting the benchmarks, while fourteen states scored 6 or below. Those states with large Latino U.S. born and immigrant concentrations failed to meet or barely met the benchmarks (Arizona, California, Texas, New Mexico and Florida received a score of 4; New York received a score of 6) (National Institute for Early Education Research 2007).

3. During the 2000–2001 school years, Latino children in the West and Northeast were most likely to attend publicly funded pre-K programs that were 60 percent minority, in which 75 percent or more of the children qualified for free or reduced lunch. In contrast, NHW children were more likely to attend schools with lower minority enrollment and fewer students qualified for free or reduced lunch. Schools with higher minority and poverty concentrations had larger class sizes and less funding, and enrollees were less likely to be offered services such as transportation and extended care.

4. Concern for the cognitive, mental, and physical development of school-aged children and youth draws attention to opportunities to engage in

after-school extracurricular activities and time spent in unsupervised activities. Latino children are much less likely (35.4 percent) than NHW (63.3 percent) and Asian (51.2 percent) children to participate in arts, sports clubs, and community activities from pre-K to eighth grade and more likely to watch television three or more hours a day.

These trends have remained relatively unchanged over the last decade (FIFCFS 2009, 103). Extracurricular activities all contribute to brain stimulation and development that are strongly associated with school performance. However for many low-income parents, limited economic resources and neighborhood safety concerns diminish these opportunities for Latino youth.

### Preschool, Literacy Activities, and Kindergarten Academic Preparation

Latinos under the age of five make up over 15 percent of their age group in the U.S. population (NCES 2003a). In proportion to the total child population, the Latino population has been increasing faster than the NHW and NHB child populations. By 2020, the census projected that one in five children will be of Latino/Hispanic origin. However, enrollment in public early schooling programs and kindergarten[6] is less likely for Latino children than NHW or NHB children at ages three, four, and five (NCES 2003a). At age three, Latinos (26 percent) are less likely to attend early schooling programs than NHW (47 percent) and NHB (60 percent). Though Latino four-year-olds are more likely to attend a center-based program than three-year-olds, Latinos (64 percent) are still less likely than White (69 percent) and Black (81 percent) four-year-olds to attend an early schooling program (see Zambrana and Morant 2009 for a review on Latino immigrant children in preschool programs).

Overall trend data for the years 1991–2005 show that approximately 40 percent of Latino children ages three to five have attended an early childhood or educational program (NCES 2006). In 2007, 43 percent of Latino children (ages 3–5) attended early childhood care and educational programs compared to 59 percent of NHWs and 66 percent of NHBs (see table 4.2).

The last decade has witnessed a plethora of research activity on the importance of early childhood education or early schooling for low-income children. Head Start was begun in 1965 and updated in 1981, yet the gap between low-income children and upper-middle-income children has widened. A general

---

6. The term *early schooling programs* is used (unless otherwise noted) to include federally funded Early Head Start, programs that serve pregnant women, infants, and toddlers from ages zero to three; Head Start, programs that serve children ages three to five; and preschool educational programs for three-year-olds and pre-K educational programs for four-year-olds that are a part of the local public school systems or otherwise funded by the state.

public consensus has been formed around the importance of early schooling programs and activities to ensure that all children are afforded a fair start, a head start, and an early start.[7] The importance of early learning activities (such as being read to) is linked to brain development and school success. Although not a new discovery, children who have educational toys, strong and positive home environmental stimulation by parents through conversation and intentional learning interactions, and extracurricular activities including structured play groups experience higher levels of social, physical and neurocognitive brain stimulation. Both home and preschool environments serve as a vital foundation for future academic performance and success and the quality of resources in these environments vary significantly by socioeconomic status of parents.

The amount of time families spend engaging infants and toddlers in literacy activities, such as reading a book, telling stories, singing songs, and visiting libraries is critical to brain development. Differences in access to early learning activities are associated with family structure, household poverty level, and mother's educational attainment. Children whose mothers did not complete high school, and children who lived below the federal poverty threshold, were exposed to fewer early learning experiences at both nine months and two years of age (Rathbun and Grady 2007).

The number of children's books in the homes of two-year-olds also distinctly varied by race and ethnicity, high school completion, poverty level, and primary home language. For example, the mean number of children's books in the home for Latino two-year-olds was twenty-six compared to an average number of books for NHW two-year-olds of sixty-seven books, almost three times as many books as Latino children had. When English was not the primary home language, two-year-olds had access to only about nineteen children's books, compared to fifty-six books for two-year-olds where English was the primary language. Two-year-olds whose families were living at or above the poverty line had almost twice as many books (fifty-five) as those who lived below the poverty line (twenty-seven). Gaps observed for the nine-month and two-year-olds persist as the children reach three- to six years of age. These findings suggest that the nature and quality of early learning activities are associated with low SES and in turn less parental economic means to purchase education-related resources that facilitate the engagement of infants and toddlers in early learning activities (Rathbun and Grady 2007). Among Latino

7. The Children's Defense Fund (www.childrensdefense.org), National Center for Child Poverty (www.nccp.org), and the Foundation for Child Development (www.fcd-us.org) have invested a substantial amount of intellectual energy and financial resources to inform researchers and policy makers about the disparities between NHW and poor, racial/ethnic and immigrant groups and to propose cost-effective and appropriate educational interventions.

children entering kindergarten, marked disparities are evident in mathematics, reading abilities, and cognitive and motor skills in comparison to other racial and ethnic groups (O'Donnell 2008).[8]

In a survey of teachers' perceptions of student performance by race and ethnicity, teachers reported that about 67 percent of Latino first-time kindergartners stay focused on tasks compared to 75 percent of NHW kindergartners and 81 percent of Asian/Pacific Islander kindergartners, and that Latino kindergartners (70 percent) were less eager to learn than NHW (78 percent) and Asian (80 percent) kindergartners. Finally, teachers observed that Latino kindergartners (62 percent) were least likely to pay attention in class compared to NHW (70 percent) and Asian/Pacific Islander (71 percent) children (NCES 2003a). Data suggest that teacher's perceptions were similar for NHB children. These teacher observations may be related to Latino and NHB children's being less academically prepared but may also represent biased attitudes, low expectations, and lack of preparation to meet the academic needs of these students. In fact, the majority of preschool teachers do not perceive themselves to be fully prepared to meet the needs of students with limited English language proficiency or those from diverse cultural backgrounds (Brice 2002). This lack of preparedness to assist Latino students seriously impedes the quality of their education and, perhaps, their access to the necessary cognitive and social skills required to compete academically in elementary and secondary school. Low-quality preschools and limited early learning activities are associated with repeating a grade and higher school dropout rates (see table 4.2).

### High School Completion and Dropout Rates

In 2000, Latinos and Blacks each composed 17 percent of the public elementary and secondary school student enrollments, compared to 61 percent White. By 2006, Latino children and youth made up 20 percent of the school-aged population. By 2050, estimates suggest that there will be more Hispanic school-aged children than White children in the public schools (Fry and Gonzales 2008).

Latinos are less likely than Whites and Blacks to obtain a high school diploma or an equivalent credential including a general educational development (GED) credential. In 2005, 64 percent of Latinos eighteen to twenty-four years old completed high school, compared to 92 percent of Whites, 96 percent of Asians, and 84 percent of Blacks (Fry 2005; KewalRamani et al. 2007). Latinos have the highest dropout rate, almost twice the rate of Blacks, three times the rate of Whites, and almost six times the rate of Asian/Pacific Islander high school students (4 percent). Overall Latino immigrants' dropout rate was 43 percent

---

8. Children who could *not* speak English were not included in these assessments.

in 2001 and decreased to 38 percent in 2005. Central Americans (33 percent) and Mexicans (26 percent) are consistently most likely to drop out, while South Americans and Dominicans are the least likely to drop out of high school (Cosentino de Cohen et al. 2005; Kaufman et al. 2004; KewalRamani et al. 2007; White House Initiative for Hispanic Educational Excellence 2003).

Of keen interest is college completion trend data from 1980 to 2007. Table 4.3 shows a rather steep decrease in the percentage of Hispanics with less than a fifth grade education in 1980 (15.8 percent) to 2007 (6.9 percent). The high school completion rate increased approximately 9 percentage points in a fifteen-year period from 44.5 percent in 1980 to 53.4 percent in 1995, and only 7 points over another eleven-year period from 1996 to 2007. Despite these improvements, however, high school completion rates—an important economic marker—remain disproportionately low for those of Mexican origin.

Two recent reports examine the educational gap and the role of education in the pathways of Latino youth (M. Lopez 2009; Fry 2009). Factors reported as contributing to the attainment gap were lack of parental involvement and cultural differences between school personnel and students. Other explanations by respondents such as poor English skills, dislike of school, feeling that they don't need more education for the careers they want, have inherent assumptions of individual attributes rather than a focus on the fact that all too often poor Latino students sit in unsafe (physically and psychologically) spaces, outdated schools with inadequate instructional materials and school personnel with low expectations of their abilities. However, as already noted, these factors cannot be assessed without considering the SEP of parents, racialization, and institutional practices in schools.

Latino youth are more likely to be concentrated in central cities and are more likely to attend schools that are overcrowded and underfunded with little or no access to resources such as mental health counseling, college admission counseling, and mentors. In California, for example, about 16 percent of teachers in high Latino enrollment public schools are not fully credentialed, which is twice the percentage for students in predominantly White high schools (Pew Hispanic Center 2004). As observed by Kevin Kumashiro (2008) in speaking about the achievement gap and school resources,

From its history of differentiating education by race, to its current system of unequal funding by district, the education system has worked to disadvantage certain groups, accumulating an "educational debt" that makes their achievement gap inevitable. Raising test scores does not solve the larger problem of this education debt. And perhaps that's the point. Perhaps the focus on the achievement gap is a distraction that allows the larger inequities to exist. (75)

Table 4.3. Educational Attainment by Race and Hispanic Origin, 1940–2007 (percent of population age 25 and older, by years of school completed)

| Age and Year | White[a] | | | Black[a] | | | Hispanic | | |
|---|---|---|---|---|---|---|---|---|---|
| | Less than 5 years of elementary school | High school completion or higher[b] | 4 or more years of college[c] | Less than 5 years of elementary school | High school completion or higher[b] | 4 or more years of college[c] | Less than 5 years of elementary school | High school completion or higher[b] | 4 or more years of college[c] |
| April 1940 | 10.9 | 26.1 | 4.9 | 41.8 | 7.7 | 1.3 | — | — | — |
| April 1950 | 8.9 | 36.4 | 6.6 | 32.6 | 13.7 | 2.2 | — | — | — |
| April 1960 | 6.7 | 43.2 | 8.1 | 23.5 | 21.7 | 3.5 | — | — | — |
| March 1970 | 4.2 | 57.4 | 11.6 | 14.7 | 36.1 | 6.1 | — | — | — |
| March 1980 | 1.9 | 71.9 | 18.4 | 9.1 | 51.4 | 7.9 | 15.8 | 44.5 | 7.6 |
| March 1985 | 1.4 | 77.5 | 20.8 | 6.1 | 59.9 | 11.1 | 13.5 | 47.9 | 8.5 |
| March 1990 | 1.1 | 81.4 | 23.1 | 5.1 | 66.2 | 11.3 | 12.3 | 50.8 | 9.2 |
| March 1992 | 0.9 | 83.4 | 23.2 | 3.9 | 67.7 | 11.9 | 11.8 | 52.6 | 9.3 |
| March 1993 | 0.8 | 84.1 | 23.8 | 3.7 | 70.5 | 12.2 | 11.8 | 53.1 | 9.0 |
| March 1994 | 0.8 | 84.9 | 24.3 | 2.7 | 73.0 | 12.9 | 10.8 | 53.3 | 9.1 |
| March 1995 | 0.7 | 85.9 | 23.4 | 2.5 | 73.8 | 13.3 | 10.6 | 53.4 | 9.3 |
| March 1996 | 0.6 | 86.0 | 25.9 | 2.2 | 74.6 | 13.8 | 10.4 | 53.1 | 9.3 |
| March 1997 | 0.6 | 86.3 | 26.2 | 2.0 | 75.3 | 13.3 | 9.4 | 54.7 | 10.3 |
| March 1998 | 0.6 | 87.1 | 26.6 | 1.7 | 76.4 | 14.8 | 9.3 | 55.5 | 11.0 |
| March 1999 | 0.6 | 87.7 | 27.7 | 1.8 | 77.4 | 15.5 | 9.0 | 56.1 | 10.9 |
| March 2000 | 0.5 | 88.4 | 28.1 | 1.6 | 78.9 | 16.6 | 8.7 | 57.0 | 10.6 |
| March 2001 | 0.5 | 88.7 | 28.6 | 1.3 | 79.5 | 16.1 | 9.3 | 56.5 | 11.2 |
| March 2002 | 0.5 | 88.7 | 29.4 | 1.6 | 79.2 | 17.2 | 8.7 | 57.0 | 11.1 |
| March 2004 | 0.4 | 90.0 | 30.6 | 1.3 | 81.1 | 17.7 | 8.1 | 58.4 | 12.1 |
| March 2005 | 0.5 | 90.1 | 30.5 | 1.5 | 81.5 | 17.7 | 7.9 | 58.5 | 12.0 |
| March 2006 | 0.4 | 90.5 | 31.0 | 1.5 | 81.2 | 18.6 | 7.6 | 59.3 | 12.4 |
| March 2007 | 0.4 | 90.6 | 31.8 | 1.2 | 82.8 | 18.7 | 6.9 | 60.3 | 12.7 |

Sources: U.S. Department of Commerce 2009b.

Note: — = not available.

[a] Includes persons of Hispanic origin for years prior to 1980.

[b] Data for years prior to 1993 include all persons with at least four years of high school.

[c] Data for 1993 and later years are for persons with a bachelor's or higher degree.

## High School Academic Performance Indicators: Standardized Tests

Students' academic performance and achievement is strongly associated with school attendance, good conduct to avoid suspension and expulsion, and adequate performance on standardized assessments. Latino students, from eighth grade to twelfth grade, have higher absenteeism rates than Whites. In 2000, over one-quarter of Latino students in the eighth grade, and over one-third of Latino students in the twelfth grade were absent three or more days from school, which is higher than any other racial/ethnic group. About one-fifth (20 percent) of Latino students in grades seven through twelve were suspended or expelled compared to Whites (15 percent) and Blacks (35 percent) (NCES 2003a). These relatively high rates of absenteeism and expulsion/suspension are most likely associated with higher dropout rates, the 13 percent of Latino students in grades K through twelve who repeat a grade, and less academic preparation required to excel in standardized tests.

Reasons for low high school completion are associated with academic performance indicators. Trend data for Latinos show that average scores on the National Assessment of Educational Progress (NAEP) that tracks reading, math, and science scores of nine-, thirteen-, and seventeen-year-olds continue to reflect academic underperformance. Recent trend data (1990–2007) in math and reading reveal several interesting findings:

1. All student scores in reading and math have improved on average thirty points over this time period. The pattern has remained unchanged since 1990 with Asians having the highest scores followed by NHWs, Hispanics, American Indian, and NHBs. Males tend to outperform females, although females at all grade levels had higher reading scores than males.
2. The higher the education of parents, the higher the overall achievement scores with on average a thirty-point difference in scores (FIFCFS 2009). In 2007, both reading and math scores were associated with parental educational attainment and showed that the disparity in scores by race and Hispanic ethnicity decreased when parents were college graduates (FIFCFS 2009, 50–52).
3. In the years 1994–2000, Latino high school students' number of academic and vocational course credits increased. Latinos who took advanced placement (AP) exams increased from 22 to 117 per 1,000 twelfth graders, while the number of White twelfth graders taking AP exams increased from 49 to 183 per 1,000 twelfth graders during the same period. Latino high school students are less likely than White students to complete advanced mathematics, advanced science, and advanced English courses in preparation for college enrollment, but are more likely

than White and Black students to complete advanced foreign language courses (NCES 2003a).

These data attest to the accumulation of educational disadvantage as Latino students go through the education pipeline, which suggests that a significant majority are not prepared academically for college.

### College Readiness Assessments

Table 4.4 shows average scores on the standardized assessment test (SAT)—an indicator of college readiness and criteria for entry into higher education—by race/ethnicity and Latino subgroup for high school students (1996–2006). The SAT[9] assesses students' academic preparation for higher education by measuring verbal and mathematical skills and is used as a predictor for success in college. During 1996–2006, of all racial/ethnic students who took the SAT, scores increased by seven percentage points, from 31 to 38 percent. During this period, Latino test-takers increased their scores by three percentage points (from 8 to 11 percent), compared to an increase of less than two percentage points for Asians/Pacific Islanders, an increase of less than one percentage point for NHBs, and a decrease of less than half a percentage point for American Indians/Alaska Natives. Average verbal scores fluctuated for most racial/ethnic groups, though NHWs, Asian/Pacific Islanders, and Puerto Rican students generally increased their verbal scores. The average math score increased for all racial/ethnic groups during 1996–2006 with Asian/Pacific Islanders showing the largest increase in scores. Non-Hispanic Blacks, Mexican Americans, and other Latino test-takers experienced smaller increases (KewalRamani et al. 2007).

The American College Testing (ACT) examination is another standardized test used as a criterion for college entry.[10] Scores for each section range from 0 to 36, and composite scores below 19 on the ACT indicate minimal readiness for college (NCES 2003a, b). Similar to the SAT, the percentage of ACT test-takers who are racial/ethnic minority students is increasing. Latino test-takers increased by two percentage points (6 to 8 percent) between 1997 and 2005.

Puerto Rican, Mexican American, and other Latino students showed lower scores than NHWs and Asian/Pacific Islanders in mathematics, and unlike SAT

9. The Critical Reading section of the exam includes sentence completions, passage-based reading, and analogies that measure extended reasoning, literal comprehension, and vocabulary in context. The mathematics section of the exam includes multiple-choice items, student-produced responses, and quantitative comparisons. In 2005, the SAT introduced a new writing section. Due to the lack of trend data, writing scores are not discussed.

10. The majority of students who take the ACT live in the Midwest, Rocky Mountains, Plains, and southern regions of the country. The SAT is more prevalent on the east and west coasts and in the Northeast. The ACT consists of four sections: English, Mathematics, Reading, and Science.

**Table 4.4.** Average SAT Scores for Twelfth Grade Test-Taking Population, by Race and Latino Subgroup, 1996–2006

| Subject and year | Total[a] | Non-Hispanic White | Non-Hispanic Black | Mexican American | Puerto Rican | Other Latino | Asian/Pacific Islander | American Indian/ Alaska Native |
|---|---|---|---|---|---|---|---|---|
| Verbal | | | | | | | | |
| 1996 | 505 | 526 | 434 | 455 | 452 | 465 | 496 | 483 |
| 1997 | 505 | 526 | 434 | 451 | 454 | 466 | 496 | 475 |
| 1998 | 505 | 526 | 434 | 453 | 452 | 461 | 498 | 480 |
| 1999 | 505 | 527 | 434 | 453 | 455 | 463 | 498 | 484 |
| 2000 | 505 | 528 | 434 | 453 | 456 | 461 | 499 | 482 |
| 2001 | 506 | 529 | 433 | 451 | 457 | 460 | 501 | 481 |
| 2002 | 504 | 527 | 430 | 446 | 455 | 458 | 501 | 479 |
| 2003 | 507 | 529 | 431 | 448 | 456 | 457 | 508 | 480 |
| 2004 | 508 | 528 | 430 | 451 | 457 | 461 | 507 | 483 |
| 2005 | 508 | 532 | 433 | 453 | 460 | 463 | 511 | 489 |
| 2006 | 503 | 527 | 434 | 454 | 459 | 458 | 510 | 487 |
| Mathematics | | | | | | | | |
| 1996 | 508 | 523 | 422 | 459 | 445 | 466 | 558 | 477 |
| 1997 | 511 | 526 | 423 | 458 | 447 | 468 | 560 | 475 |
| 1998 | 512 | 528 | 426 | 460 | 447 | 466 | 562 | 483 |
| 1999 | 511 | 528 | 422 | 456 | 448 | 464 | 560 | 481 |
| 2000 | 514 | 530 | 426 | 460 | 451 | 467 | 565 | 481 |
| 2001 | 514 | 531 | 426 | 458 | 451 | 465 | 566 | 479 |
| 2002 | 516 | 533 | 427 | 457 | 451 | 464 | 569 | 483 |
| 2003 | 519 | 534 | 426 | 457 | 453 | 464 | 575 | 482 |
| 2004 | 518 | 531 | 427 | 458 | 452 | 465 | 577 | 488 |
| 2005 | 520 | 536 | 431 | 463 | 457 | 469 | 580 | 494 |
| 2006 | 518 | 536 | 429 | 465 | 456 | 463 | 578 | 494 |

*Sources:* KewalRamani et al. 2007, 77.

*Note:* Scores for both verbal and mathematics range from 200 to 800. Test-takers were asked to self-identify a single racial/ethnic group. Race categories exclude persons of Hispanic origin.

[a] Total includes other race/ethnicity categories not separately shown.

math scores, ACT math scores have not increased over time. These academic performance indicators show that underperformance is more complicated than a focus on individual characteristics, as the disparities between White and Asian groups have remained relatively stable since the 1980s when these data were made available to the public. Parental constraints due to poverty, quality of schools, and discriminatory institutional practices such as lack of college counseling and/or mentorship, in confluence maintain low-income Latino and NHB students outside the opportunity structure. Improvements in academic performance such as SAT scores for Latinos are not evenly distributed by ethnic subgroup or SEP. However second-generation students of college-educated Latino families contribute to the modest increases for total Latino student scores.

In summary, the preschool through twelfth grade educational pipeline experiences of Latino students intersect with parental SEP and academic quality of schooling experiences, including availability of AP courses and college counseling, that determine the options and opportunities available for entrance to postsecondary educational institutions. Two-thirds of Latino students are enrolled in highly segregated minority school districts compared to 9 percent of NHW children. One-ninth of Latino students attend schools where almost 100 percent of the student body is minority (Pew Hispanic Center 2004). As a result, low-income Latinos often experience an extreme disadvantage for college admittance due to the inequities they confront during their earlier educational trajectory. Further, because many Latinos are from working-class or low-income families, they confront serious financial burdens in completing high school and pursuing college options.

### *Trends in Enrollment, Attendance, and Completion of Postsecondary Education*

Since 1970, among Latinos who finished high school, the rate of college attendance has increased from 25 percent to 40 percent. Latinos who are U.S. citizens are more likely than Latinos who are not U.S. citizens to enroll in a college or university. In 2000 Latinos represented about 10 percent of enrolled students in U.S. colleges and universities, compared to 74 percent of Whites and 12 percent of Blacks (NCES 2003a, b; Jamieson et al. 2001), and among eighteen- to twenty-four-year-old Latinos, 22 percent were enrolled compared to 39 percent of Whites and 31 percent of Blacks (NCES 2003b) In 2000, although enrollment rates continue to increase, Latinos continue to enroll at lower rates than their White and Black counterparts. Latino enrollment rates for two-year colleges is higher than for four-year colleges and universities. For example, in 2000, Latino students accounted for 14 percent of the students enrolled in two-year institutions, compared to Whites (64 percent) and Blacks (12 percent). Latino students accounted for 7 percent of the students enrolled in four-year institutions, compared to Whites (71 percent) and Blacks (11 percent) (NCES 2003a). There is no measurable difference between 1980 (50 percent) and 2006 (59 percent) data in the proportion of Latinos who enrolled in colleges and universities immediately after completing high school (FIFCFS 2009, 55). These data are particularly of concern since Hispanic-Serving Institutions (HSIs)[11] were designated primarily in geographic areas of high concentration of Latino students to increase enrollment of Latino students in college degree–granting programs (Vigil Laden 2001). Yet college enrollment rates have not witnessed a dramatic increase. Latino college completion rates overall witnessed the largest increase between 1980 (7.6 percent) and 2000 (10.6 percent). Yet this represents a mere 3 percent increase in twenty years, and for Latinos who completed four or more years of college it shows only a 2.1 percent increase from the year 2000 to 2007. Although 88 percent of Latino students report that college is important, only 49 percent plan to complete a college degree, and for immigrant youth only 29 percent compared to 60 percent of native-born Latinos plan to complete college. Yet their educational aspirations do not match the level of importance they place on college. For example, 74 percent of all sixteen- to twenty-five-

11. Hispanic-Serving Institutions (HSIs) are defined as colleges, universities, or systems/districts where total Hispanic enrollment constitutes a minimum of 25 percent of the total enrollment. Over half of all Latino undergraduate students in higher education (54 percent) are enrolled in less than 10 percent of institutions in the United States. This concentration of Latino enrollment in higher education was first recognized by educators and policy makers in the 1980s and contributed to the development of HSIs. It was expected that these institutions would serve as an important resource for Latino college-bound students. HSIs are still largely unknown and little understood by most educators and policymakers in the United States. Although HSIs represent almost 6 percent of all postsecondary institutions, they enroll approximately half of all Hispanic students in college, granting more associate and baccalaureate degrees to Hispanic students than all other American colleges or universities combined. Despite these impressive outcomes, a federal definition for HSIs exists only in the Higher Education Act of 1965, under Title V, as amended in 1992 and 1998. The 1998 legislation defines HSIs as accredited, degree-granting, public or private, nonprofit colleges and universities with 25 percent or more total undergraduate, full-time equivalent, Hispanic student enrollment. HSIs with this enrollment must also meet an additional criterion to qualify for Title V funds, which stipulates that no less than 50 percent of its Hispanic students must be low-income individuals.

"Total Enrollment" includes full-time and part-time students at the undergraduate or graduate level (including professional schools) of the institution, or both (i.e., headcount of for-credit students). Title V eligibility (i.e., meeting the federal definition of an HSI) is determined by the U.S. Department of Education as the first step in the application process for a Title V grant. Specifically, if your college or university has (1) a full-time equivalent (FTE) enrollment of undergraduate students that is at least 25 percent Hispanic students and (2) not less than 50 percent of all students are eligible for need-based Title IV aid, it should be an "eligible institution" for Title V. The Integrated Postsecondary Education Data System (IPEDS) identifies 265 HSIs as defined by federal law and 175 as emerging HSIs that meet the basic legislative definition (2007). (In the fall of 2006–2007, fourteen states [Arizona, California, Colorado, Connecticut, Florida, Illinois, Kansas, Massachusetts, New Jersey, New Mexico, New York, Texas, Washington, and Puerto Rico] were identified.) In an analysis of emerging HSIs, Arkansas, Indiana, Louisiana, Oregon, and Pennsylvania states are seeing significant numbers of Latino undergraduate enrollment.

For further information on HSIs see the Hispanic Association of Colleges and Universities at www.hacu.net.

year-old survey respondents who did not finish high school, or who completed high school but did not continue their education, report the primary reason as financial pressure to help support their family, and almost half report limited English language proficiency (49 percent) as a reason for discontinuance of school. For the overwhelming majority, financial affordability dampens their aspirations (Lopez 2009).[12]

Although data on adult education are limited, Kwang Kim and colleagues (2004) in their analysis of the Adult Education and Lifelong Learning Survey found that a higher percentage of Whites received employer-based financial support for education than Latinos. Latinos are less likely to receive federal financial aid awards than any other racial/ethnic group and are more likely to obtain nonfederal (commercial) and employer-based financial loans for their education (Excelencia in Education 2005). These data suggest that middle-income White students have access to resources in the economic opportunity structure that are not readily available to low-income racial/ethnic students. This social capital may be associated with commercial or private loans that are cosigned by relatively more affluent parents and access to long-term employment opportunities and employers who are willing to invest in them. Financial support during college contributes to timely graduation rates and more time to dedicate to study to promote academic success. On the other hand, limited financial resources contribute to the double jeopardy circumstance that many racial/ethnic students experience when they work part-time and attend school full-time or work full-time and attend school part-time. Holding a job while in school full-time, combined with adjustment to the college environment, inevitably increases the number of years in college and can jeopardize academic performance and college degree completion.

12. There are four primary ways to pay for college: grants, loans, work-study, and personal contributions. These four options are not mutually exclusive, and most students use a combination to pay for their college education. In addition, these types of financial aid are available from a variety of sources, including federal and state governments and colleges themselves. A majority of both Latino and all undergraduate students received some form of financial aid in 2003–2004 to help them pay for their education.

Latino undergraduates actively applied for financial aid, and many received aid to pay for college in 2003–2004. Almost 80 percent of Latino undergraduates applied for financial aid, and 63 percent of Latinos who applied for financial aid received some form of aid to pay for college. Latinos received the lowest average financial aid award of any racial/ethnic group. The average total aid award for all undergraduates in 2003–2004 was $6,890. Asians received the highest average financial aid awards to pay for college ($7,623), while Latinos received the lowest ($6,253). This pattern has not changed since 1995–1996. Federal financial aid has been a critical source of aid for Latino undergraduates. In 2003–2004, 50 percent of Latino undergraduates received federal aid, while only 16 percent of Latino undergraduates received state aid and 17 percent received institutional aid. In 2003–2004, Latinos were more likely to receive federal aid (50 percent) than the combination of all racial/ethnic groups (46 percent). Only African American students were more likely to receive this aid (62 percent). The average federal aid award for Latinos was $5,415, while the average was $6,230 for Whites, $6,145 for Blacks, and $5,995 for Asians. For further information on financial aid, student college cost profiles, and sources of financial aid, see Excelencia in Education 2005.

Latinos tend to participate more in part-time than in full-time adult education programs in U.S. colleges and universities. About 41 percent of Latinos ages seventeen and above participated in adult education in 1999 (NCES 2003b). Of this number, 44 percent of the Latinos participating in adult education were employed, compared to 53 percent for Whites. Moreover, 16 percent of Latinos enroll in part-time adult education for personal development, specifically for basic education and for English as a second language courses. Only 7.1 percent of Latinos participate in full-time college or university credential programs.[13] Overall, lack of access to financial aid resources and inadequate academic preparation persist and contribute to lower rates of college enrollment and completion and the consequent higher education gap between Latinos and other racial/ethnic groups.

Table 4.5 shows percentages of students enrolled in degree-granting institutions and degrees conferred by race and ethnicity. In 2007, 43 percent of Latino undergraduates were enrolled part time, compared to 35 percent of White, 38 percent of Black, and 37 percent of Asian undergraduates. Latinos of traditional college-age are less likely to be enrolled in college: In 2007, 26.6 percent of Latinos eighteen- to twenty-four years old were enrolled in degree-granting institutions, compared to 42.6 of White, and 33.1 percent of Black students. Latino students are more likely than other students to be enrolled part time.

Overall, Latinos are much more likely to be awarded an associate degree (11.7 percent) than bachelor's (7.5 percent) or doctoral degree (3.3 percent). In 2007, the number of Latinos receiving associate degrees increased by 110 percent; the number increased by 14 percent for Whites, 73 percent for Blacks, and 52 percent for Asians. Latinos represented 6 percent of all graduate and first professional degree[14] students in higher education compared to five percent in 1995. About 5 percent of the first professional degrees were conferred to Latinos, 72 percent to Whites, and 7 percent to Blacks. Asians earned almost 13 percent of the first professional degrees. Latinos represent a small percentage of the population earning doctoral degrees. Doctoral degrees conferred upon Latinos were 3 percent compared to 56 percent for Whites, 6 percent for Blacks and almost 6 percent for Asians (NCES 2007). Latino doctoral recipients are more likely to have majored in education (20 percent) and psychology (17 percent) than are other students (Whites, 15 percent; Blacks, 10 percent), and less likely to earn doctoral degrees in engineering and physical sciences.

13. Full-time participation in a college or university credential program or in a vocational or technical diploma program.

14. First professional degree is defined as an award that requires completion of a degree program that meets all of the following criteria: 1) completion of the academic requirements to begin practice in the profession, 2) at least two years of college work before entering the degree program, and 3) a total of at least six academic years of college work to complete the degree program. Includes degrees such as M.D., D.D.S and law degree.

**Table 4.5.** Percentage of 18- to 24-Year-Olds Enrolled in Degree-Granting Institutions and Degrees Conferred by Race and Ethnicity, 2007

|  | Non-Hispanic White | Non-Hispanic Black | Latino | Asian |
|---|---|---|---|---|
| Enrollment |  |  |  |  |
| Enrollment as a percentage of all 18- to 24-year-olds | 42.6 | 33.1 | 26.6 | NA |
| Enrollment as a percentage of all 18- to 24-year-old high school completers | 47.8 | 40.1 | 39.2 | NA |
| Part-time enrollment | 35.0 | 38.0 | 43.0 | 37.0 |
| Degrees conferred |  |  |  |  |
| Associate | 67.5 | 12.5 | 11.7 | 5.1 |
| Bachelor's | 72.6 | 9.6 | 7.5 | 6.9 |
| Doctoral | 56.2 | 6.1 | 3.3 | 5.8 |
| First professional degree[a] | 71.6 | 7.1 | 5.2 | 12.9 |

*Source:* National Center for Education Statistics 2007.

[a]An award that requires completion of a degree program that meets all of the following criteria: (1) completion of the academic requirements to begin practice in the profession, (2) at least two years of college work before entering the degree program, and (3) a total of at least six academic years of college work to complete the degree program. Includes degrees such as M.D., D.D.S., and law degrees.

College completion rates vary by Latino subgroup. Recent data show the following: (1) Twenty-five percent of Cubans ages twenty-five and older—compared with 12.6 percent of all U.S. Latinos—have obtained at least a bachelor's degree; (2) Mexican Americans (9 percent) have the lowest level of college completion; and (3) South Americans (Peruvians, 31 percent; Colombians, 30 percent) have higher rates of postsecondary educational degrees than other Latinos (Pew Hispanic Center 2009 b). As a group, Latinos lag behind Whites, NHBs and Asians in high school completion, associate degrees, and advanced degrees. Without question, Latinos are severely underrepresented in degree-granting institutions at all levels and in all major professions including law, medicine, other health professions, the professoriate in colleges and universities, and technical fields. Although modest progress has been made in high school and college completion, the institutional barriers remain significant.[15]

∽

Two observations on the importance of education and Latinos based on the data show that: The persistent notion that low-income Latinos do not value

---

15. An extensive body of work is available on factors that promote college enrollment, retention, and graduation for Latinos. Factors such as financial constraints; college adjustment (as many students come from low-income, predominantly minority communities and schools and enter into predominantly White institutions); race, ethnic, and gender bias in college life; and academic difficulty due to inadequate preparation are principal areas of investigation (Delgado Bernal et al. 2006; Gandára et al. 2006; Garrod et al. 2006; Yosso et al. 2009).

education is based on incomplete research paradigms. Disparities in early academic performance are associated with differing opportunities for early learning activities and differences in parent education and income, access to health care services, and quality of early schooling programs.

Emerging scholarship has expanded the boundaries of prior research and given us some new insights. Three conclusions can be made. First, the social construction of a racialized Latino identity is embedded in inequitable institutional school practices within resource-poor and often unsafe community environments. The social construction of Latino children as inferior and foreign adversely affects low-income children, but the social construction of identity crosses ethnic, racial and class lines. One Latino upper-middle-class college student states:

> In aiming for success, I have had to confront, like my parents, the stereotypes of Latinidad and my place within the broad pan-ethnic label of Latino. Growing up, I often felt like my ethnicity and identity were predefined. Although I am a pale-skinned, upper-middle-class, White Latino, I have experienced the struggles that many Latinos face in trying to get ahead in a society that deems Latino people underqualified. (Rodríguez 2007, 202)

Second, the discourse around school failure and success often engages in a victim-blaming approach relying on individual or cultural deterministic explanations. These foci often fail to address parental barriers to participation in the education of their children, structural and historical inequity such as the quality of economic investments in neighborhoods and schools, available academic resources, and stereotypic perceptions of educational personnel that have left unrevealed the intersections of race, ethnicity, class, and power relations in schools and society.

Third, emerging data clearly show that SEP of parents is a powerful predictor of academic performance. The accumulation of educational deficits and disadvantage over the educational pipeline has more to do with social constructions of Latino identity as underperformers and SEP than cultural explanations. The key ingredients for educational success are best stated by Lory Dance (2009): "by including economic capital and efficient funding as a policy recommendation, we simply argue that what's good for affluent students in elite private schools is good for impoverished students who attend public schools" (196). With more equitable access to social and educational resources, all children and youth can increase their chances at educational achievement and a better quality of life.

# 5

# Girlhood to Womanhood

> The same obstacles that have existed historically exist
> for us as Chicanas in society. No matter how we cut
> it, the structures of patriarchy, male domination,
> racial domination, and particularly class domination
> have not fundamentally changed. Maybe they have
> been elasticized a little bit—they've always elasticized
> to let one or two of us in—but fundamentally those
> structures remain, and we brush up against those
> structures.
>
> —Antonia Castaneda, quoted in de la Torre and
>    Pesquera 1993, 233

What do we know about the lives of Latino girls? What are the forces that shape their lives and guide their life decisions? How do life experiences in girlhood impact their life course? In this chapter, I present selected social science findings that elucidate the pathways of Latino girls and provide an overview of the profile of adult women and research on changing adult gender roles and education. To gain some insight on the lived experiences of Latino girls, I review work on gender role formation and performance and discuss the social construction of Latina ethnicity to illustrate the ways that these factors negatively shape their life chances and their transition to womanhood. A brief educational profile of girls is presented, followed by a discussion of pathways in schooling experiences and academic indicators, gender role performance, sexuality, pregnancy, and motherhood. Selective works are discussed to disrupt the discourse on how the lived experiences of Latinas are often measured outside of a social inequality context. I also showcase some recent work to expand our understanding of the intersection of Latina ethnicity, socioeconomic status (SES) and gender roles. Although not an exhaustive review of scholarship, major themes of this body of work are identified.

In discussing the research on Latina adolescents, several caveats are warranted. These studies do not reflect the lives of the majority of Latino girls. In fact, new trends show important transitions and changes. The pregnancy rates and early mothering data show strong decreases in fertility rates in the last few decades. These rates are at their lowest level. Latino girls are more likely than Latino boys to attend college—a trend that is similar across racial and ethnic groups. The number of Latino girls in gangs is minuscule as reported by the Pew Hispanic Center. It is important to interrogate what is being studied and why. What themes are being made visible for Latino girls, what is omitted in these studies, and how representative are these themes of the lived experiences of girls?

To date, the overwhelming majority of research has been conducted on low-income Mexican American and Mexican immigrant females, and a more limited literature exists on Puerto Rican girls and other Latinas. Although some of this research sheds light on the lives of low-income Mexican American and immigrant girls, sadly, the body of evidence portrays a dismal scenario of the developmental life course of low-income Latino girls. Yet it is my intention to challenge the knowledge production that misrepresents the factors associated with the effects and consequences of material conditions (poverty) on the lives of low-income Latina youth.[1] On the other hand, the harsh reality of the intersections of racial/ethnic subordination and class domination contribute to a life course trajectory that is shaped by these factors. The educational pathways of adolescents, discussed in the following sections, are a major determinant of social location in adulthood.

### Profile of Latino Girls

Latino girls account for the largest racial/ethnic female group in the United States, constituting approximately 20 percent of 7.7 million Latinas under the age of eighteen, not including the population in Puerto Rico (U.S. Census Bureau 2008). The high school graduation rate for Latinas remains lower than for any other female racial and ethnic group. In 1975 almost one-third (31.6 percent) of Latinas dropped out, compared with about 23 percent of Black and 12 percent of White girls. From 2005–2008 almost one-fifth of Latinas dropped out of high school, at almost more than twice the rate for other racial/ethnic groups. Table 5.1 depicts high school dropout rates of Latino girls' from 1975 through 2008.

A 2009 report on Latino girls states:

The statistics for Latina adolescents reveal the scope of the problem. Forty-one percent of Latinas—as compared to 22 percent of whites—fail to graduate from

---

1. This chapter focuses on girls, adolescents, and women as represented in much of the social science literature. Significant past literature that discusses fertility, family formation, and pregnancy is not covered. I include selected studies that illustrate depictions of Latina lives. I want to emphasize that these studies do not reflect the lived experiences of all low-income and working-class Latinas. The main goal in this chapter is to both show how Latinas are studied without a context of social determinants and to insert a more comprehensive perspective to understand the disproportionate number of Latinas who are adversely affected by negative representations of their lives and institutional patterns of social inequality that impede their social mobility. My intent was also to demonstrate new ways to study Latinas. Many studies of Latinas are comparative to NHW women by SES. In some ways these comparisons are necessary to deconstruct the marker of Latina as other, that is, marginalized.

**Table 5.1.** High School Dropout Rates among Females (16–24 Years Old) by Race and Ethnicity, 1975–2008

| Year | White | Black | Latina |
|------|-------|-------|--------|
| 1975 | 11.8 | 22.9 | 31.6 |
| 1980 | 10.5 | 17.7 | 33.2 |
| 1985 | 9.8 | 14.3 | 25.2 |
| 1990 | 8.7 | 14.4 | 30.3 |
| 1995 | 8.2 | 12.9 | 30.0 |
| 2000 | 6.9 | 11.1 | 23.5 |
| 2001 | 6.7 | 9.0 | 22.1 |
| 2002 | 6.3 | 9.9 | 21.2 |
| 2003 | 5.6 | 9.5 | 20.1 |
| 2004 | 6.4 | 10.2 | 18.5 |
| 2005 | 5.3 | 9.0 | 18.1 |
| 2006 | 5.3 | 11.7 | 18.1 |
| 2007 | 4.5 | 8.8 | 18.0 |
| 2008 | 4.2 | 11.1 | 16.7 |

*Source:* U.S. Department of Commerce 2009a.

high school on time with a standard diploma. Failure to obtain a high school diploma has life-long negative consequences for Latinas' health and economic well-being, as well as a long-term impact on the strength of the U.S. labor force. (National Women's Law Center and Mexican American Legal Defense and Educational Fund [NWLC and MALDEF] 2009, 15)

Limited educational attainment is closely associated with high levels of poverty that hinder opportunities for social and intergenerational mobility. These data are compelling because education is often a prerequisite for entering higher-paying occupations, and Latinas' earnings are greatly affected by the education they have attained. Among Latinas age eighteen years and over in 2007, those with less than a high school diploma represent the largest group and are the most likely to be poor by race and ethnicity. For example, among U.S. born Latinas with no high school completion, their expected median earnings are $21,182 versus a median earning of $35,644 with some college or more (Fry 2010). Schooling experiences oftentimes open or block the pathway to access to the economic opportunity structure.

## Pathways of Latinas: Girlhood, Schooling Experiences, and Academic Indicators

The majority of work on Latino girls has been in the developmental life stage of adolescence. Adolescence is that turbulent life stage when a person is dealing with identity, mastery, competence, and achieving social status, as s/he is neither child nor adult. For many low-income Latino girls, struggles in school and with parents and limited knowledge and access to resources, mentors, and options circumscribe their opportunity of successful resolution of the task of identity formation. Although some work has been conducted on the resiliency (the ability to bounce back and defy the odds of structural barriers) of Latina populations, these studies, although important, focus on the rare instances of success rather than on the structural factors associated with the greater number of low-income Latina adolescents who do not complete their education (Arellano and Padilla 1996; Griffin et al. 2007; Portes and Fernandez-Kelly 2008; Zalaquett 2006). New paradigms have emerged to examine the lived experiences of low-income Latinas.

The 1990s witnessed an incorporation of feminist and gender critiques by Latino scholars to include the intersection of gender roles, socioeconomic position (SEP), and structural inequality as a key focus in understanding socialization processes in the study of girls and women (Amaro 1995; Bettie, 2003; de la Torre and Pesquera 1993; Hurtado 1996; Sandoval 2000). These authors argued that to understand the choices and lived experiences of Latino females, researchers needed to examine multiple factors including the intersection of social and family material conditions on the lived experiences of girls in unresponsive school systems, the effect of racialized, gendered identity constructions, and how the confluence of these factors shaped decisions to have children and form families. The life course connections among early adolescent experiences, major life events, and individual choices have a powerful impact on social location in adulthood. Understanding these connections deepens our understanding of Latina life course transitions.

Three landmark reports on the plight of Latino girls and educational attainment tell a compelling story of the stark realities and lived experiences of the inequities embedded in Latina lives (NWLC and MALDEF 2009; Ginorio and Huston 2001; National Alliance for Hispanic Health 1999). These reports confirm that the gender role stereotypes of Latinas as submissive underachievers and caretakers of elder and younger family members are often reinforced by family, school personnel, and media and contribute to Latinas' oftentimes poor educational performance (Romo 1998; Ginorio and Huston 2001). In schools, a major socialization agent, teachers often reinforce negative stereotypes such as inherent "low" potential attributed to Latino girls (Marlino and Wilson 2006; NWLC and MALDEF 2009). Consequently Latinas may feel devalued and misunderstood (Flores 2006), do not foresee their possibilities for doing well in school and pursuing postsecondary education or careers, and leave school and start a family due to lack of encouragement to pursue education.

Some studies find that girls are more influenced by family expectations than boys (Gaarder et al. 2004). Although mothers are significant sources of personal influence on career aspirations, followed by fathers and the media, persistent and accumulating evidence shows that low maternal education combined with community context, low expectations of school personnel, and limited or absent college advising is associated with mental health problems (e.g., depression) and educational underperformance. The trends over the last three decades urgently signal a need to examine school factors. Although a significant portion of prior research examined ethnic- and gender-specific educational deficits, emerging research has focused on institutional factors such as poor quality of public educational systems in low-income Latino communities, low teacher expectations, and other forms of racism and discrimination that plague Latino students (Gándara et al. 2006b; Hyams 2006; Lopez 2009; National Council of La Raza [NCLR] 1998; Reyes 2006). A persistent trend among Mexican American girls is leaving school earlier than Black and White girls to assist their families economically with the care of siblings or due to early marriage and motherhood (National Center for Education Statistics [NCES] 1995; Zambrana and Zoppi 2002). School environments for low-income Mexican American and Latino girls are not conducive to academic achievement (Segura 1993; Dance 2009). Experiences of Latinas, from elementary to postsecondary education, show that teachers often overlook, ignore, and avoid Latinas in the classroom, while preferring to interact with Anglo males (Solorzano and Delgado Bernal 2001). Attitudes of instructional personnel in the schools and limited access to mentors, professional women, and positive role models in the home, school, or community are factors that greatly hinder educational achievement among Latinas. Factors such as lack of available after-school educational and recreational programs, lack of encouragement to participate in extracurricular activities, and inadequate school counseling services are also long-standing barriers. Frequently Latina adolescents are steered into vocational education for jobs with little career or income potential that are known to limit future options (Romo and Falbo 1996). In other words, educational achievement is linked with access to social capital in the form of translators, bridges to information, guidance, role models, and respect for culture and language that signals equality in ethnic group membership. The absences of these forms of social capital are barriers to Latina educational achievement (Segura 1993).

School resources are highly linked with geographic region and residence of students. About one-third of Latino youth live in poverty and attend inner-city or rural schools where both school and home environments lack educational materials such as computers and books. In the twenty-first century, lack of family economic resources and inadequate school resources combined with lack of access to technological resources are major contributors to educational underperformance. Latinas are less likely than any other racial/ethnic group to have a home computer, Internet and broadband access; Mexican girls are the least likely among all subgroups to have Internet access at home and more likely to access Internet at public libraries. Latinas born outside the United States and those who speak only Spanish at home are least likely to use technology (Fairlie and London 2006, 178). New data show that the use of these technologies is highest among college educated Latinos (Livingston et al. 2009). On all academic indicators, Latino girls underperform in comparison to White and Black girls but tend to perform better than Latino boys (see chapter 6).

Generally, Latino girls outperform Latino boys in multiple areas. In the fourth grade, Latinas score higher than Latinos in reading and history; by the eighth grade, they score higher in math and reading. Finally, by the twelfth grade, they score higher in science and reading (White House Initiative for Hispanic Educational Excellence [WHIHEE] 2003).

*Academic Indicators*

In comparison with their White and Asian counterparts, Latinas are less likely to take the SAT, and those who do score lower on average than other racial/ethnic girls (KewalRamani et al. 2007). Compared with their female peers, Latinas are underenrolled in gifted and talented education courses and underrepresented in advanced placement (AP) courses (Ginorio and Huston 2001). Empirical work has focused on articulating the multiple individual, family, and institutional factors associated with Latina educational underperformance (Arellano and Padilla 1996; Brice 2001; Gándara 1995, 1999).

High school grade point average (HSGPA), AP courses, and the perception of an individual's ability and prior encouragement from school personnel are major criteria to ensure college readiness and entry and access to higher education. These indicators are set as standards in understanding racial/ethnic disparities, yet these indicators often reflect the outcomes of inadequate schooling experiences rather than actual academic potential (Farkas 2003; Teranishi et al. 2004). Using the HSGPA to predict academic success in various fields shows that both White and Black girls tend to have higher HSGPA than Mexican American girls. HSGPA however is strongly associated with school resources, geographic location, and attitudes of high school personnel towards racial/ethnic students (Teranishi et al. 2004). Academic disparities between Latina students and other racial/ethnic students begin as early as kindergarten and remain through age seventeen. Examining individual and school factors helps to explain gaps in achievement between Latina and other racial/ethnic females.

Although Latinas have high aspirations for themselves, their achievement is compromised by a variety of factors, including poverty, a lack of participation in early schooling programs, attendance at poor-quality elementary and high schools, placement into lower-track classes, poor self-image, limited neighborhood resources, the absence of role models, and gender role attitudes (Evelyn 2000; Ginorio and Huston 2001; NCLR 1998; Niemann et al. 2000; Nieto 2000; Zambrana, Dorrington, and Bell 1997). Most important, all these factors are highly associated with the high rates of reported depression and suicide attempts among Latina adolescents (Canino and Roberts 2001; Rodriguez-Trias and Ramirez de Arrellano 1994; Zayas et al. 2005).

*Psychosocial Developmental Stressors*

Negative school experiences and community context influence one's sense of self-esteem and—combined with intergenerational conflict with parents and other stressful developmental tasks—may lead to sadness and depression. Compared to other racial/ethnic groups, Latinas showed the highest decline in self-esteem from elementary to high school: 79 percent in elementary school, 59 percent in middle school, and 38 percent in high school (AAUW Educational Foundation 1995). A sense of self-esteem may also be diminished if an adolescent feels unable to control or cope with their immediate stressors such as family conflicts. Intergenerational conflict has been extensively researched and is a normal process within families but becomes exacerbated within low-income Latino families. Parental fears and concerns for the safety of their daughters, lack of access to emotional and social support resources combined with the real risks of experiencing and witnessing violence in the community context (Sanders-Phillips 2009) intensifies intergenerational conflict and places girls at higher risk of depression and attempting or committing suicide at a younger age than other racial/ethnic girls. Persistent worries by the adolescent—coupled with high rates of poverty and limited resources, including adverse community and school environments—contribute to feelings of limited hope and depression. Depression, suicide attempts, and completed suicide may be exacerbated by stressful life events such as fear for safety in schools, ridicule by peers, and accumulated family stress (Hovey and King 1996; National Alliance for Hispanic Health 1999; Zambrana and Silva-Palacios 1989; Zayas et al. 2005).

Luis Zayas and colleagues (2005) provide an overview of the data on suicide attempts by Latino girls; the increased risk was first observed among young Puerto Rican girls in the 1960s and has been substantially confirmed by prevalence data from the Youth Risk Surveillance Survey since 1995. The authors affirm that suicide attempts are not restricted to one Latina group but show "increasing numbers of female attempters" in many Hispanic subgroups (276). To understand suicide attempts, Zayas et al. (2005) propose the following:

> In addition to acculturation, the socioeconomic disadvantage of many suicide attempters, their traditional role socialization, their ethnic identity, and adolescent parental conflict seem to converge in the suicide attempt, which raises questions of whether the suicide attempts are distinguishable by generational status and the psychological and family profiles. (279)

As Rodriguez-Trias and Ramirez de Arellano (1994) noted in reference to Latino youth, especially females, "the fact that suicidal behavior is so prevalent in the face of deterrents such as religious values suggests that a significant proportion of Latino youth are in despair and unable to get the help they need" (127).

Higher rates of depression among Latino girls may be related to lack of participation in school and the workforce. What is most surprising is that the percentage of Latinas who were not in the workforce or in school in 1970 has declined very little as of 2007. Hopelessness and depression may partly explain recent findings that show that:

> One in five young Latino females was neither in school or the labor force in 2007, a level of disengagement from school and work in excess of young Black males. Some of the young Latino females who were not in school or the labor force were mothers. In 2007, about 9 percent of young Hispanic females were mothers who were not in school or labor force and another 11 percent who were not in school or labor force were not mothers. (Fry 2009, 14)

These data provide a glimpse into the material as well as mental health conditions that disproportionately impact young Latinas. In addition trend data including high school completion and depression rates have shown little change but represent important factors in understanding the impact of structural racism on the educational performance and options of low-income Latino girls. When a lack of educational options blocks the aspirations of low-income adolescents, for some young Latinas other viable pathways such as early family formation are sought. Exploring the formation and influences on gender role performance, schooling, and motherhood at an early age within a family and community context best captures the multiple levels of factors associated with the Latina life course.

### Gender Role Performance and Sexuality

Adolescence is an important yet difficult developmental stage in which an intensification of gender-related socialization occurs (Raffaelli and Ontai 2004). Female adolescence is a period marked by increased independence, strong relationships with friends, and experimentation with adult behavior (O'Sullivan and Meyer-Balhburg 2003). The empirical work to date on young Latino girls and women has been on sexuality, fertility, and reproduction with an emphasis on culture as associated with traditional gender roles and limited parental communication as explanatory factors for decisions to engage in unprotected sex and early childbearing. Latino girls show increased risk markers in terms of their emotional, social, and physical health. These risk markers are an important standpoint from which to assess the consequences of being young, poor, racialized, and ethnic with a culturally marked identity in U.S. society.

A significant number of studies on Latino girls have investigated the detrimental consequences of early school leaving (Fry 2010; Lopez 2009; NCLR 1998, NWLC and MALDEF 2009; National Alliance for Hispanic Health

1999; WHIHEE 2003). Culture-bound, traditional gender roles and lack of communication with mothers are factors that inform the conventional discourse on Latina sexuality and early family formation. A closer look at these studies show that the majority of these investigations have been conducted with low-income families residing in resource-poor communities. Critical assessment of past research provokes a set of questions: What is being studied? How are the results being interpreted? Do the findings advance our knowledge about the lives of Latino girls? Do the data provide an understanding of the multiple factors that are associated with life options and experiences? Do they identify root causes beyond culture than can remedy the concern?

Two family factors that have been found important in early family formation are (1) romantic socialization and (2) a lack of communication with parents and knowledge of sexuality and sexual behavior. Lucia O'Sullivan and Henyo Meyer-Balhburg (2003) conducted a study of adolescent girls residing in urban neighborhoods characterized by poverty and crime, who are at considerably higher risk for early sexual unprotected activity that contribute to sexually transmitted infections (STIs) and pregnancy. Their study of Latinas between the ages of seven and nine found that cultural scripts guide Latina girls' romantic and sexual development as they begin to express romantic interests in boys, and between nine and eleven years old, they begin having boyfriends. The findings revealed that Latinas reported being more supervised in their interaction with boys; hid that they were interacting with boys from family members, especially their mothers; reported being reprimanded for having a boyfriend; and displayed more idealized and romantic views of sexual relationships than African American girls display. Yet, Latino girls compared to African American girls displayed less understanding of sexual behavior; were less frank and open in talking about sex; emphasized pressure to remain virgins yet described more pressure to "find a man," marry, and have children; were more likely to exhibit shame and degradation; and were judgmental toward more sexually active girls.[2]

In contrast to former studies about lack of communication with parents, other studies show that direct communication about male–female relationships and its consequences occurs with both fathers and mothers with Latina adolescents. In a study of Mexican immigrant fathers, Gloria González-Lopez (2004) observes that fathers' fear of raising their daughters in new, urban environments is associated with concerns that their daughters will become pregnant out of wedlock, experience sexual violence and abusive relationships, contract sexually

---

2. Sociologists have focused on Latina sexuality scholarship only within the last twenty years. A limitation of this chapter is that it does not address such crucial themes as lesbian adolescents and women, transgendered peoples, and lesbian marriage. For exemplary studies on Latino homosexuality, gender identity/sexual orientation, Latina adolescent sexuality, and their sense of agency in sexual behavior decision-making, see Arend 2005; L. Garcia 2006; Guzman 2006; Rosario et al. 2004.

transmitted infections (STIs) including HIV/AIDS, and become involved with crime and gang violence. Thus, fathers' fears were strongly associated with their understanding of the negative consequences for daughters of early sexual activity, such as not completing their education, becoming poor, being abandoned, and being stigmatized as single mothers. Similarly, Latina mothers emphasized the extreme aspects of sexual activity including pain, shame, and humiliation and stressed that sex led to pregnancy, possible abandonment, and obstacles to life goals. The study findings show that Latina mothers held harsh views about men and taught daughters to be constantly on guard to protect themselves against men and to avoid a life of exploitation and victimization, stressed finding a responsible man, and exaggerated the pain associated with sexual intercourse and childbirth. While mothers urged their daughters to disclose information about their sexual activity, mothers and daughters adopted antagonistic positions that closed down communication lines (O'Sullivan et al. 2001).

Other studies find that mothers send contradictory messages to their daughters that involve both a critique and loyalty to women's traditional gender roles. These messages balance reality and possibility: the reality of gender oppression and the possibility of transcending strict gender roles (Ayala 2006). Mothers realize their possible selves through their daughters and emphasize the importance of education, independence from men, and risk-free sexuality. Often mothers discuss sexuality within a discourse of danger, violence, and victimization to encourage their daughters to focus on their education (Ayala 2006). In a study of 279 Latina girls who participated in an adolescent pregnancy prevention program to lower pregnancy rates and encourage safe-sex behavior in Los Angeles County in California, 63.1 percent of the girls reported that they felt comfortable talking to their mothers about sex, 58.7 percent discussed not getting pregnant, and 67.6 percent discussed delaying sex until older. Not surprisingly, only 2.3 percent of young Latinas felt comfortable talking to their fathers about sex (Guzman et al. 2006).

A consensus in more recent scholarship shows that the parents of low-income, Latina adolescents mistrust males and heavily restrict their daughters' contact with them. Most girls report that their parents establish rules of no contact with boys, provide few opportunities to date, and exact an age limit to begin dating (Raffaelli and Ontai 2001). This extreme position perhaps reflects a protective parenting standpoint and suggests that parents are engaged in parental practices to prevent their daughters from early sexual activity and pregnancy. Low-income Latino parents may use this strategy if, for example, they feel unable to articulate these fears and concerns with an alternative range of extracurricular options or resources such as participation in sports to delay early sexual activity. Fathers in particular may assume a more authoritarian, distant role as has been proposed in the past. Yvonne Caldera and colleagues (2002) investigated co-parenting strategies among lower- to middle-class Latino and White families, and the results "defied the traditional view of Latino fathers as uninvolved in parenting" (123). Latino families, similar to White families, engaged in co-parenting, and fathers were actively involved with their children. In both groups, fathers were firmer in discipline than mothers, which may explain why Latino girls are less likely to talk with their fathers about sex. Knowledge of options and communication regarding sex education are important parental skills in the prevention of early pregnancy and are associated with higher levels of parental education.

In low-income Latino families, discussions about "biological" topics infrequently accompanies conversations about sexual activity, while in more middle-class families a fuller exploration of the topic ensues. For example, Marcela Raffaelli and Lenna Ontai (2001) report that in their study, 27 percent of Latina adolescents reported discussion of physical development with parents, 36 percent discussed intercourse and pregnancy, and 68 percent discussed menstruation. Although the girls reported discussion of appropriate behavior with parents (91 percent), boys and dating (82 percent), and moral aspects of sexuality (59 percent), dating was reported to be a source of tension and guilt and parents were usually not supportive of dating. Yet sex education (e.g., use of contraception) was not a fully explored topic in parent adolescent conversations. In a secondary analysis of the 1995 National Survey of Family Growth (NSFG) data on risk factors for HIV infection among Puerto Rican and Mexican American women ages fifteen to forty-four, 60 percent of respondents reported receiving no sex education from their parents and very limited exposure to sex education in the schools (Zambrana et al. 2004). It is unlikely that sex education from parents or schools has increased significantly since 1995 in light of both the economic downturn and the popularity of abstinence only programs.

Overall these studies support the notion of parents as important transmitters of sexual knowledge, which is embedded in a "culture of sexual fear" defined as a mistrust of males by Latino parents and a lack of biological discussions of sex. This is not especially surprising given the material conditions and lack of resources such as adolescent health clinics for girls in their communities. Low-income parents themselves have limited knowledge of sex education yet understand its negative outcomes. One can argue that their approach values preventing early family formation, which contests arguments on cultural emphases on early marriage and childbearing. Although we do not know a lot about what is communicated to Latino girls whose parents are college graduates, it is expected that middle-class parents similarly communicate the negative consequences of early parenthood to their daughters but also emphasize the options and opportunities.

Some investigators argue that gender role socialization and cultural scripts, acculturation (the process by which immigrants adopt dominant culture values), and neighborhood effects play an important role in sexual activity among young Latinas (Upchurch et al. 2001). English-speaking U.S.–born Latinas are more likely to use contraceptives than foreign-born Latinas. Although differences have been attributed to acculturation, demographic data inform us that U.S.–born Latinas are more likely to be high school graduates than foreign-born Latinas and that patterns of sexual activity and pregnancy vary by subgroup. In effect, low-quality educational experiences, depression, and lack of sex education, combined with parental fears for daughter's safety and limited alternative options, may all contribute to many low-income U.S. born and immigrant Latina adolescents seeking an identity or social status that has value in society such as early motherhood.

## Early Childbearing and Family Formation

Over the last two decades, although fertility rates have drastically declined for all U.S. women, Latina adolescents and women have the highest fertility rates, and about 30 percent of Latino children are born out of wedlock (Moore et al. 2006). In 2000, the adolescent pregnancy rate was 137.9 per 1,000 for Latinas ages fifteen to nineteen, compared with 83.6 per 1,000 for the overall U.S teenage population (Child Trends 2006). Mexican-origin adolescents have the highest birth rate of all Latinos (124.6/1,000) compared to Puerto Ricans (89/1,000) and Cubans (29.2/1,000) (Kaplan and Cole 2003). Of note, these birth rates decrease for all subgroups as the level of education increases.

Risk factors identified for initiation of early sexual activity include the following: teens living in single-parent households; teens who report higher levels of parental control; and teens living in perceived "ambient hazard" neighborhoods where social disorder, breakdown in social relations, personal threat, and physical deterioration are present (Upchurch et al. 2001). Other factors including lack of knowledge of contraceptive options and lack of health insurance or money to purchase or get a prescription for contraception are serious barriers for low-income girls. A lack of access to contraception information and to comprehensive sex education are long-standing issues for Latino males and females.

Not surprisingly these barriers are associated with reported low use of family planning clinics and contraceptives and low abortion rates among Latinas all of which contribute to higher birth rates compared to other racial/ethnic youth (Kaplan and Cole 2003). Latinas are least likely to report use of condoms, a factor in teenage pregnancy. Among Latino girls almost 50 percent report using a condom compared to 55.6 percent of NHW and 62.1 percent of NHB girls (Mosher et al. 2005). Latino girls are more likely to use unreliable methods of contraception during sexual intercourse or none at all, with Mexican-origin girls the least likely to have discussed sex or contraception use with anyone (Flores et al. 2002; O'Sullivan et al. 2003).

Due to material conditions where few role options exist for Latina adolescents, gender identity is most likely associated with a motherhood role.

Motherhood is a universal ideal that cannot be ascribed to any one cultural group. Rates of pregnancy are inversely associated with economic and social development of a country and the educational and work opportunities available to women. In other words, less educated women tend to have higher fertility than more educated women worldwide. Historically and persistently, Latinos have been characterized as valuing family, placing great importance on the role of motherhood, relying on close connections to extended family, and having more traditional feminine and masculine gender roles (Sciarra and Ponterroto 1998; Raffaelli and Ontai 2004). These values have been associated predominantly with higher fertility and larger family size without distinctions by SES or the educational level of women. It is incomplete to explore the factors underlying Latina adolescents' sexual decision-making behaviors and their consequences without taking into account the material conditions (SES) and its impact on a adolescent's perception of life options and pathways to a recognized social status. As Julie Bettie (2003) explains, "Teenage pregnancy is more often a result, not a cause of, academic failure" (104). The symbols, discourses, and practices that are intertwined in the school setting (as discussed in chapter 9) are important to decode to understand the multiple ways that young women come to understand themselves as Latinas with limited options. A key question is how or does culture play a key role in early mothering?

A cultural ascription model is observed in the analyses of girls' choices as predicated by acculturation. The assignment of the variable acculturation as predicting Mexican-origin girls' decision to engage or not engage in unprotected sex is more likely a proxy for low SES. For example, studies report that increased sexual activity is positively associated with acculturation level (Kaplan et al. 2002; Flores et al. 1998; Tschann et al. 2005) which supports Raffaelli and Ontai's (2004) idea of cultural scenarios and social scripts. These studies reify how a collective cultural orientation paradigm explains the ways that Latinas understand themselves as interdependent members of their social groups, especially the family, and are many times willing to give up their personal needs for the needs of their families (Flores et al. 2002). Other studies challenge the applicability of these findings to all Mexican-origin or Latino females. In fact, caution is being encouraged by many researchers because these studies are conducted with relatively small Mexican-origin samples, in specific geographic regions, and at one moment in time.

Drawing from these studies, the major set of findings shows that highly acculturated girls are more likely to be sexually active and rely on their boyfriends for sexual information while less acculturated girls are more likely to do what their parents say and have friends who are not sexually active. Although culture seems to anchor these findings, simultaneously it contradicts the conclusions. It is expected that highly acculturated girls are English language proficient, are more likely to be U.S. born, and would most likely choose not to foreclose educational options if they were available. Further, birth rates show that immigrant Latina adolescents are more likely to marry at a younger age and assume a mothering role than U.S.–born adolescents. However, the proportional differences may not be as significant since both low-income U.S.–born and immigrant adolescents who perceive few alternative life pathways and experience limited educational success are more likely than high-income U.S.–born Latina or immigrant adolescents to become mothers at a young age. Although these studies proffer that community values and social norms (scripts) highly value virginity before marriage and motherhood and wife roles, this discourse is disrupted by new understandings that SES and neighborhood context jointly affect the conditions under which young Latinas perceive their role options and make life choices. These conditions offer more powerful explanations than the acculturation factor in understanding the thwarted educational pathways of Latino adolescents and decisions for early mothering.

Empirical work on low-income Latinas has tended to use theories of acculturation and the theory of reasoned action (predicts that behavioral intent is caused by two factors: attitudes and subjective norms) to explain decision making regarding sexual activity. These theories often fail to incorporate the intersection of school context, community resources, and family SES. A substantial body of social science work can be misleading because it fails to link the associations among gender roles, low education of parents, neighborhood effects, and school context. By not looking at the context in which Latina youth make life decisions, a scientific opportunity is missed to identify structural causes of academic underperformance and insights on how to explain and how to prevent early motherhood and family formation. These multiple intersecting factors require simultaneous analyses to provide accurate insight into adolescent choices regarding sexuality and early motherhood. Otherwise, low-income Latino parents and their daughters are persistently marked in social science research as "social problems" since acculturated or unacculturated status has similar adverse outcomes in distressed and poor communities, and few studies have been conducted on girls who avoid early motherhood.

Scholars typically frame discussions of abstinence and early sexual activity in terms of cultural values such as reserving virginity and avoiding pregnancy rather than the effects of SEP. In a study examining Hispanic teen pregnancy and birth rates, Suzanne Ryan and colleagues (2005) propose that Hispanic teens who abstain from sex base their decisions on strong motivations to remain virgins to avoid pregnancy (32 percent) and argue that this reason is more significant than religious or moral values (25 percent). The authors conclude:

> Although virgin Hispanic teens cite fear of pregnancy as their primary motivation for remaining abstinent, the tendency among all Hispanic teens to hold less negative views of teen pregnancy than teens in the overall population may be one factor contributing to Hispanic teens' high pregnancy and birth risks. . . . [I]f some

sexually active teens do not feel a strong aversion to becoming pregnant, they likely will not be as careful to avoid it. (Ryan et al. 2005, 6)

Ryan et al. (2005), unintentionally perhaps, stereotype "all Hispanic teens" as holding "less negative views of teen pregnancy." These representations of all Latino girls contribute to the social construction of all Latino girls as non-normative, highly sexualized, or unaware of consequences of early pregnancy. Yet, Latino adolescents fifteen to seventeen years of age are more likely to be sexually abstinent than NHW and NHB girls. Latinas who have options and plans for college, for example, are less likely to engage in unprotected sex (Flores et al. 2002). Jill Denner and colleagues (2001) report that Latina adolescents who have options in and outside their community coupled with support from strong community-based organizations are more likely to complete school and delay pregnancy. Decisions to delay pregnancy are highly related with increased education level, increased use of condoms and contraceptives, less traditional gender roles, family support, and neighborhood effects (Donovan 1998; Darroch and Singh 1999). Information about sexual arousal, desire, and intimacy that promotes healthy sexual decision-making is important for all adolescents but particularly for low-income adolescents. Gender-specific programs can build on existing strategies to help adolescent and young adult females develop a sense of their own power and to protect themselves (Amaro 1995; Denner and Dunbar 2004).[3]

Studies on Latino girls in the last decade have shifted their lens from a totally culturally bound set of gender roles that determined girls' lives to a broader cultural script (albeit still one) that impacts the actions of Latino girls. The lens used to explain girls' sexual behavior and decision making persisted in ascribing the cultural values of collectivism and *familism* and the importance of virginity as major factors in shaping girls' sexual experiences (Raffaelli and Ontai 2001; O'Sullivan et al. 2003). These cultural attributions require interrogation

---

3. An ideal example of a successful outreach project is Chicago's peer-education program Shero's, which uses a cultural-strength approach to promote sexual health. Run by Project Vida, Shero's is an eight-week group-based sex health promotion program for girls aged twelve to twenty-four. Five culturally specific categories are identified as (1) sexual/reproductive health, (2) sexual pleasure, (3) role of religion and pregnancy, (4) sexual assertiveness and communication, and (5) gang culture and affiliation (Harper et al. 2006). Shero's deploys the method of "subverting culture" by focusing on critical interventions of aspects of culture that help and obstruct prevention efforts (Harper et al. 2006); for example, cultural narratives such as *machismo, marianismo,* and other double standards are counteracted by shifting the message of sexual intervention and prevention programs to a new narrative of sexual health that promotes knowledge of disease prevention. This narrative of sexual health empowers young Latino women to be active agents in their sexual lives and to form new social support networks. Alternatively the assumptions underlying the model seek to shift gender role performance from a passive to active agency and expand real opportunities and perceived options for girls and women through knowledge and skills.

because culture per se is not necessarily the yardstick that guides all choices—SES and ascribed social location also shape gender role performance and the lived experiences of girls who become young mothers. How cultural scripts vary by national origin, social class, and gender have not been well examined and thus key differences on factors that shape girls' decisions are omitted in the discourse. In effect, researchers and practitioners generalize the extant body of knowledge on predominantly low-income Mexican American and Puerto Rican girls to all Latino girls as cultural fate. Future studies can increase our understanding of the how and why adolescents make decisions to engage in protected sexual activity by building on the evidence that parental, SES, community, and school factors all have a role in adolescents decision-making to delay early family formation. The evidence also clearly shows the importance of examining differences within and across groups by SES (Cauce and Domench-Rodriguez 2002; Harwood et al. 2002, 51).

## Expanding Knowledge Boundaries: Inserting Neighborhood Effects

A new body of scholarship has emerged in the last decade that examines with reflexivity the challenges confronted by Latino girls and expands the boundaries of their gender role identity to include the effects of structural, representational, institutional practices and neighborhood effects. Investigators have moved beyond cultural deficit models that placed the onus on individuals and have identified external social and structural factors that shape gender role performance, educational achievement, and social mobility. As observed by Jill Denner and Bianca Guzman (2006), a significant portion of the research on Latino girls depicts them as girls who make poor choices and engage in risky behavior, such as teenage pregnancy, suicide, and violent behavior. Emerging scholarship seeks to reconstruct a positive gender role identity for Latinas by exploring how they negotiate family relationships, institutional barriers, access to institutional support, and develop initiative.

Multiple socialization institutions—namely, family, school, and media—play a central role in the opportunity structure of an individual. Access to social capital as proffered by family material conditions greatly determines the transmission of social norms and expectations and is a marker of access to the opportunity structure. Denner and colleagues (2001) define *social capital* as the "parental and kin support, relationship networks that provide collective supervision and resources for youth" (5). Economic means to participate in extracurricular activities such as sports, tutoring, and volunteer work are important to enhance adolescents access to the opportunity structure. Deborah Marlino and Fiona Wilson (2006) identified significant sources of personal influence on the career aspirations of Latinas: mothers, fathers, and the media (in that order); mentors and professional women to give career advice; and teachers. However, barriers to success have also been identified in the form of disciplinary power. Some teachers reinforce negative stereotypes that link Latinas with "low" potential labels.

Racial profiling of Latinas as less capable and less intelligent extends to the classrooms where some teachers act on these false assumptions (Bender 2003; Rolón-Dow 2005) contributing to the high rate of high school dropouts (ostensibly they are high school students who have been pushed out) (Zambrana and Zoppi 2002; Dance 2009; Flores 2006). For example, low–income Latinas are more likely to be tracked into noncollege or vocational courses, limiting their opportunities for higher education (Marlino and Wilson 2006; Bettie 2003), and they experience sexual harassment in schools more than any other group (Romo et al. 2002). Girls who are harassed are subject to sexual comments and jokes, sexual rumors, leering, and unwanted physical contact that leads girls to stay home from school, cut class, and not contribute in their courses (Romo et al. 2002). Although studies suggest that Latinas use a "conformist resistance" to balance school expectations and negotiate gender advancement, these structural forces are not easily overcome by the majority of low-income girls (Cammarota 2004, 55). For some young Latinas without college or career possibilities, having a baby is a marker of adult status, and they look forward to this marker of adulthood, motherhood, responsibility, and respect. Their partners, predominantly working-class men of color and usually of similar SES, may experience difficulty in economically supporting their families (Bettie 2003). In effect, much scholarship demonstrates that residence in low-income, hypersegregated communities and limited access to resources place Latinas at risk of educational underperformance and early school leaving, unprotected sex, and early family formation.

Critical theorizing around community and neighborhood effects provides a more balanced, intersectional lens to understand the lives of Latina youth. Neighborhood processes have powerful effects on early and unprotected adolescent sexual activity and pregnancy rates (Browning et al. 2004; Upchurch et al. 1999, 2001; Gilliam 2007). Neighborhood effects include the proportion of Hispanics in a given neighborhood, social support, neighborhood density (which supports social networks and cohesion), and SES factors that impact sexual behavior among youth. Importantly, linking neighborhood effects as determinants of early sexual activity show racial and ethnic disparities. Neighborhood socioeconomic data, such as lower educational attainment, lack of financial independence, and increased poverty (Gilliam 2007), are associated with early sexual activity (Ramirez-Valles et al. 1998; Browning et al. 2004). In one study, neighborhood quality explained two-thirds of racial differences in premarital childbearing (Browning et al. 2004). Adolescents living in economically and socially disadvantaged neighborhoods tend to exhibit poorer outcomes in comparison to their counterparts and other ethnic groups from more economically advantaged neighborhoods (Upchurch et al. 1999). However, protective effects—such as parental monitoring, family support, and parent and child emotional closeness—can counteract physical deterioration, threats of violence, and other neighborhood negative conditions (Upchurch 1999; Browning 2004).

These aforementioned studies insert neighborhood effects as potential mediators in delaying early adolescent sexual behaviors by suggesting that "high density Latino communities provide higher levels of intergenerational closure and strong informal social support to monitor and control teens" (Upchurch et al. 2001, 1160; Kirby 2001). Although these findings may be true in some cases, generally material conditions (poverty) and institutional patterns of inequality often prevent community members from accessing the types of resources necessary to improve the lives of their youth.[4] Other studies explicitly theorize that neighborhood effects on the lives of minority youth represent a trajectory of accumulated disadvantage in their neighborhoods as a result of inadequate early schooling programs, low-resource schools, few recreational spaces, and the hypercriminalization of Latino youth (Rios 2006; Timberlake 2007; Acevedo-Garcia et al. 2008).

This information on the lived experiences of adolescent Latinas is important because it moves beyond individual decision-making paradigms and culture to show that the neighborhood context in which these girls live shape their developmental life course and their life options. Thus, low-income young Latinas who may become the mothers of young Latino girls have limited economic resources to invest in their daughters. Education and labor force profiles of Latinas, especially U.S.–born Latinas, have witnessed only modest progress

---

4. Attention has recently been focused on Latino female gang membership and incarceration. The racialized labeling and representation of Latino girls as gang members and prisoners in the social science literature is troubling. I concur with Richard Fry (2009) regarding his concern of highlighting girls in prison or gangs when he states: "Among young women in 2007, fewer than 1 percent were either in the armed forces or incarcerated in correctional facilities, and thus little clarity is sacrificed by not enumerating these very small female populations" (2). These studies are important to the extent that institutionalized racist practices as they are applied to Latino girls and women are documented. These studies show that despite the recent increases in the number of females sent to juvenile detention centers, these Latina adolescents do not have access to gender specific programming or language translators (Hunt 2000), and 20 percent of incarcerated women had difficulty accessing services due to language difficulties (Gaarder et al. 2004). A lack of resources results in many girls being sentenced to adult prison without going through the juvenile system first (Gaarder and Belknap 2002). For girls that are in the juvenile system, an analysis of case files reveals a bias in probation officers when dealing with women; 20 percent of girls were depicted as promiscuous and 16 percent as liars and manipulators (Gaarder et al. 2004). Nonetheless concerns are warranted regarding the interpretations of such studies. The study of Latina youth in the juvenile and criminal justice system would help advance our understanding of Latinas life course by embedding these data in a discourse of social inequality, racial profiling, and community and school surveillance of marginalized groups and neighborhood effects to counteract the prevailing representations of Latinos as criminals and deviants.

in increasing educational attainment, labor force participation, and occupational mobility, which parallels the life course trajectory of Latino girls and adolescents.

## Girlhood to Womanhood

### Profile of Latino Women

Information on who Latino women are, including their level of education, median earnings, and occupational status, is important because it dispels myths about a homogenized group of women, shows differences between and among women by national origin and nativity (see chapter 2), and demonstrates how low SES shapes the life course trajectory of adult women's roles and options. Equally important, it reveals those groups of Latino women who are at an economic and social disadvantage compared to more privileged Latino women and why they are.

About half of all Hispanic women are U.S. born, and about 52 percent are foreign born, the majority of whom arrived after 1990. Foreign-born Hispanic women are older, more likely to be married, less likely to be employed, less likely to have a high school diploma, and less likely to speak English well (Gonzales 2008). Mexican American and Central American women tend to be concentrated in unskilled service labor markets such as domestic work and the garment industry. Not unexpectedly, Latino women (22 percent) are twice as likely to live in poverty as White women (11 percent) and have the lowest percentage of high school graduates (64 percent) compared to all other racial/ethnic females.

Hispanic women account for 12 percent of the total employed female population and are more likely than White women to be employed in blue-collar, service occupation, and office and administrative positions. U.S.–born Latino women's full-time median weekly earnings are 34 percent less than White women although slightly higher than Hispanic immigrant women (Gonzales 2008). Puerto Rican women are the most likely to be single head of households, and Cuban and Mexican-origin first-generation women are the most likely to be in two-parent family households. Cuban women are the most likely to have college degrees. The subgroup patterns are similar across generational status, although for native-born Puerto Rican and Mexican American one observes increases in female householder rates (Landale et al. 2006, 150).

The scholarship on adult women has been developed around themes similar to adolescent girls. Many of the educational and social barriers experienced in youth with respect to lack of access to major resources shape Latinas' opportunities and options in adulthood. Nonetheless a substantial body of work has been developed over the past two decades on health, including maternal and child health, sexuality, and transmission of infectious diseases (see chapter 7) and on employment. The past two decades have produced a larger body of work on Latinas in higher education and the professions (Marcano 1997; Loque and Garcia 2000; Niemann et al. 2002). A more modest body of knowledge has focused on family processes with a foci of interest in cohabitation patterns, changing gender roles, and child-rearing values (Manning and Landale 1996; Organista 2007).

Furthermore, a strong feminist (albeit small) body of work has explored the lived experiences and social constructions of Latino women in blue-collar occupations such as cannery work, domestic workers and transnational motherhood (Hondagneu-Sotelo and Avila 1997), and garment work (de la Torre 1993; Pesquera 1993; Romero 2002). For example, a study of the social and economic conditions of Latina domestic workers compared the power of the workers with their female employers on the emotional and mental labor involved in this occupation. Mary Romero (2002) found that Latinas are constructed as ideal domestic workers, forming gendered, classed, and racialized occupations of Latinas. The author found that employers seek Latina domestic workers because of their perceived docility and passivity, humble attitude, and eagerness to work more for less. Romero defines these perceptions of predominantly middle-class White households as the "commodification of personhood" (19). Since a significant number of Latino women have a triple day—working outside the home, caring for children, and doing housework—yet yielding limited economic resources, questions such as how they negotiate their work and family roles, how gender roles and behaviors play out in the domestic sphere, and whether there are differences by SES represent new and important areas of inquiry.

### Changing Gender Roles

Gender role attitudes and behaviors are in transition among Latino women. Adult women's lives are powerfully shaped by economic necessity, access to education that in turn provides access to alternative life options and perspectives, and changes in social gender norms. Gender-focused scholarship in the last two decades has shifted the discourse on gender role attitudes by inserting the role of increased education and SES in the study of gender role behaviors and family processes.

Changes in gender role attitudes and behaviors can be observed over time as education level increases. Latino women are performing their gender roles differently than in the past. Yet for low-income Latinas traditional gender roles persist similar to other low-income women regardless of race and ethnicity. More egalitarian gender role attitudes are highly associated with increased levels of education, SES, and exposure to differing life options and choices. The higher the education levels of Latino family members, the more similar the heteronormative gender role behavior is to their educated middle-class counterparts. Not surprising is that women are more quickly adopting less traditional gender role attitudes than males as they increase their education, enter the labor market, decrease their fertility, and have more options in accessing resources. These factors all contribute to varied family patterns and processes. A few studies are described below to illustrate the continuum of gender role performance in Latino families by SEP and subgroup.

Studies of gender role attitudes among Puerto Rican and Mexican American college students and professional women have reported more egalitarian gender role attitudes (Cofresi 1999; Franco et al. 2004; Gowan and Trevino 1998; Toro-Morn 1995). Maura Toro-Morn (1995) conducted in-depth interviews with seventeen married Puerto Rican working- and middle-class women who migrated to Chicago in the late 1960s. Distinct class differences were reported in terms of both reasons for migration and gender role performance. Working-class women viewed the migration as a family project to deal with economic problems, while the professional women perceived migration as "a joint family project" and "had an agenda of their own" (718). Both groups of women migrated as part of a family migration, but working-class women viewed employment as a temporary necessity and held more traditional gender roles.

Professional women placed their career goals alongside their family responsibilities and held more egalitarian gender roles. These women were able to juggle multiple responsibilities and negotiate tasks with husbands due to their middle-class position, similar to NHW women. Options for child care were different based on family SES. For working-class women, child care was addressed in various ways; for example, leaving their children in Puerto Rico with grandmothers, bringing over relatives to help, or using informal friend or family care during the day as a way to lessen their multiple responsibilities as worker, wife, and mother. Professional women exercised different options: They were able to hire help, postpone having children, and organize their schedule to be compatible with their children's activities. These data demonstrate gender role variability and different life choices that are attendant with education and economic privilege (SES).

In a study of thirty Central American women in the Washington, D.C., area, Terry Repack (1997) found that women's employment and economic contribution to the family enabled them to renegotiate gender roles. The interviewees reported that their partners shared in household work and childcare responsibilities. The study also confirms that changes and acceptance of new gender role performance is highly associated with level of education of the woman, prior working status in country of origin, marital status, SES, rural versus urban prior residence, and opportunity in labor market structure for men. Although the women reported that these changes caused family tensions and family disruption such as divorce, they "relished the freedom from community pressures and sanctions that were an integral part of life in small Central American towns" (253). Not unexpectedly, when Latino immigrant working-class women in the United States establish family households, expectations reflect change as family members respond to the changing demands of dual-wage earner families and different societal expectations and gender privileges in the United States.

In another study on low-income Black, White, and Latino women ages fifteen to forty, Linda Burton and colleagues (2009) examined partner relationships and cohabitating patterns and women's interpersonal trust of men. Using in-depth qualitative interviews, results showed that the majority of women had a generalized gender distrust of men. The women's early life course was characterized as having experienced poverty, prior physical and sexual abuse, mental and physical health conditions, and other uncertainties and corollary risks that permeate the lives of impoverished women (1109). This complex study seems to confirm the "culture of fear" that is transmitted from mother to daughter in low-income Latino families. These fears that I have already discussed in the adolescent section are related to gender role socialization messages that perceive potential partners/spouses as unreliable men likely to abandon family and having limited ability to provide economic security. These messages do not differ significantly by race and ethnicity among low-income groups. Since low-income women tend to select partners from their own SES and racial/ethnic group who experience similar economic and social risks, family material conditions for the next generation will most likely not change significantly.

Increases in labor force participation and education have had a strong effect on gender role performance for both native-born and immigrant Latino women. However, for low-income Latino women, low-wage work, triple shifts, and inequity in access to educational resources maintain their economic disadvantage and limit their gender role performance.

### Latinas and Higher Education

Access to higher education is a relatively recent phenomenon among Latino women (Arellano and Padilla 1996; Brice 2002; Gándara 1995; Trueba 1999; Zambrana 1987). In a 2009 review of Mexican American women's entry into higher education, it was noted that the first significant cohort of Mexican American women to enter into institutions of higher education occurred in the 1960s (Zambrana and MacDonald 2009). In the past two decades, new avenues of inquiry have been pioneered by examining family and institutional factors and how the intersection of race, ethnicity, gender, and SES are associated with academic and professional success (see Garza 1993; Molina 2008; Zambrana, Dorrington, and Bell 1997). Yet, issues of recruitment, admissions, and retention have remained critically important. As Sylvia Hurtado (2009) states: "More than two decades ago, scholars began to sound an alarm signaling that advancing Latinos in higher education was critical to U.S. national interests" (545).

Since 2000, increasing equity in access to higher education has been taken up again. Although modest progress has been made with more Latinas entering institutions of higher education, low-income, historically underrepresented Mexican American and Puerto Ricans, and first-generation college-bound students are lagging behind. Latino intergroup differences in access to higher education are mainly associated with higher parental SES. High parental SES translates into Latinas going to better schools, living in better neighborhoods, and having access to and engagement in extracurricular academic activity. SES is a major ingredient in the accumulation of academic skills and experiences that promote Latinas staying in school, delaying motherhood, and enhancing academic preparation for a competitive application for college entry. Stories of the higher education experiences of, in particular, low-income Mexican American women suggest that they experience significant stressors due to ethnic, racial, and class discrimination. This discrimination stems from educators' low expectations of ability and performance of Latino students as well as a lack of Latino faculty and administrators who can provide mentorship and emotional support to them during their higher education experiences. For many low-income, first-generation college-bound Latinas, the educational disadvantages experienced in adolescence and racialized institutional practices in the K–12 pipeline continue to shape their college experiences.

In two recent collections on higher education, the authors focus on institutional practices in colleges and universities and lack of representation of Latino faculty and administrators that would measurably increase access and opportunity for Chicana/Latina women. The authors argue for expanding opportunity in higher education for Latino students to address the crisis of higher education. The premise for these arguments is that higher education is and has been an inaccessible right and privilege and an unwelcoming location historically for Latino students (Delgado Bernal et al. 2006; Gándara et al. 2006a). Although historical documentation of the denial of access to secondary and higher education institutions for Mexican Americans exists (Johnson 1995; MacDonald 2004), few investigations account for these historical antecedents.

Complementing these collections, a series of articles that represent the voices and lived experiences of Latino students are recounted in two publications (Yosso et al. 2009; Garrod et al. 2007). The narratives reveal that stereotypes and feelings of marginality continue to present serious barriers to positive experiences in undergraduate institutions and to degree progress. The stories tell of racism, of strength and resiliency, and of struggle. They tell us about institutions that do not have academic programs of U.S. Latino Studies, of lack of recognition of Latinidad in these major institutions, and of creating new intellectual spaces and discourses. Although these stories are predominantly being told by students born in the United States after the Civil Rights era, they have not changed considerably from those of prior generations.

Higher education is an important pathway to social mobility, and access to higher education is highly dependent on prior schooling experiences. As discussed in chapter 4, the educational experiences of many low-income Latinas in the K–12 educational pipeline do not prepare them academically to compete for college admission. If they are prepared, often family financial barriers prevent young women from attending college. So, one cannot separate information on higher education participation and degree completion from family SES, prior experiences in the educational pipeline, and institutional practices. Further experiences of discrimination are prevalent for many Latinos based on stereotypic notions of ethnic inferiority in higher education. These factors contribute to the underrepresentation of Latinas in higher education. Below I offer trend data on the college attendance and completion rates of Latinas.

In 1980, Latinas represented only 2.4 percent of all bachelor's degrees, and 1.7 percent of all doctoral degrees in all fields. In 2003–2004, 7.1 percent of bachelor's degrees were awarded to Latinas, and 3.9 percent of the doctorates. In 2007, 29 percent of Latinas were high school graduates with no college attendance; 15 percent had some college, but no degree; 7 percent had associate degrees; and 12 percent were college graduates (KewalRamani et al. 2007). Foreign-born immigrant women from South America have the highest levels of education, with 43 percent having attended college compared to 16.3 percent of immigrant Central American women and 38.5 percent of Caribbean-born Hispanic women. South American women are twice as likely as Central American women are and three times as likely as Mexican immigrant women to have some college education. Native-born Latino women have higher rates of labor force participation (64 percent) than NHW women (61 percent) and Hispanic immigrant women (54 percent). However, a closer look at these data clearly shows that Mexican American progress is disproportionately lower than for other Latino subgroups. Table 5.2 presents degrees granted by degree-granting institutions in 2001–2002 to women by race and ethnicity. About 7 percent of all college graduates were Latina, and 5 percent received a professional degree. The post-secondary degree most likely to be received by a Latina is an associate degree.

**Table 5.2.** Percentage of Degrees Granted to Women by Race and Ethnicity

|  | Latina | Non-Hispanic White | Non-Hispanic Black | Asian |
|---|---|---|---|---|
| High school graduation 2007 (%) | 64 | 86 | 82 | 86 |
| Associate degree 2001–2002 (%) | 10 | 69 | 13 | 5 |
| Bachelor's degree 2001–2002 (%) | 7 | 73 | 10 | 6 |
| First professional degree 2001–2002 (%) | 5 | 70 | 9 | 13 |

*Source:* KewalRamani et al. 2007, 117.

In 2004, Latinos represented about 11 percent of all students in higher education, more than doubling the 5 percent in 1990. Latinas are entering and completing college at higher rates than Latino men. Modest increases in completion of higher education degrees are reflected in occupational categories. For example, in 1994, Latino women represented only 4 percent of women in managerial or professional positions and by 2004 that percent had risen to 6.3 percent or 1.5 million Hispanic women in professional and managerial positions.

As noted in chapter 2, higher education degrees do not easily translate into higher median income, and Latina median income is much lower compared to the median income of other racial/ethnic women (Fry 2010). The high cost of higher education, less access to employment-based education benefits, academic disadvantage accrued in the educational pipeline, elimination of affirmative action policies, discriminatory practices in higher education, and family formation patterns are major impediments in securing higher education degrees.

～

In this chapter I examined what we know about the lived experiences of Latino adolescents and what factors shape their transition from girlhood to womanhood. Several findings help us to understand these experiences and transitions. Neighborhood effects, poor-quality schools, negative perceptions of Latinas, and low parental SEP have contributed to early family formation for some and few alternatives for social mobility for a large number of Latinas. These circumstances form a weak social and economic foundation for the transition from girlhood to womanhood and constrict available life options. Latinas face greater challenges than other racial/ethnic females in completing high school, obtaining high-wage jobs, and accessing higher education. These material conditions contribute to high rates of depression in both Latino adolescents and women that adversely impact family processes. Early life circumstances all too often limit options and alternatives in adulthood and promote intergenerational family cycles of inequality.

Latino women's gender roles in the family are in transition, and changes are highly associated with higher education. Higher education provides women with improved material conditions and opens up new ways to perform their gender role and provides different life options. For Latino women who have achieved higher education, the data show similar gender role attitudes to educated dominant culture women. Higher educational attainment generally results in higher labor force participation, lower unemployment rates, and increased resources for investment in the future of one's children.

Modest gains have been made in the last four decades in increasing the educational and occupational status of Latinas and in decreasing early pregnancy and motherhood (Fry 2009). I conclude that most research on Latina gender role performance along the developmental life course trajectory has been shrouded by an opaque veil of cultural determinism without accounting for SES, neighborhood effects, and school contexts. Emerging scholarship, however, is contesting cultural deficit models and reframing new ways to think about how young low-income Latinas negotiate structural and representational barriers. Future research must move beyond the sole cultural focus on the Latina to embedding her lived experiences in the social context of the forces that shape her decisions and gender role performance.

# 6

# Boyhood to Manhood

> Adolescents from Latino, African American, and
> immigrant families are more likely to live in poor
> neighborhoods with high crime and few resources.
> Neighborhood quality and school quality are strongly
> linked in the United States, which means that these
> youth attend schools of poor quality with less skilled
> teachers and fewer advanced programs. It is difficult to
> imagine how students from Latino immigrant families
> and those from African American families can raise
> their high school completion and college attendance
> rates without a significant improvement in the quality
> of the schools that they attend.
> —Fuligni and Hardway 2004, 111

We know very little about Latino boys and men except what we view on television and in movie theaters and what is filtered through the news media. In this chapter, I explore how Latino adolescents and men are portrayed in the social sciences and other disciplinary literature. The questions I ask are many and varied. For example, What is Latino masculinity? What is the role of the family in male gender role socialization? What are the facts and rationale behind the persistent stereotyping of Latino boys and men as gang members and as "foreign" or fringe members of our society? What is the role of schools in promoting favorable life options for Latino boys? What are the lived experiences of Latino males as students, sons, and fathers?

The last decade has witnessed an increase in scholarly work on gender that has included a focus on masculinity and men. The work on Latino men has clustered around cultural values of *machismo* and relationships, HIV/AIDS, immigration, and deviant behavior such as gangs and criminal activity. Similar to the body of scholarship on Latinas, the overwhelming majority of research has been conducted on low-income Mexican American and Mexican immigrant males, and a more limited literature exists on Puerto Rican males. As discussed in previous chapters, few studies of Latinos distinguish by socioeconomic status (SES) and subgroup, and this is also the case with Latino males. Once again the lived experiences of Mexican American and Puerto Rican adolescents and men are not contextualized within their social location and the segregated, low-resourced communities in which they live. Like for Latino girls, more recent work focusing on early adolescence and young adulthood fails to capture the intersection of social and family context on the experiences of Latino boys in unresponsive school systems, their decisions to form families, and the material conditions and lack of access to the opportunity structure for many of these young men. It is important to examine how boys and men are singularly affected by these factors.

In this chapter, I identify major themes in research and how these works capture the lived experiences of Latino boys and their transition to adulthood in the United States. I examine the literature on gender role performance, schooling, employment, fathering, and the intersection of social and family conditions on the life choices of boys and men. While chapter 2 offered important demographic indicators, this chapter begins with some demographic information on levels of schooling and continues by engaging the discourse around the construction of Latino masculinity and its relationship to family formation and gender role performance. This selected review of the literature offers important insight into the social and economic position of Latino boys and men in U.S. society.

## Brief Educational Profile

Overall, Latino males complete an average of 10.6 years of schooling compared to a national average of 12.2 years for non-Hispanic Black males (NHB) and 13.3 years for non-Hispanic White (NHW) males. In general, U.S.–born Hispanics complete an average of 12 years of schooling, while foreign-born Hispanics are less likely to complete high school and to have parents who are high school graduates than those who have U.S.–born parents (Pew Hispanic Center 2004; Federal Interagency Forum on Child and Family Statistics 2007).

High school dropout rates have slightly declined in recent years, among both Latino males and females ages sixteen through twenty-four. Trend data from 2004 to 2008 show Latino males dropout rates have declined from 28.5 percent in 2004 to 19.9 percent in 2008. However, dropout rates remain four times higher than that for White males (5.4 percent) and two times higher (8.7 percent) than that for Black males (NCES, 2009a). Among adults ages twenty-five and over, 60.6 percent of Latino men have a high school diploma (compared to 63.3 percent of women)(U.S. Department of Commerce 2009). Latino men are less likely to have a high school diploma (compared to 8.0 percent of the U.S. total population) and significantly less likely to have a bachelor's or postgraduate degree (12.5 percent of Latinos compared to 30.1 percent of U.S. total population).[1] Among Latino males, similar to

1. Across Latino subgroups, high school completion rates vary widely by country of origin. Among U.S.–born children of Hispanic immigrants, 40 percent have less than a high school

females, South Americans and Cubans are the most likely to be college graduates and to speak English (Pew Hispanic Center 2008b). Educational disadvantage coupled with racialized and negative representations of Latino boys and men "as dangerous machos" in the public imagination often forecloses positive identity development processes and access to the opportunity structure.

## Theorizing on Latino Masculinity

Excessive, and often aggressive, masculinity, *machismo,* and patriarchy are generalizations attributed to Latinos, particularly Mexican men. Dominant paradigms of Latino masculinity have largely been framed and reinforced within the disciplines of social science and family studies. Cultural scripts of gender roles have portrayed Latino boys and men as hypermasculine or machos. *Machismo,* which can be translated into provider, protector, and head of family unit, has been used as an organizing principle to theorize about males in Latino families. Negative conceptualizations of *machismo* portray masculinity as being represented by a man who is an aggressor and domineering patriarch. Despite this heavily racialized and negative notion of *machismo,* studies show that in many Latino families, males contribute to the reproductive work of household chores and child care and hold egalitarian views similar to Whites (see chapters 3 and 5). Scholars have interrogated this stereotypic cultural script of Latino gender roles (Mirande 1997; Torres 1998). While notions of *machismo* may lead, in some cases, to unhealthy behaviors or beliefs, culturally specific and overemphasized conceptions of Latino masculinity have shaped powerful narratives that misrepresent entire communities of men and their role in the family. For example, Pierrette Hondagneu-Sotelo (2000) found that prolonged spouse separation as a consequence of transnational immigration significantly transformed patriarchal authority and traditional division of labor. Men who lived with other men in nontraditional living arrangements found themselves taking on more traditional feminine tasks such as cooking and washing clothes. For example, Mexican men who immigrated post 1965 lived in male communities and lived longer periods without their wives. These social and material conditions provided the impetus and need for creating new ways to perform their gender roles.

Jose Torres (1998) in his study of Puerto Rican men posits that negative connotations of men that include male dominance, aggression, authoritarianism, and oppressive behavior toward women and children ignore the positive attributes of the male gender role as responsible and economic providers for their family. The author argues that these negative attributions of Latino males have negative effects on their physical, social, and mental well-being. The

---

education, 12 percent have a college degree, and 18 percent live in households with annual incomes of $75,000 or more (Fry 2009).

construction of Latino manhood as negative power undermines their role as respectable partners, fathers, and citizens and reinforces differential treatment, for example, by school and law enforcement officials. Alfred Mirande (1997) argues that a continuum of masculine gender role exists that reflects a variety of "modalities" and forms of masculinity. In interviews with 105 Mexican men from California and Texas who were married and had a child between four and eighteen years of age, Mirande found that participants lacked spaces and opportunities to express their feelings and were very aware and dissatisfied with popular conceptions of Latino masculinities.

Theorizing on essentialization of *machismo* has extended into the area of sexuality. A 2004 study analyzed data from a sample of 1,880 boys drawn from the National Survey of Adolescent Males. The data showed that boys with more traditional masculine values (superior male status and antifemininity) were less likely to support condom use and male responsibility to prevent pregnancy (Pleck et al. 2004) and that strong links exists between "masculine ideology" or masculinity and hyperheterosexuality, explaining sexual behavior of some Latino youth. For example, the study argues that youth who hold "traditional" masculine beliefs, such as condoms decreasing sexual pleasure, often had sexual encounters that led to unplanned pregnancies and sexually transmitted infections (STIs) (Pleck et al. 2004). Yet, although Latino adolescents are less likely than NHB and NHW youth to use condoms, these types of arguments overlook key factors such as SEP, religious values, youth impulsivity, failures of contraception, access to and economic means to purchase condoms as well as knowledge regarding the use of preventive or post-intercourse remediation measures such as morning after pill. Although these are all plausible explanations for all low-income youth across racial and ethnic groups, particularly economic considerations, few studies take the latter into account, and most studies make implicit assumptions regarding culture as the sole-driving force in Latino male early sexual activity and family formation.

Marking behaviors such as gender role values of sexual practices as cultural and group-specific rather than associated with SES pathologizes males and contributes to the marginalization of Latino boys and men as a group.

The omission of structural inequality as represented in lack of sex education in the schools, lack of availability of quality health care services, and lack of economic resources underestimates the multiple factors associated with safe-sex preventive practices. Poor young males regardless of race, ethnicity, and national origin are more likely than boys from college educated, upper-middle-class families to engage in unprotected sex. Furthermore, in the latter case, higher SES boys and their partner would most likely know of and have access to options not easily available to low-income boys, such as the morning-after pill or abortion. Unacknowledged in these narratives of hypermasculinity is the effect that these ethnic-specific attributions have on the mental health of

Latino adolescents and young men, such as higher rates of depression and attempted suicide.

## Gender Role Performance, Family, and Community

Gender role performance for Latino boys and men has been portrayed as embedded in a cultural-bound script of *machismo* characterized by authoritarianism, hyperheterosexuality, and abusive relationships. In 1997, Mirande produced the first significant work on Latino masculinity whose "overriding goal was to undertake a study of Latino men that did not begin with the premise that Latino culture and Latino masculinity were inherently negative and pathological" (6). The author used multimethods that included personal observations, interviews, life experiences, and historical materials to contextualize the concept of Latino masculinity. Mirande (1997) investigates differing perceptions and meanings of *machismo* among Mexican men and the construction of a son's male identity within the family and culture. He distinguishes between traditional and revisionist views of the meaning of masculinity and affirms differences on male gender role performance associated with regional, economic, and occupational position. Mirande's findings show that masculine ideology is not unique to Latino men; it is fluid and contradictory at times; and no one mode of masculine gender performance exists but rather a complicated and diverse continuum of male gender role performance is observed.

His principal conclusions are that the lived experiences of the Latino men he studied contradict prevailing social science literature and public perceptions. He advocates for a pro-feminist approach to the study of the construction of male identity, one that is inseparable from the construction of female identity. In other words, as structural and material conditions change (such as the need for both partners to work or increases in educational level), gender role performance, too, changes.

In another important work on masculinity, *Muy Macho,* by Ray Gonzales (1996), male writers provide insight into how they view themselves as men within the concept of what it means to be *macho*—the catchword for adult Latino manhood. The men in the anthology write "about their fathers, sexuality and the cult of silence between men—a literary task taking place for the first time" (xiii). The question of whether Latino males are different than other men in America is one of the central themes of the book, and it addresses issues that complicate the expression of Latino manhood: the implications of "a strict Catholic upbringing, language barriers that keep many Latinos from being more assertive about what they want, and the relative *passivity of many Latino women [sic]*" (xv). The author challenges stereotypes that have been forced on males by their own culture and U.S. society and offers evidence on the ways in which alienation has contributed to the construction of their male identity, both heterosexual and homosexual.[2] The author speaks to racism as a major factor in the ways that their individual and collective identities have been shaped. Both of these landmark studies show that structural factors such as poverty, lack of opportunity and racism, and the psychological burden of difference and inequality in an unwelcoming environment have contributed to the marginalization of Latino boys and men in the United States.

Yet the strength of these lived experiences as powerful frameworks for understanding the experiences of young Latino adolescents and men has been ignored in social science literature. Latino masculinity has been socially constructed based on historic, cultural-bound stereotypes of predominantly low-income, non English-speaking Latinos. These stereotypes are consistently reconstructed and reinforced through the narrow lens of social science literature and institutional reenactments of racist practices for both U.S.–born and immigrant Latino boys and men who constitute a racially, stigmatized group (Lopez 2002; Morris 2005). For example, there was a multipart series of articles on Hispanics in the United States in the *Washington Post* (December 7 and 9, 2009) featured as "Struggles of the Second Generation." One story was about the experiences of a former gang member, now with a partner and child, who is trying to be a responsible father and citizen. The second, entitled "An Undesirable Inheritance," featured an undocumented Mexican immigrant family and their life illegally living in the United States (Aizenman 2009a, b). Both articles, perhaps unwittingly, reinforce two very common Latino male stereotypes of criminalization and illegality. In response to these articles, an editorial entitled "Reinforcing Racial Stereotypes" concluded with the following statement:

> I appeal to you to reconsider such articles. I have tutored and mentored many children and I know that such articles don't motivate them. Rather they undermine the high expectations that many of us attempt to inspire. Our children deserve encouraging stories that will facilitate their hope and dreams. (*Washington Post,* December 9, 2009)

There are several flaws in these print media representations that continue to fuel negative identity markers for Latino males. First, the overwhelming majority of Latino boys and men are neither gang members nor illegal immigrants, but these stories have a strong effect on generalizing these misconceptions. For example, popular notions of "wilding," along with car-jacking, gang-banging, and

---

2. Scholarship on Latino gay men is an emerging and important area of inquiry. Although a limited body of work was available prior to 2000, significant visible research has emerged post 2000 under queer studies, sexuality studies, and cultural studies; see, e.g., Diaz 1998; La Fountain-Stokes 2009; Nesvig 2001; A. Cruz 2002.

other media inventions, become one more excuse to distrust people of color, thus justifying racial discrimination in the criminal justice system (Welch et al. 2004; Bender 2003). Second, these stories do not stimulate the humanitarian concerns of the American public imagination but rather reinforce the need for targeted and racialized institutional practices and policies and promote anti-Latino and anti-immigrant sentiment. Third, as noted in the editorial, these stereotypes send a message of discouragement, group failure, and a future without hope to Latino girls and boys. Similarly, these perceptions are mirrored in the mainstream social science literature, which often excludes the prior literature predominantly by Latino scholars who have inserted different perspectives.

Although there are few studies on Latino males, the majority of studies are clustered around three themes: family and school failure, delinquency and gang membership, and a more recent emphasis on boys and men who impregnate adolescent girls. Studies have examined the relationship among the family (economic resources and communication), educational failure, and male delinquency (Driscoll 1999; Davalos et al. 2005). In a study of Mexican American and White students, the results found a relationship between perceived parental school support and family communication and likelihood of committing delinquent acts (Davalos et al. 2005). An analysis of the 1995 National Longitudinal Survey of Adolescent Health found that children from single-parent families are more delinquent than those from two-parent families (Demuth and Brown 2004). In contrast Patrick Tolan and colleagues (2003) found that single-parenting does not increase the chances of youth delinquency, and they argue that family environments can be considered only in conjunction with macro-level factors such as poverty to understand causes of delinquency. However, parental support has been found to be more effective in dissuading girls from participating in high-risk behavior than boys (Gaarder et al. 2004). Yet boys may have different sources of influence compared to girls in their communities that make the difference in engaging in high-risk behavior. For example, Julio Cammarota (2004) in his ethnographic study of forty Latino boys and girls between the ages of seventeen and twenty-four years of age found that boys had weaker ties with their mother than girls and perceived even weaker support from their fathers. The results show that a Latino male has a greater likelihood of graduating from high school and pursuing college with the help of a fellow Latino community member. These studies reinforce the importance of mentors and community support in academic success.

In contrast, research on gangs shows that gangs function as "fictive kin" for many males. While Latina gang members identify real family members as the most important people in their lives (Hunt et al. 2000), boys concerns about personal safety in their community coupled with adolescent needs to belong to a group may have a stronger impact on their decisions for affiliation. An unprecedented focus has been placed on Latino boys and adolescents as gang members. Only about 3 percent of Latino boys report ever being a gang member (Pew Hispanic Center 2009d, 89). Yet these same adolescent processes of belonging, experimentation, and identity development represent normal stages in the transitions from boyhood to manhood but take on in the American public imagination a different interpretation and symbolic, gendered meaning in racialized and poor communities. Community structural characteristics are highly associated with neighborhood social processes and influence the developmental ecology of urban male youth and their opportunity structure. Tolan and colleagues (2003) build on the ecological work of the sociological tradition that showed in the 1940s that community characteristics such as poverty, ethnic heterogeneity, and residential mobility (especially in urban communities) was highly associated with delinquency and violence. In their study of Latino and African American male participants between eleven and fourteen years of age from economically disadvantaged inner-city neighborhoods in Chicago, the investigators evaluated how both structural characteristics and neighborhood social processes related to the level of individual involvement in violent behavior through examining micro-level factors such as parenting influences and deviant peers.

The data reveal that adolescents and their caretakers residing in inner-city communities are more likely than those in other poor urban communities to perceive higher levels of problems and lower levels of neighborliness (e.g., sense of belonging), which are social processes thought to buffer risk. Not unexpectedly, parenting practices provided limited protective benefits in these disadvantaged communities and did not directly affect the role of gang membership. While Tolan et al. (2003) conclude that their "model is far from complete," one important contribution of this study is a broader ecological perspective about parenting. Parenting practices cannot be examined outside the context of structural characteristics of community, which provide the social, economic, and institutional context (such as schools) that is closely associated with youth outcomes. Further, the social construction of Latino families as "negligent" and of gang membership as solely a dangerous threat to U.S. society both misrepresents the situations of families and applies a different standard for normal adolescent group affiliation and formation to Latino males (as will be discussed in chapter 8). The inseparable, almost synonymous links between poor, Latino racialized communities and their proclivity toward violence, criminality, and immorality are ongoing themes in the American public imagination and are reenacted on a daily basis in public spaces such as schools.

## Social Construction of Masculinity in Schools

Gender-based stereotypes influence the ways teachers, school officials, and other authority figures perceive and treat Latino boys. Teachers often express

biased views and hold negative perceptions of Latino boys, yet school personnel extend unearned academic privileges to NHW and Asian boys. Latino boys
are perceived as hypermasculine, dangerous, problematic, and threats to society (Katz 1997; Cammarota 2004; Morris 2005). Multiple studies have found
that teachers and school personnel have low expectations of Latino students
and proffer less quality teaching to Latino boy and girl students based on their
perception of low intelligence and incompetence. Cammarota (2004) found
that boys tended to not attend class to avoid teacher harassment and conflicts
over language and culture. Another racialized, discriminatory perception is the
assigned identity marker of "gangsta" (gang member) to Latino boys, which
contributed to continuous surveillance and disciplinary measures on the part
of school personnel. In contrast, NHW and Asian boys were rarely disciplined
for the same infractions or violation of school rules such as dress code or getting out of seat without permission compared to Latino boys. Latino boys in
the school setting "endured adult assumptions that because of their race and
gender, they had the potential for danger and should be monitored and disciplined accordingly" (Morris 2005, 44). These data show a clear link between
negative school environments and male Latino (both U.S.–born and immigrant) poor academic performance.

Schools are a central socialization mechanism, and teachers and school
personnel have an important role as sources of support and role models for
students. Welcoming academic environments in schools can result in a sense
of attachment, belonging, and support; help to form positive aspirations
and goals; and create a positive identity and status for Latino boys. However, Latino immigrant boys report weak school-based relationships that influence their engagement in school and communication with teachers. Many
U.S.–born and immigrant Latino boys voiced a strong peer pressure to reject
school, and many formed oppositional relationships to school-based identities.
A study of generational differences in dropout rates found that the following factors influence high school dropping out: parental expectations, home
resources, family income, and number of siblings (Driscoll 1999). Despite the
importance of the association between SES and high school dropout rates, the
improvement in SES from one generation to the next does not always lead to
a lowering of the dropout rate among second- and third-generation Latinos.
Driscoll argues that these findings support the theory that "higher generation
immigrants are more likely to perceive structural barriers to success and have
less faith in the ability of education to serve as a route to economic success"
(Driscoll 1999, 871).

More recent data on Latino immigrant boys (predominantly Mexican and
Central American) show that, similar to U.S.–born racialized Latinos, they fare
less well in the educational system and confront racism, negative stereotypes,
and peer pressure. Schools with large numbers of students that are limited-

English proficiency (LEP) are racially and ethnically segregated, have higher levels of children living in poverty, and employ more inexperienced teachers. Compared to teachers in non-LEP schools, the teachers are less likely to be certified and have less academic preparation (Cosentino de Cohen et al. 2005). Minority male students are more likely to be viewed as having behavioral problems than other groups. Dominican and other Caribbean students are often criminalized in the school context (Lopez 2002) or viewed as problems (Fine 1991). Teachers all too often have low and negative expectations of Latino male youth that promote a hypervigilant, authoritarian, and inauthentic caring attitude.

Initial findings from the Harvard Longitudinal Immigrant Student Adaptation Study (LISA) confirmed previous research on Latino immigrant boys that shows that they are less engaged with the educational process, have lower grades, and have poor relationships with teachers (Suarez-Orozco and Qin-Hilliard 2004). Compared to their female counterparts, immigrant boys have lower grade point averages and lag behind in language arts, math, and science. Teachers reported that 44 percent of immigrant boys performed poorly academically and socially. The unequal treatment of Latino immigrant boys (compared to Latina girls) by school officials and administrators contributes to the educational gender gap. For example, immigrant boys reported more conflict with administrators and teachers, were more likely to witness their male friends in negative interactions with security guards and other authority figures, and were more likely to perceive school as a "prison." In addition, immigrant boys reported more racism than girls, reported feeling less support, and perceived school as a negative, hostile, and racist environment. These factors contributed to immigrant boys "checking out" of the academic process (Suarez-Orozco and Qin-Hilliard 2004).

Another perspective on weak ties to schools among Latino boys is the hypervigilance that schools engage in regarding Latino boys and the absence of tolerance for the lack of material and human capital (including methods of dress and comportment) of low-income and working-class racialized youth combined with a perception of "dangerousness." Studies reveal that low-income Latino and African American children are labeled as problems from an early age and are criminalized for any infraction. Two studies suggest that schools presume Latino boys to be guilty and encourage a delinquent identity from elementary school (Katz 1997; Rios 2006).

Feelings of marginalization and alienation as a result of living in communities with limited resources, parents who worry about community conditions, and schools who do not welcome them all contribute to the higher risk of Latino males attempting or committing suicide at a younger age than African American and White youth (Hovey and King 1996; NCHS 2004).

## Schools, Juvenile Delinquency, and Closing the Opportunity Structure

Schools are central sites that initiate the labels of delinquency and deviant behavior. As observed by Marion Wright Edelman, founder and president of the Children's Defense Fund, "schools become a breeding ground for prisons" (September 11, 2009). The unprecedented emphasis on Mexican American youth as gang members and delinquents transgresses the role of community and reflects how discriminatory institutional behaviors negatively affect the lives of Mexican American and Puerto Rican youth. Although the location of much of this work has been in California and other southwestern Mexican-origin communities, studies suggest the following: students that drop out (pushed out) of high school may be more likely to engage in delinquent behavior (Davalos et al. 2005). Latino adolescents are more likely to report the presence of gangs at school and to be involved in gang activity and youth violence (Chandler et al. 1998; Tolan et al. 2003).

The labeling of Latinos as gang members is a social problem that has tremendous repercussions and consequences for Latino adolescents in exercising life options. Thus, the label itself and the contributing factors in these group memberships need to be addressed. Gang membership can be formulated as group membership and as an identity process that is a normal part of identity development. Alternatives for group membership, for example, in hockey club, 4-H club, or sports clubs are not readily available options in low-income communities. Although most adolescents have groups of friends with whom they engage in activities, the naming of these memberships in low-income communities as "gangs" needs to be interrogated and reframed within a broader social and economic context and a developmental trajectory of adolescent identity markers.

Studies on gangs show that many contextual factors contribute to involvement in gangs: isolation from mainstream society, poverty, family stress and crowded households, peer pressure, and the struggle for self-identity. Gang membership also represents a sign of hopelessness and self-destructiveness (Vigil 1988; Rodriguez 1993). Although Brown and Benedict (2004) report that immigrant students are more fearful of weapons than nonimmigrant students, this may be a result of Mexican immigrant students having fewer economic resources and a greater fear and mistrust of law enforcement officials than U.S.–born persons. The focus of most studies on gang membership has been on Mexican-origin and Salvadoran gangs.

Popular representations of Latino youth have conflated friendships and gang membership (Way 2004). In her study of urban youth and their friendships, Way challenges assumptions of universal gang membership of Latino male youth by demonstrating that male relationships are integral to the lives of these young men. Way finds that contrary to "activity-centered" studies that argue that boys are less reliant on intimate friendships, teenage boys yearn for close and loyal friends and struggle to find and maintain these close ties (Way 2004). Latino boys consider a close friend someone who will protect them, show concern, and help them from getting in trouble. Some are closest to those friends whom they consider like "brothers" (Way 2004). Conventional modes of masculinity that emphasize independence, emotional neutrality, and autonomy do not benefit Latino boys, and instead boys should be allowed and encouraged to seek close and intimate friendships that could possibly keep some from dropping out of high school and engaging in other risky behavior (Way 2004). Although in some cases intense same-sex friendships are highly discouraged, punished, and judged as immature, Latino boys value close male friendships and struggle to find and maintain these close ties. The majority of all adolescents value friendship and seek peer groups. Yet for Latino male adolescents, these normal adolescent processes are pathologized and viewed as nonnormative and dangerous.

The reality in many low-income communities is that young Latino males are in jeopardy of interacting with law enforcement officials as a result of peer relationships interpreted as gang membership and the school's readiness to file charges for any infraction. These perceptions by schools and law enforcement officials are driven by popular media stereotypes of many Latinos as gang members. Perhaps what is most concerning is the underlying nature and longevity of these stereotypes of Latinos as dangerous. As Bender (2003) observes, "Most of these stereotypes...date back to the nineteenth century Southwest" (12). High poverty rates, inadequate education, a lack of academic extracurricular and recreational activities, and perceived or actual gang involvement are all factors that contribute to the overrepresentation of Latinos in the juvenile and criminal justice system (see chapter 8). As a result, juvenile and adult incarceration rates have risen dramatically over the last few decades for Latino youth and men, particularly in states with the highest Latino concentration—Texas, California, Florida, and New York (Mauer 2007; Hinton Hoytt et al. 2002a,b). Unquestionably, high school suspension rates, peer ridicule, institutional discrimination, and stereotypes of hypermasculinity, "dangerousness," and criminality strongly contribute to Latino male youth not persisting in the school system, which often leads to early fathering and family formation.

## Masculinity, Sexuality, and Family Formation

Variability in male expression and gender role performance in family patterns and processes have been studied predominantly by Latina scholars, yet these studies have remained invisible in conventional social science research (see Hurtado 1995). In this section, my goal is to provide examples of prior and recent studies on variability of Latino male gender role attitudes and gender role performance.

Almost three decades ago, Lea Ybarra (1982) conducted a study of Mexican American working-class couples in California and found a range of gender roles, with most men participating in household division of labor; that is, helping with domestic chores. Maxine Baca Zinn (1980, 1982) examined variation in male contributions in household division of labor and confirmed Latino men's active roles in household work. Although household division of labor is higher among professional couples than working-class couples regardless of race/ethnicity, the myth of Latino males as authoritarian patriarchs has been repeatedly disproved (de la Torre 1993; Gonzalez 1996; Mirande 1997; Pesquera 1993). Two other studies conducted with 62 Mexican American male and female undergraduate and graduate students (Gowan and Trevino 1998) and 444 men of whom 146 were professional Hispanic men (Long and Martinez 1997) provide some insight into Latino male gender role attitudes. In the first study, males reported more traditional gender role attitudes regarding the role of females in the workplace and toward parental views for child care than their female counterparts. However both male and females disagreed with traditional attitudes toward family and career roles. The authors in comparing their results to other NHW samples conclude that SES is the primary determinant of attitudes toward gender roles rather than ethnicity (1091). In the second study, Long and Martinez (1997) report higher masculinity scores among the Hispanic professional men compared to non-Hispanic men and graduate students. Interestingly, Latino professional men reported higher masculinity scores without the corresponding high self-esteem and high self-acceptance scores. The authors seek to interpret this inconsistency as the "struggle of trying to balance U.S. majority cultural values with ethnic identity and with ethnic cultural values" (Long and Martinez 1997, 487). In other words, the compensatory efforts of higher Latino masculine gender role identity are perhaps associated with perceived racism and structural/institutional obstacles to upward mobility. This is an important area of inquiry among professional Latino men. Two important observations from these studies: Gender role attitudes vary by SES among both Latino males and females, and Latino women report less traditional gender role attitudes than the men. Despite such studies, the representation of Latino men as having traditional gender roles persists.

Few studies have been conducted on Latino males, family functioning, and adolescent fathering. Lesser and colleagues (2001) note that "compared with adolescent mothers, little is known about adolescent fathers. Nonetheless there is a growing body of literature indicating that adolescent fathers share similar concerns with their female partners about the well-being of their child and a desire to be actively involved in child-rearing" (331).

One phenomenon that has been explored is men's involvement in teen pregnancy to assess the association between gender role attitudes and pregnancy. In a study of 307 predominantly U.S.–born Mexican Americans in the Los Angeles area with a mean age of 18.5 and mean educational level of eleven years of school, Goodyear and colleagues (2000) measured developmental variables (age, parental alcohol use, child abuse and neglect, satisfaction with childhood quality), gender-related attitudes, affect regulation, dating characteristics, and sexual behavior (sexual activity and contraceptive use). Men were grouped into those who had impregnated an adolescent girl and those who had not. The results show that male gender role ideology increased with age and that inexpressiveness of feelings was directly related to number of pregnancies. The two main behaviors that contributed to pregnancy were coercive sexual behavior (which was associated with family neglect) and the use of ineffective birth control methods. The authors conclude "that many Latino men and women would probably not perceive a situation as coercive in which a man insists on sex when the woman is not interested" (Goodyear et al. 2000, 464). The authors report that their findings account only for a small amount of variance (16 percent), which suggests that many other factors such as low SES and poor self-esteem can better explain these behaviors. In another study of adolescent pregnant African American and Latino couples (n = 53), the association between relationship factors and parental dysfunction was examined. The females were between fourteen and nineteen years old, and the males were between fourteen and twenty-four years of age, and about 67 percent were still in high school (Florsheim et al. 2003). The Latino fathers had a mean age of eighteen, had completed on average ten years of school, and 80 percent were working full- or part-time and had low incomes. Similar to the Goodyear et al. (2000) study, quality of relations with parents and partners, parenting stress, child abuse potential, physically punitive behavior, relationship status, and SES were measured. Overall, the Latino men had similar sociodemographic characteristics as the African American men. However, Latino men were more likely to have been raised in dual-parent families, to have dropped out of school and to be working, and to have lower scores for abuse and physically punitive behaviors. The authors also found high levels of stress among the young parents in adjusting to their parental role. Those respondents who had positive relationships with their own parents were at lower risk of dysfunction.

Although the sample sizes were small and some African American and Latino fathers appeared to disengage from the relationship after two years, the authors conclude without substantial evidence that "these findings support the possibility that how young couples adjust to parenthood may depend on culturally specific norms and expectations regarding couple's relations and parenting behavior" (Florsheim et al. 2003, 76). In neither of these studies (Goodyear et al. 2000; Florsheim et al. 2003) was neighborhood effects or SES taken into account in the interpretation of the data. Yet racial/ethnic or cultural attributions for behaviors were implied for these groups of men that in so many ways continue to portray men as irresponsible, culturally bound machos from abusive backgrounds who have options in their decision making regarding child support. For many low-income boys and men regardless of race and ethnicity, traditional gender role attitudes and behaviors are class linked and serve as the guide for interpersonal, heterosexual partnerships. Unfortunately the question of what it means to these young men to be fathers (which is discussed later) is often not asked, nor are young Latino boys aware of the economic burden and psychological investments required in child rearing. We can perhaps argue that all too often lack of knowledge, search for a masculine role identity, perceived limited life options and alternatives, and their intersection with traditional gender role expectations lead low-income adolescents into early parenting. For young low-income Latino men, fatherhood may represent a social status and a role that provides them with a sense of manhood that is not readily accorded to them in society. An equally important point is that the majority of adolescents and young men do not choose early family formation. Vigilance is thus necessary to not assume that these studies represent the choices and options of all Latino adolescents and men. If adolescents and young men can successfully negotiate the educational pipelines, other pathways are available.

## Alternative Pathways for Latino Boys and Their Transition to Adulthood

Several recent reports provide in-depth analyses of pathways for Latino youth. In a comprehensive analysis of four decades of Census Bureau data by the Pew Hispanic Center (2009d), the good news is that as of 2007, 86 percent of Latino youth are engaged in work or school, which represents a significant increase from past generations. The trend data show that: "The growth over time in the share of youths involved in such market-oriented activities is not limited to Latinos. Similar changes have occurred among Black and White youths. But the Latino trends are particularly noteworthy because their share of the young adult population has increased so dramatically during this period—to 18% in 2007, more than triple their 5% share in 1970" (1). Overall, U.S.–born males are more likely to be involved in school and work activities than foreign-born males although this varies by nativity. Among Latino males, labor force participation increased from 65 percent in 1970 to 68 percent in 2007. For Latino males without a college degree, the pathway to middle-class status has virtually vanished with the decrease in manufacturing jobs (Fry 2009, iii).

For those boys who complete high school, two options can ensure their social mobility: enrollment in higher education institutions and/or enlisting in the military. College enrollment among those who complete high school differs by generation. For the years 1997 through 2000, Fry finds that the highest rates of college attendance among high school graduates is for second-generation Latinos (17.1 percent) followed by "third-generation or more" (12.4 percent) and foreign-born Latinos (8.1 percent). Although Latinos who do graduate from high school have high rates of college attendance, the numbers of students who graduate from college are reduced by factors such as part-time enrollment, attendance at two-year institutions, and prolongation of time toward completion of degree. Rates for minority enrollment in college can also be deceptive because minority populations are younger (Fry 2002). All too often, college is not an alternative for young low-income Mexican American and Puerto Rican males or other low-income Latinos and thus military service is a viable option.

Military service is a pathway into adulthood that can improve educational achievement, provide health care benefits, and provide specialized training that increases one's life work and career prospects. In 2002, 10 percent of military personnel were Latino. They had the highest participation in the Marines (comprising 15 percent) and the lowest participation in the Air Force (6 percent). Among Latinos in the military, 18 percent are in combat, 45 percent are in technical occupations, and 37 percent are in administrative (and other) positions (Segal and Segal 2004). The military pathway as a bridge to adulthood for all racial/ethnic young adults has decreased since 1970 with voluntary military enrollment, although the "propensity to serve" is still high among Hispanics; that is, among those Hispanics who indicate interest in serving. Yet, Latinos are less likely to be commissioned officers or attend any of the three federal military academies: U.S. Military Academy at West Point, NY, U.S. Air Force Academy at Colorado Springs, CO, and the U.S. Naval Academy at Annapolis, MD. Officer training usually requires more formal education such as college degrees or Reserve Officers' Training Corps (ROTC) during college education. As noted by Segal and Segal (2004):

> As with blacks, the commissioning of Hispanics as officers has lagged well behind their recruitment into enlisted ranks and falls below their share of civilian college graduates. Four percent of officers are Hispanic, compared with 6 percent of college graduates ages 31 to 35 and 10 percent of enlisted personnel. Hispanics are more likely than blacks to be in combat specialties, and less likely than blacks to be in administrative or supply occupations. Hispanic officers in the Army, Navy, and Marine Corps are more likely than either white or black officers to be at the lowest officer grades (23).

Voluntary service for both males and females in the military can provide benefits such as education allowances, medical care, and housing purchase assistance. However for the majority of enlisted Latinos who may be in combat, physical and mental health consequences may decrease their future life options. Important questions of how participation in military service among Latino men and women contributes to educational and employment opportunities over the life course and to social mobility and how it impacts family formation and processes are significant areas to explore.

Differences in life pathways by gender were also found. Gender, school, and work comparisons are important because available pathways influence decisions on family formation and gender role attitudes. Noteworthy in comparison to Latino males, U.S.–born Latino females have experienced the greatest increase in work and school activities. The largest gender gap (females attending school more than males) occurs in the second-generation, which is also the group with the highest rates of college attendance. Among second-generation Latinos, 14.7 percent of male high school graduates attend college compared to 19.5 percent of females. The gender gap for those that are foreign-born (with males at 7.1 and females at 9.2) and "third-generation or more" (with males at 11.2 and females at 13.4) are also significant (Fry 2002). With the increases in Latino female high school completion, college enrollment, increasing labor force participation, declining motherhood, and the increasing economic and educational disparity between Latino and White males, gender transitions are evident. These transitions are setting a new course for the reconstruction of masculinity and feminine gender roles in patterns of marriage and family formation, and those narratives have yet to be written. Increasingly the accumulated body of evidence shows that SES and social location in the economic opportunity structure is a more significant predictor of gender role attitude than race or ethnicity. What this chapter so far shows is that the study of Latino adolescents and men has not been sufficiently developed and thus has not provided a balanced view of the continuum and varied set of experiences.

## Normalizing Masculine Identity for Latinos

Emerging scholars have initiated a new discourse on Latino boys and men. Many of these studies reviewed below embed their descriptions of males in their lived experiences, their ethnic and gender identity, and their perceived marginality. The studies speak to men's lives as the men themselves tell their story of dreams, aspirations, values, and gender relations. Each study provides some insight on one area of a man's life such as an economic provider role or a father role. Shifts in gender roles in the United States have less visibly affected the traditional gender roles of Latino men because of limited opportunities for education and segmented labor markets. Yet new constructions of femininity and masculinity, institutional and discriminatory practices in school and the labor market, and changing economic opportunity structures for men and women have *unsettled the only bastion of power left for Latino men*—their home, family, and interpersonal relationships. In the following section, I describe an emerging body of evidence that informs our understanding of alternative conceptions of Latino masculinity. The studies are mainly ethnographic interview studies with small sample sizes. These studies contribute by giving voice to men's experiences as male providers and fathers, which expands the lens through which we can understand who they are and what factors they perceive to most profoundly affect their gender role performance.

In a small quasi-life history study of poor and working-class Puerto Rican men born in Puerto Rico and residing in the northeastern United States, Weis and colleagues (2002) explored the construction of masculinity. The authors focus on the ways in which these men are staking out their identity in the United States as well as the social context in which this social construction is taking place. The authors provide a social, economic context of Puerto Ricans in the United States and acknowledge the "perched marginality" of these poor and working-class men. The authors claim that "Puerto Rican men are staking their identity as 'hombres' [men] holding on to a form of being Puerto Rican rooted in patriarchal authority in their everyday actions" (289). Consistent themes of dignity and autonomy are linked to notions of family and kin and are equally associated with economic participation, freedom from discrimination, and cultural citizenship. This "refers to attitudes and practices that affirm the right to equal treatment and participation in the society through the right to cultural difference and dual allegiance" (291). The article covers a broad range of critical topics such as gender violence, violence in family of origin, and racial categorization. The authors conclude that these men are reconstructing traditional gender role regimes based on their own family experiences (although critical of the violence in their families of origin). The authors expand the lens on Latino men by framing the discourse on men within the U.S. racialized context: "Without the material conditions that allowed men to be men, these men are stripped of their language, access to material goods, jobs, a place in the economy, and increasingly a place as head of household" (Weis et al. 2002, 300).

The authors contextualize this study within the reality of postindustrial economic restructuring in U.S. society, its impact on the role of poor and working-class men and the factors that shape gender role attitudes and (as observed in the following study) an opportunity to parent differently from how they were fathered.

In an ethnographic study of adult noncustodial Latino fathers, perceptions of fatherhood and provider role were assessed among Mexican Americans (n = 17) and African Americans (n = 13) in Los Angeles (Becerra et al. 2001). Men were recruited from those enrolled in work training programs. Interview data were gathered on relationships with family of origin, communities in which they spent their formative years, educational, employment and marital/relationship history, and their relationship with their children. There were few differences by race and ethnicity. All the men were employed and had been raised in low-income, inner-city neighborhoods where poverty, gangs, and violence were prevalent. A common characteristic of participants was that they loved being fathers and having a relationship with their children. The fathers perceived the emotional component of the relationship with the child as important and wanted to engage in the type of parenting that was not provided to them by their own fathers. Many fathers owed a significant amount in back child support (arrearages). Reasons cited included unemployment and the father's limited understanding of the child support enforcement process. For example, few knew that the child support order was based on current earnings and could be modified when earnings changed or if they were unemployed. These investigators conclude that the overwhelming majority of fathers (75–80 percent) participate in the noncustodial parenting role, feel close to their children, and want to contribute to the parenting role (emotionally and financially) (29). These qualitative data provide an oppositional ethnic portrait to the conclusions of prior studies and is embedded in an understanding of the intersections of the social location of low-income Latino men, the limited options known and available, and institutional practices.

Similarly, in a study by Lesser and colleagues (2001) where the researchers explored young Latino fathers' feelings about their fathering role and perceptions of HIV risk, context and social location were central in the analysis and therefore led to a more thoughtful social and ethnic portrait of their lived experiences. The young men were fifteen to twenty-five years of age, fathers or expectant fathers, living in inner-city California. Focus groups were conducted with forty-five men, and in-depth interviews were conducted with ten men. Three main themes were identified in the lives of these young men or adolescents transitioning to adulthood: (1) a childhood entrenched in poverty, social oppression, violence, and alcohol and drug abuse (mainly marijuana); (2) the role of the gang; and (3) taking on the paternal role. Importance of social relationships is deeply embedded in each of these themes. These authors, similar to other investigators, confirm the finding that joining the gang in early adolescence represented a search for self-identity and "a place to belong for young people whose options have been restricted and as a reaction to a childhood filled with discrimination, violence (community and family) and feeling alone" (333).

The young men report that fatherhood was a way to break from the gang, gain empathy from others, and modify perspectives on male–female relationships to include equality. These young men want something different from what they have experienced, but are not always able to break the negative internalized images of themselves that have been transmitted by teachers, school officials, and lived experiences. Fatherhood can be a positive role for young men if it provides the impetus for a positive transition to manhood. These results suggest that indeed fatherhood can motivate young men to seek viable employment, return to school, and be an equal partner in child rearing. On the other hand, if other options were available, fatherhood would most likely be delayed.

The studies presented in this last section were driven by an intersectional approach that examined multilevel processes at the individual, familial, and institutional level to construct a meaningful "cultural portrait" of these men. Acknowledged were the role of power relationships with dominant society and the "spirit-breaking" cycle of internalized oppression that Jerry Tello (1998) describes: "It occurs over generations, whereby the true nature and resiliency elements of a culture have broken down by the dominant's society uncompromising pressures (racism, poverty, poor educational systems, alcohol promotion and violent neighborhoods)" (35).

∽

In this chapter, I have offered a glimpse into the ways Latino males live and the ways they are studied. Oppositional narratives exist side by side: traditional Latino male portraits are more characteristic in conventional social science and other disciplines, while an emerging scholarship that blends with prior U.S. Latino research naturalizes and inserts the social forces that contribute to the varied experiences of Latino males. Even in the modest amount of work compiled in this chapter, several findings extend our knowledge about Latino males.

First, the transition from boyhood to manhood is shaped by childhood and adolescent experiences in family, school, community, and work that shape (mold) dreams and aspirations. During these early years, boys build or do not build social and human capital (education and skills) to use in their adulthood years. *Social capital* is broadly defined as access to networks and connections that are provided by parents, schools, and community resources. If neither of these forms of capital is accrued, options to access the economic opportunity structure are limited in the transition to adulthood. The accumulation of disadvantage and consequent low social location are significant and cannot be attributed solely to individual behavior or culture, as the lived experience narratives and data so powerfully show. Second, the range of gender role behaviors of Latino males have not been yet fully represented in the social science literature, and Latino boys and men experience numerous social and economic disparities due to family SEP, neighborhood processes, and institutional practices that limit their life experiences and options.

An emerging body of work has developed on theorizing around new and normalized definitions of masculinity to extend our knowledge of male gender roles including fatherhood. This new scholarship focuses on reconstructions of

Latino masculinity using an intersectional lens that takes into account structural constraints to create normative gender role boundaries and a definition of masculinity with explicit assumptions. A primary assumption is that the social constructions of masculinity and femininity are fluid, dynamic, and are shaped by region, national origin, education, SES, and occupational status and by the material conditions and prior experiences in family of origin. For example, a men's movement that is fueled by the notion of manhood as honorable but has received limited attention is called Circulo de Hombres (circle of men), a National Compadres Network of Mexican-origin men. The movement is "taking a head-on look at a key element of Latino cultural identity: *machismo*." One of the founders, Alejandro Moreno, states:

> There is a whole other side to the word than womanizer who talks big and wears big chains. It means doing right by his wife, children and companions. We are trying to take the word back and teach it to all who will listen. It represents a critical look at old ways and confronting the stresses with a new U.S. culture and upward economic mobility in new ways. (Wood 2001, 1)

This emerging body of knowledge is providing us with new ways to think about how Latino men construct their masculinity or sense of manhood and how fathers transmit these gender role socialization messages to their sons (and daughters). The role of economic provider is a major marker of manhood regardless of race, ethnicity, and SES, and this role is often denied to poor and working-class men. To elucidate gender role family socialization processes beyond culture requires an examination of the economic opportunity structure, including equitable access to resources, structural barriers, and racialized social constructions of male dangerousness and criminality. How Latino men respond, adapt, and reconstruct their masculinity is strongly associated with the opportunity they perceive to exercise their masculine role as provider, protector, and advocate for the family. In other words, Latino men seek to perform those male roles that are extended "to all men." The question left unanswered is, What is at stake here if we change these Latino male perceptions of difference and inequality?

# 7

# Physical and Mental Well-Being through Adulthood

> Of all forms of inequality, injustice in health care is the
> most shocking and inhuman.
> —Martin Luther King, Jr.

Health is a crucial asset that enables women, men, and youth to perform their daily responsibilities such as go to work and school, engage in so-cial relationships, form families and parent children. Up until the 1960s access to health care was essentially a privilege of those who worked in good jobs or who could afford to pay for health care. While we've seen a general expansion of health care access since then, the disparity between poor and rich is evident now more than ever. Differences in rates of diseases such as tuberculosis, high blood pressure, diabetes, or sexually transmitted infections (STIs) are unques-tionably related to having enough money or health care insurance coverage to visit a medical provider.

The study of Latinos and health has traditionally focused on poor and low-income women and pregnancy, on lack of health care insurance coverage, on adolescent risk behavior, and on differences between U.S.–born, English-speaking Latinos and foreign-born, non–English-speaking Latinos. The same focus continues today in much of the research. Moreover this research, as with most of the other disciplinary research on Latinos, is often interpreted using a cultural explanatory lens. A growing body of research, however, is moving beyond traditional cultural presuppositions to help us better understand the multiple forces that impinge on one's health. An important feature of this re-search is the acknowledgment that social determinants—where we live, where we play, where we work, what we can afford to eat, and how much stress we experience in our daily lives—all play an important role in our physical health and mental well-being. In this chapter, I bring together various bodies of health knowledge to create a profile of what we know about Latino health and mental well-being by gender through the life course. The overwhelming majority of this research is on poor Latinos and thus little is known about the health of middle-income, college–educated, professional Latinos.

*Health* is defined as a sense of well-being and freedom from disease and discomfort. Good health is the foundation for child and family well-being and is one of society's priorities. Many indicators are used to measure physical and mental health that span from more commonly discussed indicators such as birth weight to less discussed topics such as rates of intentional injury. Regardless of type of indicator, one conclusion that can be drawn is that the health of America's children, families, and adults is linked, often intersectionally, to educational level, socioeconomic status (SES), race and ethnicity (due to its economic implications). I draw on available data to disentangle the role of ethnicity, social determinants of health disparities, and their intersection with structures of inequality. The major themes that I discuss are maternal and child health, child health, adolescent physical and mental health, and adult physical and mental health by gender.[1] A brief overview of major access indicators and their association with adult morbidity (chronic conditions) and mortality (death rates), health access, and health behaviors is also included. National data are presented as an aggregate with few exceptions, and additional data are included from regional and specific geographic areas to inform on different health disparities for each subgroup.[2]

Health studies represent the largest body of intellectual inquiry on Latino populations as interest in this group has increased with the new emphasis on disparities in the twenty-first century. Economic, contextual, and institutional factors are implicated as potential explanations for disparities within the Latino community. Disparities in health and health care access across race, ethnicity, and SES in the United States are well documented (Atrash and Hunter 2006;

---

1. Each of the substantive areas covered in this chapter represent an entire subfield of medicine and public health such as maternal and child health and HIV/AIDS in male-to-male transmission and mother-to-child transmission. Other areas of importance such as domestic violence, public health interventions, and health care policy and practice are important areas of inquiry but beyond the scope of this brief review.

2. Multiple limitations in health data have been identified (National Research Council 2004). Since 2000 national surveys collect data only on Mexican Americans, and prior to the year 2000, surveys were administered only in English (Zambrana and Carter-Pokras 2001). Health trends data and comparative data by subgroup are not generally available. Data are drawn from multiple sources, including population-based studies for different years and thus are not always consistent across sources. National data are not representative of the experiences of specific Latino subgroups such as high SES, college educated Latinos or in specific geographic concentrations such as migrant farm workers (of whom Latinos comprise nearly 80 percent), *colonia* residents living in the unincorporated areas along the two-thousand-mile U.S.–Mexico border (that often lack sewers and running water) (Azevedo and Ochoa Bogue 2002), and inner-city distressed neighborhood residents. Data on Puerto Ricans who reside on the island of Puerto Rico are not used for national comparisons but are available in separate reports.

Clancy and Chesley 2003; LaVeist 2005; Satcher and Pamies 2006; Smedley et al. 2003; Thomson et al. 2006). Despite progress in the overall health of Americans, the 2007 *National Healthcare Disparities Report* found that disparities varying in magnitude by health access indicators and medical condition have remained unchanged or worsened in the Latino community (Agency for Health Research and Quality [AHRQ] 2007).

Health care access is usually measured by health insurance coverage, which is a major factor in health care disparities in the Latino community. The consequences of being uninsured and having low socioeconomic status (SES) include receiving less preventive care such as Pap smears, diagnosis at more advanced disease stages, and receipt of less therapeutic care once diagnosed (Henry J. Kaiser Family Foundation 2001). Having health insurance is associated with having a usual place to obtain health care. While 42 percent of the uninsured lack a health care provider, only 19 percent of the insured do not have one. The major reason why Latino individuals do not have health insurance coverage is the low level of employer-sponsored coverage. Only 43 percent of Latinos get coverage through their own employer or that of a family member, well below the national rate of 64 percent (Quinn 2000). Further, although Latinos have high rates of labor force participation (78.4 percent), they are more likely to work in minimum-wage or below-minimum-wage jobs without health-linked benefits (Angel and Angel 2009). Hispanics who are least likely to have a usual source of health care are men (36 percent), young adults (37 percent of eighteen- to twenty-nine-year-olds), and the less educated (only 32 percent of those without a high school diploma).

Generally, Latinos who are foreign born and/or Spanish speakers are also at a disadvantage: 30 percent of those born outside of the fifty U.S. states, 32 percent of Spanish speakers, and 43 percent of immigrants who are neither citizens nor legal permanent residents lack a regular health care provider (Livingston et al. 2008). For Latino immigrants, recent policy changes in immigration laws, welfare reform, and health care reform have heightened the barriers to access to health care. The fundamental issues of limited access to health care services are related to health policies and economic and structural factors that contribute to disparities (Cordoba 2007; Fuentes-Afflick et al. 2006, 624; see also Rios 2005).

Health care disparities are associated with numerous factors including patients' perceived discrimination (Krieger et al. 2010; Office of Minority Health 2000; Perez et al. 2009); perceived social acceptance (Portes 2000; Arcia et al. 2001); mistrust of the health care system (Coleman-Miller 2000; Hunt et al. 2005); poor or ineffective communication between patient and physician (Alegría et al. 2009; Armstrong et al. 2007; Vermeire et al. 2001); provider's lack of ethnic knowledge and competence and sensitivity to material conditions of patient (Geiger 2001; Physicians for Human Rights 2003; Rutledge 2001); SES (House and Williams 2000; Krieger 1999; Galobardes et al. 2006; Kennedy et al. 1998; Alan Guttmacher Institute 2008); race discordance between doctors and patients (Oliver et al. 2001; Wissow 2003); access to health care, literacy, and communication barriers (Bustamante et al. 2009; Carrillo et al. 1999; Rodríguez et al. 2009); and quality of health care (Ong et al. 1995; Parchman and Burge 2004; Pippins et al. 2007). Patient's language, SEP, and health literacy level are major determinants of compliance with recommended treatments and preventive screenings (Brach and Fraser 2002; Cooper et al. 2003; Epstein and Hundert 2002; Institute of Medicine [IOM] 2001, 52). In other words, patients must be able to communicate with their doctor, explain their symptoms, understand the doctor's instructions, and have the means to act on the provider's recommendations such as to buy prescription medicine or rest. If these processes do not occur due to the patient's low SES and language or literacy issues, then the health condition, particularly if the person has no health insurance coverage, may worsen. Often researchers look only at what the person does rather than why the person did or did not take action (e.g., get a prescription filled, show up for a follow-up appointment).

Using paradigms that fail to take into account all these factors provide limited knowledge on persistent health disparities and inequalities in the Latino community. Similar to the social science disciplines, public health and medicine implicitly attribute Latino ethnicity and culture as primary determinants of health care disparities and have often treated Latinos as a monolithic ethnic group (Brown et al. 2003; Kimbro et al. 2003; Harris 2004; Weinick et al. 2004). As a result of this aggregation of Latinos in most health-related research studies, only in the past decade do we have information on specific health needs by age, gender, and subgroup. Although it is important to understand the culture of patients, social determinants such as education, income, health literacy, and access to health insurance are more significant contributors to health disparities than culture. Considerable interest in understanding the causes of health disparities among Latino subgroups has generated a large body of work that has centered on the concept of acculturation as an organizing principle.

## Paradigms for Understanding Health Disparities

Multiple perspectives have been proffered to explain health disparities for racial and ethnic groups. Health disparities refer to differences in morbidity, mortality, and access to health care among population groups defined by factors such as SEP, gender, geographic location, race, and ethnicity. Theorists have identified a racial-genetic model, a health behavior model, a socioeconomic status model, a psychosocial stress model, and a structural-constructivist model (Dressler et al. 2005). Studies have provided some insights on these different explanatory models, yet minimal understanding of the reason for disparities between and within Latino groups has been achieved. Most health research on Latinos in the last four decades has centered on what is referred to as the "Hispanic epidemiologic paradox" and acculturation.

The observation in the 1960s and 1970s that Mexican-origin persons have, on average, better health and mortality profiles than non-Hispanic Whites (NHWs) despite lower SES has been referred to as the "Hispanic epidemiologic paradox." The paradox refers to the inconsistency between low SEP, limited access to health care services, low use of preventive and primary care services yet more favorable health outcomes such as normal range birthweight infants (Hayes-Bautista 2002; Patel et al. 2004; Markides and Eschbach 2005; Franzini et al. 2001; Hunt et al. 2003; Palloni and Arias 2004). Although this paradox uses the aggregate term *Hispanic/Latino,* most of the research that yielded this conclusion is based on young, reproductive-age Mexican-origin immigrant women. Although Mexican-origin and by association all Latinos have been viewed as "healthy," most health indicators (particularly health care access and quality) are worsening for Latinos and Mexicans (AHQR 2007).

Acculturation studies have been steadily increasing over the past forty years. Latinos are the most studied group under the rubric of culture, acculturation, and immigrant status, especially Mexican-origin groups (see chapter 3). The study of Latino health care disparities using acculturation indicators has yielded inconclusive and conflicting portraits of Latino health. The major methodological problems are the lack of scientific consensus on how to measure acculturation, and its use as a proxy for SEP (Zambrana and Carter-Pokras 2010; Acevedo-Garcia and Bates 2008; Viruell-Fuentes 2007; Hunt et al. 2004; Jasso et al. 2004). In general, better health is "more closely associated with social advantage than with social disadvantage" (Galobardes et al. 2006, 95).

Socioeconomic status (SES) is well recognized as a principal social determinant of health status; low SES is associated with lack of access to health care and increased risk for many conditions including mental illness, infectious diseases, and early death. As noted in the Office of Minority Health report in discussing the role of SES and health: "The literature . . . is replete with examples of the associations between socioeconomic status (SES) and morbidity/mortality and the significant implications of SES for health" (2008, 11). Education is commonly thought to capture "knowledge-related assets of individuals" and, in part, reflects circumstances of early life and country of educational experience. For example, the more favorable health status observed for Cuban and South American groups as an aggregate is associated with higher levels of education that is generally linked with employment and health insurance coverage. One study among Central and South American immigrants in Maryland found that higher levels of education were associated with higher perceived health status (good to excellent) (Logie 2008). Building on insights from disparity and social determinants research, new paradigms are being used to uncover the multilayered causes of Latino health disparities.

The primary theoretical assumptions that guide an understanding of health disparities emerge from an intersectional analysis that helps to explain the persistence of patterns of inequality.[3] This approach challenges researchers to pay attention to structural mechanisms such as social and material conditions. The three primary assumptions include the following:

1. Social determinants of health associated with poverty are more powerful predictors of health care disparities than individual attributes. Poverty is the threshold below which families or individuals are considered to be lacking the resources to meet the basic needs for healthy living—having insufficient income to provide the food, shelter, and clothing needed to preserve health—and is primarily the result of the unequal distribution of society's goods and resources (DeNavas-Walt et al. 2007).
2. Race, ethnicity, and geography matter, especially as they intersect with SEP, and together they determine *access* to social and economic resources.
3. Residential segregation, hypersegregation, and housing environment are key indicators of pathways that contribute to health disparities among low-income and racial/ethnic groups (Ellen and Turner 1997; Acevedo-Garcia 2001; Subramanian et al. 2005; Acosta et al. 2008). For example, Dolores Acevedo-Garcia (2001) examined residential segregation and its role in tuberculosis rates among four racial/ethnic groups. Looking beyond individual-level factors, the authors examined zip code–level risk factors and rates of tuberculosis. The data showed very high tuberculosis rates for African Americans and Latinos who resided in poor-quality environments in comparison to NHWs and Asians who resided in higher-quality living environments. Poverty and hypersegregation in resource poor neighborhoods all contribute to the accumulation of health disadvantage over the life course.

Beginning before birth and continuing into old age, lack of access or access to inadequate health care and adverse material conditions have a deep impact on each person and his or her family.

## Maternal and Child Health

The last forty years have witnessed a near scientific obsession with the field of Latino reproductive health. Although the study of Latina adult health and disease has been growing, a disproportionate number of studies has been conducted

3. For a complete examination of intersectional analysis and the relationships among health, economic conditions, race, ethnicity, culture, and gender, see Schulz and Mullings 2006.

on pregnancy and pregnancy outcome among reproductive-age women fifteen to forty-four years of age. These studies have investigated fertility patterns, adolescent pregnancy, use of prenatal care, determinants of low birth weight (LBW is defined as less than 2,500 grams or 5.5 pounds), and health behaviors during pregnancy. Studies have explored subgroup differences in foreign-born versus U.S.–born women in birth outcome by low birth weight, and infant mortality). Overall trends show similar patterns of findings since 1970, which include: Mexican-origin and Puerto Rican women tend to have children at an earlier age (less than twenty years of age) than NHW and other Latino subgroups. Mexican-origin women have similar birth outcome rates to NHW women despite the fact that they are less likely to initiate early prenatal care and more likely to have low incomes. Foreign-born Mexican women have more favorable birth outcomes than U.S.–born Mexican women yet are less likely to have health insurance, are more likely to speak Spanish, and are less likely to initiate early prenatal care. Cuban women, who have birth outcomes similar to NHW women, are more likely to initiate early prenatal care, to have health insurance, and to speak Spanish.

During the prenatal period and the breastfeeding period, a mother's health has a direct impact on her child's physical and emotional health. One indicator that illustrates this influence is *birth weight,* which represents one of the most important measures of a nation's health. Low birth weight (LBW) has been strongly linked with living in highly segregated and unsafe communities, stressful life events, economic stress (low SEP) and limited social supports (Mullings and Wali 2001). Non-Hispanic Black (NHB) women have consistently shown the most adverse outcomes compared to all other racial/ethnic women. Among Latino women distinct differences on major maternal and infant indicators exist by group and across racial/ethnic groups. Table 7.1 shows recent maternal and child health indicators by race and Latino subgroup. Mexican American women are the least likely to have LBW and VLBW infants, to initiate early prenatal care (among Latino subgroups), and to smoke. Mexican American mothers are 2.5 times as likely as NHW mothers to begin prenatal care in the third trimester or to receive no prenatal care (CDC 2007b). Mexican American and Puerto Rican women are the most likely to have a child under twenty years of age compared to other Latina subgroups and NHWs. Young Latinas with the exception of Cuban women are almost twice as likely as NHWs to have a child, and to be unmarried. The infant mortality rate ranges from 4.6 per 1,000 live births for Cubans to 7.8 per 1,000 live births for Puerto Ricans compared to 13.6 per 1,000 live births for NHBs. Puerto Rican women have consistently had the highest incidence of LBW (less than 2,500 grams) among all Latina subgroups, and are most likely to have very low birth weight (VLBW; defined as less than 1,500 grams) infants, to have children when they are younger than twenty years of age, to be unmarried, and to smoke (Ventura et al. 2001; CDC 2007b).

**Table 7.1.** Maternal and Child Health Indicators by Latino Subgroup and Race

| Health indicator | All Hispanics | Mexican American | Puerto Rican | Cuban | Central/ South American | White | Black |
|---|---|---|---|---|---|---|---|
| Infant characteristics | | | | | | | |
| Low birth weight (less than 2,500 grams) | 6.7 | 6.3 | 10.0 | 7.0 | 6.7 | 7.1 | 13.6 |
| Very low birth weight (less than 1,500 grams) | 1.2 | 1.1 | 2.0 | 1.4 | 1.2 | 1.2 | 3.2 |
| Preterm birth (less than 37 weeks' gestation) | 11.9 | 11.7 | 13.8 | 11.8 | 11.4 | 11.3 | 17.8 |
| Infant mortality rate | 5.6 | 5.5 | 7.8 | 4.6 | 4.7 | 5.7 | 13.6 |
| Maternal characteristics | | | | | | | |
| Prenatal care in first trimester | 77.4 | 76.5 | 81.1 | 92.0 | 79.0 | 88.8 | 75.9 |
| Births to mothers less than 20 years | 14.3 | 15.3 | 17.9 | 7.9 | 8.3 | 7.5 | 17.4 |
| Births to unmarried mothers | 45.0 | 43.7 | 59.8 | 31.4 | 46.0 | 23.6 | 68.5 |
| Mothers who smoked during pregnancy | 2.7 | 2.0 | 7.9 | 2.4 | 1.1 | 14.3 | 8.3 |

*Source:* Centers for Disease Control and Prevention 2007b, table 2.

Acevedo-Garcia et al. (2007) analyzed data on maternal nativity (foreign born versus U.S. born) and education level to assess whether these factors confer a protective effect in LBW across U.S. Latino subgroups (Mexicans, Puerto Ricans, Cubans, and Central/South Americans). Foreign-born Latino women are less likely to have LBW infants than U.S.–born Latino women, but a weaker relationship exists between education level and LBW for foreign-born women. In contrast, among U.S.–born Latinos by subgroup, LBW rates generally decease as education level increases (Acevedo-Garcia et al. 2007). Maternal education matters as women with higher education levels are more likely to have health insurance coverage, have the necessary skills, health literacy, healthy eating, and economic resources to engage in self-care practices that promote maternal and child health during pregnancy and decrease the risk of LBW infants. Parents, especially mothers who are the main caretakers of children, can most effectively care for their children when they have adequate economic resources and access to quality health care—both of which are associated with emotional, psychological, and physical well-being.

The well-being of children is directly influenced by the economic well-being of their families (SEP) and family structure (single-parent vs. dual-parent households). These factors are highly associated with the mother's physical and mental health status during pregnancy (Ventura and Taffel 1985; Wasserman et al. 2007; Koniak-Griffin et al. 2002; Zuñiga de Nuncio et al. 2003; Bender et al. 2001). Low-income women are more likely to report fair or poor health and to report the presence of chronic conditions and physical limitations. For example, 40 percent of women with annual household incomes of less than $10,000 reported fair or poor health compared to 15 percent of women whose incomes were more than $50,000 (Misra 2001). Fair or poor health was reported by 29 percent of Latinas, 20 percent of NHB women, and 13 percent of NHW women (Henry J. Kaiser Family Foundation 2001). Mothers below the poverty level who head single-parent families and are coping with illness are burdened by physical and psychological distress that may hinder adequate parenting and access to quality health care and support resources such as child care.

In addition, prior undiagnosed health conditions and the cumulative effects of poverty during each developmental period of a woman's life are central factors in maternal and child well-being. Aida Giachello (2001) notes the gaps in Latina maternal and child health:

> There is a need to study biological, behavioral, environmental and social processes, including community norms, that determine the physical, emotional and cognitive growth of Latinas from the moment of inception and through transitions of infancy, childhood and adolescence, which set the foundation for conditions, diseases, and behaviors that impact human reproduction and ultimately lead to disparities (152).

The maternal and child health field is replete with redundant studies that all seem to explore the "paradox" without contextualizing the lives of Latino women. Much reproductive health research has omitted representational and structural factors such as racial, ethnic, and gender biases of providers on outcomes. In a synthesis of what we know about preconception, prenatal, and postnatal health, Carol Korenbrot and Nancy Moss (2000) stated that our limited understanding of the field of maternal and child health reflected the "failure to consider women's lives and their health before they become pregnant, and after they give birth, unnecessarily limits our understanding of maternal health in pregnancy and childbirth, and the impact on pregnancy outcomes" (7). After several decades of impressive public health efforts to improve the health of infants, health indicators suggest that only modest progress has been made in improving infant health, particularly for poor and racial/ethnic groups. In fact, according to the United Nations infant mortality ranking of all countries, the United States is ranked 33 (6.3 deaths per 1,000 births). The ability of a nation to give the next generation a fair and healthy start is premised on a nation's political willingness to change the material conditions under which children live and thrive—which involves access to quality health care services for mothers and children.

### Children's Health Status

The health status of Latino children is strongly linked with poverty and parental employment (Zambrana and Logie 2000). In 2006, 28.9 percent of Hispanic children lived in poverty, almost three times the proportion of NHW children (11.3 percent) but similar to poverty levels experienced by NHB children (36.1 percent) (Pew Hispanic Center 2008b). Increases in Hispanic poverty from 1970 through the 1990s are partially explained by the lower educational and economic attainment of Latino families despite having the highest level of workforce participation of any group in the United States (DeNavas-Walt et al. 2007). However many Latinos are employed in unskilled and semi-skilled occupations and in informal labor market sectors such as landscaping, restaurants, and domestic work, jobs which generally do not have employment-based health insurance coverage (Angel and Angel 2009). In 2006, 22.1 percent of Hispanic children did not have any health insurance, compared with 7.3 percent of NHW children, 14.1 percent of NHB children, and 11.4 percent of Asian children (DeNavas-Walt et al. 2007).

Overall, Latino children are the least likely to (1) have a usual or regular source of health care by income status (poor, near poor, and non-poor); (2) have had a health care visit during the previous year; and (3) to be immunized. In addition, Latino children may be more likely to use emergency rooms as a source of primary care compared to other racial/ethnic children (Flores et al. 2002; Zambrana et al. 1994; Zambrana and Carter-Pokras 2004a). Latino children report lower ratings of self-perceived health status, with about 60 percent reporting excellent health or very good health compared to 90 percent of NHW children; have higher prevalence rates of tuberculosis and type 2 diabetes (Mexican American children), lower rates of physical activity, and higher rates of sedentary activity that are associated with obesity (Flores and Vega 1998; Flores et al. 2002). In 1976 to 1980, only 6 percent of all children ages six through seventeen were overweight. By 1988 to 1994, this percentage had risen to 11 percent, and it continued to rise to 15 percent in 1999 to 2000. In 2005 to 2006, 17 percent of children ages six through seventeen years old were overweight (Federal Interagency Forum on Child and Family Statistics [FIFCFS] 2009).

Obesity and its links to early onset of diabetes and long-term health consequences represents a serious health concern. Although obesity is framed as an individual health behavior, environmental, geographic residence, SES, and neighborhood processes (all social determinants), play a major role in Latino childhood and adolescent obesity. Access to grocery stores with healthy fresh foods, recreational areas around home and school, and neighborhood safety and physical activity programs in schools all play a central role in the healthy physical and mental development of children and youth.

### Adolescent Health and Mental Health Indicators

Health data on adolescents reveal an adverse health profile. Nationally, Latino adolescents are twice as likely as NHB adolescents and three times more likely than NHW adolescents to be uninsured. For example the 1999–2002 National Health Interview Survey (NHIS) reports striking differences in health insurance coverage by Latino subgroup (National Center for Health Statistics, [NCHS] 2002). For example Central/South American (30 percent), Mexican (38 percent), and Puerto Rican (28 percent) adolescents were more likely than NHW youth (20 percent) to be uninsured (Callahan et al. 2006). Lack of access to health care is associated with less use of preventive and screening services, less likelihood of early detection and treatment of medical conditions such as STIs and diabetes, and less likelihood to obtain information on health risk behaviors.

Table 7.2 presents health risk behaviors for adolescents by gender and race/ethnicity. Latinos are more likely to be overweight and less likely to engage in physical activity than NHW males and females. Among twelve- to nineteen-year-old Latinos, Mexican American males had higher rates of overweight compared to NHW and NHB males. Among females, NHB adolescents had the highest percentage of being told they were overweight compared to NHW and Mexican American females (Ogden and Tabak 2005). Generally, an inverse relationship between income and obesity is observed; that is, as personal incomes rise above the poverty level, obesity levels decrease. Although one, recent data found no clear association between SEP and obesity among Latino children (Wang and Zang 2006), national data report differences in overweight and obesity by race and ethnicity. In assessing the role of poverty in being overweight, several factors may account for the disparities in weight such as less extracurricular activity and television watching. Latino youth compared to NHW and NHB youth are less likely to be engaged in outside school activities such as the arts, academic activities, scouts, and team sports and less likely to live in residential areas where public recreational spaces are available. Children whose families live below the poverty level are less likely to participate in after-school activities than children whose families live at or above the poverty level (FIFCFS 2007). Although NHB youth have the highest rates of television watching, greater than three hours per day, 45.8 percent of Latino males and females watch television more than three hours per day. This activity may be the result of living in unsafe neighborhoods, restrictions by parents to remain home due to safety concerns, lack of recreational spaces, and lack of economic means or access to sports and other extracurricular activities in their communities (Zhu and Lee 2008; Burdette and Whittaker 2005; Weir et al. 2006; Lumeng et al. 2006; Lindsay et al. 2009; Gordon-Larsen et al. 2006; Roemmich et al. 2006; Powell et al. 2006). These behaviors represent a serious health risk that may be reflected in self-perceived health status. For example, Latino females (ninth- through twelfth-graders) are more likely to report fair or poor health (12.9 percent) than Latino males, NHW females, and NHB females. Although long-term health problems are more prevalent among NHW females (13.5 percent) compared to Latino males and females (8.5 percent and 8.7 percent) respectively (Carter-Pokras and Kanamori 2010), undiagnosed and untreated conditions may be present among Latino youth who are least likely to have access to providers. Obesity and overweight represent a risk or precursor for adult health conditions such as diabetes and cardiovascular disease.

For all adolescents (ninth through twelfth grade), illicit drug and alcohol use and early unprotected sex impact well-being (Flores and Sheehan 2001). Although risky behaviors are more likely in all adolescents compared to other age groups, Latino males compared to other racial/ethnic groups seem to engage in more health risk behaviors. Table 7.2 shows that NHB and Latino males are less likely than NHWs to wear a seatbelt and less likely to wear a seatbelt than females, across race/ethnicity which may account for higher male mortality due to accidents. Latino adolescents are more likely than NHB and NHW youth to have driven when drinking alcohol or driven with someone who had been drinking (Baker et al. 1998; Kann et al. 2000). Latino and NHW males are also more likely to be current smokers and alcohol users compared to NHB males. Among adolescent females, data show overall decreases in smoking rates for NHW females, increases in rates for NHB females, and no change in rates for Latino females (19.2 percent) over the last decade (CDC 2006).

**Table 7.2.** Selected Adolescent Health Behaviors by Gender, Race, and Ethnicity

| Health behavior | Hispanic | | Non-Hispanic White | | Non-Hispanic Black | |
|---|---|---|---|---|---|---|
| | Male | Female | Male | Female | Male | Female |
| Overweight,[a] 12–19 years | 20.0 | 17.1 | 17.9 | 14.6 | 17.7 | 23.8 |
| Watched TV ≥ 3 hrs/day | 45.8 | 45.8 | 30.2 | 28.1 | 63.5 | 64.5 |
| Rarely or never wears seatbelt | 12.5 | 8.7 | 11.5 | 7.2 | 17.7 | 9.4 |
| Drove when drinking alcohol | 14.6 | 6.4 | 12.4 | 10.1 | 6.5 | 3.5 |
| Current cigarette use | 24.8 | 19.2 | 24.9 | 27.0 | 14.0 | 11.9 |
| Current alcohol use | 48.9 | 44.8 | 47.0 | 45.9 | 29.6 | 32.5 |
| Currently sexually active | 36.3 | 33.7 | 30.6 | 33.5 | 51.3 | 43.8 |
| Condom use | 65.3 | 49.8 | 70.1 | 55.6 | 75.5 | 62.1 |
| Abstinence among age 15–17 years | 57.0 | 75.0 | 75.0 | 70.0 | 47.0 | 59.0 |

*Sources:* National Center for Health Statistics 2004; Mosher et al. 2005; Ogden and Tabak 2005.
[a] See the 2000 Centers for Disease Control and Prevention Growth Chart for definitions of *overweight* versus *obesity,* http://www.cdc.gov/growthcharts.

Safe sex practices are necessary to both prevent pregnancy and protect against sexually transmitted infections (STIs). About one-third of Latino and 30 percent of NHW youth are sexually active in ninth through twelfth grades—compared to about half (51.3 percent) of NHB males, and 43.8 percent of NHB females. Non-Hispanic Black males are the most likely to use condoms followed by NHW and Latino males. Over 50 percent of Latino and about fifity-five percent of NHW females use condoms, with NHB females being the most likely to use condoms. A study of Mexican American college students found that the expectancy of enhanced sexual performance and experience were associated with involvement in sexual risk behaviors due to drinking (Zamboanga 2005). Abstinence rates among fifteen- to seventeen-year-olds show Latino males were much less likely to be abstinent than Latino females. NHB males had the lowest rates of abstinence at 47 percent and NHWs had the highest rates of abstinence at 75 percent (Mosher et al. 2005). Early age engagement in unprotected sexual activity all too often contributes to early childbearing. Additional responsibilities of parenting at a young age in distressed economic circumstances combined with other health behavioral risks capture a profile of Latino youth under psychosocial distress.

Multiple factors affect the mental health status of Latino youth. Interfamily tensions, racism based on language accent, intergenerational differences, fear in their neighborhoods and schools, community violence, and unwelcoming environments in the schools contribute to a sense of not belonging (see chapters 5 and 6). Interfamily tensions have been attributed to several factors: Latino youths' ability to acquire English language proficiency at a much faster rate than their parents and to their exposure to different values and behaviors of peers and those of American society through English media. These differences

**Table 7.3.** Mental Health Indicators for Children and Adolescents (< 18 Years of Age) by Gender, Race, and Ethnicity

| Mental health indicator | Latino | | White | | Black | |
|---|---|---|---|---|---|---|
| | Male | Female | Male | Female | Male | Female |
| Has severe emotional difficulty or problem with concentration | 4.7 | 2.6 | 6.6 | 3.8 | 8.3 | 2.7 |
| Felt sad or hopeless (9th–12th grade) | 26.0 | 46.7 | 18.4 | 33.4 | 19.5 | 36.9 |
| Made a suicide plan (9th–12th grade) | 10.7 | 18.5 | 9.7 | 15.4 | 5.5 | 13.5 |
| Attempted suicide (9th–12th grade) | 7.8 | 14.9 | 5.2 | 9.3 | 5.2 | 9.8 |

*Source:* National Center for Health Statistics 2004.

in family members' "level of assimilation can become a significant source of intergenerational stress that undermines family relationships" (National Research Council 2002, 19) and can be exacerbated by worries about their parents' health and economic situation (Zambrana and Silva Palacios 1989).

Among children and adolescents, the most frequently diagnosed mood disorders are major depressive disorder and bipolar disorder. Because mood disorders such as depression substantially increase the risk of suicide, suicidal behavior is a matter of serious concern for clinicians who deal with the mental health problems of children and adolescents (U.S. Department of Health and Human Services [USDHHS] 2001a). As shown in table 7.3, although Latino males (ninth through twelfth graders) are less likely than NHW and NHB to experience severe emotional difficulty or problems with concentration, they are much more likely than NHW and NHB males to report feeling sad or hopeless and also more likely than other males to make a suicide plan and attempt suicide. Close to half of Latino females (46.7 percent) reported feeling sad or hopeless and had the highest rates of suicide attempts compared to Latino males and NHW and NHB females. High levels of economic, environmental, and interpersonal stress are most likely linked to the high level of psychosocial distress reported among Latino adolescents (National Alliance for Hispanic Health 1999; National Research Council 2002; Schulz et al. 2006). High rates of sadness and suicide ideation and attempts among Latino youth offer us insights into the hopelessness and alienation being experienced by these youth especially Latina adolescents. Their lived experiences as described in chapters 5 and 6 contextualize their everyday experiences that threaten their sense of self and dampen their hopes and dreams. Perceptions of powerlessness and not belonging are constantly reinforced through schools and media.

For adolescents and their families, limited access to physical and mental health care services combined with poverty and low-resourced community environments can contribute to a low sense of control in their environment; limit cognitive and intellectual stimulation; and leave serious health and mental health conditions undiagnosed. Undiagnosed and untreated conditions contribute to depression, anxiety, substance use, and poor school performance. Untreated youth and parental physical and mental health conditions contribute to increased mental distress during adolescence. For Latinos the most indubitable marker of the effects of this stress is the increases in attempted and completed suicide rates. Of utmost significance, the chronic stress of everyday life experiences that adolescents confront, including racism and barriers to health care, influences their health status as an adult.

### Adult Health Behavior Indicators

The physical and mental health status of Latino adult women and men are associated with multiple factors including SES, access to health care insurance, health behaviors, and mental health status such as depression. *Health behaviors* or self-care practices are important contributors to mortality and morbidity. These behaviors include use of tobacco, alcohol, and drugs; sleep patterns; nutrition and diet; physical exercise and leisure time; use of preventive screening practices such as mammography and oral health care. Although public health and medical science investigators generally view health behaviors as an individual responsibility, material conditions, lack of health insurance, and other social determinants often serve as barriers to appropriate self-care practices.

Gender differences in health beliefs and health risk behaviors are consistent across several racial and ethnic groups (Ashton et al. 2003; van Ryn 2002). Two general trends in health behaviors by gender have been observed: (1) women are less likely than men to engage in risky health behaviors, and (2) women are more likely than men to visit physicians and to obtain periodic physicals, screenings, and self-examinations (Courtenay et al. 2002; Courtenay 2000a, b; Courtenay and Keeling 2000; Courtenay 2001). Trends in health behaviors are important to understand health disparities. Table 7.4 displays selected health care behavior indicators for women by race and ethnicity. Smoking rates are highest for NHWs and lowest for Asians. Although data tend to vary by survey, between 1999 and 2001, the percentage of women ages eighteen and older who reported currently smoking cigarettes (defined as having smoked at least one hundred cigarettes in her lifetime and currently smoking) ranged from a low of 6.7 percent (Asian women) to a high of 22.2 percent for NHW women (Schoenborn et al. 2004).

Smoking prevalence varies by Latino subgroup (data not shown), with Puerto Rican women most likely to smoke and Mexican American women least likely to smoke. Between 1999 and 2001, 27.3 percent of Puerto Rican women, 17.5 percent of Cuban women, 16.9 percent of Central/South American women, and 15.6 percent of Mexican-origin women reported that they smoked during the previous month (CDC 2004b). Eliseo Perez-Stable

Table 7.4. Selected Health Care Behavior Indicators for Women by Race and Ethnicity

| Indicator | Latina | White | Black | Asian |
|---|---|---|---|---|
| Never smoked | 76.2 | 57.6 | 67.7 | 86.5 |
| Current smoker | 12.0 | 22.2 | 19.5 | 6.7 |
| Abstain from alcohol | 48.8 | 25.6 | 43.7 | 61.8 |
| Heavy alcohol consumption | 7.0 | 12.9 | 5.5 | 4.2 |
| Marijuana use in past year | 7.4 | 8.9 | 8.4 | — |
| Cocaine use in past year | 1.4 | 1.7 | 1.6 | — |
| Drug-induced deaths | 5.6 | 78.8 | 13.9 | 0.8 |
| Had a Pap test within past year | 54.0 | 53.0 | 60.0 | 45.0 |
| Had a mammogram in past 2 years | 61.4 | 72.1 | 67.9 | 53.3 |
| Blood pressure checked in past 2 years | 78.0 | 92.0 | 92.0 | — |
| Cholesterol screened in past 2 years | 51.0 | 60.0 | 58.0 | — |

*Source:* Office of Research on Women's Health 2006.

et al. (2001) found that as Hispanic women and immigrant Latinas become more integrated in the United States, their prevalence of smoking increased compared to less acculturated (foreign-born) Hispanic women, and a similar pattern is observed among adolescents; that is, smoking rates increase with acculturation (measured by numbers of years in the U.S. and/or ELP) (Epstein et al. 1998; Otero-Sabogol et al. 1995; Sanchez-Johnson et al. 2005).

Lung cancer deaths are three times higher for Hispanic men (23.1 per 100,000) than for Hispanic women (7.7 per 100,000). The rate of lung cancer deaths per 100,000 was higher among Cuban-American men (33.7) than among Puerto-Rican (28.3) and Mexican-American (21.9) men (American Cancer Society 2007). Declines in the prevalence of smoking have been greater among Hispanic men with at least a high school education than among those with less education. Given the lower rates of insurance and access to health care services, Latino smokers may be less likely to be advised by health care providers or have access to smoking cessation treatments (Houston et al. 2005).

Other important health behaviors include use of alcohol and illegal drugs, physical exercise, consistent sleep routines, and nutritional habits (USDHHS 2001b). Overall, U.S. Latinos are reported to have high levels of alcohol consumption per capita (Caetano and Galvan 2001). Although the rate of binge drinking among U.S. Hispanics has increased from 18 percent in 1991 to 24 percent in 2003 (Substance Abuse and Mental Health Services Administration [SAMHSA] 2004), heterogeneity in drinking patterns vary by country of origin and gender (Nielsen 2000). The percent of women abstaining from alcohol consumption (defined as having consumed less than twelve drinks in a lifetime) are consistent with those reporting lifetime alcohol use. Asian women are the most likely to report being lifetime abstainers, compared to almost one-half of Hispanic women, 43.7 percent of NHB women, and 25.6 percent of NHW women (Schoenborn et al. 2004). Blacks whose ancestry is Caribbean consumed less alcohol compared with U.S. Blacks. Cox et al. (2005) found that similar to national data on all Hispanic adults, 60 percent of Central/South American men and women report no alcohol use in the past thirty days.

Use of drugs is low among all racial/ethnic women. However NHW women are slightly more likely to use marijuana or cocaine and are significantly more likely to die from a drug-induced death than other racial/ethnic women (see table 7.4). Between 1999 and 2001, 5 percent of Hispanic females ages twelve and older reported having used an illicit drug in the past month. Among subgroups, 6.6 percent of Puerto Rican females, 4.8 percent of Mexican females, 2.9 percent of Central/South American females, and 2.2 percent of Cuban females reported illicit drug use. Hispanic females younger than age twenty-five were more likely than those ages twenty-six and older to have used illicit drugs (SAMHSA 2002).

Screening practices are important to early detection, diagnosis, and treatment of conditions in early stages of disease including cervical and breast cancer (Lim 2010). In 2000, among Latino women ages forty and older, only 40 percent had mammograms in the last year—37 percent of Mexican Americans, 42 percent of Central or South Americans, 46 percent of Puerto Ricans, 47 percent of Cuban Americans, and 52 percent of Dominicans (Gorin and Heck 2005). In table 7.4, 2005 data show that Latinas are equally as likely to have pap smear as NHWs but less likely to have a mammogram than NHWs or NHBs. Asian women are the least likely to have a pap smear or a mammogram. Although Latinas are reported to have lower rates of cancer overall, the incidence rate of cervical cancer is almost one and a half times higher than the rate for NHW women (Erwin et al. 2010; Office of Research on Women's Health 2006; Wingo et al. 1998). Fewer Latinas are diagnosed with breast cancer than NHW women, but they are more likely to be diagnosed at a more advanced stage and are more likely to die from breast cancer. Although national data suggest higher rates of screenings since 1990, intergroup variations show differences by subgroup associated with health care insurance coverage and age (Freedman et al. 2010; Yin et al. 2010; Zambrana et al. 1999). Several studies have also found differences by geographic area. For example in Los Angeles, California, in 2003, breast cancer was the leading cause of cancer death among Latinas (Cordoba 2007). More Central/South Americans, Mexican Americans, and Puerto Ricans had tumors larger than one centimeter than did NHW women, which Heeden and White (2001) explained by the lower rates of mammography screening in the Latino population. In another study, Central American and Cuban women compared to Mexican American and Puerto Rican women were reported to have more positive attitudes toward cancer, but these attitudes were not predictive of mammography and Pap smear screening behaviors (Ramirez et al. 2000a, b). Screening practices are an important health behavior that require time and health insurance coverage.

Physical activity and leisure time use are important in maintaining good physical and mental health. Yet, low-income families are far less likely to have the economic resources to purchase healthy yet expensive nutritional foods and/or to have access to recreational spaces in their neighborhoods to exercise (Morland et al. 2002; Powell et al. 2007). Consistently, Hispanic men and women report the lowest levels of physical activity in national surveys. The National Health and Nutrition Examination Survey (NHANES) 1999–2000 and 2001–2002 data demonstrate continued increases in the prevalence of obesity and overweight among all age groups, especially Hispanics. Another indicator of physical activity is the use of leisure time, which is associated with SEP. In a study of leisure time use, Central Americans were more likely than Anglo or Mexicans to be in organized groups and more acculturated Latinos tended to visit more with friends and less with extended family (Juniu 2000). Physical activity and use of leisure time may be associated with decreases in stress levels and lower rates of sleeping disorders.

Consistent sleeping patterns and seven to eight hours of sleep a night has been found to restore the body's processes. Sleep deprivation, one of the consequences of sleep disorders, has been associated with depressive disorders, low productivity, and higher risk of occupational and motor vehicle injuries. A study in Los Angeles, an area including a large Latino population, found an overall prevalence of current or previous sleep disorders of 52.1 percent, including a 42.5 percent prevalence of insomnia, 11.2 percent nightmares, 7.1 percent excessive sleep, 5.3 percent sleep talking, and 2.5 percent sleepwalking. The importance of sleep in the relationship between SES and well-being has been examined in a number of large-scale surveys (Gellis et al. 2005; Young et al. 2002; Anderson and Armstead 1995; Moore et al. 2002; Riedel and Lichstein 2000). Studies show that noise levels are higher in crowded housing or in high-rise apartments and in low-income communities where traffic and emergency and police vehicle noise is more prevalent, which contributes to poor sleep quality. Not unexpectedly, decreased sleep quality and sleep-related well-being are associated with decreases in mental and physical health.

Lastly oral health has been identified as important in maintaining good health. Hispanics in general have less favorable oral health indicators than NHWs or NHBs.[4] Hispanics as a group are less likely to have visited the dentist in the previous year than other groups. Mexican American adults have the lowest report of dental visits and the lowest rates of dental coverage. Among Latino women in 2000 to 2003, 54 percent of all Latino women reported having visited a dentist in the previous year. Among subgroups, Mexican women (49.3 percent) were least likely to have visited a dentist, whereas Cuban women (63 percent) and

---

4. For further information see Ramos-Gomez et al. 2005.

other Latino women (65.2 percent) were most likely. Central or South American women and Puerto Rican women were equally likely to have seen a dentist (58.8 and 58.9 percent, respectively). During the same period, 70.2 percent of NHW women reported having visited a dentist in the preceding year (Scott and Simile 2005). Mexican Americans are more likely than Cuban and Puerto Ricans to have a higher number of decayed teeth, but less likely to have filled teeth and total tooth loss. Data from the third National Health and Nutrition Examination Survey (NHANES III) showed that Mexican Americans were more likely to have decayed teeth but have less tooth loss than NHWs and NHBs. Low tooth loss concurrent with higher untreated decay is associated with Mexican Americans' limited access to dental care and less likelihood to wear dentures.

Overall, low-income Latinos are more likely to report poor to fair health status; are less likely to be insured (especially Mexican native born and immigrants); less likely to have screening examinations including oral health care; and less likely to engage in leisure time physical activity than their NHW and NHB counterparts. Further, for low-income Latinos, they are more likely to have low health literacy and health knowledge, live in low-resourced communities, and experience chronic stress such as money worries and everyday racism (that often accompanies poverty), placing them at higher risk of chronic physical and mental health conditions (Aguirre-Molina et al. 2003: Aguirre-Molina and Pond 2002; Stewart and Napoles-Springer 2003; Carrillo et al. 2001; National Center for Health Statistics [NCHS] 2004). These factors contribute to disparities in mortality by gender, SES, and subgroup.

## Physical Health Status

The most important health conditions in the Latino community often are identified through an examination of mortality and morbidity data. In this section, I present leading causes of death and major chronic conditions by gender and race/ethnicity. Table 7.5 presents leading causes of death by gender,

**Table 7.5.** Comparative Ranking of Leading Causes of Death by Gender, Race, and Ethnicity

| Cause of death | Latino | | White | | Black | |
|---|---|---|---|---|---|---|
| | Male | Female | Male | Female | Male | Female |
| Heart disease | 1 | 1 | 1 | 1 | 1 | 1 |
| Cancer | 2 | 2 | 2 | 2 | 2 | 2 |
| Accident | 3 | 5 | 3 | 6 | 3 | 6 |
| Stroke | 4 | 3 | 5 | 3 | 4 | 3 |
| Diabetes | 5 | 4 | 6 | 8 | 6 | 4 |

*Source:* Adapted from National Center for Health Statistics 2006, 187–89.

race, and ethnicity. Heart disease and cancer are leading causes of death for all groups. The third leading cause of death for men is accidents, while for women it is strokes. For Latino and NHB women, diabetes is the fourth leading cause of death. Regardless of race or Hispanic subgroup, men have higher overall mortality rates than women. Puerto Rican men are at a particular disadvantage, with higher mortality rates than NHW men between the ages of twenty-five and sixty-four years (Carter-Pokras and Kanamori 2010). In Gopal Singh and Mohammad Siahpush's (2001) analysis of the National Longitudinal Mortality Study, all-cause death mortality rates were lower for immigrants than U.S.–born persons. While the top two leading causes of death are similar across gender and racial/ethnic groups, disparities in morbidity, early diagnosis and treatment, and premature death are more likely in low-income NHB and Latino men and women than NHWs.

Latino adults (eighteen years of age or more), similar to NHB adults, are more likely to report fair or poor health than NHWs regardless of gender (see table 7.6). In 2005, about one-fifth of Latino and NHB females reported fair or poor health. Persons who report fair or poor health status also have higher rates of medically attended injury and poisoning episodes than persons who have excellent, very good, or good health (NCHS 2007). Among males, Latino men were more likely to report fair or poor health compared to NHW men but less likely than NHB men. Self-reports of previous physician diagnosis of coronary heart disease (CHD) show that the rates were higher for NHW men (8.5 percent) than for Latino and NHB men (6.6 percent and 5.7 percent, respectively) while the rates for Latino and NHW females (5.2 percent and 5.1 percent) were similar but lower than for NHB females (6.6 percent). Females were more likely than males to report asthma and arthritis with NHB females more likely to report these conditions. Hispanics were 1.5 times as likely as NHWs to die from diabetes (NCHS 2007). However, other data show

**Table 7.6.** Self-Reported Health Status and Chronic Conditions for Adults 18 Years of Age and Older by Gender, Race, and Ethnicity

| Health indicator | Latino | | White | | Black | |
|---|---|---|---|---|---|---|
| | Male | Female | Male | Female | Male | Female |
| Self-reported health status fair/poor | 15.7 | 19.9 | 10.1 | 10.9 | 18.7 | 20.4 |
| CHD | 6.6 | 5.2 | 8.5 | 5.1 | 5.7 | 6.6 |
| Diabetes | 9.6 | 10.2 | 7.3 | 6.2 | 11.2 | 11.5 |
| Stroke | 2.5 | 2.0 | 2.3 | 2.2 | 2.8 | 4.0 |
| Asthma | 3.5 | 7.3 | 5.6 | 9.4 | 5.2 | 10.7 |
| Arthritis | 14.4 | 19.1 | 19.2 | 25.4 | 15.0 | 26.0 |

*Source:* Adapted from National Center for Health Statistics 2006.

that Mexican American adults were 2 times more likely than NHW adults to have been diagnosed with diabetes by a physician.

Cardiovascular disease (CVD), hypertension, stroke, and diabetes are the leading health conditions for Latinas. Additional health conditions include arthritis, asthma, and osteoporosis (Henry J. Kaiser Family Foundation 2001). According to the American Heart Association (2009), prevalence rates for CVD were highest for NHBs (45 percent for both sexes) compared to Hispanics (26 percent for males and 32 percent for females) and NHWs (38 percent for males and 33 percent for females). Hispanic females have higher CVD rates than males and also are more likely to have diabetes, to live below the poverty level, to lack health insurance, to report depression, and to have hypertension that places them at risk for CVD. More than three-quarters (78 percent) of Latinas surveyed in 2001 had their blood pressure checked within the past two years, compared to 92 percent of both NHW and NHB women. In 2001, more than half of NHW, NHB, and Latino women reported having a cholesterol screening in the past two years—60, 58, and 51 percent, respectively (Wyn et al. 2004).

In a study of national hypertension-related mortality (HRM), data for the periods 1995–1996 and 2001–2002 show that HRM was highest among Puerto Rican and Mexican American women, and increased significantly for the latter during the two time periods (Zambrana et al. 2007). Mexican-American women (22.3 percent) are the most likely to have higher blood pressure rates compared to NHW women (19.7 percent) but lower rates than NHB women (36.4 percent) (NCHS 2004), and most likely to have lower control rates (management of hypertension) than both NHW and NHB women (Crespo et al. 1996). Puerto Rican women are more likely to experience high rates of serum cholesterol and asthma (Ledogar et al. 2000). High blood pressure and serum cholesterol are associated with overweight/obesity, stress, and lack of leisure time physical activity (Kurian and Cardarelli 2007). Yet Latino women are the least likely to have blood pressure and cholesterol screening than NHW and NHB (see table 7.4) that places them at risk for CVD conditions. Latino women have been understudied with respect to CVD.

One disease condition that has received enormous attention and funding is HIV/AIDS. Trend data summarizing the diagnoses and prevalence of HIV/AIDS by race/ethnicity from 2004–2007 shows HIV/AIDS diagnoses declining or remaining relatively stable (CDC 2009).Of the total U.S. population, 1.1 million people (0.37 percent) have been diagnosed with HIV/AIDS at the end of 2006 (CDC 2007a). Non-Hispanic Blacks have the highest rates (44.1 percent) followed by NHWs (35.3 percent) and Latinos (19.1 percent). Mean age range of those with HIV/AIDS is twenty-five to forty-nine, which constitutes 69.6 percent of people living with this condition in 2006. Among the total population of people with HIV/AIDS, 18 percent have no health care coverage while 58 percent of non-Whites have no health care insurance, and of the 52 percent who have public health insurance, 61 percent are non-White (Battacharya et al. 2003). Multiple factors contribute to the transmission and progression of HIV/AIDS in the NHB and Latino communities, including lack of health insurance, lack of access to medications and treatments that are effective in managing and treating this condition, lack of available specialists in their community health network, and physician bias. Social determinants such as community context and segregation, education level that is associated with individual knowledge of where to go and how to negotiate health care systems, poor nutrition, and everyday stressors are important yet understudied factors in understanding the transmission and progression of HIV/AIDS.

Latinos represent approximately 16 percent of the U.S. population, and the latest CDC estimates show that they account for an estimated 18 percent of people living with HIV in the U.S. (194,000 persons), and an estimated 17 percent of new infections each year (9,700 infections) (CDC 2009). In 2006, rates of AIDS cases were 47.6 per 1,000 for NHBs, 15.6 for Latinos, and 5.4 for NHWs in the fifty states and the District of Columbia (CDC 2009). The largest proportion of HIV/AIDS cases are Latino males (21 percent) compared to Latino women (18 percent). More than 25 plus years into the HIV/AIDS epidemic, more than 85,000 Latinos with AIDS have died.

Women account for more than one-quarter of all new HIV/AIDS diagnoses. Latino and NHB women are disproportionately affected by HIV infection and AIDS. In 2006, the rate of new HIV infections among Latino women was nearly four times that of NHW women (14.4 percent and 3.8 percent respectively). For NHB and Latino women the most likely mode of transmission is high-risk heterosexual contact (HRHC). Transmission through injection drug use is almost twice as likely among NHW women (30 percent) compared to NHB and Latino women (17 percent each). Puerto Rican women report the most cases of HIV infection and AIDS. Explanations for the higher rate of AIDS among Puerto Rican women, similar to NHB women, are that they tend to be of lower SES and partner/marry largely within their ethnic subgroup (sexual networks), which contributes to the spread of HIV/AIDS. For women who engage in substance use, they tend to use intravenous drugs within the context of needle-sharing networks that are racially and ethnically homogeneous (Office of Research on Women's Health 2002). Most research has been conducted on Latino male sexual behaviors and modes of HIV/AIDS transmission.

Studies conducted with Latino males in HIV/AIDS have focused on male sexual behaviors, health risk behaviors, and the use of screening exams (Lesser et al. 2001; Díaz 1998; Díaz et al. 1999; Ramirez-Valles et al. 1998). Trend data for HIV/AIDS show that between 1981 and 2004, rates for men have been decreasing while rates for women have been increasing; rates for NHW groups have been decreasing while rates for NHBs have been increasing; and rates for Latinos increased until 1995 and have remained stable. HIV mode of transmission for Latino men include men having sex with men (MSM) (49 percent), intravenous drug use (IDU) (30 percent), MSM/IDU (5 percent), and HRHC (16 percent) (CDC 2009). For NHW men the most likely mode of transmission is MSM (76 percent), as is for NHB men (43 percent). Forty-four percent of Latino men and 45 percent of NHW men fifteen to forty-four years old have been tested for HIV. Overall, 67.2 percent of Latino men at least eighteen years of age, 69.7 percent of NHW men, and 54 percent of NHB men have been tested for HIV. A study of 1,052 Latino men during 1999 to 2001 found high lifetime testing rates (76 percent). However, only 45 percent had been tested during the past year (Fernandez et al. 2002). Although some information on prevalence, mortality, and testing rates for HIV/AIDS is available, much less is known about factors that contribute to disease progression, comorbid conditions, the extent of access to specialized services, and the impact of HIV/AIDS on family processes among racial/ethnic MSM and bisexual men.

A comprehensive review of the health status of Latino men was conducted by Olivia Carter-Pokras and Mariano Kanamori (2010) and is briefly summarized here. Latino men, particularly low-income men, are less likely to have a physician visit and to be vigilant about their health self-care practices. Among Latino men, similar to Latino women, they are less likely to have insurance coverage, to have a usual source of health care, and to receive screening procedures. In 2005, 36.5 percent of Latino males less than sixty-five years of age did not have health insurance, which was higher than any racial/ethnic group. Among adults at least eighteen years of age, Latino (32.7 percent) and NHB men (32 percent) were the least likely to report having visited a physician during the past year, compared to 22 percent of NHW men, and less likely to have visited a dentist during the past year. For those men who had seen a physician, Latino men were much more likely to report never seeing a physician (4.2 percent) than NHW (0.6 percent) and NHB men (1.2 percent). Lower rates of health care use are associated with lower rates of all screening procedures. Latino men are less likely to have received testicular exam (32.6 percent) than NHW (38.7 percent) and NHB (50.3 percent) men. Only 53 percent of Latino men over the age of forty reported having received a digital rectal exam, a standard exam for prostate and colorectal screening, while close to half reported never having heard of the procedure (Talavera 2002). Married fifteen- to forty-four-year-old Latino (4.4 percent) and NHB men (5.1) are also less likely to have received a vasectomy than NHW men (16.2 percent). As discussed for Latino adolescent males, Latino men are more likely to be overweight, to drink alcohol compared to NHW and NHB males, equally likely to smoke as NHW males, and less likely to receive any clinical screening procedure.

An adverse cardiovascular profile is suggested by the fact that one out of every four Latino men has hypertension, three out of four is overweight, and three out of five do not exercise in their leisure time. All these data suggest that Latino men may be at major risk for CVD (Carter-Pokras and Kanamori 2010). The health of Latino men is clearly an understudied area that requires more attention to prevent middle age disability due to chronic conditions, premature death, and mental health conditions such as depression.

## Mental Health Status of Adults

One cannot separate good health from good mental health. Mexican American adults are more likely to report depressive symptoms, alcohol use, and suicidal ideation than Mexican immigrants (Cuellar et al. 2004). Positive mental health status of Latinos tends to deteriorate with time spent in the United States and age of arrival. Ethel Alderete and colleagues (2000) found that Mexican immigrants residing in the country for less than thirteen years had lower rates of mood and anxiety disorders than Mexican immigrants living here more than thirteen years. Psychiatric disorder prevalence rates are reported to be higher among Hispanics who had migrated to the United States before the age of thirteen or after the age of thirty-four than among those who had migrated at other ages (Alegría et al. 2007).

Based on Peter Guarnaccia and colleagues' (2005) review of three national mental health studies—the Hispanic Health and Nutrition Examination Survey (HHANES), the Los Angeles site of the National Institute of Mental Health Epidemiologic Catchment Area (ECA) program, and the Mexican American Prevalence and Services Study (MAPSS)—important statements about the mental health status of Latinos in the United States may be made. Guarnaccia and colleagues (2005) noted that in comparison to Cubans and Mexican Americans, Puerto Ricans had higher rates of both symptoms of depression and depression cases, and a greater prevalence of a major depression episode (a major mental health disorder). In their analysis of the National Latino and Asian American Study (NLAAS), Alegría and colleagues (2007) observed that Puerto Ricans had the highest overall lifetime and past-year prevalence rates of psychiatric disorders (e.g., depressive disorders, anxiety disorders, substance use disorders, and overall psychiatric disorders) in comparison to Cubans, Mexicans, and other Hispanics. Perceived sense of discrimination, low SEP, and limited economic mobility may be factors that negatively affect the mental health status of Puerto Ricans.

Most studies are consistent with previous research (excluding Central and South Americans) showing that Latino women are more likely to experience moderate to severe depression; experience depression in their lifetime; be at risk of experiencing depression; and have higher prevalence of depression

**Table 7.7.** Depression Indicators by Gender, Race, and Ethnicity for Adults 18 Years of Age and Older

| Indicator | Latino | | White | | Black | |
|---|---|---|---|---|---|---|
| | Male | Female | Male | Female | Male | Female |
| Feel sad all or most of the time | 2.6 | 6.0 | 2.2 | 3.0 | 3.8 | 5.8 |
| Feel hopeless all or most of the time | 2.1 | 4.1 | 1.3 | 2.1 | 2.0 | 2.7 |
| Feel nervous all or most of the time | 2.5 | 6.4 | 3.4 | 5.0 | 2.8 | 4.6 |

*Source:* Adapted from National Center for Health Statistics 2004.

than Latino men (Rouse 1995; Collins et al. 1999; Alderete et al. 2000; Vega and Alegría, 2001; González and González-Ramos 2005; Stone et al. 2004). Table 7.7 presents data on depression indicators by gender, race, and ethnicity. Latino women are twice as likely to report feeling sad all or most of the time and hopeless all or most of the time compared to NHW women but have similar rates to NHB women. Latino females are more than twice as likely to report feeling nervous all or most of the time compared with Latino males, and higher than NHW or NHB women. Latino women have similar self-reports of depression symptoms as Latina adolescents.

Low-income Latinos often mistake depression for nervousness or tiredness, and they think of depression as something that is temporary: *"I'm a bit down; it will pass," "It's just my nerves, that's all"* (Vega et al. 2010). Low-income Latinas (17 percent) are much less likely than NHB (36 percent) and NHW women (58 percent) to report a mental health care visit (Alvidrez 1999). Low use of mental health care services is often associated with lack of health insurance coverage, low SEP, and less knowledge of the symptoms of depression and its consequences. High rates of depression among Latino women may also be a consequence of gender role constrictions, neighborhood effects, sense of loss, or work experiences outside the home associated with gender, ethnic, and class discrimination. For example, women feel (and often have) less control in their lives, and immigrant women may experience a sense of loss in the relocation to a foreign country. Additionally, all too often low-income Latinas have multiple caretaking roles yet lack the resources to cope with their physical and emotional roles and demands. These multiple roles without adequate coping resources place them at risk for depression. The role of caretaker for sick or disabled relatives, combined with work and child-rearing responsibilities is especially relevant for women. More than half (54 percent) of women caregivers had one or more chronic health condition, compared with two-fifths (41 percent) of other women. Caregivers also reported higher rates of mental health concerns. The demands of caregiving may take a toll on caregivers' health status and well-being. One of four women (25 percent) caring for sick or disabled family members rated herself as being in poor or fair health, compared with one-sixth of other women (17 percent).Although the role of caregiver falls on women uniformly, regardless of income, race/ethnicity, or even marital status, the extent of their responsibilities varies with family economic resources (Collins, Schoen, Joseph et al. 1999; Lee et al. 2003; Shaw et al. 2003).

~

My goal in this chapter was to provide a contextualization of how social determinants, especially SES and lack of health insurance coverage, affect Latino physical and mental health by gender and life course stage. Several observations are noteworthy. First, the higher the SEP, the better a person's physical and mental health as a result of both more likelihood of having health insurance and access to timely, quality health care. Multiple health care barriers faced by Latinos in the United States have been persistent: poverty and socioeconomic stress, racism and discrimination in health care delivery and public health policies, living in low-resourced communities, high rates of depression, and compromised access to quality health care. While access to quality health care, including diagnoses and treatment, undoubtedly plays a role in excess mortality, excess morbidity is complicated by the effects of the physical and psychological stressors related to economic and neighborhood conditions for both Latino men and women. In effect the inequity in social conditions contributes to a disparate risk of becoming ill, which is then compounded by disparate access to health care—including screening, diagnosis, and treatment—once a person becomes ill.[5] Thus patterns of physical and mental health status cannot be separated from material conditions and their effects on family and individual well-being.

For low-income Latinos who are least likely to have health insurance coverage and experience unequal access and treatment, the accumulation of health disadvantage over the life course of all family members is a major lesson that can be extracted from the research. In looking at the physical and mental health profile of Latinos from birth to late adulthood, we obtain a better picture of how SES decidedly determines and shapes physical and mental health status and its impact on family well-being. Physical and mental health conditions within a family seriously impact their ability to work, social mobility, ability to optimally parent, and opportunities to engage in physical and social activities that enhance their individual health and family well-being. Findings further inform us that depression—which is associated with life circumstance and multiple role performance—is a major condition from adolescence to adulthood and a comorbid condition of major chronic illnesses (Israel et al. 2002).

A wide spectrum of evidence from multiple disciplines suggests social and economic strategies to decrease racial/ethnic disparities. If health disparities

5. See Aguirre-Molina et al. 2003; Zambrana and Dill 2006.

among U.S.–born and immigrant Latinos are a consequence of social and economic determinants, then the solutions have to address the findings. Examples of evidence-based policy solutions include instituting a living wage for all workers in the United States (i.e., not $7.25/hour but $12.00/hour); providing universal health care; focusing on prevention; coordinating local, state, and federal resources to ensure long-term success of equitable public health services in all communities; increasing the proportion of underrepresented U.S. racial/ethnic minorities in the health professions; and increasing the number and role of community health workers.

The ways in which Latinos are studied in the fields of public health, medicine, health psychology, and other health-related disciplines require extending the paradigm to decenter culture and center social determinants. Perhaps, the unremitting focus on culture rather than inequality in access to health care resources, material conditions, and neighborhood effects has derailed knowledge production on Latinos and contributed to increasing health disparities.

# 8

# Public Service Systems as Sites
# of the Reproduction of Inequality

It is undeniable that welfare policy is inextricably
intertwined with gender and race. However gender
and race are necessary, but not sufficient, explanatory
elements in an attempt to understand the evolution
of welfare policy.... [I]t is the overriding need to
distinguish between the able-bodied poor and
the disabled poor, between the "deserving" and
"undeserving poor," be they men or women of any
racial and ethnic group, that is the driving force behind
welfare policy. It is the able bodied, whatever their
ascriptive status that present the moral dilemma to
the modern capitalist state because they challenge the
legitimacy of its economic and civic order.
—Handler and Hasenfeld 1991, 7

The last two decades have witnessed extensive research and documentation
of racial profiling, unequal treatment in health, juvenile, and criminal justice, urban displacement of the poor with little or no replacement of adequate
housing, welfare reform with more stringent and inhumane restrictions, and
failing schools. Examining data on who uses and interfaces with public service
systems and how the poor are treated illuminates what Joel Handler and Yeheskel Hasenfeld (1991) have aptly labeled the "moral construction of poverty." The poverty discourse focuses on the moral justification for why people
are poor, services available to assist those in poverty, their treatment in these
programs, and the consequences of being poor.

The thinking for this chapter emerged from personal experience, observation, and interdisciplinary study that showed that public service systems serve
a similarly socially marked population with a disproportionate, visible number being Black and Latino. Herein, I present a brief historical snapshot of
the silent issues and underlying assumptions that drive the debates on public
assistance programs and data on who uses or are involved in public service

systems. I also discuss empirical studies on institutional practices of health and human services programs financed by the local, state, and federal government. These programs include public welfare including work-related supports, public housing, child welfare, schools, juvenile justice, and adult correctional systems. The intent is multifold: to provide information that is not easily accessible or meaningful without syntheses and interpretation; to reveal who is most likely to be served in each system through examining the overlap, or what I will term cross-overs, in these public service systems; and to illustrate contemporary instances of unfairness that contribute to discriminatory treatment of non-Hispanic Blacks (NHBs) and Latinos in public service systems. Moreover I seek to dispel myths about the "poor as lazy and unwilling to work" through the use of facts and to unveil how these public systems use disciplinary power—that is, regulation and state authority—to undermine the human capital of the very individuals they were created to help and in effect maintain and reinforce their marginalized social location.[1]

Historically, public service systems were designed as a safety net or a form of "public patriarchy" for those individuals, who were temporarily unemployed, disabled, or female widows. These programs have always been a moral dilemma for both the State and the recipients of public assistance. As Handler and Hasenfeld (1991) so eloquently articulate, the normative underpinnings of welfare policy had several moral constructions derived from implicit assumptions that included "work as an individual responsibility" and "many people are poor because they choose a way of life that makes them poor" (10). In other words, the moral definitions of the *deserving poor* included those who worked but for any reason were temporarily unemployed, while the definition of the *undeserving poor* included those who could not work or had limited education and skills and were unable to find work. These definitions served two important social functions: (1) "affirming the values of the dominant society (industrial discipline, two-parent family and individual responsibility and work ethic) by stigmatizing the outcasts" (16) and (2) defining what is deviant, with the poor as the enemy to the existing social order. The distinctive emphasis on individual responsibility precludes historical antecedents of slavery and colonialism, segregation laws, racism, and other structural barriers. Although

---

1. The fields of social work/social welfare and sociology have a long intellectual history in the study of public assistance programs including child welfare, juvenile justice, and criminology, a subfield of sociology. Handler and Hasenfeld (1991) provide a synthesis of the historical welfare programs from poor houses established in the United States in the English tradition to establishment of welfare policy and its continuous reformations. An incisive history around welfare policy is provided through 1988. Post 1960 an extraordinary amount of study was conducted on the Johnson-era War on Poverty programs and their effectiveness. In this chapter, I provide a glimpse into scholarship that has used an intersectional lens rather than on those scholars who uphold the implicit ideology of the moral construction of poverty.

these antecedents remain silent, they drive the underlying moral construction of poor and racial/ethnic poor as nonnormative or deviant individuals who are undeserving of fair, quality treatment.

Thus the "deserving poor" are those men, generally speaking, who had some connection to the labor force sector but had experienced some event, such as job loss or disability. For women, the deserving poor were those who had been connected to a male worker in the formal labor market sector, such as widows. These latter groups of poor represented the hegemonic understanding of deserving poor under the moral construction of poverty; that is, of individuals or families deserving of public service benefits. Up until the 1960s, the majority of poor, particularly NHB and Latino (Mexican American and Puerto Rican), had been restricted from access to both education and high-paying labor market sectors due to segregation and discriminatory policies and laws. These racial/ethnic groups represented the poorest groups in the United States and those most in need of public assistance. A major debate given impetus by the civil rights movement in the 1960s and 1970s was whether individuals who are unable to work for physical or mental health reasons or lack of skills to obtain a suitable job were entitled to public cash assistance and supplementary benefits to acquire the skills necessary to secure a job. The push was to expand the 1935 Aid to Families with Dependent Children (AFDC) to the poor including health benefits; namely, Medicaid. Although legislation was passed as part of the Johnson-era War on Poverty programs, resistance and criticism have continued to characterize the implementation of public assistance programs. Handler and Hasenfeld (1991) describe the public assistance program as "A program mired in controversy and moral ambiguity. The social security widow is treated with respect and dignity. The AFDC...woman is more often than not treated with suspicion and contempt" (1).

The debates on deserving and undeserving poor implicitly center the core issue of rights that has plagued U.S. policy since its creation as a nation. The debates dismiss structural inequality and how poverty, race, gender, and ethnicity intersect and shape the power relations between poor and nonpoor, non-Hispanic White (NHW) and racial/ethnic underrepresented minorities. The harshness of the policy debates continue unabated regarding distinctions between the deserving and undeserving poor, with the *undeserving poor* increasingly representing the face of Black and Latino families. There are two cooccurring silent or implicit assumptions in contemporary debates that shape how programs are designed and delivered. First, the notion that poverty is a behavioral problem among the poor that can be fixed by instilling "proper American values" and by women "being proper wives and mothers" (as reflected, e.g., in the abstinence and healthy marriage initiatives in early 2000). The second implicit assumption is that in our democracy all willing workers should be able to get a job and those who don't work or are unable to find a job do not deserve dignified treatment.[2] Even though the Social Security Act of 1935 clearly states that being treated with equity is a right, Daniel Moynihan (1995) argued that welfare (public assistance) is not a right but instead "a commitment by the Federal Government to match state spending on programs that states devise" (184).

The implementation of state policy is the social location where differential and unequal treatment of Blacks and Latinos is most evident. The moral foundation of these programs is reflected in two ways: by the amount and quality of resources that states allocate to programs, and by the ways in which official state representatives such as caseworkers and probation officers implement program benefits and use disciplinary power (e.g., barriers to services, personal treatment of clients) to ensure that recipients are aware of their ascribed status. These differences in state allocation of resources and how agency officials and caseworkers implement the program is often overlooked in the study of these systems (see, e.g., Reich 2005; Watkins-Hayes 2009). What is well-known is the disheartening paradox between the goals of the program to instill industrial discipline, work ethic, and self-sufficiency and the meager resources allocated for these goals with the power of individual states to design adequate or inadequate programs with limited federal regulation and oversight. As a result of lack of federal monitoring, states policies vary widely in the level of benefits provided, and many instances of biased and unfair implementation have been recorded; for example, in the State Children's Health Insurance Program (SCHIP), schools, juvenile and criminal justice, and public assistance programs (see, e.g., Bender 2003; American Civil Liberties Union [ACLU] 2007; Jones-DeWeever et al. 2009).

Overall, public assistance programs serve a small group of the poor and exclude many who need assistance. States determine how much individuals and families get in economic assistance, which varies by race, ethnicity, and gender, and is often inadequate to promote self-sufficiency. Increased study of these programs reveals that rather than helping poor families, they curtail citizenship rights; are morally degrading, intrusive, and humiliating; segregate and stigmatize groups of individuals as deviants; treat men more harshly and in more mean-spirited ways; and subject recipients to frequent administrative regulations. "At the same time, these institutional practices send a message to the poor who are not on welfare, by signifying the types of ceremonies they are likely to be subjected to if they do apply for welfare" (Handler and

---

2. For excellent histories of failed public policies for the poor, see Sealander 2003; Miller and Roby 1970. France Fox Piven and Richard A. Cloward's pivotal works, *Poor People Movement: Why They Succeed, How They Fail* (1977), *The New Class War* (1982), *Regulating the Poor: The Functions of Public Welfare* (1993), and numerous others challenged the investments in the war on poverty that failed to change structural conditions.

Hasenfeld 1991, 12). As a result, the many reforms of these programs have contributed little to their transformation from their original punitive design, and research has been more likely to focus on people failures than system failures.

Social scientists in past decades in their study of poor racial/ethnic populations initiated a scientific legacy that perpetuated a view of public welfare programs, particularly AFDC, as creating a "welfare culture" or a "culture of dependency and irresponsibility," which they claimed failed to hold people accountable that is to provide for themselves economically. Handler and Hasenfeld (1991) poignantly address the use of these social science theories in policy making. They state: "Justifying or debunking welfare policy on moral grounds while using social science research and theory to buttress the moral argument is the key attribute of moralistic theories" (7–8). The outcome of much of this research with some important exceptions reinforces prior historical representations of poor and Black and Latino peoples as deviant, an "underclass," and undeserving of assistance. Social scientists represent both sides of the debate. For example, some scholars discuss the failures of public assistance programs, while others denounce the differential treatment, discrimination, and unfairness of the system. Those studies that are most consistent with dominant hegemonic thinking are lauded as credible, while those studies that challenge hegemonic thinking are often ignored. The potential power of a unified scholarly political voice is hindered by the fact that critical discourses are often located in different disciplines. Thus intellectual silos are created, which fail to disrupt the institutional practices and policies that are engaged in the reproduction of inequality.

Although we have historically focused on public assistance as a site of inequality, it can be argued that all public systems (e.g., juvenile justice, child welfare) have a basic value system and "myths and ceremonies" that promote minimal subsistence service, deny basic civil rights, and often falter in common sense and basic decency in dealing with all poor but especially Blacks and Latinos.

## Profile: Who Are the Poor?

The poor are defined in the United States by a median income for individuals or a family household income, which is highly associated with years of education completed and participation in the labor force. The poverty thresholds and poverty guidelines differ in terms of what they are used for, who determines them, and how they are calculated. For example, in 2008, the federal poverty threshold was $10,997 for one person and $22,017 for a family of four (U.S. Bureau of Labor Statistics 2008). The poverty guidelines set forth by the U.S. Department of Health and Human Services (USDHHS) in 2009 was $10,830 for one person and $22,050 for a family of four ($424.00 a week).[3]

Table 8.1 displays economic indicators of the U.S. civilian noninstitutionalized population sixteen years of age or older by race and ethnicity. Median household income is lowest among Blacks and Latinos and highest for Asians with a median household income of $57,518. The highest rates of labor force participation are among Whites, Latinos, and Asians, while Blacks have the lowest employment rates and the highest unemployment rates. Among Blacks and Latinos, 11 percent have been in the workforce for twenty-seven weeks or more but still live below the poverty level, and for those with a high school diploma or less over one-third (36 percent) of Blacks and about one-quarter (26 percent) of Latinos live below the poverty level compared to 19 percent of Whites' and 15 percent of Asians. Blacks and Latinos are almost three times more likely to be poor than Whites and 2.5 times more likely to be poor than Asians. Black (33 percent) and Latino (27 percent) children have exceptionally high poverty rates compared to White and Asian children. Interestingly, overall all groups have close to or over a 60 percent employment rate, yet Blacks and Latinos with a high school diploma are more likely to be unemployed than Whites and are much more likely to live below poverty level compared to Whites and Asians. These data confirm that given similar levels of education, Whites and Asians receive more median earnings (see chapter 2), and Blacks and Latinos have less access to those higher-paying jobs, which places them at risk for higher unemployment and poverty. Those most in need of government public support services are Black and Latino families who are disproportionately poor. Further, poor Blacks and Latinos who are more likely to have a main economic provider who works in low-paying unskilled labor or seasonal jobs or who has sporadic employment are also more likely not to have health insurance. Families who require economic assistance due to inability to find work require access to public assistance to maintain the economic and social well-being of their families.

3. There are two basic versions of the federal poverty measure: the poverty thresholds (which are the primary version) and the poverty guidelines. The Census Bureau issues the poverty thresholds, which are generally used for statistical purposes—for example, to estimate the number of people in poverty nationwide each year and classify them by type of residence, race, and other social, economic, and demographic characteristics. The Department of Health and Human Services issues the poverty guidelines for administrative purposes—for instance, to determine whether a person or family is eligible for assistance through various federal programs. http://aspe.hhs.gov/poverty/faq.shtml#differences.

**Table 8.1.** Income, Employment, and Poverty Indicators by Race and Ethnicity

|  | Total | White | Black | Latino | Asian |
|---|---|---|---|---|---|
| U.S. population, 2006 (millions) | 299,399 | 221,335 | 37,051 | 44,252 | 13,101 |
|  | (100%) | (74%) | (12%) | (15%) | (4%) |
| Individuals below poverty line, 2006 (%) | 12 | 8 | 24 | 21 | 10 |
| Children below poverty line, 2006 (%) | 17 | 14 | 33 | 27 | 12 |
| Median household income ($) | 46,326 | 48,977 | 30,134 | 34,241 | 57,518 |
| Median personal income ($) | 32,140 | 32,919 | 27,110 | 23,613 | 36,152 |
| Civilian noninstitutional population 16 years and older, 2007 (millions) | 233,156 | 188,657 | 27,603 | 31,554 | 10,625 |
| Employment-population ratio, 2007 (%) | 63 | 66 | 58 | 64 | 64 |
| Unemployment rate (16 years and older) (%) | 5 | 4 | 9 | 6 | 4 |
| Not in labor force (16 years and older) (%) | 34 | 34 | 37 | 33 | 31 |
| People in the labor force for 27 weeks or more, below poverty level, 2004 (%) | 6 | 5 | 11 | 11 | 4 |
| People in the labor force for 27 weeks or more, below poverty level with high school diploma or less, 2004 (%) | 22 | 19 | 36 | 26 | 15 |

*Sources:* Adapted from U.S. Department of Labor 2006; U.S. Census Bureau 2008.

## Government Public Assistance Programs

In 1935, in the wake of the Great Depression when all U.S. citizens were exposed to the risks of poverty, the Aid to Families with Dependent Children (AFDC) was the landmark public welfare program that initiated the provision of economic and social resources and assistance to families in need. *Public assistance,* best known as *welfare,* is commonly defined as *government benefits distributed to impoverished persons to enable them to maintain a minimum standard of well-being.* The public assistance infrastructure provides economic, housing, food stamps, and health benefits to poor citizens in order to assure a minimum standard of well-being. During its first twenty-five years, AFDC caseloads were predominantly White widows and, in the late 1950s and 1960s, increasing numbers of NHBs and Latinos. As the "color" of the public service programs changed, so did the scrutiny of those who applied.

The public welfare system underwent a major reform under the Clinton administration, from Aid to Families with Dependent Children to Personal Responsibility and Work Opportunity Reconciliation Act (PRWORA) of 1996. The welfare reform was powerfully influenced again by social pressure and criticism from individuals and groups who perceived the system as responding to and serving deviant, nonworking but capable individuals. In 1994, former President Clinton addressed the concern of the "welfare culture" and proposed that to change the system it must begin with responsibility, implying government and personal responsibility: "We can strengthen our communities if we can give every person on welfare the dignity, the pride, the direction, the strength, and sheer person power" (Clinton 1994, 24). PRWORA included government policies designed to help working and low-income families become economically self-sufficient. Programmatic components included the earned income tax credit (EITC), health insurance such as Medicaid and SCHIP, food assistance through food stamps and the Women, Infants, and Children (WIC) program (access to prenatal care and child health for mothers and children), child care subsidies, work support benefits, and public housing vouchers. Work support benefits were included to decrease the probability that when welfare participants transitioned from welfare to work, their jobs would not leave them earning below or near the poverty line (Daponte et al. 1999; Marchevsky and Theoharis 2006; Urban Institute 2006a, b). Although former president Clinton's rhetoric focused on family strengthening and supports, the design of the program with a five-year restriction to reenvision your life, develop new skills, increase your education, and find a job above the poverty level reflected a reconstruction and reinforcement of the moral arguments of the undeserving poor. PROWRA, however, paid little attention to the effects of accumulated economic and social disadvantage over the life course and its impact on family structure and processes. Much disappointment was expressed in the shortcomings of this regressive reform, which mandated change in strengthening communities but did not require structural change and investment of significant government resources to remedy the lives of marginalized populations.

## Temporary Assistance for Needy Families (TANF)

Temporary Assistance for Needy families (TANF) was created under PRWORA and replaced the AFDC, Jobs Opportunities and Basic Skills Training (JOBS), and the Emergency Assistance (EA) programs (USDHHS 2006a, b, c). The purposes of TANF are to provide financial assistance to needy families so that children can be cared for in their own homes (to avoid children becoming wards of the state); reduce the long-term dependency of needy parents by promoting job preparation and work opportunities; and promote and maintain two-parent families (USDHHS 2006c). Federal funds are provided to states as a block grant that allows States to implement their own TANF programs and develop state-determined needs standards (Currie 2006; USDHHS 2006b).

TANF has specific federal work requirements to receive cash assistance, including at least thirty hours of work a week for single parents and thirty-five to fifty-five hours a week for two-parent families. Failure to participate in work requirements can result in a reduction or termination of benefits. TANF also includes a five-year limit for receipt of cash benefits; an optional state-determined family cap, which denies benefits to children born to welfare recipients once in the program; limited child care stipends for those participating in work programs; and provisions that deny most forms of public assistance to legal immigrants for five years or until they attain citizenship (USDHHS 1996, 2006c). Most recipients of TANF are eligible for Medicaid, which provides access to health care, hospital care, and prescription drugs (Kaiser Commission 2007). In 2005, the Deficit Reduction Act was passed, which requires states to engage more TANF cases in productive work activities that lead to self-sufficiency and the reduction of the TANF caseloads (USDHHS 2006b).

Table 8.2 presents data by race and ethnicity of recipients of public benefits. During the 2006 fiscal year, there were close to two million families and two million recipients of TANF benefits, of which approximately three million were children. Thus, one million adults out of the total U.S. population received public assistance. Blacks made up about 36 percent of all TANF recipients, followed by Whites (33 percent) and Latinos (26 percent) (USDHHS 2006c). Another component of public assistance is the food stamp program, which aims to help alleviate hunger and malnutrition (otherwise referred to as food insecurity) by providing coupons and electronic benefits that can be used to purchase food at grocery stores. To be eligible, households must have a net monthly income below the poverty line; 41 percent of all food stamp recipients lived in a household with earnings below the poverty line (U.S. Department of Agriculture [USDA] 2007). More than 55 percent of food stamp recipients are children or the elderly (over the age of sixty). Approximately 35 million participants are estimated to be eligible to receive food stamps and approximately 25 million receive this benefit, a take-up rate of about 70 percent, which is considered successful according to the federal government. These benefits are considered to be "well targeted to intended beneficiaries" with an identified need to improve the knowledge about and the use of nutritional food options among its recipients (U.S. Office of Management and Budget and Federal Agencies 2003). However, this also means that 10 million people or more may be experiencing food insecurity; that is, they do not have enough to eat on a daily basis.

In 2006, the participation rate for those who received food stamps was inconsistent with the eligibility rate. For example, only 8 percent or approximately twenty-three million Whites would qualify for food stamps based on income, but they constitute 43 percent of the recipient pool, placing their take-up rate at about 46 percent (about eleven million Whites received these benefits in 2006) (USDA 2007). Therefore 46 percent of all eligible Whites, based on income, receive food stamps compared with 11 percent of eligible Blacks and 8 percent of eligible Latinos (USDA 2007). Although Whites have the highest median income compared to Blacks and Latinos, Whites access the highest percentage of benefits in food stamps, unemployment insurance, Medicaid, and EITC. Blacks, who have the lowest median personal income, are much less likely to use food stamps, unemployment insurance, and Medicaid

**Table 8.2.** Recipients of Public Benefits by Race and Ethnicity

|  | Total | White | Black | Latino | Asian |
|---|---|---|---|---|---|
| Families receiving TANF, 2006 | 1,802,567 (100%) | 33% | 36% | 26% | 2% |
| Food stamp receipt, households, 2006 | 11,315,000 (100%) | 46% | 31% | 13% | 2% |
| Food stamp receipt, participants, 2006 | 25,595 (100%) | 43% | 33% | 19% | 2% |
| Households with elderly individuals | 2,024,000 | 50% | 24% | 18% | 7% |
| Child care subsidies (children 0–6 years not in kindergarten and below poverty line), 2005 | 15% | 17% | 24% | 5% | N/A |
| Unemployment insurant, 2007 (average weekly claim total) | 2,532.9 | 58% | 18% | 16% | 2% |
| Medicaid recipient, 2003 | 52,000,000 (100%) | 41% | 22% | 19% | 3% |
| EITC, 2005, Full Credit Eligibility Tax Analyst, 2005 | 100% | 60% | 15% | 18% | N/A |
| Average credit | $679 | $721 | $564 | $638 | N/A |
| Percent with less than full credit because earnings too low | 30% | 18% | 50% | 46% | N/A |

*Sources:* U.S. Department of Agriculture 2007; U.S. Department of Labor 2006; U.S. Bureau of Labor Statistics 2008.

but are more likely to use child care subsidies. Latinos have similar patterns to Blacks in use of public welfare services, but are less likely to use child care subsidies. The higher use of public services by Whites may be associated with their ability to better negotiate the system, experiencing less discrimination based on race and ethnic group membership, and/or may highlight the significant yet invisible poor Whites that are not acknowledged in national data systems (see Henderson and Tickamyer 2009).

Although Latinos are the least likely to use food stamps and public health insurance coverage, they are also at the highest risk of food insecurity and lack of access to health care services. In a study of low-income children at a pediatric clinic, Margaret Kersey and colleagues (2007) found that U.S.–born Latino children who have at least one Mexican-born parent are at especially high risk for hunger and household food insecurity (6.8 percent) compared to nonimmigrant, non-Latino children (0.5 percent). Another study found an upward trend during 1983 to 2003 in no health insurance coverage among U.S.–born Hispanics, driven by a decrease in private coverage with no increase in public coverage (Rutledge and McLaughlin 2008). Available public health insurance coverage programs, such as Medicaid and SCHIP, are not effectively reaching uninsured Latino children (Flores et al. 2002). Among Latino women, a study explored the impact on the use of prenatal care following the enactment of PRWORA in three states: New York, California, and Florida. Although Florida was the only state to restrict eligibility, women in all immigrant subgroups were two to four times more likely to have inadequate prenatal care than U.S.–born citizens in New York (Fuentes-Afflick et al. 2006).

Access barriers to most public services and low participation rates are not new. What is new is the research and discourse that highlights unequal access to services. Factors that contribute to the low participation rates for racial/ethnic minorities include lack of knowledge about the programs and eligibility requirements and perceived and real difficulties concerning completing the application process (such as language barriers, literacy levels, time commitments, fear of deportation, and differential treatment by public service workers). Although studies on participation suggest that stigma may contribute to lower participation, other studies have found that few people expressed that they did not want to be associated with the program due to stigma or not needing the services (Daponte et al. 1999; Marchevsky and Theoharis 2006; Urban Institute 2006a).

### Goals of Public Assistance and Unequal Treatment

The goals of TANF are to move welfare recipients from welfare to work to increase family economic self-sufficiency and to decrease state welfare caseloads—a task for which states are held accountable for and receive incentives from the federal government (USDHHS 1996). The unprecedented and rapid decrease in welfare rolls in many states post 1996 sparked attention and inquiry. State reports and data from the National Survey of American Families indeed showed evidence of discrimination and mistreatment based on race and ethnicity (Jones-DeWeever et al. 2009; Marchevsky and Theoharis 2006; Urban Institute 2002a; Zedlewski 2003). While welfare and TANF caseloads have decreased, Black (41 percent) and Latino (51 percent) women continue to be more likely to remain on welfare than White (27 percent) women for longer periods of time (up to sixty months) and are more likely to be negatively affected by time limits. Kristen Harknett (2001) analyzed differences in welfare and labor market participation among White, African American and Hispanic welfare recipients in Riverside, California. The author found that in the absence of welfare-to-work interventions, African Americans and Hispanics worked as much or more than Whites but were less likely to leave welfare. Two factors may account for this disparity: lower marriage and cohabitation rates among African American and Hispanic welfare recipients and less financial assistance from social networks and paternal child support.

Female-headed households are the largest percentage of households receiving TANF benefits and are likely to experience the most racial/ethnic and gender discrimination within the welfare system (Urban Institute 2002a). Two examples illustrate instances of discrimination: Latino and Black women are more likely than NHW women to be asked sexually invasive questions and to experience sexual harassment at their assigned work activities. For example, one study found that 41 percent of all women reported being asked questions such as their sexual orientation, their relationship with their children's fathers, if they were sexually active, and if they were taking birth control (Gordon 2001). Alejandra Marchevsky and Jean Theoharis (2006) studied Latino and immigrant women and reported that participants were often denied, dropped, or had their benefits reduced but were unsure of the reason for the decision. Caseworkers would often make inappropriate and racially charged comments to participants.

For example, "After discovering that her family's food stamps had been terminated, [Delia] called the welfare office several times and finally spoke to a caseworker who offered to reinstate a monthly food stamp allotment of $68 (she previously had received $260). As Delia recounted she asked, 'Why $68?' and explained to the caseworker that her family needed to eat. You people always are asking for help when you don't need it, you should be happy with what you have or go back to Mexico, Delia backed off, fearful that the caseworker would take away even the $68 in food stamps she had first offered" (164).

The work requirement of TANF is another area where discriminatory practices are observed. Adults receiving TANF report barriers that significantly reduce work activities: almost 45 percent had at least one barrier to work, and 14 percent had two or more barriers to work. These barriers include poor mental or physical health (35 percent), having less than a high school diploma (42 percent), a three or more year gap in employment (30 percent), having a child under the age of one (19 percent), and requiring an interview in Spanish (10 percent) (Zedlewski and Holland 2003; Urban Institute 2002a). Other circumstances that make it difficult for recipients to work include severe mental distress as a consequence of domestic partner violence, inadequate child care, lack of transportation, and the lack of availability of jobs and training programs (Jones-De Weever et al. 2009; Savner 2000; Marchevsky and Theoharis 2006).

In general the public assistance system has proved to be an unfriendly and unfair environment for eligible racial/ethnic minorities, poor individuals, and families. What has been documented in the last decade is that Blacks and Latinos are not given access to resources that provide a solid foundation for economic self-sufficiency and family well-being. Disparities exist in access to and receipt of services across racial and ethnic lines, especially in areas where caseworkers are given the discretion in the services they offer recipients. In one study of interactions between welfare recipients and caseworkers, Whites (59 percent) were more likely than Blacks (36 percent) to state their caseworkers were helpful in providing information about potential jobs. Further, while 41 percent of Whites indicated that they were encouraged to go back to school and continue their education, no Blacks reported the same (Savner 2000). The

National Urban League (2002) found that the type of work option available to recipients varied by ethnicity and race, with 72 percent of Latinas and 65 percent of Black women working at unpaid jobs to receive welfare benefits, while only 46 percent of White women were working at unpaid jobs in exchange for benefits (U.S. Commission on Civil Rights [USCCR] 2002). As a result, White women are more likely than Blacks and Latinas to leave public assistance with employment that may help them transition to economic self-sufficiency.

Overall NHWs (25 percent) are more likely to leave public assistance with paid employment, compared to NHBs (17 percent) and Latinos (9 percent). This disparity cannot be attributed to the culture or work ethic of racial/ethnic minorities but rather to employer preferences (Holzer and Stoll 2003). Employers are less likely to hire Black and Hispanic welfare recipients, even when they have more education than White welfare recipients, and among temporary employment agencies there was "extensive evidence of racial discrimination in hiring for entry-level jobs" (USCCR 2002, 2). Furthermore, NHW women (48 percent) were more likely to receive the necessary subsidies (child care, transportation assistance) to transition to work and increase their level of education, while less than 30 percent of both Latino and NHB women received such subsidies (National Urban League 2002).

For the small number of language minority eligible families, language continues to be a barrier while trying to navigate the welfare system. Nationally, over 50 percent of survey respondents reported they needed translation services but none were available, even though federal regulations required "welfare agencies to provide interpretation when a significant portion of the client base speaks a language other than English" (Gordon 2001, 35). In New York City, where the majority of the TANF recipients are Latino (36 percent), that percent was significantly higher, with 70 percent of respondents indicating they needed translation but none was made available to them. Among TANF recipients, whose first language was a language other than English, 62 percent reported experiencing significant language barriers while seeking welfare services, completing the application process, and trying to obtain employment opportunities. In fact, many Spanish-speaking welfare recipients were denied access to English language–learning classes because space was not available, and to job training courses, including vocational training and resume-writing classes, due to a lack of accommodations for students who were not English speakers (National Urban League 2002).

National data show that more TANF families' cases were closed due to failure to comply (20 percent) than employment (18 percent), which suggest that decreasing caseloads do not necessarily represent entry into labor force or economic self-sufficiency (USDHHS 2006c). Further, a multistate study of welfare recipients that transitioned out of the TANF program found severe discrepancies coinciding with race for the reasons the recipients left welfare.

In a study conducted across three states from 1997 to 1999, 54 percent of racial/ethnic minority cases were closed due to failure to comply compared with 39 percent of NHW cases. In a similar study conducted in Florida, 8 percent of Whites had their cases closed due to compliance issues compared with 22 percent of Blacks (Savner 2000). The Center on Budget and Policy Priorities (CBPP 2002) found that recipients receiving sanctions resulting in a reduction or discontinuance of benefits were more likely to suffer from incidences of domestic violence, had greater barriers to employment such as disabilities or limited education, and were more likely to experience multiple barriers.

Discriminatory institutional public assistance state practices and policies impede NHBs' and Latinos' access to resources that could increase their skills and economic sustainability of families. These practices are detrimental to the lives of the people intended to be served and are compounded by racism in the larger society, particularly work sites. As observed by Holzer and Stoll (2003), the conditional demand for NHB and Hispanic welfare recipients lags behind their representation in the welfare population and seems affected by employer preferences and location suggesting "minority welfare recipients face more serious employment barriers than their NHW counterparts" (219). Although Robert Preuhs (2007) tries to make a case for increased Latino representation and legislative incorporation as a means to influence social welfare policy, the author acknowledges that scholars continue to find evidence of racial backlash in public policy decisions. We can conclude that public welfare programs are not making the human capital investments required to ensure that racial/ethnic minorities and low-income NHWs can lift themselves out of poverty. Access to quality housing and community resources plays an important role in buttressing or diminishing one's life options and the quality of family life. Without access to safe neighborhoods and quality educational and recreational resources, the social location of the poor remains relatively unchanged.

### Housing, Community, and Neighborhood

Housing is the largest expense of the typical American household, and housing conditions are often reflective of other financial and educational opportunities (Bowdler 2004). Residential location and the quality of housing have a significant impact on the lives of individuals and families. Specifically, what are the characteristics of the neighborhood in which low-income and poor families are able to live when using public assistance programs? Limited government assistance is available to help low-income families and individuals with the cost of housing. The U.S. Department of Housing and Urban Development (HUD) administers financial support for free or limited cost public housing for low-income residents and includes a mandatory community service requirement by the tenants. These supports are provided through Section 8 certificates and

**Table 8.3.** Characteristics of Public Housing Residents by Type of Housing and Race and Ethnicity

| Characteristic | Section 236 | Section 8 | Public housing |
|---|---|---|---|
| Number of subsidized units | 440,329 | 1,817,360 | 1,282,099 |
| Average monthly tenant rent ($) | 254 | 226 | 202 |
| Average household income ($) | 11,200 | 10,600 | 10,000 |
| Female-headed households (%) | 76 | 84 | 77 |
| White (%) | 45 | 39 | 31 |
| Black (%) | 37 | 41 | 46 |
| Latino (%) | 13 | 16 | 20 |
| Asian (%) | 4 | 3 | 2 |

*Sources:* U.S. Department of Housing and Urban Development 1997, 2008a.

vouchers and through Section 236, which subsidizes the interest payments on mortgages for rental or cooperative housing owned by private, nonprofit, or limited profit landlords and rented to low-income tenants (HUD 2004).

Latinos are less likely than Whites and Blacks to receive any housing benefits and are proportionately less likely when accounting for poverty level and average housing costs to access these benefits. Racial/ethnic minorities who receive governmental funding for public housing are more likely than Whites and Asians to live in a neighborhood that is economically disadvantaged.

Table 8.3 presents data on HUD–supported subsidies by family structure (single-parent households), income, and racial and ethnic characteristics of residents (HUD 1997; 2008a, b, c). Noteworthy, over 75 percent of all residents are female-headed householders. Whites and Asians are more likely to have Section 236 vouchers, and Blacks and Latinos are more likely to live in public housing. Those with incomes of $10,000 or less were the most likely to reside in public housing and to have the lowest rental payments.

The location of different housing options makes a marked difference in access to a social and economic opportunity structure. The average poverty rate for the neighborhoods in which public housing is located was 37 percent higher than the averages for both Section 8 and Section 236 (20 percent). Further, Section 8 (40 percent) and Section 236 (33 percent) recipients were more likely to live in neighborhoods with higher single-family detached homeowners than recipients of public housing (26 percent) (HUD 1997). Latinos and NHBs are the least likely to live in "neighborhoods of opportunity," which are determined by the neighborhood's availability of sustainable employment, healthy environments, access to high-quality health care, adequate transportation, high-quality child care, and high-performing schools. Dolores Acevedo-Garcia and colleagues (2008) propose that NHB and Latino children typically live in a neighborhood environment that is much more disadvantaged than the neighborhood environment of the average NHW child. Using the 2000

Census data from the one hundred metropolitan areas with the largest child population, the authors show that a typical Latino child lived in a neighborhood with a poverty rate of 19 percent and unemployment rate of 9 percent, and where 35 percent of the adults did not have a high school diploma. The data for a typical Latino child living below the federal poverty line shows a much bleaker profile: Children are living in a neighborhood with a poverty rate of about 26 percent, unemployment rate of about 11 percent, and where more than 42 percent of the adults in the neighborhood lack a high school diploma.

In one study of neighborhood effects (see chapter 5 for a description of neighborhood effects), Jeffrey Timberlake (2007) estimated racial and ethnic inequality in the amount of time children can expect to live in poor and nonpoor neighborhoods throughout childhood. Using the 1990s as a benchmark, the average NHB child can expect to spend 50 percent of his/her first eighteen years in neighborhoods with poverty in excess of 20 percent versus 40 percent for Latino and 5 percent for NHW children.

Neighborhoods are an important context to understand the intersection of economic opportunity structure, poverty, and race/ethnicity. Of the twenty cities with the highest Hispanic population, only four have rents and owner costs lower than the national average (Bowdler 2004). Almost 70 percent of Hispanics are concentrated in five states; two of them are California and New York, which are among the top five least affordable states to live. Nationally about 26 percent of a household's income is spent on rent, with NHBs (28 percent) and Latinos (27 percent) spending more of their income on rent than NHWs (25 percent) and living in less desirable neighborhoods (U.S. Census 2004c). Hispanics were more likely in 2000 than in 1989 to be quoted a higher rent than their NHW counterpart for the same unit (Urban Institute 2002b). In 2003, Hispanics were overrepresented as home renters and in categories of negative housing indicators (e.g., housing hazards, crime, vandalism, exposure to toxins) and are disproportionately exposed to worse living conditions than the population as a whole (U.S. Census 2004c). Latinos live in residential spaces that are smaller and more crowded than the overall population, and they are disproportionately represented among those who live in older, deteriorated housing with severe physical problems, leading to higher exposure to environmental triggers of asthma, lead paint, and asbestos (U.S. Census 2004c; Carter-Pokras et al. 2007).

Institutional practices in the housing market show that the greatest share of discrimination for Latino and NHB home seekers is omission of information such as being told units are unavailable or being shown and told about fewer units than a comparable nonminority home seeker. Hispanics are more likely than NHWs and NHBs to be discriminated against in their quest for housing (HUD 2006). Consistent patterns of housing discrimination show that (1) NHW applicants were consistently favored over Hispanics more than 25 percent of the time in relation to requests for additional information and inspection of available housing units, and (2) Hispanics experienced adverse treatment compared to equally qualified NHWs 50 percent of the time when they visited real estate or rental offices to inquire about the availability of housing advertised in major metropolitan newspapers (Urban Institute 2002b).

Inequality in access to quality housing and residence in hypersegregated communities with limited education, employment, and recreational resources perpetuate chronic stress due to a lack of food, money, and crowded spaces. Access to housing is linked to the health and well-being of individuals and families. When a market lacks a sufficient supply of affordable housing, lower income racial/ethnic families are often forced to limit expenditures for food, medical care, and other necessities in order to pay rent (Anderson et al. 2003).

These factors contribute to child neglect and intervention by child protective services (CPS, a public agency that investigates child abuse and neglect cases). These structural processes of inequality, such as inadequate public assistance and poor housing options, maintain the marginalization of low-income NHBs and Latinos outside the economic opportunity structure and are disruptive to healthy family functioning and processes. Moreover, many of the poor who reside in public housing often become the targets of racialized institutional practices due to implicit moral social constructions of the poor by public systems bureaucratic guardians as "morally unfit and deviant" and inadequate parents.

### Child Welfare System

*Child welfare* refers to the physical, mental, and social well-being of a child and is highly associated with family SES and community resources.[4] Multiple

---

4. Child abuse and neglect is broadly defined as "the physical or mental injury, sexual abuse, negligent treatment, or maltreatment of a child under the age of eighteen by a person who is responsible for the child's welfare under circumstances which indicate that the child's health or welfare is harmed or threatened thereby" (Giovannoni and Becerra 1979, 12). The majority of child welfare cases fail under the category of neglect, that is, children who may not have enough to eat, may not have adequate clothing, or may be left home alone with older siblings due to parents having to work. The breakdown of substantiated child abuses cases in 2000 was 63 percent for neglect, 19 percent for physical abuse, 10 percent for sexual abuse, and 8 percent for psychological abuse. The rates of child abuse vary by race and ethnicity with NHWs at 51 percent, African Americans at 25 percent, Hispanics at 15 percent, American Indians/Alaskan Natives at 2 percent, and Asian/Pacific Islanders at 1 percent (US Department of Health and Human Services 2000). In 2008, the National Child Abuse and Neglect Data System reported that 73.2 percent of victims of child abuse suffered neglect including medical neglect (2.2%), while 16 percent were victims of physical abuse, an estimated 9 percent experienced sexual abuse and 7.3 percent were emotionally or psychologically maltreated (http:/www.childwelfare.gov/systemwide/statistics/index. cfm). These national rates may be different by state and region. The policies and laws applied in

factors are associated with child maltreatment, such as poverty, inadequate parenting skills including physical and mental health conditions, substance use, and chronic family stressors. Racial/ethnic minority children compared to NHW children are more likely to receive more intensive and punitive services, are more likely to be reported more often, and are more likely to remain in CPS for longer periods of time (Church 2006; Harden 2008). Unlike higher-income families, poor families are more likely to be involved with public service systems, and therefore they are more likely to be under scrutiny and have their cases reported to CPS (Children's Defense Fund [CDF] 2005).

The number of Latino children entering the child welfare system increased during the last decade. Children who live in poverty are the most likely to interface with the child welfare protective services system. African American and Latino children have historically been disproportionately overrepresented in the child welfare system and experienced unequal treatment (Sealander 2003; Zambrana and Capello 2003; Harden 2008). Though poverty is not the sole cause for child abuse and neglect, children who live in families with annual incomes of less than $15,000 are twenty-two times more likely to be abused or neglected than children living in families with annual incomes of $30,000 or more (CDF 2005, 115). A large percentage of families involved with the child welfare system are Black and Hispanic. In 2005, Hispanics made up 17 percent of the children in foster care nationally and 40 percent of the children in foster care in California (Annie E. Casey Foundation 2006; Douglas-Hall et al. 2006).

Poverty and chronic economic stress are associated with barriers to parents fulfilling their normative parenting responsibilities including the provision of food, clothing, health care, and paying bills. Latino parents frequently face multiple barriers in accessing and effectively using public social services, such as fear of removal of their child from the home; social services that are inaccessible or of low quality; insufficient bilingual personnel and inappropriately

---

each state vary and are differentially applied by the Child Protective Service (CPS) agencies designated to implement investigations. This inconsistent application of guidelines is associated with qualifications and potential biases of caseworkers and the unclear guidelines provided under CPS guidelines. As noted by Giovanni and Becerra (1979) and other scholars (Reich 2005; Zambrana and Dorringinton 1998; Zambrana and Capello 2003), the vague statutory definitions that have historically characterized the definition of child abuse and neglect would not pose serious problems if there were clear-cut criteria and standards for interpreting them available to those who must make judgments about specific cases. There is substantial evidence that such criteria do not exist. "Whether from the standpoint of statutory definitions or from professional guidelines such as those above, the burden of interpretation ultimately falls on the various professionals, who must make decisions about whether individual cases belong under the broader rubrics of neglect and abuse" (Giovannoni and Becerra 1979, 10–11). This role of interpretation by caseworkers, many of whom are not trained or licensed in the field of child welfare, has left poor and racial/ethnic families and children in particular in unpredictable and disruptive circumstances.

written informational materials; inadequate family support; and social services that lack cultural competence (Ortega et al. 1996). Children placed in foster care frequently have behavioral and physical disorders (Santiago 1995). One study found that 84 percent of children adopted in New York in 1992 to 1993 and 95 percent of children adopted in California in 1993 to 1994 had one or more physical or emotional problems (Simms et al. 1999). Families who interface with the child welfare system often experience other difficulties such as substance abuse, mental health problems, children with special needs, and domestic violence. The Children's Defense Fund (CDF) notes that "poverty, domestic violence, and involvement in the child welfare system are often inextricably linked" (2005, 117).

Table 8.4 presents national data for all states combined on percent of children in foster care and rates of child maltreatment. Overall, the rates of maltreatment for NHWs and Latinos are slightly over 10 percent compared to almost double that rate for Black children. White and Black children are almost twice as likely to be placed in foster care as Latino children (USDHHS 2009). However, for Latinos in states where Latinos constitute a larger proportion of the total population, rates are estimated at over 40 percent (CDF 2005). When parents are deemed unfit to care for their children due to lack of financial resources, abuse, or neglect, the children are removed from the home. Once a child has been removed from their home, they are either placed with another family member (i.e., kinship care) or in the care of the state in a temporary foster home until the family can be reunited or the child can be placed in long-term alternative housing (such as a group home). Black children are the most likely to be removed from their home and placed in foster care, and Asian children are least likely. Racial/ethnic minority children are generally overrepresented in the foster care system and between 30 and 40 percent of the children in foster care also receive special education services.

Racial and ethnic disparities are prevalent in the lack of substantiation for specific cases, placement patterns, and service utilization among children in foster care. Although cases reported for abuse and neglect are relatively proportionate for Hispanics and Whites, substantiated cases are more likely to occur with Hispanic children (Suleiman 2003; Church et al. 2005). Children in foster care face several barriers to receiving the education, health care, and required special education services needed to help them transition into successful, productive adults. Black and Latino children are also less likely to be reunited with their parents than White children and are less likely to be adopted, resulting from economic inequalities and racial bias within the foster care system (CDF 2005).

An exploratory study of family reunification of foster care children in California found that family structure (single- vs. two-parent families) played an important role in family reunification. Black single-headed households are at a

**Table 8.4.** Foster Care and Child Maltreatment Rates by Race and Ethnicity, 2006

|  | White | Latino | Black | Asian |
|---|---|---|---|---|
| U.S. child population | 55.3 | 22.8 | 14.7 | 4.4 |
| Rates of child maltreatment, 2006 | 10.7 | 10.8[a] | 19.8 | 2.5 |
| Children in foster care, 2006 | 40.0 | 19.0 | 32.0 | 1.0 |

*Source:* U.S. Department of Health and Human Services 2009.
[a]In states where Latinos make up a greater population, such as California, New Mexico, Texas, and Arizona, their rates are over 40 percent.

significant disadvantage regarding the likelihood of family reunification compared with White and Latino families. In two-parent families, being Hispanic conferred a significant advantage in timeliness of family reunification compared to being Black or White (Harris and Courtney 2003). Since many of the Black and Latino children in the child welfare system live in single-parent family households, these findings suggest that race/ethnicity and family structure intersect to shape family reunification services and processes. An adverse outcome for many youth who have been placed in foster care is that if they reach the age of eighteen without having been reunified with their families or adopted, they are less likely to be prepared for self-sufficiency due to high rates of early high school leaving and a lack of work experience.

Not surprisingly, children that experience child abuse and neglect are more likely to become involved with the juvenile justice system. The Children's Defense Fund maintains that abused and neglected children are 1.5 to 6 times more likely to be involved in delinquent behavior and 1.25 to 3 times more likely to be arrested as an adult (CDF 2005, 117). A study of school-aged children reported for child abuse in ten California counties after 1990 revealed three interesting findings: (1) Black and Latino children who received in-home or foster care services after the index investigation had a lower risk of incarceration than those whose cases were closed after the investigations; (2) among females, the rate of incarceration was highest for those who experienced foster or group care placements; and (3) children initially reported for neglect were more likely to be incarcerated than those reported for physical or sexual abuse (Jonson-Reid and Barth 2000). These data suggest the need for more specific attention to children whose cases are closed prematurely or who are reported for specific issues within the home (e.g., neglect) to ensure that appropriate interventions are made to reunite the family and prevent future interactions with public systems such as law enforcement.

Questions prompted by the data above include the following: How do we invest in families to strengthen and optimize their parenting role? What types of services do they need to enhance family functioning? What services do the children/youth need to stabilize their lives after a family crisis? Child welfare systems, similar to other public service systems, are not designed to make the necessary human capital investments required to remedy disadvantage over the life course. What we know is that many low-income children who enter the child welfare system had difficult lives, and the services rendered are more often than not insufficient to make their transition to adulthood easier. Yet, NHB and Latino children are less likely than NHW children to receive the social and psychological interventions needed to address family problems in order to enhance family functioning and progress toward family reunification. Wesley Church's (2006) conclusions are representative of scholarly themes in the literature:

> [T]hese findings strongly reinforce the conclusion that extended out-of-home placement is deleterious to the development and well-being of children and their families.... [D]ifferential treatment of ethnically diverse children, as manifested in the precipitous removal of these children from their homes, could "largely be the result of unwarranted, inaccurate, and racist assumptions of parent inadequacy and family instability (1021, quoting Close 1983, 14).

Thus child welfare services and their in/effectiveness cannot be understood without taking into account the intersection of race, ethnicity, class, and structural inequality that results in an unfair disadvantage for these children's developmental pipeline and that places them at high risk for disciplinary measures in schools and interface with law enforcement officials.

## Schools as Pipelines for Prison

Quality education is a major determinant of economic, social, physical, and mental well-being and is a strong predictor of a child's range of future options and quality of life. Why has the expression "schools as pipelines for prison" been coined? This link between schools and prisons is related to several findings regarding institutional policies and characteristics of schools where Latino and NHBs are in the majority: (1) low-performing schools; (2) a high rate of students receiving free or reduced lunch (an indicator for low SES); (3) strong disciplinary policies that are enforced; (4) constant threats to civil liberties (such as personal searches and security guards from the local police jurisdiction); and (5) high rates of school suspensions and expulsions (Dinkes et al. 2007; ACLU 2007; Snyder and Sickmund 2006). Marion Wright Edelman, a youth advocate, depicts the lived experiences of poor racial/ethnic minority youth in schools:

> High school dropouts are almost three times as likely to be incarcerated as youths who have graduated from high school. But dropouts are not the only ones who encounter entryways into the prison pipeline. Many middle and high schools have full-time police officers who can independently arrest children on school

grounds for any number of infractions like disorderly conduct, malicious mischief and fighting that just a few years ago would have been handled by families, the schools or community institutions. And now, children as young as five and six are being hauled down to police stations in handcuffs. I think we adults have lost our common sense and sense of plain decency. (Edelman 2009)[5]

Differences in discipline policies at the school level, such as the zero tolerance policy,[6] arrests for minor, noncriminal violations of school rules, and gang prevention programs have a disproportionately negative effect on NHB and Latino youth, resulting in these students being penalized more regularly and more harshly for committing acts that tend to be normal or average for their grade and age level (ACLU 2007). For example, Francisco Villarruel and Nancy Walker (2002) found that NHB and Latino students (12 percent each) were not significantly more likely than NHW students (7 percent) to have ever belonged to a gang. However, NHB (41 percent) and Latino (48 percent) students were significantly more likely than NHW students (23 percent) to attend a school where gangs were present (Snyder and Sickmund 2006). Furthermore, Latino students (10 percent) were more likely to report being threatened or injured with a weapon on school property, compared to 7 percent of NHW and 8 percent of NHB students. Latino youth (18 percent) were also more likely to report that they have been in a physical fight at school compared to 12 percent of NHW students (Dinkes et al. 2007).

Thus schools that NHB and Latino youth attend are more likely to have violence and other crimes because they are located in highly segregated poor

5. See www.childrensdefense.org. Children's Defense Fund (CDF) president Marian Wright Edelman writes a weekly Child Watch column.

6. Since the 1980s the phrase *zero tolerance* has signified a philosophy toward illegal conduct that favors strict imposition of penalties regardless of the individual circumstances of each case. Zero tolerance policies deal primarily with drugs and weapons and have been implemented by most school districts in the United States. Two federal laws have driven zero tolerance, but state legislatures have also been willing to mandate similar policies. Supporters of zero tolerance policies contend that they promote the safety and well-being of school children and send a powerful message of deterrence. In addition, supporters believe strict adherence to these polices ensures that school officials do not treat individual children differently. Critics of zero tolerance believe that inflexible discipline policies produce harmful results. Moreover, school administrators have failed to use common sense in applying zero tolerance, leading to the expulsion of children for bringing to school such items as an aspirin or a plastic knife. School principals, who must administer zero tolerance policies, began to suspend and expel students for seemingly trivial offenses. Students have been suspended or expelled for a host of relatively minor incidents, including possession of nail files, paper clips, organic cough drops, a model rocket, a five-inch plastic ax as part of a Halloween costume, an inhaler for asthma, and a kitchen knife in a lunch box to cut chicken. Outraged parents of children disciplined by zero tolerance policies protested to school boards, publicized their cases with the news media, and sometimes filed lawsuits in court seeking the overturning of the discipline. Courts generally have rejected such lawsuits, concluding that school administrators must have the ability to exercise their judgment in maintaining school safety (Heitzeg 2009). For these definitions see http://legal-dictionary.thefreedictionary.com/Zero+Tolerance.

communities. Latino and NHB students are more vigilant in school settings and more likely to be harshly punished at school. The most frequent discipline issues that were rated as serious or moderate problems by school principals were tardiness, absenteeism, and physical conflicts that often led to expulsion or suspension (Office for Civil Rights 2002). Although Latinos represent 18 percent of elementary and secondary school enrollment, they account for 16 percent of out-of-school suspensions and 20 percent of school expulsions. In 2003, 28 percent of NHWs under the age of seventeen reported that they at some time were suspended from school, compared to 56 percent of NHBs and 38 percent of Latinos (Snyder and Sickmund 2006).

Higher rates of suspension, expulsion, and applications of the zero tolerance policy have negative consequences that contribute to poorer school climate, higher dropout rates, lower student achievement, and more punitive consequences for NHB and Latino youth compared to NHW students (Heitzeg 2009). These schools are also more likely to have inexperienced teachers and refer NHB and Latino students to CPS and to the police. Stereotypic perceptions associated with the social construction of the "danger posed by these youth" to the school community contribute to the marginalization and criminalization of these students that eventually narrow their life options and chances to improve their lives.

### Race/Ethnicity, Neighborhood, Public Safety, and Law Enforcement

Public safety has always been a concern of the U.S. government, and public funds are used for the protection of individuals, families, and neighborhoods, through police presence and the criminal justice system, which prosecutes and tries people who are thought to be a danger to public safety. Public safety is not only a concern of law enforcement but also of low-income racial/ethnic residents who care about personal safety and crime in their neighborhoods. In the 2005 American Housing Survey conducted by the U.S. Census Bureau, 15 percent of those polled reported crime in their neighborhoods, and 24 percent of those polled stated that the crime was bothersome enough for them to want to move. Latinos (36 percent) were the most likely to state that neighborhood crime was troublesome enough for them to want to move. However, Latinos (19 percent), NHBs (25 percent), and those living below the poverty level (20 percent) reported a higher incidence of neighborhood crime than the total group (U.S. Census 2006). Thus, regardless of the level of police presence or crime prevention programs, Latinos, NHBs, and those living below the poverty line do not feel safer as a result of law enforcement efforts. Rather, NHB and Latino males all too often find themselves as targets of biased law enforcement practices.

Policing practices in poor, racial/ethnic communities became more aggressive during the 1980s War on Drugs when Latino and NHB males in the public imagination were perceived to be the most likely to carry and use drugs. These practices, referred to as *racial profiling,* are commonly practiced on U.S. highways as well as in communities where NHBs and Latinos are unfairly and disproportionately targeted and accused by police of committing crimes (Oboler 2009, 6; Rights Working Group 2010). The ACLU has been involved in lawsuits against several states including Arizona, California, Maryland, Massachusetts, Minnesota, New Jersey, New York, and Rhode Island for violating individuals' rights by racial profiling. In Texas, a state that is heavily populated by Latinos, a survey of the law enforcement records by the *New York Times* found that NHBs and Latinos were significantly more likely to be stopped by the police than NHWs, and were also 3.5 times more likely to be searched (Barnes 2004). The ACLU (2007) contends that racial profiling is largely ineffective, causes resentment in the targeted communities, and is becoming a common practice. The ACLU advocates that racial profiling be eradicated or at least minimized with the use of data collection tools that allows stakeholders to monitor who is being stopped, how often certain groups are stopped, how those who are stopped are being treated, and the results of the police stopping (2007).

In a 2009 National Survey of Latinos by the Pew Hispanic Center (2009d), among a sample of 2,012 Hispanics sixteen years of age and older, questions were asked regarding risky behavior such as carrying a weapon, being threatened with a weapon, being in a fight, and being questioned by police. Not unexpectedly, U.S.–born Latino males were almost three times as likely as girls to report risky behaviors, and 29 percent of males reported being routinely questioned by police. Surprisingly, although few Latina girls reported engaging in risky behavior, about 13 percent of the females were also routinely questioned by police. Although data are not available for racial/ethnic comparison, these data may suggest that Latino females have come under surveillance in recent years although they engage in risky behaviors at a lower rate than seems warranted by police questioning. In contrast, immigrant Latinos were less likely to engage in risky behaviors and less likely to be questioned by police (15 percent) compared to second-generation (26 percent) and third-generation and higher (26 percent). High school graduates or those in school were less likely to engage in risky behaviors and less likely to be questioned by police (25 percent) than those Latinos who were not high school graduates and who were not in school (32 percent). Of interest, only 3 percent of young Hispanics say they are in a gang, but 31 percent say they have friends or family members with gang involvement. Among Latinos, Mexican-origin groups are significantly more likely to have a family or friend who is or was involved in a gang (37 percent) than other Latino groups (19 percent) (82–86). These data challenge national law enforcement data and perceptions of significant members of Latino youth as gang members, yet police surveillance for both males and females is prevalent in these poor communities (PEW Hispanic Center 2009d).

Another form of racial profiling is the hypersensationalism and social constructions fueled by the media of gangs as unique and specific to Latino and NHB adolescents and as threats to neighborhood safety.[7] Interestingly, although "crime had significantly dropped between 1993 and 2000, it continued to dominate both the news and entertainment media. Hence, the power of media lies not only in its ability to project fear but also its capacity to convey a highly racialized picture of crime to the public" (Morín 2009, 24).

The media fuels fear that is then translated into public policy. For example, in 1996 the U.S. legislature passed the "Violent Youth Predator Law" offering millions of dollars to states to implement harsh juvenile justice policies. This law lowered the age from sixteen to fourteen to be tried as an adult for a crime and legislated mandatory sentences for violent youth offenses (Rios 2009b, 101). How these images are projected and inform public policy speaks to racialized institutional practices for maintaining social control over NHB and Latino males, who have historically been perceived as dangerous to the social order. The intersecting roles of media, public policy, and allocation of federal resources show how hegemonic ideology shapes the power relationships between poor, racialized minorities and society. In other words, as the fear of the racial/ethnic minority poor, including immigrants, became part of the American public imagination, restrictive and punitive legislation was passed both in public assistance (e.g., 1996 PROWRA) and law enforcement systems.

Simultaneously in 1996, the National Youth Gang Survey implemented a survey of "law enforcement agencies to identify the presence and assess the extent of the youth gang problem in jurisdictions throughout the United States" (v). For the purposes of the National Gang Youth Survey study a *gang* was defined as follows:

> A group of youths or young adults in your jurisdiction that you or other responsible persons in your agency or community are willing to identify or classify as a "gang." DO NOT include motorcycle gangs, hate or ideology groups, prison gangs, or other exclusively adult gangs. Thus, the National Youth Gang Survey measures youth gang activity as an identified problem by interested community agents. This approach is both less restrictive and self-determining, allowing for the variation in gang definitions across communities. (U.S. Department of Justice [USDJ] 2006, 4)

---

7. For a historical and contemporary overview of these stereotypes and their influence on incarceration rates of Latinos, see Bender 2003. For the most recent data on Latinos in the juvenile and adult correctional system, see Pew Hispanic Center 2009c, e.

The most striking aspect in the above quote is the operational definition of a "youth gang" used for the purposes of the survey.[8] Unsettling is the vague and often contradictory data. The trend data show that Latino youth in 1996 constituted about 45 percent of all gang members, and in 2006, Latinos were reported to represent 49.5 percent of all reported youth gang members. Approximately 731,000 gang members in over 21,500 gangs were estimated to be active in the United States in 2002. This latter figure reflects that a gang is defined as three or more individuals with a name, some form of identity, style of clothing, graffiti, and hand signs. Conflicting data are presented in the report. For example, 29 percent of the agencies reported that on average the majority of identified gang members were neither Latino nor NHB. Several patterns are reported from 2002–2008: prevalence rates of youth gang problems remained high in the largest cities; reports of gang presence increased steadily in suburban counties and smaller cities, and then decreased between 2007–2008; and little change is observed in gang-problem prevalence rates for rural areas where less than 5 percent of the total number of gang members are located (USDJ 2010). In large cities, half or more of the reported young gang members remained in the gang for less than one year, and older youth (18+ years) are remaining for longer periods. The report states that in the absence of viable social and economic opportunities (e.g., employment) the upper age limit of gang membership is extended (USDJ 2006, 20). Focused concentration in poor, racial/ethnic inner-city communities characterizes this report. Yet the ambiguous definition of gang membership seems to mark as dangerous a whole racial/ethnic community on state enforcement definitions of three or more individuals constituting a gang. These definitions are then implemented based on the perception and social constructions of law enforcement officials and geographic region (Durán 2009).

In a large survey of middle school students across eleven large cities among reported gang members, 25 percent were Latino, 31 percent were NHB, and 25 percent were NHW. Among these gang members, 10–20 percent are reported to be females, which inflates the reported 3 percent of female gang

8. Conflicting definitions of the term *gang* exist. The U.S. Department of Justice *defines* the term *gang* as "an ongoing group, club, organization, or association of five or more persons: (A) that has as one of its primary purposes the commission of one or more of the criminal offenses described in subsection (c); (B) the members of which engage, or have engaged within the past five years, in a continuing series of offenses described in subsection (c); and (C) the activities of which affect interstate or foreign commerce" (18 USC § 521[a]).

Current federal law *describes* the term *gang crime* as: "(1) A federal felony involving a controlled substance (as defined in Section 102 of the Controlled Substances Act (21 USC § 802)) for which the maximum penalty is not less than five years. (2) A federal felony crime of violence that has as an element the use or attempted use of physical force against the person of another. (3) A conspiracy to commit an offense described in paragraph (1) or (2)" (18 USC § 521[c]). For more information see http://www.nationalgangcenter.gov/Survey-Analysis.

members in 2001 (Bender 2003, 38). Further the PEW study reports that a minuscule number of Latino girls are gang members (Fry 2009). The conclusion is that considerable variation was observed across the sites and that "site selection shapes the image of gangs and gang members; they are a reflection of their communities" (Esbensen and Lynskey 2001).

Interrogating these figures is important. Robert Duràn (2009) observes:

> The majority of gang members across the United States have been racially and ethnically identified by police officers as Latino (47 percent) or African American (31 percent) and they have been mostly poor (85 percent). Self-reported data indicate that Whites identify as gang members at a higher rate than is captured by police data. Many states legally define gangs as three or more people engaged in criminal activity individually or collectively. This neutral definition has resulted in an application of the label to people who are considered non-white (144).

The social construction of gang membership is closely linked with poverty. As I discussed at the beginning of this chapter, the moral construction of poverty is associated with the negative identity marker of criminality, delinquency, and dangerousness or the "racial/ethnic minority threat." This representation of Mexican Americans predominantly in Los Angeles, Chicago, and other large urban areas represents a historical marker of lawlessness. As Steven Bender (2003) recounts the legal legacy of Latinos, he states: "The current legal standards applicable to racial profiling by government do not sufficiently discourage these law enforcement practices—enough leeway resides in present law to disguise profiling or, in some circumstances, to rely explicitly on racial and ethnic profiles to justify interrogatory steps" (53). Bender provides the example of the 1855 California Vagrancy Act, popularly known as the Greaser Act, and notes "the racist potential of this early anti-loitering law survives today in loitering, anti-gang, anti-day laborer, and curfew statues and ordinances that are racially neutral on their face yet give law enforcement officials great discretion in their application" (55). Contemporary studies document the persistent practices of marking Latino youth as dangerous to the social order.

Duràn (2009) illustrates the application of police discretion in poor communities. In an ethnographic study over a five-year period of Mexican American communities in Ogden, Utah, and Denver, Colorado, he explored the gang suppression model and how it becomes practiced in the profiling and interactions between police and inner-city Mexican Americans. His findings showed that the actual practice of gang enforcement included: (1) racialized profiles, (2) fabricated intelligence, and (3) suppression of marginalized communities (163). The author concludes that young, poor Mexican American boys and men are perceived as a threat for gang membership and that "structurally vulnerable areas become targeted with concentrated aggressive gang enforcement that supported gang assumptions and fueled moral panic by labeling non-gang members as gang members (ecological containment)" (164).

In addition, observations revealed that Whites were treated more leniently by police and that vigorous "lock-up" (prison) approaches remained the key action of police departments, particularly in large cities with a gang problem (Duràn 2009). Labeling and time spent in juvenile justice facilities and/or prisons have serious life course consequences for a group of young boys and men who already have economic and educational disadvantage stacked against them. The "lock-up" approach channels many Latino youth into the juvenile justice system (153). Two major events have contributed to the increase in the incarceration rates of Latinos compared to Whites: (1) the intentional and punitive laws in the 1990s; and (2) gang definitions and policy, surveillance, and racial profiling in poor, Latino communities. Victor Rios (2009b) describes that "the development of punitive juvenile justice policy in the 1990's was influenced by racialized constructions of Black and Latino youth as "super predators" by intellectuals, politicians and the media" (101).

### Juvenile Justice: Latino Overrepresentation

Hispanics are most often classified by the juvenile justice system as Whites, with 92 percent of Hispanic juveniles being classified as White.[9] Villarruel and Walker (2002) found that inaccuracies in the reporting of Latinos as Whites contribute to Latinos being undercounted. Lack of racial and ethnic identifiers in federal and state corrections data systems continue to make Latinos an invisible group in the prison population (Community Service Society 2008). Census data indicate that about 3 percent of young U.S.–born Hispanic males and 2 percent of foreign-born Hispanic males were incarcerated in 2008 compared to 1 percent of young White males and 7 percent of Black males. About 70 percent of U.S.–born Latinos are placed in local and state correctional facilities, while 70 percent of Latinos in federal facilities are non–U.S.-born Latinos. Since 1970 incarceration rates have increased from 1.5 percent to 3.1 percent for native born and from 1.5 percent to 2.1 percent for foreign-born Latinos (Pew Hispanic Center 2009d, 87–88).

9. The U.S. Department of Justice does not regularly maintain data for prison inmates by race and ethnicity in local and state correctional facilities. However, special reports on local jail inmates from 2002 and state prison inmates in 1991 provide some insight on Latino representation in these facilities. Since the U.S. Marshall Service (USMS) reports arrest data by race only, percentage of Latinos arrested by the USMS for drugs is not available. Villarruel and Walker (2002) found that juveniles at the federal prison level were overcounted in the White race category with 58 percent of the inmates being classified as White, but when ethnicity was controlled for, only 31 percent of the juvenile prison population was White.

Latino youth who enter the juvenile justice system are less likely to be high school graduates, more likely to be poor, more likely to live in urban neighborhoods that are not "neighborhoods of opportunity," and more likely to be under surveillance by law enforcement personnel. As observed the zero tolerance policy and surveillance of the school that the youth attends also increases his/her probability of incarceration. In addition, these youth come from families who lack the resources to provide extracurricular activities and opportunities that keep youth actively engaged in educational and labor market experiences and deter youth from becoming involved with the juvenile justice system (Arboleda 2002; Acevedo-Garcia et al. 2008). Racial profiling and racial stereotypes that infer that all Latinos are gang members and are more likely to commit crimes than other groups increase the arrest and conviction rates of Latino youth (Durán 2009; Rios 2006). The following quote from a nineteen-year-old Latino speaks to this disproportionate rate and racial profiling that contributes to higher incarceration rates for Latino youth:

> I heard a lot of friends from around here say "Maybe you should let the White guy drive because the police will pull you over and search your car." I've been searched twice…and they put me in handcuffs.…and put me on the sidewalk and didn't find anything and let me go. (Pew Hispanic Center 2009d, 88)

## Trends in Incarceration Rates and Unequal Treatment

Once Latinos enter the juvenile justice system, there is also evidence that they do not receive the same treatment as NHWs. From 1985 to 2001, the number of youth in detention centers doubled. Latino youth are three times more likely than NHW youth to be incarcerated (Hinton Hoytt et al. 2002a). In 1985, NHW youth were detained at the rate of 45 per 100,000, while NHB and Hispanic rates were 114 and 73, respectively. By 1995, detention rates for NHWs had decreased by 13 percent, while the rates for NHBs (180 percent increase) and Hispanics (140 percent increase) had skyrocketed (Wordes and Jones 1998). For example, in Texas for the years 2002 to 2003, the number of prisoners under eighteen more than doubled (112 percent increase) (USDJ 2004a). Nationally 190 out of every 100,000 NHW juveniles were in custody in a juvenile facility compared to 348 out of every 100,000 Latino youth and 754 out of every 100,000 NHB juveniles (Snyder and Sickmund 2006). In a thirty-six state study on disposition of cases, three findings are important. Latino admission rates to custody after being found guilty were thirteen times higher than for NHW youth for drug offenses, five times higher than the admission rate for Whites for violent offenses, and twice the rate of White admission for property offenses. Second, Latino youth (average 305 days) were more likely to serve longer sentences than NHB youth (average 254 days) and NHW youth (average 193 days). Third, Latino youth were treated more harshly for the same crime (Villarruel and Walker 2002).

The increased racial profiling of girls in low-income communities coupled with a lack of economic resources to retain private counsel results in many girls being sentenced to adult prison without going through the juvenile system first (Gaarder and Belknap 2002). Although the data on Latinas suggest that girls are experiencing similar aggressive racial profiling and law enforcement "lock-up" approaches, although the percent is very small, social science researchers unfortunately have begun to focus on girls as deviant gang members.[10] In fact, many of these boys and girls are not gang members but are perceived as a threat to the social order (Rios 2009b). Laurie Schaffner (2009) in her study of Latina adolescents in juvenile detention, many of whom were first- or second generation, describes the girls' background:

> Similar to other reports reflecting the troubled lives of detained young women, the youth who participated in this research came from depleted and disadvantaged backgrounds: 58 percent had already dropped out of school; 46 percent reported having experienced some form of physical abuse; 40 percent reported sexual harm due to interpersonal violence; and 83 percent claimed to self-medicate or were substance-dependent. (117)

For both males and females, high poverty rates, lack of adequate education and recreational activities, perceived and actual gang involvement by law enforcement, depression, and discriminatory judicial practices are all factors that contribute to the overrepresentation of Latino youth in the juvenile justice system and in local and state corrections systems (Arboleda 2002; Driscoll 1999; Davalos et al. 2005).

This unprecedented increase in Latino youth and immigrant imprisonment, also part of what is referred to as the "prison-industrial complex," (D. Hernández 2009, 43), has been of concern to social scientists, community activists, and families of these youth (Cartagena 2009; Oboler 2009). For example, questions of how masculinity is informed in prison systems are important. Victor Rios (2009a) examines how policing, incarceration, and probation offer "masculinity making resources" that confer on a prison inmate or ex-inmate permanent criminal credentials that virtually close off options for participation

---

10. Research on Latino women in prison is important. In the edited volume by Oboler (2009), two articles—one by Juanita Díaz-Cotto, Chicana(o) Prisoners: Ethical and Methodological Considerations, Collaborative Research Methods, and Case Studies, and the other by B. V. Olguín, Toward a Pinta(o) Human Rights? New and Old Strategies for Chicana(o) Research Activism—propose approaches for the study of race, ethnicity, and gender in penal studies.

in the labor market and the "development of a specific set of gendered practices (response to police treatment and institutional racism with a tough front of physical aggression and hypermasculinity), heavily influenced by interactions with police, detention facilities, and probation officers" (151).The author concludes that "gender is one of the processes by which the criminal justice system is involved in the reproduction of inequality" (160–161). These gender processes are inserted into the lives of youth who have already experienced by virtue of their circumstances, poverty and at every stage of their interaction with public systems, unfair treatment and inadequate quality of services. As discussed in previous chapters, these life experiences contribute to a sense of hopelessness and depression associated with suicide attempts and undetected emotional and behavioral conditions such as attention deficit hyperactivity disorder (ADHD) that are exacerbated by incarceration (Canino and Roberts 2001). Unfortunately juvenile arrests most likely contribute to future imprisonment. The Department of Justice estimates that the lifetime chances of a person going to prison are higher for NHBs (19 percent) and Latinos (10 percent) than for NHWs (3 percent), with an estimated 17 percent of all Latino males likely to enter state or federal prison during their lifetime compared to 6 percent of NHW males and 32 percent of NHB males (USDJ 2000).

## Local and State Correctional Facilities

For young adult Latinos the probability of serving time in a detention center or local prison is highly associated with (1) parental economic resources and levels of knowledge regarding legal rights, (2) inadequate legal representation because most public defenders are overburdened with cases and are unable to prepare a strong defense or an appeal, and (3) the judicial representatives' perception of Latino youth as gang members and a threat to society, so that judges are less likely to approve their release. Those who serve time in state and local correctional facilities tend to be less educated than those convicted and incarcerated by the federal prison system. In 2002, the Department of Justice reported that while 27 percent of federal inmates had obtained some high school or less, this was the highest level of education attained by 40 percent of state inmates and 47 percent of local jail inmates. Latinos (53 percent) were the largest group of state prison inmates who had not earned a high school diploma or a GED compared to 27 percent of NHWs and 44 percent of NHBs. Those inmates whose families had received welfare or lived in public housing represented about 41 percent of the state inmates and were most likely to not have completed high school (47 percent) than those whose families did not receive these public services (35 percent) (USDJ 2003a, b). In 2002, 30 percent of local jail inmates reported they were not employed before their arrest, and of those that were employed approximately 40 percent reported their income was less than $1,000 a month (USDJ 2004b).

In 2003, nearly 60 percent of persons in local jails were racial/ethnic minorities: 15 percent were Hispanic and 40 percent were Black. In state jails in 1991, racial/ethnic minorities were more sharply overrepresented, with 65 percent being non-White inmates (USDJ 1997; USDJ 2004b). States with highest Latino populations are also the states with the highest prison populations: Texas, California, Florida, and New York (USDJ 2004a). Among prisoners who are not U.S. citizens, 62 percent are held in state prisons and 38 percent are held in federal facilities. On a state level, noncitizens composed 12 percent of prisoners in California, 6 percent of those in Texas, 12 percent of those in New York, and 6 percent of those in Florida (USDJ 2004a).

Table 8.5 displays national data on percent of inmates by race and ethnicity and offense in local and state prisons for the year 2002. Whites are slightly more likely to have prior offenses and to be charged with violent, property, and public disorder offenses. Blacks are more likely to be charged with violent offenses and drug charges at both local and state levels. Latinos are most likely to be in state and local prisons for drug charges but least likely to have prior offenses.

The encounters with the criminal justice system that lead up to incarceration, such as arrest and pretrial detainment, have important impacts on incarceration rates. Hispanics experience multiple disadvantages associated with incarceration. Hispanic defendants are 25 percent *less likely* than non-Hispanic defendants to be released before trial (22.7 percent compared to 63.1 percent), substantially *more likely* to be detained before trial than non-Hispanics (90.6 percent compared to 53.5 percent), and *least likely* of all groups to have a criminal history (56.6 percent compared to 75 percent and 60.6 percent for Blacks and Whites, respectively) (Arboleda 2002). Even though Hispanics are *slightly less likely* to be drug users than non-Hispanics (10.1 percent of Hispanics as compared to 10.9 percent of NHBs and 11.2 percent of NHWs), they are *highly likely* to be convicted for drug offenses and the *least likely* to be convicted for violent offenses (42.6 percent of drug-offenders were Latinos and only 9.5 percent of offenders convicted for violent offenses were Hispanic). For those convicted of violent offenses, Latinos served sentences that were fourteen months longer among those with the same offense. Latinos and NHBs (27 percent) were more likely than NHWs (22 percent) to be serving time for violent offenses and drug offenses (31 percent of NHBs and 28 percent of Latinos compared to 19 percent of NHWs) (USDJ 2004a). These data do not suggest that Latinos and NHBs commit these crimes more often than NHWs but show that they are more likely to be racially profiled, arrested, incarcerated, and serve time for committing these crimes than their NHW counterparts.

**Table 8.5.** Profile of Jail Inmates by Offense and Race and Ethnicity, 2002

| | Violent | | Property | | Drug | | Public order | | Percent with prior offenses |
| | Local prison | State prison | Local | State | Local prison | State prison | Local | State | Local |
|---|---|---|---|---|---|---|---|---|---|
| Non-Hispanic White | 22% | 49% | 28 | 30 | 19 | 12 | 31 | 8 | 61 |
| Non-Hispanic Black | 27 | 47 | 24 | 22 | 31 | 25 | 18 | 5 | 58 |
| Latino | 27 | 39 | 18 | 21 | 28 | 33 | 28 | 8 | 51 |

*Source:* U.S. Department of Justice 2004b.

## Federal Prison

U.S. federal law enforcement agencies including Customs and Border Protection, Drug Enforcement Agency, Federal Bureau of Prisons, Marshall Services, Federal Bureau of Investigation, and Customs and Immigration Enforcement arrested suspects for violations of federal laws (violent offenses, property damage, theft, immigration, drug, weapons, and other illegal acts) (USDJ 2003a). Those in federal prison tend to be more educated than those in state and local prisons, with approximately 50 percent of them having a high school diploma (27 percent) or a postsecondary degree (24 percent) (USDJ 2003b). These data generally represent NHW with drug offenses, professional corporate, and "white collar" inmates, while most Latinos in federal prison are incarcerated for immigration violations. In 2003, noncitizens of the United States comprised 23 percent of all inmates held in federal prisons.

Table 8.6 displays federal prison inmate population by offense and race and ethnicity. In 2003, similar to 2006, Latinos represented 32 percent of the federal prison population, compared to 39 percent of NHBs and 58 percent of NHWs (USDJ 2003a, 2007). Latinos were the largest group serving time for immigration offenses (90 percent), the least serious offense. Latinos were the *least* likely compared to NHBs and NHWs to be serving time for violent offenses (USDJ 2003a). Latinos are *more likely* to be federal prison inmates than inmates in state facilities due to the high rate of immigration and drug cases that are handled by the Federal agencies (USDJ 2000; Pew Hispanic Center 2009). For Latinos, increased arrests are most likely associated with renewed anti-immigrant policies in the twenty-first century.

In 2003, Latinos constituted 33 percent of federal inmates serving time for drug charges, compared to 54 percent of NHWs and 46 percent of NHBs.

**Table 8.6.** Profile of Federal Prison Inmates by Offense and Race and Ethnicity, September 2003

| Race | All offenses | Violent | Fraudulent | Drug | Weapon | Immigration |
|------|------|------|------|------|------|------|
| White | 58 | 45 | 63 | 54 | 43 | 95 |
| Black | 39 | 43 | 34 | 45 | 55 | 4 |
| Latino | 32 | 7 | 13 | 33 | 10 | 90 |
| Asian | 1 | 1 | 3 | 1 | 1 | 0.4 |

*Source:* U.S. Department of Justice 2003a, table 7.10.

During October 2002 to September 2003, most arrests for drug charges were made by the Drug Enforcement Administration (DEA) and the U.S. Marshall Service (USMS). The majority of arrestees for drugs were NHW (70 percent) and Latinos (43 percent), with NHBs (28 percent) being least likely to be arrested by the DEA. Noteworthy, 40 percent of drug arrests made by the DEA were in Texas (12 percent), California (11 percent), Florida (11 percent), and New York (7 percent)—all states that are heavily populated by Latinos. Among the federal prison population, about 97 percent of NHWs were arrested for drugs and about 4 percent of NHBs for immigration violations (USDJ 2003a). Approximately 90 percent of those serving a sentence for federal immigration offenses are Latino. Yet 95 percent of those Latinos are racially classified as White, which underestimates the way that immigration policy and the criminal justice system are adversely affecting the Latino community (USDJ 2003a).

In summary, the overrepresentation of NHBs and Latinos at all levels of the prison system have contributed to considerable concern, and increasing scholarship has emerged on the prison-industrial complex that seeks to unveil the forces of structural inequality for low-income, historically underrepresented groups and the institutional practices used to exclude marginalized and immigrant groups (see Oboler 2009). Petit apartheid[11] has been used to explain racial profiling in the war against drugs, regulating and policing public spaces, underrepresentation of persons of color in law enforcement, and the use of racial derogation in prosecutors' closing arguments (Romero 2006; Martinez 2007). The investment in a prison-industrial complex is a macro-aggression toward Latino and NHB communities. The critical question is why has society not invested in community and neighborhood development and human capital to improve the material conditions and expand the economic and social opportunity structure to Latino and NHB communities? The overwhelming

---

11. *Petit apartheid* refers to the hidden, informal types of racial bias that permeate various stages of the criminal justice system. Notably, these informal practices are not included in most evaluations of racial discrimination. For more information see *Petit Apartheid in the U.S. Criminal Justice System: The Dark Figure of Racism* by Dragan Milovanovic and Katheryn K. Russell-Brown (2001, Durham: Carolina Academic Press), which offers the first detailed consideration of petit apartheid through a series of essays by criminal justice experts.

majority of youth and adults (male and female) who enter the juvenile and correctional systems were born into distressed communities.

~

Historical moral constructions of poverty and their intersection with race and Hispanic ethnicity have driven the development, implementation, and quality of U.S. public service systems. These stratification systems are characterized by disinvestments in poor and racial/ethnic communities, and in the last two decades by more restrictive and discriminatory polices including PROWRA, the Violent Youth Predator Act, and federal and state immigration policies. Public service systems reinforce those very moral hegemonic constructions of poverty that both create the material and social conditions of poverty and develop punitive public systems to maintain the poor and marginalized outside the social, economic, and civic opportunity structure. These institutional practices are then justified by mainstream narratives about individual, cultural, or racial/ethnic irresponsibility.

Several observations emerge from these data. First, being poor and a racial/ethnic minority is a negative identity marker that places a person at risk of interacting with public service systems at multiple stages of their life course. These systems predominantly serve the same populations, and thus individuals often have crossovers into different parts of the public systems throughout their life course. Second, the public service system does not often serve as a safety or support net for poor people to promote economic self-sufficiency and social mobility. The intergenerational cycle of poverty is more often a reflection of structural failure than individual or family failure. Structural processes of inequality include the provision of unfair and inequitable access to quality services, such as schools and housing, and the use of disciplinary power by bureaucratic guardians who often embrace a hegemonic view of the poor as deviant and representing a "culture of irresponsibility," requiring social containment and control.

Third, neighborhoods are the locus of control where issues of social inequality and citizenship rights are inextricably linked to disciplinary power that maintains low-income families in marginalized social locations. Neighborhoods are where federal and state policies such as school enforcement, law enforcement, and immigration policies are most likely to target community members. For example, the trajectory from racial profiling, to policing strategies in low-income neighborhoods, to incarceration and probation has serious consequences for Latino youth and adults in every domain of their life. For low-income Latino youth and their families, inadequate neighborhood resources, low-quality public systems, and a mutually constituted negative Latino identity marker projected by media sensationalism that makes visible predominantly only foreignness, gang membership, and pregnancy forecloses access to the economic opportunity structure and reinforces inequality on a daily basis.

# 9

# Persistent Images and Changing Perceptions in the Twenty-First Century

> In short, the U.S. political experience, viewed
> historically, has been far more concerned with finding
> means to exclude and discourage many groups from
> civic engagement and political participation than with
> promoting inclusion and encouraging engagement
> and participation. At every level of U.S. government,
> groups have had unequal access to participation and
> power within civil society itself. Throughout U.S.
> history the concept of democracy as an inclusive process
> has been contradicted by policies of racial exclusion.
> —Gerstle 2001, 319

The gaze of the media is powerful. It tells us what to believe and transmits images and messages as indisputable truth. The media has not been an ally of Latinos, and less so of racialized, low-income Latinos (Subervi-Veléz et al. 1994). Rather, media has historically, and to the present, made visible Latinidad as a negative identity marker and maintained invisible Latinidad as a rich and diverse group of U.S. citizens. Latinos have persistently been depicted as alien, different, backward, and resistant to modernization. Patricia Hill Collins (2000) has explained these representations as a result of hegemonic power, which refers to the cultural ideologies, images, and representations that both shape group and individual consciousness and justify policies and practices in the structural and disciplinary domains. She argues that through the manipulation of this dominant ideology, social institutions use disciplinary power as exemplified through organizational practices such as racial profiling of alleged gang youth that impact the everyday experiences of racialized people in the United States (284). This ideology is consistently reinforced through media and social science research that influences the ways that Latinos are viewed and depicted in the society at large and the expectations associated with these depictions (Dávila 2001; Bender 2003). Intersectional analyses challenge us to interrogate those ideologies and representations, to locate and uncover their origins and multiple meanings, and to examine the reasons for their existence and persistence. A substantial body of evidence calls into question the role of the media and social institutions in promoting negative stereotypes of Latinos.

Dominant representations of Latinos build on and elaborate ideas, images, and stereotypes that are deeply rooted in U.S. history and become the rationale for the differential treatment of groups and individuals (Portes 2000; Bender 2003). Stereotypes and generalizations occur along the dimensions of power, strength, competence, prestige, and numeric size and are deeply embedded in the historical modes of incorporation into a society. Given the history of conquest and colonialism of Mexican-origin peoples and Puerto Ricans, these stereotypes reflect and reinforce images of subordination and incompetence as shown in a group's ability to fully embrace dominant Western cultural values and behavior. In effect, these images are represented through the media as Latinos are often portrayed as accented "foreigners," aberrant in their lack of English, and the women as overly emotional and highly fertile, the men as handsome and hypersexualized.

In this chapter, I provide a mere glimpse into the nature of these representations and provide examples of selected scholars who have questioned the social and political ideologies behind these practices. I give a brief overview of the links between social science knowledge production and media representations and its antecedent role in maintaining and promoting the discourse and visibility of Latino negative identity as a homogeneous foreign group. Further the images and representations of Latinos in varied mass media illuminates the underlying dynamic that has contributed to a persistent cultural production of images of Latinos as a singular and unacculturated group. Interrogating these stereotypic representations challenges the essentializing of U.S. Latino groups. Lastly, I present a portrait of Latino markers of integration and economic success that remain invisible in the U.S. public imagination. Extensive data are available that show that Latinos have achieved economic success and wealth asset markers as shown by rates of home ownership, rates of civic and voting participation, political representation at local, state, and federal levels, and intergenerational differences in values and behaviors that are associated with increased education. The new discourse on Latinos has convincingly shown that family socioeconomic position (SEP), geographic and national origin, and prior experiences in both countries of origin and the United States all shape Latinidad and its social location in the United States. These trends refute the discourse on Latinos as a static, unacculturated, immigrant group and unveil the role of dominant hegemonic ideology in infusing the American public imagination with biased and distorted representations.

I make two major arguments regarding hegemonic images of Latinos. First, these cultural representations are laden with political and social meaning fulfilling the hegemonic ideology of a particular historical moment and the need for group subordination. Second, dominant–subordinate power relations and social control are inherently linked to the representational practices of Latinos in the United States. The most damaging aspects of media representations are that it misinforms the public, contributes to unfair and discriminatory public policies, and denies Latino families and communities, especially children and youth, their history and positive images and role models for their growth and development. The dominant discourse on negative identity markers requires transformation as U.S. Latino groups embrace and strive for privileges of citizenship such as improved material conditions and fair employment and housing practices.

### Popular Images and Representations of Latino Men and Women

An important mechanism for socialization in any society is the media and how television, film, books, and magazines represent different members of society. In other words, what do the powerful look like? What are the privileges of the powerful? Who are the contributors to the making of this great nation? What are the characteristics of the powerful, and who are the beneficiaries of the economic and social privileges accorded in U.S. society? Visual and textual images represent ideas and attributes of groups that become ingrained in public attitudes and contribute to the conscious and unconscious perpetuation of the myths that infuse hegemonic thought. Channels of communication—such as newspapers, magazines, social science research, and news media—influence public opinion and in turn public policy (Bender 2003). In many instances, the output of social science knowledge is appropriated and translated through the eyes of representatives of the media, popular magazines, and news stories as cultural artifacts of Latino family life.

The Latino intellectual community has responded in two ways: one is to challenge the persistent negative identity marker of Latinidad in the media, and the second is to resist the persistent degradation of the culture as backward, particularly with respect to gender representations. Cultural stereotypes have persisted for the Latino population as a whole, with distinct cultural attributions by gender. *Stereotypes* are social constructions that are strongly interconnected with race, ethnicity, gender, and socioeconomic status and are embedded in historical contexts. For example, Debra Merskin (2007), in her analysis of the role of Gabrielle Solis (played by Eva Longoria) in the popular network television show *Desperate Housewives,* provides a profound critique of mass media and its insistence on reproducing stereotypes of the "Hot Latina." The major argument is that mass media produces stereotypes to maintain White/Anglo racial superiority, and these hegemonic social control tools are psychological and require the consent of those ruled. Merskin posits: "Consent is evident in the normalization of stereotypical, one-dimensional representations that under other circumstances would seem at the least, inappropriate if not all together harmful and misleading" (135).

For Latinos the striking persistence of negative stereotypes is notable. As noted by Steven Bender (2003):

> Historically, while negative stereotypes have centered on Mexicans and Mexican Americans, over time these same stereotypes have encompassed other Latino groups, particularly Puerto Ricans and Cuban Americans. A 1949 study of American attitudes found that Puerto Ricans were viewed as extremely promiscuous, that "the men carry knives and use them unrestrainedly, that all Puerto Ricans are ignorant and stupid because they do not speak English." (13–14)

Sociologists and media, legal, and popular culture scholars have investigated the long-standing stereotypes of Latinos in Hollywood, the marketing of the image of the Latino, and the intersection of these representations and the treatment of Latinos in society. For an excellent review of the historical to contemporary development of mainstream media forms and their treatment of Hispanics, see Federico Subervi-Vélez (1994). For example, Clara Rodríguez (2004) conducted historical analyses of Latinos in Hollywood from the early 1900s to the early twenty-first century to "build a new awareness of Latino culture and history as part of the full range of diversity in the United States" (v). The author embeds the role of Latino actors in film in the economic and political climate of the era and seeks to intersect film literature and racial/ ethnic literature. Her three major findings are: (1) Latino history in Hollywood has been both "glorious and problematic" in that a few Latino actors were successful yet many had to change their names (e.g., Raquel Welch, born Jo Raquel Tejada) and many others were excluded or played minimal roles (x); (2) despite demographic increases, Latinos still remain severely underrepresented in film and in prime-time television; and (3) stereotypic characterizations of the male "Latin lover" and exoticized, eroticized females still prevail. Rodríguez summarizes the compelling effects of these stereotypes: "Despite the increase in the number of actors, and in portrayals in central and starring roles, many observers are left wondering: Where are the Latinas who are intelligent, accomplished, and powerful in areas other than sex?" (243).

Another focus of research has been the marketing of these stereotypes and the faces behind the representations of Latinos. In an in-depth study of popular culture and media, Arlene Dávila (2001) explores the social, political, and cultural dynamics affecting the representation of Latinos and the pitfalls of Latinidad. She uncovers that the owners of Spanish-media channels are predominantly Latin American and Cuban who perceive their marketing as cultural productions to reinforce the central values of the Latino culture of language, family, and children and that promote racial and ethnic hierarchies, most specifically by privileging whiteness (168). The media market develops a transnational cultural production that is developed for both U.S. Latino and Latin American audiences but inevitably leaves "little space for material that fully addresses U.S. Latinas' concerns and sensibilities, particularly regarding issues of race and gender" (162). The major arguments presented in this media market discourse are that ethnic markets are designed to commodify ethnic identity and authenticate and reinforce cultural difference between Latinos and a larger hegemonic American culture. Dávila (2001) observes:

> One underlying assumption of ethnic marketing is that each group has a distinct, identifiable culture that is unique, bounded, and separate from United States culture, this is simultaneously constructed as homogeneous, and mainstream. Thus the ethnic media selectively "cleanses" ethnic constructs by embracing affluence, authenticity, "coming of age" and cosmopolitanism and in the process erases the realities of the Latino groups such as racism and poverty. (234–35)

Ethnic media also maintains Spanish in its "purest" form so as not to taint the culture and to maintain separateness from U.S. "Spanglish"-speaking Latinos (237). Raquel Rivera's (2002) work confirms the suppression of English as part of the American context to define Latinos as foreign subjects. She discusses how the music industry overlooks English-language music by New York Puerto Rican rappers. Complex discourses occur regarding English use as an Anglocentric or African American creative expression without inserting the distinct cultural identity of second- and third-generation Puerto Ricans who are English dominant.

Another important dimension of the ethnic marketing is a staunch focus on family values. Hispanics have been marked as the most family-oriented, most brand loyal, most religious, and most rapidly growing minority group. Ethnic marketing strives to highlight these qualities for all racial/ethnic marginalized groups: Dávila (2001) provides an answer to the *why* ethnic marketing is necessary. She states:

> It is not surprising given that the family values and morality of minority populations have historically been under scrutiny by the dominant culture as compelling proofs of their stability and worthiness as targets of advertising compared to their White consumer. United States minorities are all subject to stereotyping as low-income, unskilled, uneducated, crime-ridden, unemployed, and in some cases perpetual foreigners, and, whether more or less family oriented or brand loyal than other market segments, they are always required to prove their worth and compensate for their tainted image. (217)

In contrast, English-speaking media reinforce the negative cultural aspects by distinct characterizations of Latinos as lazy, criminal, drunkard men and willing, sexually available Mexican and Puerto Rican women, who are overly fertile and welfare-driven (Gutierrez 2008; Lopez 2009). English-speaking media has a long and destructive history of dehumanizing and exploiting Latino subjects for entertainment (Bender 2003, 64–75). The history of "Latin" images in the public imagination can be traced back to Latina performers such as Lupe Velez (1920/1930s), Carmen Miranda (1940/1950s), and Rita Moreno (1960/1970s). These women represented a form of racialized gender and hyper-Latinidad that attached a certain level of excessiveness or exoticism that continues to represent Latinas in the contemporary era as melodramatic, promiscuous, and gaudy along with other excessive traits (Rodríguez 2004). Consensus among scholars is that negative and culture-bound representations dismiss within- and across-group differences and formulate a static national identity of Hispanicity while simultaneously promoting negative stereotypes by gender.

Print media (popular and text books, magazines, and other literary works) have a strong influence on Latino children and youth's self-identity and self-esteem. Invisibility in print media combined with negative images in entertainment media negatively influences the perceptions of Latino youth as a group. Several studies have examined print media to assess the quantity and quality of representation of Latinos. Data show that Latinos were featured disproportionately (2–3 percent) below their national representation. The omission conveys to students the message that their ancestors are not part of U.S. history and that Latinos have not played an important role or made significant contributions to the United States (Barry 1998; Cruz 2002). The underrepresentation of Latinos as contributors to society in print media is further undermined by the inclusion of problematic stereotypical images whereby Latinos and Latin Americans are depicted as siesta-takers, lustful Latin lovers, or violent people (Cruz 2002). Charles Weaver (2005) examines how the perceptions of Hispanic Americans have changed over time, drawing from the National Opinion Research Survey conducted from 1990 to 2000. The results show that perceptions of Latinos regarding wealth, work ethic, and intelligence have improved substantially, but there was no change in their image of proneness to violence. Perhaps a more startling finding is that Latinos in the United States themselves did not perceive any change in how they were viewed in any of the categories! These findings suggest that media representations erode the self-confidence of the Latino community in themselves as individuals and in their group.

The strongest critique of media representations in popular culture is the commodification of the bodies of Latinas in culturally scripted gender roles. In a study conducted with Latino women about the role of women in *telenovelas* (Latino soap operas), respondents perceived the *telenovelas* as reinforcing language and culture of origin, and reminded them of the centrality of religion and family that helped them sustain their own traditions. The respondents also reported that Spanish media naturalized their lives as an everyday, normal part of life in contrast to mainstream U.S. programming that infrequently depicts Latino life. However, the respondents wanted to see powerful female characters in the Spanish media instead of *mujer sufrida* (suffering women) who are represented as dependent on men, long-suffering, and submissive (Barrera and Bielby 2001).

In another study, Viviana Rojas (2004) asks: How do Latinos consume popular television culture? The author interviewed twenty-seven immigrant and U.S.–born Latino women in Texas to understand the ways they perceive women's representations in English- and Spanish-media programming. The respondents critiqued the lack of inclusion of U.S.–born Latinos in Spanish-language media. Middle-class Latinas critiqued the construction of Latino cultural unity as a popular depiction of working poor Latinos and limited representation of middle-class Latino families in English-speaking media. Respondents were also highly critical of the commodification and oversexualizing of Latinas (e.g., Univision and Telemundo). Rojas (2004) reports that many women reported feeling attacked, insulted, offended, and embarrassed. Further they observed the "whiteness and blondness" of the hosts of popular Spanish-language television shows in contrast to English-speaking media.

Social constructions in popular culture have traditionally used symbolic images such as nation, beauty, and sexuality to portray Latino women (Rodriguez 2000, Molina Guzmán 2006). Isabel Molina Guzmán and Angharad Valdivia (2004) examine the politics of representation surrounding three "hypercommodified Latinas" (Jennifer Lopez, Frida Kahlo, and Salma Hayek). The authors argue that visual and narrative tropes attached with female Latinidad are couched in the ideological processes of engendering and racialization of Latinas who fall outside the confines of racialized whiteness and blackness. Yet these three women with ambiguous racial identities become the symbols of female Latinidad globally to the exclusion of the Black Latina as a public representation of Latinidad (Quiñones Rivera 2006). In contrast, Spanish media has centered visual and narrative tropes attached specifically to White female Latinidad. In this brief overview, the complexity of media and its representations are not fully explored. However, Rojas (2004) argues that these images disempower, subject viewers to ethnic subordination, and produce class and ethnic divisions among Latinos. The strong awareness of the detrimental effects of these images are illustrated in the anthology *Latino/a Popular Culture* by Michelle Habell-Pallán and Mary Romero (2002). The authors provide critical analyses of different forms of popular culture domains with the "fervent hope that collections such as this one will challenge social inequality, marginalization, and cultural denigration that continue to exist in the economic, political and cultural spheres" (16).

## Impact on Communities, Youth, and Women

Television and print news media build on hegemonic conceptualizations of Latinos that draw from historical perceptions, individual cognitive social worlds, and social science. Since Latino youth are the most frequent consumers of media (close to four hours per day), Rocia Rivadeneyra and Monique Ward (2005) conducted a study of 186 high school students in Los Angeles (mean age=16.3 years) to assess their attitudes about traditional gender roles. They hypothesized that Latino youth were most vulnerable to absorbing narrow definitions of gender roles due to amount of TV (English and Spanish media) consumption. Adolescent Latinas who watched the most TV were more likely to express traditional gender roles, which suggests how media representations powerfully affect girls' view of available gender role options. Extending the findings of the study, Molina Guzmán (2006) explores the relationship among media texts, culture, power, and discursive formation of identity. She argues that popular representations of Latinidad occur on multiple levels and sites as a way to authenticate the Latino culture.

Media representations are often filtered through a lens of racialized gender. For example, in a content analysis of youth violence and race in print media, Michael Welch and colleagues (2004) tracked the use of the word *wilding* between 1989 and 1998 in four New York City newspapers to illuminate elements of racism deeply embedded in prevailing criminal stereotypes. Terms such as *wolf pack, gangs, beasts, thugs, animals, hoodlums,* and *mobs* were used to characterize criminal subjects, who were most likely African American or Latino youth. The authors argue that this media sensationalism seeks to promote moral panic and notions of social disorder that symbolize a threat to the prevailing political economic order and signals to the criminal justice establishment that the "upper classes" must be protected from the lower, so-called dangerous class (Welch et al. 2004). Central to gendered representational mass media sensationalism is symbolizing Latinidad with depictions of illegal immigration, Latino sexuality, poverty, and crime. These assertions are confirmed by Charles Weaver (2005) who found that only 2 percent of prime-time programming includes Latinos and the few representations relegate them to uncomplicated characters of maids and criminals.

Francisca Gonzalez (2001) challenges these messages and the hegemonic ideology of marking difference as abnormal and evil, shifting the focus from one of pathology of Latino youth to a critical view of discriminatory educational and social practices (642–44). Gonzalez (2001) found three pervasive views about Latinas in social science literature and media: (1) Chicana/Mexicana/Latina students were part of a Hispanic dropout problem; (2) immigrant women were demonized as dark and associated with deviance; and (3) Latinas were associated with a deterioration of morals, ethics, and standards. She argues that these images manipulate people's fears of difference and social change. Her intersectional lens is "a looking prism of critical race theory, Latino critical theory and feminist perspectives embodying multiple complexities, contexts and meanings" (644) embedded in historical and contemporary facts. The utility of her lens is illustrated by its application to actual policies and laws in California that show how institutional and structural features reflect racial power via color-blind ideology and contribute to the sexual oppression and social displacement of Latinas in the school system. For example, teachers expect girls not to have the academic skills or resources to attend college and do not encourage attendance in higher education. Gonzalez concludes that "educational discourses cannot be divorced from minority identities and material conditions in particular Chicano identity and Chicano Studies" (653). In her study of adolescent Chicanas she describes social processes that she calls the *cultura mestiza* (defined as "mixed" or interracial cultural lived experience) and discusses how critical race theory applies to discrimination against Latinas who are most affected by discrimination in the legal sphere (public policy and laws) as well as in the media.

Elena Gutiérrez in her book *Fertile Matters: The Politics of Mexican-Origin Women's Reproduction* (2008) explores the popular and long-standing public stereotype that portrays Mexican American and Mexican women as "hyper-fertile baby machines" who "breed like rabbits." The author examines socially constructed ethnic, racial, gender, and class stereotypes and how existing institutional mechanisms such as media, mainstream organizations (e.g., Zero Population Growth, Inc., and its offshoots), health and human service professionals, and legal professionals have produced a public discourse on the control of reproduction for Latino women. She argues that the hegemonic discourse essentially contributed to the implementation of federal and state policy in response to these stereotypes or negative representations for an entire group of people, especially Mexican-origin women. She historicizes the trajectory of ideas about Mexican-origin groups and the ways in which these ideas contributed to the implementation of sterilization policies and practices by the medical profession among Mexican-origin women and Puerto Rican women[1] (Lopez 2009).

Drawing on several theoretical traditions to elucidate the development and perpetuation of stereotypes or racial politics through her integrated theoretical lens, Gutiérrez uses social constructionist approaches, racial formation theory, and feminist studies of the racial politics of reproduction. She describes the

---

1. Iris Lopez provides a historical account of sterilization practices of Puerto Rican women in both New York and Puerto Rico. She describes the results of her longitudinal intergenerational ethnographic study, giving voice to the lived experiences in five households and embedding these institutional practices in an historical and power-relations discourse.

voice and agency of women who endured sterilization abuse and discusses the role of the media, organizations who constructed and perpetuated the racialized ideology, and scholars who supported or challenged racialized politics. This interplay of multiple actors and voices using illustrative text from multimedia and empirical sources embeds this work in a rich tapestry showing the structural forces that have shaped the views of Mexican-origin and other Latino women in the American public imagination. The gender analysis is unique, incisive, and seminal in its illumination of the multiple sites and forces that converged to curb the fertility of Latino women in the West and Southwest via nonconsensual sterilization practices similar to those used with Puerto Rican women on the East coast and in Puerto Rico (Lopez 2009). This description of the convergence of multiple social forces vividly illustrates how hegemonic ideology is formed and reinforced through the media, public policy and institutional practices.

In prior chapters I have already discussed how powerful pathological images of Latino men and youth as authoritarian and macho patriarchs, criminals and gang members, unskilled workers, and foreigners or illegal immigrants are a persistent image in the media, including print and news coverage. In his Network Brownout Report 2005, Federico Subervi and colleagues state:

> Acceptable news coverage of Latinos is an issue of fairness and accuracy. Stories on illegal immigration or Latino gangs may not be inaccurate, but this becomes unfair when it comprises an overabundance of coverage. The issue of accurate news coverage is crucial because more than 30 million people watch the evening news and are influenced by these programs. While the media landscape is dramatically changing, the evening news still plays a prominent role in determining issues covered across a range of media platforms. The networks' coverage has failed to reflect the changes in U.S. society. (3)

The propagation of these stereotypes instilled in the American imagination permeates the disciplinary power of officials who interact with Latino families, children, and youth in major institutions such as schools and courts. Bender (2003) convincingly argues that the media's derogatory stereotypes have plagued Latinos since or before the conquest of 1848 and have shaped social attitudes that contribute to the legal maltreatment of Latinos under U.S. law (1–7).

The lessons drawn from these studies bear witness to how the social construction of the Latino family and its gender representations project images of Latinos as different and unequal. These negative identity markers that continue to present "Latinos as social problems" do not acknowledge the structural and historical inequalities that exist or the contemporary heterogeneity of the Latino community. Few studies or media representations focus on the Latino middle class (Weaver 2005; Rojas 2004; Bender 2003). Strong evidence suggests that a number of factors have converged in the twenty-first century to ensure the uplift of Latinos. The social mobility of the Latino population and attendant indicators of success have been overshadowed by the continued negative and visible representations of all Latinos as immigrants. Yet, the growth of the Latino population as a demographic and significant consumer market, the increased education of Latinos, and the growing Latino middle class, with increased disposable income for recreational and other luxury items, have made Latinos a strong political and social group. In uncovering this information I am struck by the invisibility of positive identity markers for Latinos in both media images and social science production. Inevitably, the question must be asked why these data have neither been in the forefront of media images nor reflected in the work of the purveyors of knowledge production. The following section aims to provide a snapshot of the data that show these positive markers of success.

### Trends in Geographic Mobility, Intergenerational Patterns, and Rise in Middle Class: Integration Indicators

Trend data on Latinos in the United States show a more positive picture than what is provided by the gaze of the media and social science research. Positive trend indicators such as income, wealth, and home ownership rates show significant change in home ownership patterns, intergenerational patterns of upward mobility, and increases in middle-class status. Over the last two decades, changes in the subgroup composition of Latinos representing over twenty sending countries, unprecedented geographic mobility, and new Latino settlements (or what is referred to as a Latino Diaspora) in the United States have been observed (Marotta and Garcia 2003; Fry 2008a). However, the largest numbers of Latinos (50 percent) are still heavily concentrated in California and Texas. In a report entitled *Latino Settlement in the New Century* (2008a), Richard Fry noted three key findings:

1. Hispanic population growth in the new century has been widespread.
2. The Hispanic population continues to be much more geographically concentrated than the non-Hispanic population.
3. Hispanics are more geographically concentrated than the nation's non-Hispanic Black population.

Currently, the U.S. Hispanic population represents 15 percent of the U.S. population and is projected to reach approximately sixty million by 2020, an increase of 18 percent (Suarez 2007). Over two-thirds of Latinos are second- and third-generation. As the second and third generation grows, their income and proportion of the population with access to middle-class status also increases.

Intergenerational trends have been observed in values and attitudes and in intermarriage rates. In a 2004 telephone interview survey of 2,929 self-identified Hispanic/Latino persons, attitudes and experiences on a variety of topics and issues were explored (Pew Hispanic Center/Kaiser Family Foundation 2004a). Language use was measured as a proxy indicator of *assimilation*, which the authors defined as the process by which many "newcomers" adopt values, beliefs, and behaviors more similar to U.S. culture than to the culture of the country from which they or their ancestors originate (1). Primary language by generational status showed that 72 percent of first-generation immigrants were Spanish-dominant, while none in the third generation or higher were Spanish-dominant. Among the second generation, only 7 percent were Spanish-dominant, 46 percent were English-dominant, and 47 percent were bilingual. Attitudes regarding social values, gender roles, and the importance of family, work, and attitudes toward government were measured with a two-item response option: agree/disagree or acceptable/unacceptable.

English language use was a predictor of attitudes closer to those of non-Latinos. For example, among Spanish-dominant individuals, over 80 percent found sex between same-sex adults and abortion unacceptable, and 50 percent found divorce unacceptable; 59 percent reported feeling less control over their lives when asked whether they agreed or disagreed to "it doesn't do you any good to plan for the future because you don't have any control over it" as a measure of fatalism. Group differences between English-dominant Latinos and non-Latinos were also observed. English-dominant Latinos were slightly less likely than non-Latinos to report divorce, sex between two adults of the same sex, abortion, and willingness to work long hours at the expense of personal life as acceptable, but were equally likely to disagree that husbands should have the final say in family matters. Latinos were slightly more likely than non-Latinos to agree that elderly parents should live with their adult children and that relatives are more important than friends. They were also twice as likely as non-Latinos to agree to pay higher taxes to support larger government. These data corroborate recent scholarly work on changing gender role attitudes and family values among Latinos (see chapter 3).

*Intermarriage*

Nancy Landale and colleagues (2006) report subgroup and generational differences in patterns of ethnic marriage and parenthood. Marriage to a member of your own ethnic group (endogamous marriage) is highest among Mexican groups and lowest among other Latinos. For first-generation Latinos by subgroup, Mexicans (91.5 percent), Cubans (82.5 percent), and Puerto Ricans (70.6 percent) are the most likely to marry someone from their own group. For second-generation Latinos, Cubans (32.6 percent) and Central/South Americans (37.2 percent) are the least likely to have in-group marriage, and 49 percent of Cubans and 42.1 percent of Central/South Americans marry NHWs. The data on exogamous marriages (i.e., marrying outside one's own ethnic group) of native-born, native-parentage Latinos to NHWs follow a similar pattern to endogamous marriage: Mexican Americans (24.2 percent) and Puerto Ricans (33.8 percent) are the least likely to marry NHWs (46.7 percent) and Central/South American (40.3 percent) and other Latinos are most likely. For all married Latino women, the percentage of women with NHW husbands increases with each generation. Cubans and Puerto Ricans are the most likely to marry Latinos from other Latino subgroups, and Mexicans are the least likely to have an exogamous Hispanic marriage. Native-born of native parentage Puerto Rican (12.6 percent) and Central/South American (5.6 percent) are the most likely to marry a non-Hispanic Black (NHB).

These trends reveal that those subgroups who generally have higher education levels—namely, Cubans and South Americans—are most likely to interact in school and workplaces with NHWs, which increases the likelihood of marriage to NHW partners. Puerto Ricans who tend to coreside, attend school, and work in more highly concentrated and segregated areas with NHBs are more likely to marry, cohabit, and parent with NHBs. Based on these data, the authors conclude that Mexican Americans are most likely to maintain a distinct ethnic identity and culture as a result of high endogamous marriage patterns. Other Hispanic group marriage and parenting patterns with both NHW and NHB mates may blur future boundaries of Latino ethnic identity among the offspring of these unions (Landale et al. 2006, 172). Overall intergenerational patterns show that higher generational level is associated with higher education, higher income, higher rates of intermarriage (although these vary by subgroup), and gender and family attitudes that are not significantly different from non-Latinos. These data also show that future intermarriage patterns within Latino ethnic subgroups and across racial groups will further complicate the identity constructions and meanings of Latinidad in the United States.

### Middle Class, Income

Middle-class Latinos are defined as having annual earnings between $34,000 and $74,000 (Wheary 2006). Elizabeth Suarez (2007) reports that 31 percent of Hispanic households earn over $50,000 annually; 13 percent earn over $75,000 annually; and 6 percent earn over $100,000 annually. This last group experienced a 126 percent growth spurt between 1991 and 2001, compared to only 77 percent in the general U.S. population. Median income among Latinos grew 27 percent from 1995 to 2001, while the middle-class sector increased approximately 80 percent between 1990 and 2000—three times the national growth rate of 7.4 percent. Much of the gains in the Hispanic middle class are indicative of increases in the Latino population due to births and not immigration, with increases in second- and third-generation groups. Length of time in the country and levels of economic integration also contribute to increases in the Latino middle class. Disparities between Latino middle class and NHW middle class are based on the observation of groups in the aggregate. When age and migration status is not accounted for, Latinos overall appear to lag substantially behind NHWs and other groups. If the 40 percent of the Hispanic population that is foreign-born—a group that tends to be younger and to have lower income levels, lower net worth, and lower rates of home ownership—were taken into account, the increasing numbers of Latino middle class and home owners would be evident.

Between 1990 and 2000 the buying power of Latino families tripled, especially in the concentrated areas of Latino residence (Humphreys 2002). In 2004 Latino purchasing power has also increased with gains in income and education and has witnessed steady gains in assets and wealth. U.S. Hispanic purchasing power has surged to nearly $700 billion and will reach as much as $1 trillion by 2010. The substantial gain in median income among Latinos is associated with increases in lending activities for home mortgages to Latino homebuyers.

## Housing, Home Ownership, and Wealth

Home ownership is a crucial factor in securing middle-class status and remains a challenge for Latinos living in the United States. As of 2008, 74.9 percent of NHWs owned homes, compared with 59.1 percent of Asians, 48.9 percent of Latinos, and 47.5 percent of NHBs. Home ownership rates among Latino households outpaced the nation between 1991 and 2001 by 70 percent, compared to 20.9 percent for the nation (Bowdler 2004). Though there were large increases in the 1990s, home ownership rates among Latinos leveled out in 2001, with a peak of 47.3 percent. Close to one-half of all Latinos own a home, and the other half rent, with an increase of 25 percent of renter-occupied households between 1995 and 2005 (Ready 2006). Among all Latinos, about 44 percent own their own homes—an indicator of wealth and a growing middle class.[2] Native-born Hispanics increased their home ownership rates from 47.2 percent in 1995 to 56.2 percent in 2005. Foreign-born Latinos increased

2. Much of the information regarding Latinos and home ownership is centered on the Latino group as a whole and does not include income breakdowns within the group. Further, information on middle-class minorities tends to focus on the lags between all minorities and their NHW counterparts. The challenge of identifying the middle-class Latino home owner rests on unreliable data that are not disaggregated by income and, in some cases, race. Studies address income gains among the Latino population that represent middle-class status, but few provide a multidimensional lens to inform on how the middle-class Latino home owner is faring.

Yet Latinos are also significantly more likely to live in crowded households than NHWs or NHBs (see chapter 8 for housing characteristics). In 2003, 26 percent of Latino households lived in crowded conditions compared to 8 percent of NHBs and 4 percent of NHWs (McConnell 2008).

their home ownership rates from 36.9 percent in 1995 to 44.7 percent in 2007 (Kochhar et al. 2009). Several reasons may account for increases in Latino home ownership. Based on Latino households' ability to live in extended familial settings and pool their earnings to qualify for mortgages, additional families may seek home ownership and forgo inner-city living for suburban neighborhoods (Nasser 2006). Another alternative is the increase in family members who request the support of an older family member to cosign for a mortgage (Cohn 2005). Studies show that the higher the age group, the higher the home ownership rate. For Latinos between ages thirty-five and forty-four, home ownership rates jumped almost 50 percent, and among sixty-five- to seventy-four-year-olds, nearly seven out of ten (70 percent) Latinos are home owners. Overall, home owners are more likely to be middle aged; second- or third-generation and/or immigrants with long-term residency in the United States; and employed and to have higher education and skill levels.

Based on 2005 data, Latinos have a disproportionately higher percentage of low-income households than high-income households (Wheary 2006) that overshadow higher income Hispanic earners. Aggregating the data among Hispanic household income groups makes invisible the large percentage of Latino home owners who may be struggling to maintain their mortgages given the plummeting housing market and financial crisis (Cohn 2005).

Latino home owners are concentrated in five states: California, Texas, New York, Florida, and Illinois (Bowdler 2004). Southeastern states such as North Carolina, Arkansas, Georgia, Tennessee, and Nevada are also experiencing significant gains in Latino households. Furthermore, these households are distributed equally between the suburbs and central city: In 2001, 45.9 percent of Latino households were located in central cities, 45.8 percent in the suburbs, and 8.2 percent in rural areas. Ten years earlier the numbers of Latino households were higher in central cities (51 percent), lower in the suburbs (38 percent), and higher in rural areas (10 percent).

In 2001, Hispanic households paid more than 33 percent of their monthly income on housing, similar to 32.5 percent for NHW families (Bowdler 2004). Between 1991 and 2001, 41.8 percent of Hispanic households paid over-market value for housing, compared to 29.7 percent of households nationally. In the twenty top cities with high percentages of Latino home owners, housing was abnormally high except for four cities where housing costs were lower than the national average (Bowdler 2004). Much of these high costs are associated with not only "hot" housing markets but also persistent barriers that represent ongoing discriminatory practices in the mortgage industry. Still at stake is the industry's ability to fully tap its most emerging consumer market and Hispanics' ability to realize the American dream of owning a home.

The latest information on home ownership shows the following: (1) native-born Hispanics and NHBs are among those who experienced the sharpest reversal in home ownership in recent years; (2) immigrant householders did not experience similar losses in home ownership and are less likely to be home owners; and (3) NHBs and Latinos remain far more likely that NHWs to borrow in the subprime market where loans are usually higher priced. In 2007 27.6 percent of home purchase loans to Hispanics and 33.5 percent to NHBs compared to 10.5 percent for NHWs showed that the annual percentage rate for a thirty-year typical fixed conventional mortgage loan was on average 2.5 points higher for Hispanics and 3 points higher for NHB's (Kochhar et al. 2009). In 2007 Hispanics and NHBs borrowed higher amounts than did NHWs with similar incomes, confronting the likelihood of higher price borrowing and higher debt relative to income. Interestingly, the gap between racial/ethnic minorities and NHWs is greater among high-income households than low-income households. It makes sense that racial/ethnic minorities across SES are at greater risk of losing their homes due to unemployment and/or foreclosure.

What do we know about the characteristics of Latinos who have assets and wealth? Among Hispanic households, wealth increases with age, and it peaks at age sixty-five. In 2002 the wealth of older Latinos (thirty-four to sixty-five) was fourteen times the wealth of Hispanic households between the ages of twenty-five and thirty-four (Kochhar 2004). Economically, Latino families have had a large impact on the housing economy with over sixty-one billion dollars spent on housing in 2000. Foreign-born Latinos have lower home equity than U.S.–born Latinos (Krivo and Kaufman 2004). The home ownership rates among immigrants from the Dominican Republic, Mexico, and Cuba are lower than the rates among U.S.–born Latinos and NHWs (Borjas 2002; McConnell 2008).

Latinos are gaining a foothold in the housing market because their numbers are soaring in suburban communities, such as in the Baltimore/Washington metro area (Cohn 2005). The confluence of current changes and biases in the mortgage market, media skepticism and speculation, the backlash against U.S. Latino families (English language proficiency, immigration), institutionalized discriminatory practices such as subprime mortgage lending practices, and particularly the economic recession and crisis of 2008–2010 has significant implications for the future of Latino families' ability to achieve middle-class status and accumulate wealth assets. "Like the U.S. population as a whole, Latinos are feeling the sting of the economic downturn" (1). Yet, increased civic participation as well as increases in material assets have provided the basis for the emergence of Latinos as a potential electoral constituency of importance.

## Civic and Political Participation

Civic and political participation has often been a marker of social and political capital for the wealthier and more educated dominant culture groups.

However, for Latinos, their recognition as a potential political force has only in the late twentieth century received any attention. Therefore, "the scholarly study of Latino civic and electoral participation, Latino political attitudes, and the political dimensions of naturalization is a relatively new phenomenon" (DeSipio 2006, 449). Active participation at national, state, and local levels represents important channels to express needs for services and propose agendas for social change and social justice. Limited data are available to understand long-term trends in civic and political participation[3] of the Latino community, and data on Latino representation in elected office has been available only since 1984. Several important studies have been conducted in the last decade on Latino political participation and issue concerns, with the Pew Hispanic Center providing the most comprehensive analyses of the 2004 and 2008 elections. The following sections outline what we know generally about Latino voting patterns and representation in political and civic offices.

*Latino Voting Patterns*

Voting is both a civic duty and the most important mechanism to ensure that those who are elected can adequately represent those issues that are most important to us individually and as a racial, ethnic, gender, sexual, religious or disability identity group. Historically and even in contemporary times, NHBs and Latinos have confronted formidable barriers to their political participation (see Frasure and Williams 2009).

In this section I present data on eligible voters, the gap between registration and voter turnout, socioeconomic characteristics of Latino voters, and intergroup partisan differences. These are salient issues that inform our understanding of who participates in the voting process and their voting patterns, and may provide some insight into the perceived political clout of the Latino electorate. The trajectory from eligibility to vote, registering to vote, and actually voting represents important processes of political engagement and potential national impact. Voter registration and voter turnout are two direct forms of citizen engagement and participation among eligible voters (Lopez 2003).

---

3. Lorrie Frasure and Linda Williams (2009) provide definitions of *civic engagement* and *political participation:* "Civic engagement is defined as informal political and nonpolitical activities engaged in through voluntary organizations such as citizen and community associations and charitable groups. Civic engagement enables individuals, families, and groups to influence issues and factors that affect them and to experience the value of collective action. It should be noted that civic engagement allows people to participate who might otherwise be disconnected or shut out from political participation (for example, noncitizens). Political participation is defined as formal political activities such as voting, volunteering, working for and contributing to political campaigns, and membership in explicitly political organizations. Political participation falls squarely in the realm of the electoral-representative system and enables individuals, families, and groups as part of an active citizenry to elect public officials and influence formulation and implementation of public policy solutions to societal problems" (322).

Significant differences are reported in the percentage of Hispanics registered to vote and those that actually turn out to vote.

For the years 1992 to 1996, Latino voter registration increased by 27.9 percent, and it increased 16.3 percent among those who voted (U.S. Hispanic Leadership Institute 1999). During the 1996 election, 75 percent of all eligible Latinos who registered to vote participated in the electoral process. Over the next decade, due to demographic growth, Latino engagement in the political process was expected to increase Latino electoral clout (Lopez 2003). A growing number of reports have been analyzing recent trends in voter turnout (de la Garza 2004).

In 2000, Latinos represented thirteen million eligible voters (64.8 percent of Latino citizens), percentages significantly lower than for NHBs, who in 2000 represented a similar population size as Latinos but accounted for twenty-three million eligible voters (78.3 percent of NHB citizens) (Pew Hispanic Center/Kaiser Family Foundation 2004b; Lopez 2003). In 2000, 5.5 million Latinos participated in the electoral process, a substantial increase from 1996, with 4.9 million eligible voters. The increase in Latino voter turnout from 1996 to 2000 is linked to increased levels of educational attainment.

In 2000, of the 64.8 percent of the Hispanic population registered to vote, 79.3 percent voted. The 79 percent participation rate for eligible Latino voters in 2000 is slightly lower in comparison to NHW (86.9 percent), NHB (85.3 percent), and Asian (83.8 percent) voters (Lopez 2003). In March 2003, 15.7 million Hispanics, 40 percent of the Latino population, were eligible to vote in comparison to 73 percent of the non-Hispanic population (Pew Hispanic Center/Kaiser Family Foundation 2004b). Although lower eligibility among adult Latinos is often attributed to noncitizenship, age is a more important factor because 34 percent of the population is less than eighteen years old compared to 23 percent of non-Hispanic populations (Pew Hispanic Center 2004b).

In 2008, Latino eligible voters accounted for 9.5 percent of all eligible U.S. voters, up from 8.2 percent in 2004. Similarly, the share of eligible NHB voters slightly increased from 11.6 percent in 2004 to 11.8 percent in 2008, and eligible Asian voters also increased from 3.3 percent in 2004 to 3.4 percent in 2008. In contrast, the share of eligible voters who were NHW fell from 75.2 percent in 2004 to 73.4 percent in 2008. The levels of participation by NHB, Hispanic, and Asian eligible voters all increased from 2004 to 2008, reducing the voter participation gap between themselves and NHW eligible voters. This was particularly true for NHB eligible voters. Their voter turnout rate increased 4.9 percentage points, from 60.3 percent in 2004 to 65.2 percent in 2008, nearly matching the voter turnout rate of NHW eligible voters (66.1 percent). For Latinos, participation levels also increased, with the voter turnout rate rising 2.7 percentage points, from 47.2 percent in 2004 to 49.9 percent in 2008. Among Asians, voter participation rates increased by

2.4 percentage points, from 44.6 percent in 2004 to 47.0 percent in 2008. Meanwhile, among NHW eligible voters, the voter turnout rate fell slightly, from 67.2 percent in 2004 to 66.1 percent in 2008. The expectation that Latinos would become more politically engaged has materialized as voter turnout has consistently increased over the last two decades. Yet the need to continue to increase voter turnout is important to ensure that the Latino agenda becomes visible at the national level (Lopez and Livingston 2009).

### Socioeconomic Position Determines "Most Likely to Vote"

Demographic characteristics of Latino voters show that adults fifty-six years of age and older (86.3 percent) have higher voting rates than all other Latinos, followed by those thirty-one to fifty-five years of age (77.3 percent). Central and South Americans (88 percent), followed by Cuban Americans (87 percent) were the most likely to participate in the electoral process, while Puerto Ricans (80 percent) and Mexican Americans (76 percent) were less likely to participate in the electoral process (Lopez 2003).[4]

Knowing who votes and why is as important as knowing who does *not* vote. So who are the registered Latinos who do not turn out to vote? Rodolfo de la Garza (2004) examined why registered Latinos had low voting turnout. In looking at the characteristics of those Latinos who did not show up to vote, he found that an overinvestment in getting Latino citizens registered to vote was not followed up by mobilization to get those same citizens to the polls. Latinos who are less likely to vote are characterized as younger, less educated, and with lower incomes (de la Garza 2004; de la Garza and DeSipio 2006; Pew Hispanic Center 2006; Lopez 2003; Minushkin and Lopez 2008; Suro et al. 2005). Distinct differences can be identified by education level and income, which are exacerbated by racialized voting patterns and structural barriers (Frasure and Williams 2009).

Although Latinos have historically voted at lower rates than NHWs and NHBs at comparable educational levels, voting rates increased with educational achievement. For example, only 51 percent of Latinos who had a bachelor's degree voted compared to NHWs (77 percent) and NHBs (71 percent); 41 percent of Latinos with some college or an associate degree voted compared to NHWs (64 percent) and NHBs (59 percent); 29 percent of Latinos with a high school diploma or a GED voted compared to NHWs (53 percent) and NHBs (49 percent); and 15 percent of Latinos with less than high school completion participated in voting compared to NHW (37 percent) and NHB (42 percent) peers (NCES 2003a).

4. For additional information on Latino voting patterns, see Lopez and Livingston 2009; Taylor and Fry 2007. For information on Latino public opinion about the 2008 election and the candidates, see Minushkin and Lopez 2008. All available at www.pewhispanic.org.

Educational attainment and income are highly associated with voting patterns. For example, during the 2006 midterm elections, 39.5 percent of Latinos with less than a high school education voted, compared to 84.2 percent of those with advanced degrees (Heine 2008). Based on income, 48.3 percent of those with family incomes less than $20,000 a year voted, compared to 81.3 percents of individuals with family incomes over $100,000. Among Latino voters in 2000, Cuban Americans—with the highest voter registration rates (79 percent) and the second highest voter turnout rate (87.2 percent)—were more likely to be Republican, wealthier, older, and home owners and to have higher levels of education.

Older Latinos with higher incomes and higher educational attainment are also more likely to be targeted by political campaigns or asked to vote. Following the 2000 election, mobilizing Latino citizens was slanted toward higher socioeconomic groups in states that represented significantly higher proportions of Latino populations, such as California, Florida, Texas, New York, and Illinois. Overall, Latinos who earned more than $35,000, were college educated, and thirty-six years of age and older were contacted by campaigns and political parties at higher rates and asked to vote than Latinos from lower SEP groups (de la Garza 2004). A follow-up study concluded that those Latinos with higher education and higher incomes tended to vote at higher levels than those on the opposite end of the spectrum, whether or not they were contacted by political campaigns. Other non-socioeconomic indicators predictive of those most likely to vote include language, political socialization in the family, and situational factors (de la Garza and DeSipio 2006).

One sector of the Latino population that can be tapped into to close the gap between voter registration and voter turnout is the young adult group, ages eighteen to twenty-nine. Since the 1996 presidential election, 78 percent of Latinos have become old enough to vote. Among youth registered to vote, the voter turnout for those between eighteen and thirty years old was 70 percent in 2000, slightly less than NHWs (75.8 percent), NHBs (76.6 percent), and Asians (80.1 percent). Among young Latinos 60 percent said they were registered to vote, compared to 79 percent of Hispanics fifty-five years of age and older. Among this 60 percent of young voters, only 66 percent said they voted, which is substantially lower than the 90 percent of non-Hispanic groups (Lopez and Taylor 2009). More than two million more young people ages eighteen to twenty-nine voted in 2008 than in 2004. Table 9.1 shows voter participation rates among eighteen- to twenty-nine-year-old eligible voters, which increased by 2.1 percent between 2004 and 2008. Latino young adults had the lowest increases compared to Black and Asian adults. Among young eligible voters, NHBs had the highest turnout rate at 58.2 percent—a historic first (Kirby and Kawashima-Ginsberg 2009). Since the Latino population is approximately nine years younger than the average NHW, young voters can

**Table 9.1.** Change in Voter Turnout Rates among
Eligible Voters (18–29), 2004 and 2008 (%)

|          | 2004 | 2008 | Change (% points) |
|----------|------|------|-------------------|
| All      | 49.0 | 51.1 | 2.1               |
| White    | 52.3 | 52.1 | –0.2              |
| Black    | 49.5 | 58.2 | 8.7               |
| Hispanic | 35.5 | 40.7 | 5.2               |
| Asian    | 32.4 | 42.9 | 10.5              |

*Source:* Lopez and Taylor 2009.

play a significant role in the growth of the Latino electorate (de la Garza and DeSipio 2006).

Surveys to assess Latinos' attitudes regarding the economy, health care, and immigration policy can provide insight on the issues that motivate Latinos to engage politically (Pew Hispanic Center/Kaiser Family Foundation 2004b). A survey of Hispanic attitudes on key national issues reported that 54 percent said education was very important. Other important issues included the economy and jobs, health care and Medicare, and terrorism. Yet only 27 percent of Hispanics reported that immigration was extremely important in determining how they voted. Although the media proposed that immigrant reform—whether enacted or not—would create a significant impact in the Hispanic community and influence their voting patterns, this prediction was not confirmed in 2004 (de la Garza and DeSipio 2006). However the persistent anti-immigrant sentiment in the media, which continued unabated and undoubtedly contributed to backlash that resulted in harsh immigration policies, did raise the concerns of the Latino community. In 2006, 75 percent of the respondents reported that the debate on immigration reform would provoke a large turnout among Latinos in the 2008 November election. Harsh immigration policies are not viewed as bipartisan issues but rather as reflecting more conservative Republican policies. Many surveyed felt that the Republican Party was to blame for negative consequences of the immigration debates, but the political impact on voting patterns was not certain (Pew Hispanic Center/ Kaiser Family Foundation 2004b).

A 2008 follow-up study by the Pew Hispanic Center confirmed prior results of the 2006 survey that showed that 63 percent of Latinos felt pro-immigrant marches signaled a beginning to a new social movement, and 75 percent said the immigration issue would prompt more Latinos to vote. However, the 2008 survey reaffirmed that immigration was still further behind most other issues among Latino voters. Latino registered voters still ranked education, the economy, jobs, and health care as the most important issues in the fall 2008 campaign.

The years between 2004 and 2008 showed a dramatic shift in Latinos' political affiliation. In 2008, 65 percent of Latinos identified with the Democratic

Party, an increase of 20 points since 2004, while 26 percent identified with the Republican Party. In 2004, 45 percent of Latinos reported they were Democrats, 20 percent Republicans, 21 percent Independent, and 12 percent reported other or no party affiliation. The 2008 increase in the Democratic identification began to close the nonpartisan gap in 2004 (Lopez and Taylor 2009).

Besides voting, other forms of civic and political engagement include contacting public officials, print media, and broadcast media, wearing campaign buttons, writing letters to public officials, attending political meetings, signing petitions, and boycotting (de la Garza 2004). In a survey of Latinos engaged in electoral and political voice activities other than voting, Latinos demonstrated comparable percentages to Whites and Blacks. Although Latinos were slightly less likely to contact public officials, e-mail petitions, contact print media, and boycott in comparison to Whites, they were more likely to protest (Lopez 2003). Latinos with more financial resources were more likely to participate than those with fewer resources and to engage in political opportunities through institutions such as schools, work, voluntary organizations, and churches.

### Representation of Elected or Appointed Officials

Latino leadership among elected officials has a direct impact on U.S. policies. The potential political force of the Latino electorate and leadership has been referred to as a "sleeping giant." As former U.S. senator Ken Salazar, now secretary of the interior in the Obama administration, commented, "We must make sure that the sleeping giant awakes and participates" (de la Garza and DeSipio 2006). Many Latinos are interested in a form of leadership that extends beyond electoral politics to a proportionate representation of elected Latino officials at all levels of government.

Latinos are underrepresented as appointed or elected officials nationwide. Since 1981, the National Association of Latino Elected and Appointed Officials (NALEO)[5] has conducted an annual verification of the number of Latino elected officials nationwide. Comparable data on the Latino electorate is available between 1996 and 2007. However a caveat on the accuracy of these data is warranted: Some increases may reflect changes to the data collection methods between these years and updated techniques in verifying the number

5. The NALEO Educational Fund is the nation's leading 501 (c)(3) nonprofit, nonpartisan organization that facilitates the full participation of Latinos in the American political process, from citizenship to public service. NALEO members represent all political parties, all levels of government, and diverse constituencies—from metropolitan cities to rural communities working to strengthen American democracy and our community through increased political participation.

of Latinos holding national and local elected positions rather than representing progress among the group.

Figure 9.1 displays changes in Latino elected office by level of office between the years 1996 and 2007. Latino elected officers serve in forty-three states, with approximately half in Texas (42 percent) and a substantial number in California (23 percent). Including Texas and California, approximately 96 percent of Latino elected officials held offices in states with large Latino populations: New Mexico (12.8 percent), Florida (2.6 percent), New Jersey (2.0 percent), and New York (1.2 percent) (NALEO 2007). In 1996 the total number of Latino elected officials was 4,787 of whom 1,662 were women. In 2002, the number of Latino elected officials decreased to 4,624 nationwide. Party affiliation among these officials is not significantly different by gender. In 2002, among the 3,293 male officials, 1,070 are Democrats, 92 Republicans, 946 had no party affiliation, 7 Independents, and 1,178 nonpartisans (an individual in an elected position or organization in which the participants cannot declare or formally have a political party affiliation.). Among the 1,331 Latino women, 407 are Democrats, 26 Republicans, 397 no party affiliation, 5 Independents, and 496 nonpartisan. Overall, 1,694 Latino school board elected officials (men 1,119 and women 575) serve nationwide. In 2007, for all federal, state, and local offices, Latino elected officials served in 5,129 positions. Sixty-eight percent of these positions were held in either municipal or school board offices. Latinos were least likely to hold federal (0.5 percent), statewide (0.1 percent), special district positions (3.4 percent), or to serve in the state legislatures (4.6 percent). These data reflect an increase of 37 percent in Latino elected officers over the decade. Latino state wide officials experienced no change. However, at the federal level, the increase from 17 representatives to 26 is quite modest, with similar modest increments in judicial/law enforcement officials and special district officials. The largest gains are in municipal and school board/education officials followed by state legislatures and county officials. Significant changes in number of Latinos at all levels of political office, with the exception of statewide offices such as governors, occurred.

In comparison, representation of overall Latinos is a small share (33.1 percent) of elected officials. African Americans represented 63.7 percent of all elected officials, and Asian Americans represented 2.9 percent (Hardy-Fanta et al. 2005). Between 1990 and 2000, Latino elected officers experienced higher rates of growth (30 percent) than African Americans (23 percent) and Asians (4 percent). In 2005, Latinos had higher representation (82.3 percent) of elected local offices such as school board and municipal offices than African Americans (78.8 percent) and Asian Americans (67.1 percent) who held almost half of their offices at the local level and approximately half at the higher levels, which is indicative of their strong presence in Hawaii's state legislature (Hardy-Fanta et al. 2006). In terms of party affiliation, most Latinos (73 percent) are

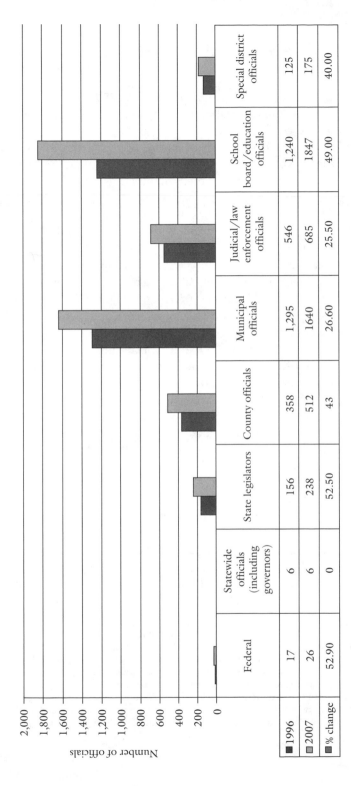

| | Federal | Statewide officials (including governors) | State legislators | County officials | Municipal officials | Judicial/law enforcement officials | School board/education officials | Special district officials |
|---|---|---|---|---|---|---|---|---|
| 1996 | 17 | 6 | 156 | 358 | 1,295 | 546 | 1,240 | 125 |
| 2007 | 26 | 6 | 238 | 512 | 1640 | 685 | 1847 | 175 |
| % change | 52.90 | 0 | 52.50 | 43 | 26.60 | 25.50 | 49.00 | 40.00 |

**Figure 9.1.** Change in Latino elected office by level of office, 1996 and 2007. *Source:* National Association of Latino Elected and Appointed Officials 2007.

not publicly affiliated and serve in offices elected on a nonpartisan basis. Of those who are affiliated to a political party, 91 percent are Democratic and only 9 percent are Republican.

By gender, Latino elected officials in 1996 were 75.8 percent males and 24.2 females, while in 2007, female representation had increased by almost 7 percent to 30.7 percent of the elected officials and men at 69.3 percent. Latino and NHB women have similar proportional representation in elected office. At the federal level, Latina representation is higher than the level for all female office holders. For example, in the House, female representatives for all racial/ethnic groups represent 16.1 percent, while Latinas represent 30.4 percent (NALEO 2007). Latinas also have high representation among Latinos in the State Senate, with 33.3 percent of State Senate seats and 25.4 percent among lower house members.

Figure 9.2 displays changes in Latino elected office in states where Latinos are geographically concentrated (1996–2007). The largest gains in increased representation were made in California (67.8 percent), Florida (81.9 percent), New Jersey (212.21 percent), Illinois (126.5 percent), and New York (60 percent). Other states combined showed a 142.1 percent increase, which included states outside of traditional areas of Latino concentration that experienced demographic growth of Latinos and mobilization efforts for an infrastructure to assist Latinos in accessing political office (NALEO 2007).

Overall representation of Latino elected officials has experienced significant gains at all levels of government.[6] The midterm elections of November 2, 2010, were historic for Hispanics. For the first time ever, three Latino candidates—all of them Republicans—won top statewide offices. In New Mexico, voters elected the nation's first Latina governor, Republican Susana Martinez. In Nevada, Republican Brian Sandoval won the governor's race and became Nevada's first Hispanic governor. And in Florida, Republican Marco Rubio won the U.S. Senate race. Despite these big top-of-the-ticket wins for Republican Hispanic candidates, Latino voters continued their strong support for Democratic candidates nationwide. Bob Menendez (D) of New Jersey remains in the Senate. Both Mel Martinez (R) of Florida and Ken Salazar (D) of Colorado served from 2005–2009; Bill Richardson of New Mexico is the only

6. "The Congressional Hispanic Caucus (CHC) was founded in December 1976 as a legislative service organization of the United States House of Representatives. Today, the CHC is organized as a Congressional Member organization, governed under the Rules of the U.S. House of Representatives. The CHC aims to address national and international issues and the impact these policies have on the Hispanic community. The function of the Caucus is to serve as a forum for the Hispanic Members of Congress to coalesce around a collective legislative agenda. The Caucus is dedicated to voicing and advancing, through the legislative process, issues affecting Hispanics in the United States and Puerto Rico." For more information, see http://chc.velazquez.house.gov/.

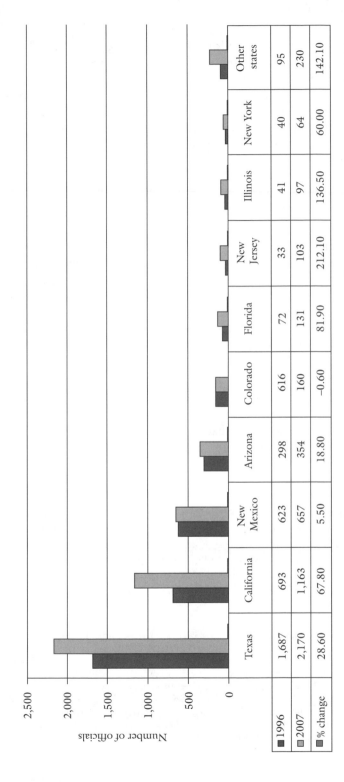

| | Texas | California | New Mexico | Arizona | Colorado | Florida | New Jersey | Illinois | New York | Other states |
|---|---|---|---|---|---|---|---|---|---|---|
| 1996 | 1,687 | 693 | 623 | 298 | 616 | 72 | 33 | 41 | 40 | 95 |
| 2007 | 2,170 | 1,163 | 657 | 354 | 160 | 131 | 103 | 97 | 64 | 230 |
| % change | 28.60 | 67.80 | 5.50 | 18.80 | -0.60 | 81.90 | 212.10 | 136.50 | 60.00 | 142.10 |

**Figure 9.2.** Change in Latino elected office by state, 1996 and 2007. *Source:* National Association of Latino Elected and Appointed Officials 2007.

Latino Democratic governor. More focused strategies will now be required to increase Latinos' elected representation in higher elected offices. Increased representation including higher percentages of Latinas can ensure advocating for the needs of the Latino community as part of the national domestic priorities, advancing a gender-equality work, immigration rights and education agenda, and serving as a national voice and presence to dispel the myths and stereotypes of Latinos as noncitizens and inassimilable.[7]

~

In this chapter, I presented visible and invisible representations of Latinos in all forms of media with demographic, economic, and conventional integration indicators to show the hegemonic perceptions that remain visible and the positive identity markers that remain invisible. Media has a powerful role in shaping how Latinos are imprinted in the American public imagination. Several key findings emerge from an examination of the English-speaking media in all its forms: (1) persistent representations of Latinos that are often grounded in projected images and a public discourse of the inferior group, racialized, and non–English speaking or heavily accented; (2) social constructions of male identity connected with major stereotypic themes of sexuality, criminality, and machismo; and (3) representations of womanhood in movies and television shows that depict Latinas as unskilled workers, highly sexualized, and emotional with little if any power or agency. In contrast the Spanish-speaking media promotes stereotypic gender role and family allegiances with themes of sensuality, emotionality, and patriarchy, but the characters are White, not ethnically identifiable, and most often well-educated, well-housed, and socially skilled. Federico Subervi-Vélez (1994) in his overview of mass communication and Hispanics concludes:

> Future generations of students—especially those who will eventually participate in the image industries—must be ever more aware of the causes and consequences of stereotyping and other forms of discriminatory inclusions and exclusions of selected segments of society. While this is especially needed with respect to mainstream media, attention should also be given to English-language as well as Spanish-language media directed to Hispanics. At times they too portray with

7. Founded in 1968, the Mexican American Legal Defense and Education Fund (MALDEF) is the nation's leading Latino legal civil rights organization. Often described as the "law firm of the Latino community," MALDEF promotes social change through advocacy, communications, community education, and litigation in the areas of education, employment, immigrant rights, and political access. MALDEF strives to implement programs that are structured to bring Latinos into the mainstream of American political and socioeconomic life; providing better educational opportunities; encouraging participation in all aspects of society; and offering a positive vision for the future. Unique to MALDEF is an approach that combines advocacy, educational outreach, and litigation strategies to achieve socio-economic change." For more information, see http://www.maldef.org/.

stereotypes an[d] exclusions Hispanics and "others," especially those of darker skin colors and/or lower social classes. (351)

The print media reproduce these social constructions and sensationalize negative identity markers of Latino immigration, poverty, gangs, and adolescent pregnancy. This postcolonial media cultural production of "tropicalism erases specificity and homogenizes all that is identified as Latin and Latina/o. Under the trope of tropicalism, attributes such as bright colors, rhythmic music, and brown or olive skin comprise some of the most enduring stereotypes about Latina/os" (Molina Guzmán and Valdivia 2004, 211). Yet these perceptions of U.S. Latinos are directly challenged by data that show a continuum of Latino narratives by SEP, national origin and White-brown-Black race, indicators of economic progress, social integration, and civic and political engagement in U.S. society.

The major conclusion is that these persistent images in all forms of media and knowledge production modalities are written and produced with an unyielding resistance to portraying the diverse material and social reality of Latinos in the United States. This portrayal of U.S. Latinos has detrimental consequences for the Latino community. Primarily these hegemonic images infuse the American public imagination at the conscious and unconscious level and serve to justify discriminatory policies and practices in the public and private institutional spheres. Second, media as a socialization mechanism conveys negative identity markers to Latino youth that is detrimental to their social and psychological well-being. Third, critical benchmarks of Latino integration, upward mobility, and citizenship status and attendant rights remain invisible in the American public imagination and are largely understudied in the current social science literature.

A transformation of the social constructions of Latino identity in both media and scholarly work is urgently needed to reverse the misinformed representations and omissions of positive benchmarks. In effect, these negative stereotypes form powerful dominant culture narratives that influence the material realties of Latinos and maintain them in a marginalized social location. Dávila (2001) expresses the harm done by these stereotypes: "What makes stereotypes so troublesome is not that they order and simplify information reducing complexities to a few limited conventions, but that in doing so, they both reflect and, more importantly, engender social hierarchies" (2001, 235).

# 10

# Capturing the Lives of Latinos in the United States

*Advancing the Production of Critical
Social Science Knowledge*

> The emergence of a significant Latina/o middle
> class that still maintains one foot in working class
> origins may signal a more ready audience for research
> on Latinas/os. There are more visible Latina/o
> scholars at the state and federal level, community
> leaders, teachers, scholars engaged in action research,
> and others who are in positions to put research on
> Latinas/os into action. Clearly there are still not
> enough of us in decision-making positions, but we
> have found roles in institutions and policy-making
> bodies that can benefit our communities based on an
> emerging Latina/o intellectual tradition.
> —Hurtado 2009, 547

As I conclude this book, I am convinced that the way Latino families and their lives in the United States is studied must be transformed. What became abundantly clear in reviewing predominantly mainstream literature was that the majority of studies on Latino families were reproducing the same data because the same people were being studied and their material conditions were not changing. Simultaneously, I experienced a sense of elation to read the "oppositional consciousness" so to speak of those scholars who were centering institutional practices that foster social inequality and decentering perceived culturally determined behaviors that allegedly maintain Latinos in their social location.

My original goal was for each of the chapters in this book to summarize multiple bodies of literature that represent the breadth though not the depth of the knowledge base on Latino families in the United States. The empirical literature surveyed draws predominantly from the social sciences but also includes scholarship in the disciplines of education, law, public policy, public health, communications, media, and cultural studies. It was important to extend the breadth of the review so as to best assess the strength of the entrenchment of the ways in which Latinos are viewed in both the scientific literature and the media. In using an interdisciplinary intersectional lens, I was able to extend its boundaries by exploring the hegemonic images of the social constructions of disciplinary and media representations and the role of public institutions and their impact in shaping the social location of U.S. Latino families.

In this chapter, I summarize major connections and links among the complex social relations that have contributed to the social construction of Latinos as a marginalized group, the societal mechanisms that continue to promote stereotypic representations of U.S. Latinos as "foreigners," and the powerful impact that these forces have had on the community. In no way does this recounting of the historical and contemporary experiences undermine the agency of Latino families and communities, but it does seek to make visible those forces that serve as barriers to increased integration and upward mobility into U.S. society. Equally important is the striking suppression or invisibility of Latino strengths and their contributions to and political struggles in U.S. society. It is precisely this paradox that maintains Latinidad as a negative identity marker in the American public imagination.

Several obstructions to advancing knowledge on Latinos were readily apparent in all the areas reviewed for this book. Primarily, I observed three pervasive undercurrents or implicit assumptions: (1) The construct of Latino identity was enveloped by a misunderstanding and ambiguous fluidity of the meaning of ethnicity, race, SEP, culture, and national origin as well as an historical amnesia of how the United States was formed and its conquests. (2) The identity category of "Latino" is shadowed by historical ghosts that inform and maintain images of Latinos as irreconcilably different from "Americans." These differences are most sharply delineated in the social sciences and the media. (3) The third striking observation was the role of major social institutions that embraced and acted on these social constructions to exercise their powers in ways harmful to Latino families, youth, and their communities. I summarize and discuss four major cross-cutting themes that in confluence shape and maintain Latinos in their social location:

- Invisible markers of Latino identity embedded in the U.S. racial formation hierarchy that intersect with socioeconomic position (SEP) and gender to shape the varying forms of social inequality.
- Empirical work that examines behaviors as if they were isolated from the social and economic context in which they occur and fuels media images.

- Role of media that shapes the representations of Latinos in the American public imagination and strongly and negatively influences how Latinos view themselves and are viewed in schools and public systems.
- Prevailing institutional practices that are inherently discriminatory and shape larger public policy.

## Making Visible, Markers of Latino Identity: The Trap of the Aggregate

An important and pervasive issue throughout the body of scholarship on Latinos was the question of whom or what is Latino/Hispanic? A significant number of books and reports described Latinos and or provided extensive narratives on history, modes of incorporation, and national origin, suggesting that these factors matter. In contrast, most of the empirical literature presented Latinos as an aggregate ethnic category, suggesting that these identity markers do not matter. The complexity of Latino identity is best illustrated in a number of ways. First and foremost is that their political and social distinction as a separate ethnic group without racial identifiers was not officially sanctioned by the federal government until the 1980s. This naming was an outgrowth of the civil rights era by the largest subgroups, Mexican Americans and Puerto Ricans. Simultaneously the influx of significant Central and South American immigrant populations was occurring that expanded the heterogeneity of Latino groups and repositioned the civil rights intent of remedy in addressing historical mistreatment of formerly excluded colonial groups. Second, Latinos as a separate identity ethnic group do not easily fit into the existing racial formations of the U.S. color hierarchy because Latinos include Black and White races and multiracial mixes (Amaro and Zambrana 2000). The identification as an ethnic group further entrenched Latinos as a cultural group while leaving race as an invisible marker. The point is that the transition from White to official designation as ethnic group for Latinos reinforced the political category of "other or different" and did not change the hegemonic racialized view of Latinos. In effect, those initial efforts to self-name and develop a politically determined category of "Hispanic/Latino" essentially yielded a cultural difference and social placement that defined Latinos (Mexican Americans and Puerto Ricans predominantly) as nonnormative in the American public imagination.

Further, important distinctions between and among Latinos are lost in what can be referred to as the "trap of the aggregate." U.S. official recognition of Hispanic/Latinos in the 1980s coincided with significant immigration flows that created one large homogenized category labeled as Hispanic/Latino. The aggregation contributes to negative stereotypes in the American public imagination in three ways: (1) it does not permit the uncovering of dimensions of inequality, such as the intersection of race, SEP, geographic concentration, and hypersegregation or community context; (2) it makes visible only characteristics of distinctly racialized and low SEP Mexican-origin and Puerto Rican subgroups as representative of all Latinos; and (3) it does not allow for the diversity within and across subgroups by SEP, nor does it include markers of privilege such as racially being White or, for some Hispanic immigrants, prior human and social capital that permits easier integration, based on SEP, into U.S. society. These factors are all important. The discourse on Latinos requires insertion of the continuum of Latino experiences within the context of racialized subgroups versus White European subgroups, and the hierarchy of color, power, and historical incorporation. These are better indicators of acculturation. In other words, acculturation can be redefined as access to resources, which is associated with color privilege, SES, and inclusionary practices. These insertions of difference, inequality, and exclusionary practices will disrupt the social problem and cultural lens discourse that prevails in the study of Latino families.

## The Lens of Knowledge Producers

Producers and guardians of knowledge had established a body of scholarship that framed Latinos as social problems. Those studies became the signifier for *all* Latino groups. As noted by Maxine Baca Zinn and Angela Pok (2002):

> The large presence of poor immigrant families in Southwestern cities gave rise to studies portraying Mexican family life as a social problem for American society. This thinking was rooted in the development of family studies as a new field. Family Studies emerged out of a deep fundamental belief in the need to study and ameliorate social problems. During the 1920s and 1930s, the social-problems approach to family life led to studies of Mexican immigrants that highlighted (1) their foreign patterns and habits, (2) the moral quality of family relationships, and (3) the prospects for their Americanization. (85)

The earlier social science discourse that had both described and created these differences continued to portray—using an essentialist and biased lens—low-income Mexican-origin and Puerto Ricans as outside the normative structure of Euro-American norms. In other words, the category "Latino" operates as a gendered, ethnic, and racial construct that converges with multiple discourses of social stratification, political national identity, and citizenship (Zambrana and Dill 2006). In the twenty-first century, major demographic shifts, immigration patterns, and economic and social domestic policy have differentially shaped family structure, social location, and neighborhood processes including the Latino Diaspora. The most fundamental theoretical conclusion is that cultural constructions of Latino groups are used to maintain systems of inequality. These fundamental cultural constructions derived from earlier empirical work on men and women, specifically on groups subordinated by conquest, are based on racial formations of difference and inferiority.

The second cross-cutting theme is that all too often empirical work examines family processes, functioning, and gender role behaviors as if they were isolated from the social and economic context in which they occur. The identity category of Latino that is shadowed by historical ghosts and analytic identity ambiguity informs how scientists define their populations. Although more recent scholarship inserts differences across groups and within groups, more often than not these differences are erased under the umbrella category of Hispanic/Latino and are still proffered implicitly as cultural determinants.

The social science discourse of Latino families has portrayed these families as underdeveloped and embedded in a traditional family archetype that has remained relatively stable over the last century. The major theorizing construct used to study family development processes has been culture. Culture has been centered as a singular, monolithic, social location that more likely than not dismisses the material conditions of Latinos as an important context that impacts family processes and gender socialization. Essentialized constructions of cultural difference without contextualization in material conditions constitute one of the major ways to maintain racial hierarchies by gender, class, race, or nation, categories that are mutually constituted.

A critical absence in the study of Latino family life course and youth development is the interrelationship between material conditions and community context or neighborhood effects. Community context is an important indicator of inequity and structural inequality that deepens our understanding of factors that influence the structures of opportunity for sectors of the Latino community. Yet, more often than not, community context is omitted as an important factor in Latino family research. When this occurs, study results compellingly demonstrate a group's shortcomings without attention to structural barriers. In locating and articulating a specific Latino voice, it is integral that we take into account the multiple histories of colonization, migration, and racial formations that exist among them (Horno-Delgado et al. 1989; Organista 2007). The overarching themes in this book show that Latinos exhibit a continuum of family structure and processes and gender role enactments that are profoundly related to educational attainment and SEP and that the context in which these processes occur are important. For example, gender role attitudes vary substantially by higher education completion and are more similar than different from non-Hispanic White counterparts. Analysis of Latino families requires shifting our construct of "Latino" as a homogeneous entity absent of economic, political, and social differences.

New theoretical and practical approaches must be deployed to advance our understanding of Latinos as a racialized group embedded in systems of inequality, which has been omitted in past work. We must challenge the disciplines to interrogate their own assumptions regarding Latinos and to include critical variables such as race, ethnicity (Hispanic/Latino subgroup), gender, and SEP to reject singular predictive variables that fail to accurately represent or explain the multicausal factors associated with the lived family experiences of poor, racialized U.S.–and foreign-born Latino women and men. Using an intersectional lens—a path to move beyond singular culture-bound theorizing to make power relations and structural arrangements visible—provides a more accurate picture of why families enact their roles in particular ways. The lack of insertion of the role of structural inequality, historically and to the present, has stagnated knowledge production on Latino families and communities. Social science and disciplinary discourses have a negative effect on the lives of Latinos. What has been clarified in this work is that the academic institutions as well as the media are central socialization mechanisms for both Latinos and the American public. How Latinos have been treated and how their lives have been recorded and described by outsiders (disciplinary scientists) becomes the filter through which the larger society views this group. Images of hypersexuality for both men and women have been common images of Latinos for decades. Social constructions of womanhood has contributed to the formation of Latino women as "commodified identities" and bodies, linked to hypersexuality, eroticism, high fertility, and perceived low intelligence. These gender formations are commonly portrayed in occupations such as domestic and food service. Strong links exist between labor and Latinas and terms such as "Mexican labor" and "dirt cheap labor" that are stratified labor by gender, race, class, and nation (Glenn 2002; Villanueva 2002; Romero 2002). These images form powerful narratives about the "proper" place for Latinas in higher education, the labor market, and society.

The social construction of Latino male identity is built on historical, racialized conceptions of Mexican and Puerto Rican males as drunkards, hypersexual and criminals. These implicit assumptions drive the research on males that represent Latino boys and men as irresponsible, dysfunctional and "gangsta." All these images form negative identity markers that place Latino boys and men at risk of being excluded from access to the social and economic opportunity structure and inhibit their ability to enact their gender roles in the family and community and to construct their masculinity as proactive, responsible men. The repercussions of conventional scientific discourses are most deeply felt in the media representations produced that infiltrate the public imagination and in the harm these representations have caused to the Latino community.

## The Powerful Gaze of the Media

The third cross-cutting theme is the role that media performs in elevating negative images of Latinos. Drawing often from the findings in the social science literature, the media reinforces these female and male images by news stories on Latino adolescent fertility, sexualized roles in television and movies, and (for males) by stories on crimes, gangs, and movies on drug wars, violence, and the Don Juan or "Latin lover" role. These images portray Latinos outside of the normative standards of the American state and fuel portraits of cultural difference and deviance. These images conform to images projected in the media and social science in the mid decades of the twentieth century (Rodriguez 2000; Bender 2003). The lesson drawn is the powerful interrelationships between historical experiences and encounters of coloniality, consequent ascribed racialized social status, and the role of major socialization institutions that persistently insert images that shape the social location of Latinos.

The media portrayal of Latinos in the United States represents an interesting polarity in images of Latinos. The pluralistic functions of ethnic media serve to create a unified Latino identity that reinforces Latinos as family oriented with mothers as loving, tolerant, and patient who value drama, closeness, and children (Johnson 2000). The family focus emphasizes cultural difference rather than cultural strengths and universalistic family values. In contrast, multiple forms of media highlight Latinos as foreign, passive and non–English-speaking, and "struggling." These images represent social constructions of negative gender and community representations that feed the American imagination and institutions that adversely affect the lives of Latino families and the community, such as through English-only laws and racial profiling. These representations have a long history with deep roots in the conquest and subordination of the Mexican and Puerto Rican people and have an adverse effect on the self-esteem of Latino girls and boys. These images influence how young Latinos think about the worthiness of their ethnic/culture group, and subsequently, they absent positive role models in their lives. Racial stereotypes in all forms of media (print, television, movies, and electronic) transcend info-tainment, influencing policy and practice. Unsettling is the unchanging message and constancy of these representations that serve to misinform, provoke animosity against the Latino community (e.g., hate crimes, and spur harsh disciplinary polices (e.g., gang and immigration policies). Another potential consequence is that law enforcement personnel may uncritically internalize these images that fuel fear and provide justification for surveillance and racial profiling.

In contrast, critical benchmarks of Latino integration and social mobility indicators—such as a strong presence of Latino middle class, home ownership, and changes in attitudes and values associated with increases in level of education and SEP—remain invisible to mainstream media and are largely ignored in the current literature. Thus a shift in the social construction of Latinos as a culturally different, poor, homogeneous group needs to occur, in both media and scholarly work, to reverse the misinformed negative perceptions of Latinos in the American public imagination. A major theoretical conclusion is that social, legal, and representational *perceptions* of society created and reinforced by science and media diminish access to the social and economic opportunity structure. These structural dimensions help to partially explain the persistent and disproportionate burden of poverty, the overall low social mobility of historically underrepresented groups, and their contemporary social location.

## The Power of Institutional Practices

Lastly, the role of public institutions, prevailing discriminatory institutional practices that drive public policy, and the use of disciplinary power are often based on negative identity markers that significantly shape the lives of Latino families and youth in schools, health care, and public assistance systems.

Public systems (schools, welfare, education, housing, child protective services) have been theoretically designed to make human capital investments and be safety nets for poor people to increase their economic self sufficiency. Yet dominant–subordinate relations of power were unveiled in the study of these systems. Most government-funded public service systems share attributes that disfavor poor/low-income Latino populations. These include an unwillingness to invest in the development of low-income families (e.g., the child welfare system's approach of removing children rather than investing in family development) and limited investments in improving quality schools while increasing gang divisions in police precincts and building more prisons. In contrast to popular belief, only about 3 percent of Latino boys and less than 1 percent of Latino girls claim membership in a gang. As a result Latinos are less likely to live in neighborhoods of opportunity, less likely to access public assistance benefits and health care, have fewer recreational facilities, and have more police surveillance.

Public system bureaucrats often think of poor people (especially Latino and NHB families) as being deviant, representing a "culture of irresponsibility," and as less likely to benefit from services. These invisible, and perhaps unconscious, perceptions are linked to a historical, hegemonic superior/inferior binary that provides the basis for differential implementation of policy and discriminatory treatment that place Latinos at an unrelenting disadvantage. In other words, public systems share a similar silent ideology of the moral construction of poverty, of deserving versus undeserving poor, that is reinforced by a racial hierarchy. The disciplinary power of officials who implement services often reinforce structural processes of inequality in the provision of inadequate services that fail to promote economic self-sufficiency, family strengthening, and access to new skills and life options for recipients.

Although often overlooked, neighborhoods are an important context for understanding how issues of quality of services and human capital investments are inextricably linked to the institutional and structural processes that maintain low-income families, marginalized and outside the opportunity structure. Researchers often engage in victim-blaming approaches relying on individual or culturally deterministic explanations to explain Latino student underperformance, early sexual activity and family formation, and gang membership without accounting for the role of low-resourced community contexts on structural inequality and the unequal treatment by public service systems designed to help them.

Several findings are worthy of mention. For low-income Latino boys and girls, location in low-resourced communities, participation in low-quality schools, racialized perceptions by teachers, more likelihood of schools to have zero tolerance policies, and low expectations all contribute to the accumulation of educational deficits and social disadvantage throughout the K–12 educational pipeline. These educational deficits are in turn often compounded by limited access to health care to address physical (e.g., vision and hearing), cognitive (e.g., learning disabilities), emotional (e.g., depression), and behavioral (e.g., ADHD) conditions and limited access to information on sex and contraceptives. In turn, this community context is fertile ground for behaviors and decisions associated with the search for a meaningful social role status, such as early formation of families and labor force participation. Although a majority of the literature addresses the problems of Latino youth, emerging scholarship is focusing on how Latino families and youth are negotiating and creating new ways to overcome barriers to access the social and economic opportunity structures.

Much of the work included in this book provides new and emergent ways of thinking about stratification and the ways in which institutional forces produce and reinforce the social location of Latinos. The research presented not unexpectedly defies the canonical social science and other disciplinary perspectives of Latinos as cultural underperformers. What I aimed to show concretely through many of the studies included were the ways in which social location is linked to hegemonic representations and how an essentialized cultural orientation in many disciplines sets up false separations of race, ethnicity, SEP, and gender rather than invoking the importance of mutually constituted identities. Equally important socialization mechanisms, community context/neighborhood effects, and institutional resources and practices informed the findings to advance our understanding of the ways in which Latinos are treated and the barriers Latinos confront in shifting their social location. What these studies have most importantly provided is some insight into *why* there is a plethora of negative findings.

The research synthesis and analysis presented show that adverse outcomes for low-income Latinos are often inaccurately characterized as ethnic- or culture-specific individual or group failures that are resistant to human capital investments by the state. The major theoretical conclusion is that attributing health, educational, and income outcomes to low-income Latino immigrants, U.S. citizens, and communities as a result of culture-driven indicators without considering the structural forces faced by these populations is not scientifically justifiable. An understanding and insertion of community context and the role of the public institutional systems in explaining the social location of Latinos provides a theoretical intervention to unmask the racial, class, and gender constructions that shape their lived experiences. In effect, these institutions serve as gatekeepers rather than safety nets to help Latinos improve their economic and social location. The omission of these forces as major factors in promoting inequality derail knowledge production on Latinos and hinder advancing our understanding of increasing disparities and the social location of Latinos.

I have used an intersectional approach as a way to show an alternative mode of knowledge production. It makes visible commonalities of inequalities and power relations across institutional systems. Using this lens shows how multiple dimensions of inequality operate simultaneously to maintain Latinos in their social location, validates the lives and stories of marginalized groups, and expands the understanding of factors associated with access to the opportunity structure. The theorizing conclusions that evolved from these analyses provide a basic set of guiding interventions for intersectional future research on Latino families, youth, and communities. Although a plethora of empirical work has been generated, particularly in the last decade, significant gaps exist in key areas of interest.

## New and Emerging Areas of Inquiry for U.S. Latino Studies

Work in U.S. Latino Studies has grown immeasurably in the last twenty years and is more publicly available. Yet scholarship on U.S. Latino experiences has a long history of production in many U.S. higher education research centers such as the Tomas Rivera Center in Claremont, California; Hispanic Research Center in New York; and other universities associated with the *Inter-University Program for Latino Research* (IUPLR), a consortium of eighteen Latino research centers based at major universities in every region of the United States. It is the only nationwide university-based research organization bringing together scholars from a wide variety of disciplines to conduct empirical and policy-relevant research on Latinos. Its primary objectives are to expand the pool of scholars and leaders, to strengthen the capacity of Latino research centers, and to facilitate the availability of policy-relevant, Latino-focused research. The IUPLR offers training programs, sponsors interdisciplinary research pertinent to Latinos and Latinas and to the nation as a whole, and creates links among scholars, policy experts, public officials, and community advocates. Much of this scholarship has been produced in reports or published in nonmainstream journals. Thus, it is unfair to say that Latino scholarship has not been produced, but rather we can say that it has not been available in the public realm of mainstream science. With this being said, I now describe areas that require additional study with an intersectional lens and other areas that require inquiry and insertion into mainstream scientific discourse.

The field of U.S. Latino Studies has made significant contributions to scholarly production. Multiple disciplines such as sociology, political science, psychology, literature, and interdisciplinary fields such as U.S. Latino/Chicano/ Puerto Rican/Dominican studies, cultural studies, sexuality studies, and Critical Race Studies have produced scholarship on the lived experiences of Latinos, but the majority of these inter/disciplines have not comprehensively integrated the Latino experience as part of the racial/ethnic discourse. Gender studies, immigration studies, and Critical Race Studies represent areas of inquiry that have yielded the largest, albeit modest, scholarly work, yet theoretical and empirical gaps persist. Most recently, Zambrana and Dill (2009) in discussing the postmodern interdisciplinary fields and their "in/exclusion of ethnic groups" state:

> Each field sought to interrogate historical patterns of subordination and domination. Thus categories of race, class, and gender were defined as major markers and signifiers of oppression with limited attention to other markers of oppression such as sexuality, nation, ethnicity, age, bodily ability, religion, and others. The last two decades have witnessed the development and maturation of a number of debates and discourses about intersectionality. (277)

Feminist scholarship that centers gender in U.S. Latino Studies can be attributed to pioneering scholars, such as Gloria Anzaldúa (1983), Anzaldúa and Cherrie Moraga (1987), Denise Segura (1993) and Maxine Baca Zinn (1980, 1982, 1994), who inserted Latina/Chicana scholarship into feminist and sociological discourses. These scholars argued that gender is a critical analytic category that has been shaped by history and social location of Latino women. An overview of feminist writings reveals that lived experiences of Latinas are markedly absent from feminist historical accounts and scholarship. Building on Black feminists' standpoint theory, Chicana feminists over the last twenty years have produced an impressive body of work that reveals the complex intersections of race, class, gender, nation, ethnicity, sexuality, and other social locations. They have formulated theories and methodologies to best insert their histories, lived experiences, and sociopolitical locations into the disciplines. Latina scholars have drawn on multiple methods to portray their lived experiences such as oral history, reflexive ethnography, empirical studies, and literary theory. These scholars sought to claim an intellectual space in gender studies, to center their experiences in the U.S. Latino discourse, and to shift the center of feminist analysis from solely on gender to examine the multiplicities of identities and mutually constituted identities. However feminist or women's studies remained a relatively White women's bastion of privilege. For example, Baca Zinn (1994) argues that Western feminism has failed to grapple with "race as a power system that affects families throughout society" (312).

In response Chicana scholars produced the narratives and research of their own lived experiences.

Chicana/Latina Studies emerged from the experiences of Mexican American women on the West coast with a focus on marginalized experiences of low-wage work and the life experiences of poor women. From this inquiry was born the field of Chicana feminism, which uniquely centers multiplicity of identities and dimensions of inequality in describing the realities of Mexican-origin women. U.S. Latina/Chicana feminist thought extended Western feminist theories to include race, nation, class, and sexuality. The major contributions of Latina feminist thought has been to center the lived experiences of a historically marginalized and underrepresented group by embedding gender studies in the historical and contemporary context of home and work life that have shaped their social location. Mexican/Chicana scholars have powerfully examined systems of inequality among Mexican women who work blue-collar jobs and face the triple oppression of gender, nationality, and class and experience employer abuses because they fear losing their jobs (Ruiz 2002; Romero 2002). In contrast to the focus of White feminists, the distinctions between public (work) and private (family) spheres are not as compartmentalized in Latino families (Hurtado 1996). Low-income and working-class Latinas have not had the privilege to experience a separation between work and family (i.e., no protected sphere of domesticity) (Baca Zinn 1994).

Tensions and debates exist within gender and women's studies regarding the continued marginalization of Latina scholars and the scholarship produced. Critical empirical gaps persist in areas of inquiry such as gender roles among professional women, role burden and overload on women in the family, dual-career and dual-worker families, socialization of children by SEP, nativity, family processes in U.S.–born and transnational families, and the role of race in definitions of womanhood and femininity. Although Latina scholars have produced scholarship on Latino women in multiple spheres, these works have not penetrated the field of Gender Studies with the expected inclusive welcome.

## Immigration, Racial Hierarchy, and Privilege

Immigration and transnational studies have occupied a powerful place in scholarly production over the last decade. Perhaps not surprising is that funding for research is often aligned with political pressure from groups as well as political interests of governing bodies. As a result some immigrant groups are more studied than others, although there is a tendency to discuss immigration as a homogeneous construct. Despite common generalizations about immigrant groups, data clearly show that some immigrant groups are at a greater disadvantage than others (Hernandez 2004; Hernandez et al. 2007; Dixon and Gelatt 2006). The term *immigrant* tends to be used as a broad category that fails to capture differences between immigrant groups: legal immigrants, temporary immigrants (such as students and professional workers with visas), undocumented workers (which usually refers to an unskilled labor force), and protected classes of immigrants (such as refugees). Clearly, immigrants are not a homogeneous group, and how they integrate socially and economically into U.S. society is highly influenced by race/ethnicity, SEP, and receptivity by U.S. society. Baca Zinn and Wells (2000) discuss Latino family heterogeneity, its boundaries, and the dynamics of Latino family life, arguing for a more systematic theorizing on the role of macro structural conditions such as globalization and "privileged im/migration" that create specific family variations across and within Latino groups. *Familism* is not a one-dimensional concept and differs across region, SEP, segmented labor markets, and nonimmigrant versus immigrant status. In many ways, Mexican Americans and Mexican immigrants are portrayed as a monolithic essentialized "other," yet significant variability exists within and across groups (Portes 2007).

The interest in and proliferation of immigrant studies have reproduced images of all Latinos as foreign subjects and detracted attention from U.S.–born, historically underrepresented Latinos who still constitute the majority of the population. Drawbacks are imminent in this empirical proliferation: Mexican immigrants have been showcased as the group who benefit from entry into the United States. Less attention has been given to their historical and contemporary contributions as a surplus labor force in the United States (and, for many, their legal resident status). The unprecedented emphasis on Mexican immigration has two undesirable outcomes. First, it targets and places all racialized Mexican-origin and other Latinos at high risk of surveillance, racial profiling, and detrimental policies by government officials (Murguia 2008); and, second, it reinforces the social constructions of all Latinos as foreigners and un-American. Equally important is that race as a social category of analysis has been markedly absent from the study of Latinos in the United States, particularly among immigrants. Yet immigrant Latinos who most closely approximate the racial (White) and SEP characteristics (college-educated) of the majority population are less likely to experience unequal treatment, and more likely to integrate into the U.S. society.

Another important area of scholarly inquiry is the role of the racial hierarchy within Latino groups. Only recently have researchers, particularly Latino researchers, begun to assess the ways in which race, ethnicity, and SEP are defined and used, as well as what constitutes meaningful comparisons within and across Latino immigrant and U.S. born groups over time. There has been a call to view race and ethnicity as markers of racial stratification (Zuberi and Bonilla-Silva 2008). Many scholars are actively seeking ways to better describe how these labels are used as proxies for institutionalized racism and how they contribute to differential treatment for specific Latino subgroups. Telles and

Ortiz (2008) in their longitudinal study of 700 of the original respondents and their 750 children included in the 2000 Mexican American Study Project found persistent educational disadvantage across generations and low integration. In a startling account of the lives of these individuals and how their racialized, ethnic minority status has served as barriers to full integration in U.S. society, the authors provide critical insight into the role of structural barriers in the persistent low socioeconomic status and social location of Mexican Americans. To understand racial identity classifications, Clara Rodriguez (2000) examined the multidimensional aspect of Latino racial identity using census data and personal interviews. She asserts that Latinos have been in large part seen as a Spanish-speaking White ethnic group who are expected to fully assimilate. Although the classification systems have changed over time, the treatment of predominantly historically underrepresented Latinos as non-Whites has remained relatively stable. Rodriguez uncovered important findings regarding Latinos and race privilege: (1) "White" Latinos experienced discrimination based on accent, surname, and dominant culture stereotypes. Rodriguez argues that there is a process of negotiation in racial formations and that "White" Latinos engage in this process for a place in the racial/ethnic hierarchy; and (2) White Latinos fare better in wages, housing, and SEP. Eduardo Bonilla-Silva (2006) extends the work on racial formations and Latinos and argues that symbolic racism has replaced biological racism with more concern with moral character and traditions of individualism. These new criteria of "color-blind racism" mask institutional practices such as market dynamics used to explain unemployment and wage disparities and cultural explanations. His focus on institutional practices and criteria for entry into White privilege ("Honorary Whites") convincingly argues that the hierarchy of racial formation in the United States buffers and maintains White privilege. The maintenance of a plural racial stratification system (mulatto, mestizo, ladino, etc.) similar to Latin America[1] upholds the system of White privilege by creating separate groups with separate political,

---

1. For a historical analysis and description of how race has been defined for U.S. Latinos (Telles and Ortiz 2008) and the racial hierarchy in Latin America, see Rodriguez 2000. The history of the involuntary immigration of African-origin peoples and integration into indigenous cultures and Spanish conquest shaped the cultural heritage of each Latin American country in different ways. Large numbers of African-origin peoples were brought to the Caribbean (Cuba, Dominican Republic, and Cuba) and Central and South America (Nicaragua [English-speaking Blacks on the east coast], Venezuela, Brazil, Columbia [Cartagena de India]). In some Latin American countries, Blacks were predominantly excluded (e.g., Argentina, Chile). After World War II, many Europeans went to southern Mexico and El Salvador, and many Eastern European Jews went to Argentina, Chile, and Bolivia. Thus some of the tensions and divisions we see in the United States today and the lack of a strong and unified political power base of the Latino community may be associated with differences in cultural background, color privilege, SEP in country of origin, modes of incorporation into home country and United States, and the status accorded by U.S. policy, law, and perception. González-Lopez and Vidal-Ortiz (2008) observe that "sociological research and theorizing on the sex lives of U.S. Latino populations is relatively recent."

social, and cultural interests. This racial hierarchy creates social and political tensions within and between Latino subgroups that may in the long run also reinforce the low social location of some Latino subgroups.

Insertion of race markers in the Latino discourse has been thwarted by several factors. These include (1) Latinos' resistance to racial identification and preference for ethnic or national identity; (2) the emphasis by Latinos and social scientists on a panethnic identity for social and political purposes; (3) the political rootedness of the Black–White binary in the United States that has disallowed the expansion of the construct of racial formations and racial inequality beyond the Black–White experience; and (4) the misuse of race as an independent predictor of social location. The use of race as a predictor has been challenged by Zuberi and Bonilla-Silva (2008) who aptly argue that the use of race as a causal variable is influenced by White supremacy methods, is inappropriately defined, and its impacts are incorrectly measured in current social science studies. The authors propose a paradigm shift from dominant White supremacy–led research methods to alternative methods. The paradigm shift suggested would center the importance of racial groups and racial inequalities and strive to be race conscious and "engaged in a systematic analysis of racial stratification and its efforts" (338). They eloquently state: "Critical social scientists on race matters can provide data, arguments, counternarratives, and all sorts of intellectual ammunition against dominant representations about racial groups and racial inequality. And to provide better ammunition for the movements against White supremacy, the sociological and social scientific efforts in this field must be race conscious and engaged in a systematic analysis of racial stratification and its effects. A neutral, or even liberal, sociology will not do the trick, as neutrality on race matters usually means support of the racial status quo: and liberal sociology fosters at best charitable views about people of color and the reformist policies on behalf of the 'problem people'" (Zuberi and Bonilla-Silva 2008, 338).

What I have learned in writing this book is that race as an analytic construct is central in the understanding of Latino family and youth social location and the material conditions and social inequality that persist. Race is a social determinant of social location because it is strongly linked with history and superior-inferior binary that has dominated U.S. hegemonic thought and contributed to the subordinate status of Latinos in the U.S. racial hierarchy. Thus, the scholarship on Latinos confirms that race, ethnicity, SEP, and gender must be examined simultaneously because they are mutually constituted categories that jointly shape access to the social and economic opportunity structure. Although the insertion of race into future studies destabilizes the notion of panethnic identity, the extant heterogeneity within and across Latino subgroups and the racial/ethnic privileged color hierarchy has transformed the notion of "one-culture, one heritage, one ethno-race." Latino identity is in flux and under scrutiny.

## Latino Critical Race Theory

The study of institutionalized racism in law and policy has been a domain of Latino Critical Theory (LatCrit). LatCrit, although largely ignored, has made historic intellectual and legal contributions. LatCrit (see www.latcrit.org) calls attention to the ways in which conventional, and even critical, approaches to race and civil rights ignore the problems and special situations of Latino people—including bilingualism, immigration reform, the Black–White binary structure of existing legal remedies (Stefancic 1997, 1510). The invisibility of Latino legal inquiry is evident in multiple fields including health, education, and child welfare. This oversight is perhaps due both to the fact that Latinos as an ethnic group were classified as White up until 1980 and to the invisibility of Latino scholars, many of whom have documented the historical legal mistreatment of Mexican Americans (see, e.g., Almaguer 1994; Bender 2003; MacDonald 2004).

LatCrit has been active in the application of critical race theory in explaining Latino lived experiences in community and legal institutions. Linking theory and practice is seen as a vital dimension of this scholarship, one that grows out of its roots in lived experience and is directed toward its goal of social justice. Recognizing that knowledge produced in the field of law affects structures of power in society, LatCrit and other legal race scholars focus the analytic lens on policies and areas of the law that have previously been overlooked. A major guiding principle is that no single community can produce a theory about intergroup justice without connections to other groups. Yet every single social justice movement has had a problem of essentialism, giving primacy to some aspects of their identity while ignoring others that intersect with and reform that primary identity (Delgado Bernal 2002). As a result, Latino identity is studied as a multifaceted, intersectional reality. LatCrit theorists, argue, that Latinos are Black, White, Asian, gay, straight, poor, wealthy, and speak many different languages. Thus the term *anti-essentialism* has particular meaning because their work is primarily focused on incorporating issues of identity, hybridism, and liberation into the analysis of law and the discourses in legal institutions and processes.

## Sexuality Studies

The intersection of ethnic, racial, national, and sexual orientation and identity are emerging areas of inquiry that require study within and across Latino subgroups and within the context of privilege and stigma (see Yarbro-Bejarano 1999; Juarez and Kerl 2003; Herek and Gonzalez-Rivera 2006; La Fountain-Stokes 2009). Sexuality and sexual orientation and identity is an understudied area both for heterosexual and same-sex Latino relationships (González-Lopez and Vidal Ortiz 2008). Sociologists have only focused on Latino sexuality scholarship within the last twenty years.

Most work on Latino men has been conducted on HIV/AIDS. A much more limited scholarship exists on Latina lesbians. Rationale for the silence around the issues of Latino sexuality has been attributed to the role of religion, culture-specific heteronormative attitudes (and in some cases hyperhetero-sexuality), and difficulty in exploring the topic of sexuality. An intersectional approach that emphasizes multiple dimensions of identity and their relationship to systems of power has been part of lesbian, gay, bisexual, and transgender (LGBT) studies, revealing the heterosexism of institutions and practices, broadening our understandings of gender, exposing the artificiality of presumed sex differences, and expanding knowledge of sexual desire, attraction and behavior. However, Latino LGBT studies have been marginalized in the field of queer studies. The absence of intersectionality has been criticized by scholars of color, in particular, because LGBT and queer studies have largely ignored race and ethnicity and failed to incorporate the insights of intersectional analysis with regard to race, ethnicity, and racialization into its larger theoretical frame (Zambrana and Dill 2009).

The study of the Latino LGBT community has been portrayed as a difficult and sensitive area of research. Recent work suggests both constraints and possible solutions to advance inquiry in this area. Latino scholars have noted obstacles in interviewing Latino subjects about issues related to sexuality. Such overt questions may alienate the respondent or involve awkward issues of translation (Herek and Gonzalez-Rivera 2006). Gregory Herek and Milagritos Gonzalez-Rivera explored the extent of homophobia in Latino communities and report that, contrary to popular belief, homophobic attitudes are not demonstrably higher than in other communities. The authors conclude that a pronounced link exists between high levels of homophobia and conservatism about traditional gender roles and gender identities.

Perceived identity and social location of individuals may also present barriers. María Zea and colleagues (2003) argue that issues of language and meaning must be considered in researching sexuality among Latinos. For example, all men who have sex with men might not self-identify as bisexual or gay. Latino men may not view that particular cultural construct as having anything to do with them because they associate it with a racialized sexuality—something more American or White-identified. To capture the lived experiences of these men, the authors suggest a multistaged methodology to explore Latino LGBT populations, including a multistep interview process with a debriefing or exit interview. Another approach to uncover their lived experiences is the use of secondary archival sources. For example, Juan Rodriguez (2003) examined the archive created through the activist work of Latino, community-based organizations, arguing that this archive demonstrates the ways in which these organizations "speak back" to dominant conversations about Latino sexualities (48). He argues that LGBT-identified Latinos in San Francisco used language and culturally encoded practices of resistance as a way to forge a community in the midst of the AIDS crisis. Rodriguez concludes that "[u]nderstanding the relationship between social context and social agents, socially constructed categories, and lived realities is crucial if we want to impact society and its (non) citizens" (2003, 46).

Female sexual orientation and identity has also received limited attention (Arguelles 1998; Martinez 1998; Perez 2003). In a 2008 issue of *Sinister Wisdom*, editor Juanita Ramos reports that the last anthology on Latina lesbians was published in 1987. In this bilingual collection, women narrate, in multiple text forms such as poetry, short stories, and art, their lived experiences in their community, their families, mother-daughter relationships, and their relationships with work and activism. An emerging body of work is developing that describes the lived experiences of Latino members of the LGBT community. Latino sexual identity is also deeply embedded in historical migration and settlements, nation, SES, and race associated with systems of exploitation, discrimination, and devalued identity markers (Hedrick 2009; Moraga 2009). Sexuality as a construct of intellectual inquiry uniquely requires its own intersectional theorizing for the LGBT community and its insertion in gender studies and Chicano/Chicana/Latino studies. As observed by Karen Mary Davalos (2008): "Two qualities of Chicana feminist thought leave me hopeful. The central role of debate and dialogue, identified by the editors of Chicana Feminisms and described by Gonzalez, allows me to anticipate conversations and alliances that will propel queer Chicana studies onto solid ground. I expect that the relative lack of attention to queer theory and experience in much Chicana feminist/studies literature will be short lived. Additionally, the transformative premise of Chicana feminism will not allow for a reversal or sustained backlash against the LGBTQ successes of the 1980s and 1990s. Unlike the disciplines from which they borrow, Chicana feminists insist on a scholarship that is accountable to social problems and that aims to root out injustice and expose artificial hierarchies and methods of exclusion" (169).

A beginning scholarship has been produced on Latino LGBT communities, but it remains modest, relatively invisible in the conventional science outlets and on the margins. Crucial areas of inquiry still remain across the life course including LGBT sexual identity expression and does it differ by SES, nation and nativity, transgendered Latinos and equally important empirical work on family formation and parenting among same-sex couples, and families processes in same-sex marriage and children of these families. These are mere examples of an area of inquiry that has vast knowledge gaps.

New frameworks and methods will require development to better understand the lived experienced of LGBT Latinos within a context of inequality and heteronormativity in the Latino community and in the larger dominant LGBT community in the context of White privilege and inequality.

## Concluding Observations: Building on Critical Scholarship, Challenging and Extending the Boundaries

Without a critical examination of the fundamental tenets of research, emerging scholars could easily repeat the same analyses and arrive at the same conclusions that have produced limited knowledge and prevented significant advances on the structural factors associated with the social and material conditions of Latinos. It is imperative to build on and draw from the findings and claims of new scholarship that extend prior conventional models of knowing. Multiple barriers exist within the academy in making a research paradigm shift. The legacy of racist scientific thought that defines the traditional uses—or, more appropriately, misuses—of race in social science and statistical analyses are well known. The assumption that objectivity characterizes scientific inquiry has been repeatedly challenged, especially by feminists, critical legal and race scholars, and revisionist social science scholars. Objectivity is grounded in the biases and values of the scientists themselves and is evidenced by the theoretical lens used, types of research questions asked, communities selected, and variables included and omitted—all of which contribute to narrow or broad interpretations of data. As Zuberi and Bonilla-Silva state: "scholars need to question the utility of an entire research methodology that has been designed specifically to make judgments regarding the superiority of one racial group over another" (19).

Conventional research, particularly in the social sciences, public health, and education among others, is largely reactive, seldom identifying root causes of social problems and rarely providing an in-depth understanding of the structural and historical factors that shape the experiences of Latino groups in the United States. A prominent issue is the general reluctance among the majority of researchers and policy makers to interrogate how culture is defined and applied within research. Culture has been and continues to be a signifier that portrays Latino group characteristics as unchangeable. Cultural discourses merely insert a biased predictor into the scientific enterprise, which maintains the marginal and unequal social location of racialized Latino subgroups in place.

Acts of resistance (which affirm and elevate culture as an asset) by Latino scholars in response to the denigrating of the Latino culture in disciplinary discourses have challenged the negative stereotyping in the dominant hegemonic discourse. Although this oppositional consciousness and resistance is scientifically valid, my scholarly concern is that it may detract from examining systems of inequality. Interestingly, challenges to mainstream hegemonic thinking by Latino scholars do not easily find a place in the public scientific discourse. Why not? In conducting research for this book, I have garnered the following observations on this problem: First, Latino scholarship that challenges hegemonic thinking tends to be published in nonmainstream journals, while scholarship that reinforces hegemonic thinking, particularly around culture, tends to be published in more mainstream journals.

Second, the producers of knowledge are concentrated in academic institutions and intellectual towers such as think tanks, both of which have few if any Latino scholars. The production of knowledge is a hallmark of faculty intellectual creativity in higher education research institutions. In 2007, Latino faculty represented about 4 percent of all college and university faculty, and Latino established senior scholars represented 1.4 percent (male) and 0.5 percent (female) of these scholars in academia (NCES 2010). The research enterprise, although interested in understanding racial/ethnic disparities, frequently circumvents the importance of the voice of Latino scholars who can serve as a cerebral hub in the concentrated activity of the production of science. Latino scholars can contribute by extending the thinking to include dimensions of structural inequalities confronted by Latino families. In spite of the small numbers, the proliferation of Latino scholarship in the last two decades suggests that new avenues of knowledge are being created and expanded. This emerging scholarship disrupts the narrow conceptualizations currently being used to understand the multifaceted factors that are associated with the diverse Latino family and community processes in the United States.

Without a doubt, the research shows that new conceptual maps—such as situated knowledge, oppositional consciousness, racial formation, racial hierarchy, racial/ethnic stratification, and "strategic essentialism" (Spivak 1988)— have been provided by feminists, Latino Critical Race theorists, and Latino and non-Latino disciplinary scholars These maps offer novel ways to theorize about difference, inequality, and diversity within and across Latino subgroups. New emphases on gender studies, sexuality studies, and masculinity studies provide an opportunity to generate an innovative line of inquiry where the social and economic conditions under which Latino men and women enact their gender roles is illuminated and differences by race, nativity, sexual orientation and identity, and SEP are duly acknowledged. This body of work has clearly affirmed that no single category (race, class, ethnicity, gender, nation, or sexuality) can explicate with profundity the human experience without reference to other categories. Therefore, intersectional scholarship embraces these understandings to deepen and extend knowledge production and to serve as a tool for social justice and social change.

More nuanced and complex understandings of identity and more fluid notions of gender, race, sexual orientation, identity, and class must be reformulated to expand the depth and breadth of Latino lived experiences. Kurt Organista (2007) contests the dominant culture's imperialism and resistance to discussion of human differences within and across cultures and calls for a discussion of difference "beyond the kind of defensive and superficial hyperbole that leaves social oppression unchallenged" (101). And, while Latino scholarship still struggles with the pull to establish either a hierarchy of difference or a list that includes all forms of social differentiation and with how to frame and place culture as a positive identity marker, it is dimensions of inequality that most deeply affect the Latino experience as cultural and legal citizens.

# References

AAUW Educational Foundation. 1995. *Growing smart: What's working for girls in school?* Washington, DC: AAUW.

Abalos, David. 1998. *La comunidad Latina [Latino community] in the United States: Personal and political strategies for transforming culture.* Westport, CT: Praeger.

Acevedo-Garcia, Dolores. 2000. A conceptual framework of the role of residential segregation in the epidemiology of infectious diseases. *Social Science and Medicine* 51 (8): 1143–61.

———. 2001. Zip code–level risk factors for tuberculosis: Neighborhood environment and residential segregation in New Jersey, 1985–1992. *American Journal of Public Health* 91 (5): 734–41.

Acevedo-Garcia, Dolores, and Lisa M. Bates. 2008. Latino health paradoxes: Empirical evidence, explanations, future research, and implications. In *Latinas/os in the United States: Changing the face of America*, edited by Havidán Rodriguez, Rogelio Sáenz, and Cecelia Menjívar, 101–13. New York: Springer.

Acevedo-Garcia, Dolores, Theresa Osypuk, Nancy McArdle, and David Williams. 2008. Towards a policy relevant analysis of geographic and racial/ethnic disparities in child health. *Health Affairs* 27 (2): 321–33.

Acevedo-Garcia, Dolores, Mah-J Soobader, and Lisa F. Berkman. 2007. Low birthweight among US Hispanic/Latino subgroups: The effect of maternal foreign-born status and education. *Social Science and Medicine* 65 (12): 2503–16.

Acosta, Luis, Dolores Acevedo-Garcia, Matthew Perzanowski, Robert Mellins, Lindsay Rosenfeld, Dharman Cortes, Andrew Gelman, Joanne Fagan, Luis Bracero, Juan Correa, Ann Marie Reardon, and Ginger Chew. 2008. The New York City Puerto Rican asthma project: Study design, methods, and baseline results. *Journal of Asthma* 45:51–57.

Acosta-Belén, Edna, and Carlos E. Santiago. 1998. Merging borders: The remapping of America. In *The Latino studies reader: Culture, economy, and society*, edited by Antonia Darder and Rodolfo D. Torres, 1–37. Malden, MA: Blackwell.

———. 2006. *Puerto Ricans in the United States: A contemporary portrait.* Boulder, CO: Lynne Rienner.

Acuña, Rodolfo F. 2003. *U.S. Latino issues.* Westport, CT: Greenwood Press.

———. 2007. *Occupied America: A history of Chicanos.* 6th ed. New York: Longman.

Agency for Healthcare Research and Quality. (AHRQ) 2007. National healthcare disparities report. USDHHS. Pub. No. 06-0017. Rockville, MD: AHRQ.

Aguirre-Molina, Marilyn, Noilyn Abesamis, and Michelle Castro. 2003. The state of the art: Latinas in the health literature. In *Latina health in the U.S.*, edited by Marilyn Aguirre-Molina and Carlos Molina, 3–23. San Francisco, CA: Jossey-Bass.

Aguirre-Molina, Marilyn, and A. Pond. 2002. *Latino access to primary and preventive services: Barriers, needs, and policy implications.* Policy Briefing. Princeton, NJ: Robert Wood Johnson Foundation.

Aguirre, Benigno E., and Rogelio Sáenz. 2002. Testing the effects of collectively expected durations of migration: The naturalization of Mexicans and Cubans. *International Migration Review* 36 (1): 103–24.

Aizenman, Nurith C. 2009a. Struggles of the second generation. *Washington Post,* December 7, Metro section.

———. 2009b. Undesirable inheritance. *Washington Post,* December 9, Metro section.

Alan Guttmacher Institute. 2008. Provider advice to women may vary by women's social class and ethnicity. *Perspectives on Sexual & Reproductive Health* 40 (1): 54.

Alderete, Ethel, William A. Vega, Bohdan Kolody, and Sergio Aguilar-Gaxiola. 2000. Lifetime prevalence of and risk factors for psychiatric disorders among Mexican migrant farm workers in California. *American Journal of Public Health* 90:608–14.

Alegría, Margarita, Norah Mulvaney-Day, Meghan Woo, Maria Torres, Shan Gao, and Vanessa Oddo. 2007. Correlates of the twelve-month mental health services use among Latinos: Results from the National Latino and Asian American Study (NLAAS). *American Journal of Public Health* 97:76–83.

Alegría, Margarita, William M. Sribney, Debra Perez, Mara Laderman, and Kristen Keefe. 2009. The role of patient activation on patient-provider communication and quality of care for U.S. and foreign-born Latino patients. *Journal of General Internal Medicine* 24 (3): 534–41.

Alliance for Excellent Education 2007. *Plan for success: Communities of color define policy priorities for high school reform.* Washington, DC: Alliance for Excellent Education.

Almaguer, Tomas. 1994. *Racial fault lines: The historical origins of white supremacy in California.* Berkeley: University of California Press.

Alvidrez, Jennifer. 1999. Ethnic variations in mental health attitudes and service use among low-income African American, Latina, and European American young women. *Community Mental Health* 35:515–30.

Amaro, Hortensia. 1995. Love, sex, and power: Considering women's realities in HIV prevention. *American Psychological Association* 30 (6): 437–47.

Amaro, Hortensia, and Ruth E. Zambrana. 2000. Hispanic/Latino and multiple race categories: Mestizo, LatiNegro, Afro-Latino, or White or Black? *American Journal of Public Health* 90 (11): 1724–27.

American Cancer Society (ACS). 2007. *Cancer facts and figures for Hispanic-Latinos 2006–2008.* Atlanta, GA: ACS.

American Civil Liberties Union. 2007. Racial profiling alert, highlights in the fight against racial profiling. http://www.aclu.org/images/asset_upload_file948_34559.doc.

American Heart Association. 2009. *Heart Disease and Stroke Statistics—2009 Update* (At-a-Glance version). http://www.americanheart.org/downloadable/heart/124025094 6756LS-1982%20Heart%20and%20Stroke%20Update.042009.pdf.

Anderson, Laurie M., Joseph St. Charles, Mindy T. Fullilove, Susan C. Scrimshaw, Jonathan E. Fielding, Jacques Normand, and the Task Force on Community Preventive Services. 2003. Providing affordable family housing and reducing residential segregation by income: A systematic review. *American Journal of Preventive Medicine* 24 (3S): 47–67.

Anderson, Norman B., and Cheryl A. Armstead. 1995. Toward understanding the association of socioeconomic status and health: A new challenge for the biopsychosocial approach. *Psychosomatic Medicine* 57:213–25.

Angel, Ronald, and Jacqueline L. Angel. 2009. Employment and benefits for working age Hispanic males. In *Hispanic Families at Risk,* 47–60. New York: Springer.

Annie E. Casey Foundation. 2006. *Undercounted, underserved, immigrant and refugee families in the child welfare system.* Baltimore: Annie E. Casey Foundation.

Anzaldúa, Gloria. 1987. *Borderlands la frontera: The new mestiza.* San Francisco: Aunt Lute Books.

Anzaldúa, Gloria, and Cherrie Moraga, eds. 1983. *This bridge called my back: Writings by radical women of color.* New York: Kitchen Table—Women of Color Press.

Arboleda, Angela. 2002. *Latinos and the federal criminal justice system.* Washington, DC: National Council of La Raza.

Arcia, Emily, Debra Skinner, Donald Bailey, and Vivian Correa. 2001. Models of acculturation and health behaviors among Latino immigrants to the U.S. *Social Science and Medicine* 53 (1): 41–53.

Arellano, Adele R., and Amado M. Padilla. 1996. Academic invulnerability among a select group of Latino university students. *Hispanic Journal of Behavioral Sciences* 18 (4): 485–507.

Arguelles, Lourdes. 1998. Crazy wisdom: Memories of a Cuban Queer. In *The Latino studies reader: Culture, economy & society,* edited by Antonia Darder and Rodolfo D. Torres. Massachusetts: Blackwell Publishing.

Arend, Elizabeth D. 2005. The politics of invisibility homophobia and low-income HIV-positive women who have sex with women. *Journal of Homosexuality* 49 (1): 97–122.

Armstrong, Katrina, Karima L. Ravenell, Suzanne McMurphy, and Mary Putt. 2007. Racial/ethnic differences in physician distrust in the United States. *American Journal of Public Health* 97 (7): 1283–89.

Ashton, Carol M., Paul Haidet, Debora A. Paterniti, Tracie C. Collins, Howard S. Gordon, Kimberly O'Malley, Laura A. Petersen, Barbara Sharf, Maria E. Suarez-Almazor, Nelda P. Wray, and Richard L. Street Jr. 2003. Racial and ethnic disparities in the use of health services: Bias, preferences, or poor communication? *Journal of General Internal Medicine* 18:146–52.

Atrash, Hani K., and Melissa D. Hunter. 2006. Health disparities in the US: A continuing challenge. In *Multicultural medicine and health disparities,* edited by David Satcher and Rubens J. Pamies, 3–32. New York: McGraw-Hill.

Ayala, Jennifer. 2006. Confianza, consejos, and contradictions: Gender and sexuality lessons between Latina adolescent daughters and mothers. In *Latina girls: Voices of adolescent strength in the United States,* edited by Jill Denner and Bianca L. Guzman, 29–43. New York: New York University Press.

Azevedo, Kathryn, and Hilda Ochoa Bogue. 2002. Health and occupational risks of Latinos living in rural America. In *Health issues in the Latino community,* edited by Marilyn Aguirre-Molina, Carlos Molina, and Ruth E. Zambrana, 359–82. San Francisco: Jossey-Bass.

Baca Zinn, Maxine. 1980. Marital roles and ethnicity: Conceptual revisions and new research directions. In *Hispanic Report on Families and Youth,* proceedings, COSSMHO's National Hispanic Conference on Families, National Coalition of Hispanic Mental Health and Human Service Organizations, Washington, DC.

———. 1982. Chicano men and masculinity. *Journal of Ethnic Studies* 10 (2): 29–44.

———. 1994. Feminist rethinking from racial-ethnic families. In *Women of color in U.S. society,* edited by Maxine Baca Zinn and Bonnie Thornton Dill, 303–15. Philadelphia: Temple University Press.

———. 1995. Social science theorizing for Latino families in the age of diversity. In *Understanding Latino families: Scholarship, policy, and practice,* edited by Ruth E. Zambrana, 177–89. Thousand Oaks, CA: Sage.

Baca Zinn, Maxine, and Angela Pok. 2002. Tradition and transition in Mexican-origin families. In *Minority families in the United States: A multicultural perspective,* edited by Ronald L. Taylor, 70–100. Upper Saddle River, NJ: Prentice Hall.

Baca Zinn, Maxine, and D. Stanley Eitzen. 2002. *Diversity in Families.* 6th ed. Boston: Allyn and Bacon.

Baca Zinn, Maxine, and Barbara Wells. 2000. Diversity within Latino families: New lessons for family social science. In *Handbook of family diversity,* edited by David H. Demo, Katherine R. Allen, and Mark A. Fine, 252–73. New York: Oxford University Press.

Baker, Susan P., Elisa R. Braver, Li-Hui Chen, Janella F. Pantula, and Dawn Massie. 1998. Motor vehicle occupant deaths among Hispanic and Black and White teenagers. *Pediatric Adolescent Medicine* 152:1209–12.

Barnes, Steve. 2004. National Briefing Southwest—Texas: Racial Profiling Found. *New York Times,* February 4.

Barrera, Mario. 1979. *Race and class in the Southwest.* Notre Dame: University of Notre Dame Press.

Barrera, Vivian, and Denise Bielby. 2001. Places, faces, and other familiar things: The cultural experience of telenovela viewing among Latinos in the United States. *Journal of Popular Culture* 34 (4): 1–18.

Barry, Arlene L. 1998. Hispanic representation in literature for children and young adults. *Journal of Adolescent and Adult Literacy* 41 (8): 630–37.

Basch, Linda, Nina Schiller, and Cristine Blanc. 1994. *Nations unbound: Transnational projects, postcolonial predicaments, and deterritorialized Nation-States.* Amsterdam: Gordon and Breach.

Becerra, Rosina M., Ward Thomas, and Paul M. Ong. 2001. Latino and African American non-custodial fathers: Perceptions of fatherhood and child support. *Journal of Ethnic and Cultural Diversity in Social Work* 10 (3): 3–30.

Bell, Derrick. A. 1980. *Brown v. Board of Education* and the interest convergence dilemma. *Harvard Law Review* 93:518–33.

Bender, Deborah E., Catherine Harbour, John Thorp, and Peter Morris. 2001. Tell me what you mean by sí: Perceptions of quality of prenatal care among immigrant Latino women. *Qualitative Health Research* 11 (6): 367–74.

Bender, Steven. 2003. *Greasers and gringos.* New York: New York University Press.

Berry, John W. 1980. Acculturation as varieties of adaptation. In *Acculturation: Theory, models and some new findings,* edited by Amado M. Padilla, 9–25. Boulder, CO: Westview.

Bettie, Julie. 2003. *Women without class: Girls, race, and identity.* Berkeley: University of California Press.

Battacharya, Jayanta, Dana Goldman, and Neeraj Sood. 2003. The link between public and private insurance and HIV-related mortality. *Journal of Health Economics* 22 (6): 1105–1122.

Blank, Susan, and Ramon Torrecilha. 1998. Understanding the living arrangements of Latino immigrants: A life course approach. *International Migration Review* 32:3–19.

Bonilla-Silva, Eduardo. 2006. *Racism without racists: Color-blind racism and the persistence of racial inequality in the United States.* Lanham, MD: Rowman and Littlefield.

Borjas, George J. 2002. Homeownership in the immigrant population. *Journal of Urban Economics* 52:448–76.

Bowdler, Janis. 2004. *Hispanic Housing and Homeownership.* National Council of La Raza Statistical Brief No. 5. Washington, DC: National Council of La Raza.

Brach, Cindy, and Irene Fraser. 2002. Reducing disparities through culturally competent health care: An analysis of the business case. *Quality Management in Health Care* 10 (4): 15–28.

Brecher, Jeremy. 1998. Popular movements and economic globalization. In *Borderless borders: U.S. Latinos, Latin Americans, and the paradox of interdependence*, edited by Frank Bonilla, 185–94. Philadelphia: Temple University Press.

Brice, Alejandro. 2001. *The Hispanic child: Speech, language, culture and education*. Boston: Allyn and Bacon.

Brindis, Claire. D., Anne K. Driscoll, M. Antonia Biggs, and L. Theresa Valderrama. 2002. *Fact sheet on Latino youth: Families*. University of California, San Francisco, Center for Reproductive Health Research and Policy, Department of Obstetrics, Gynecology and Reproductive Health Sciences and the Institute for Health Policy Studies, San Francisco.

Brown, Arleen F., Robert B. Gerzoff, Andrew J. Karter, Edward Gregg, Monika Safford, Beth Waitzfelder, Gloria L. A. Beckles, Rebecca Brusuelas, Carol M. Mangione, and the TRIAD Study Group. 2003. Health behaviors and quality of care among Latinos with diabetes in managed care. *American Journal of Public Health* 93 (10): 1694–98.

Brown, Ben, and Wm. Reed Benedict. 2004. Bullets, blades, and being afraid in Hispanic high schools: An explanatory study of the presence of weapons and fear of weapon-associated victimization among high school students in a border town. *Crime and Delinquency* 50 (3): 371–94.

Browning, Christopher R., Tama Leventhal, and Jeanne Brooks-Gunn. 2004. Neighborhood context and racial differences in early adolescent sexual activity. *Demography* 41 (4): 697–720.

Burdette, Hilary L., and Robert C. Whitaker. 2005. A national study of neighborhood safety, outdoor play, television viewing, and obesity in preschool children. *Pediatrics* 116:657–62.

Burton, Linda M., Eduardo Bonilla-Silva, Victor Ray, Rose Buckelew, and Elizabeth H. Freeman. 2010. Critical race theories, colorism, and the decade's research on families of color. *Journal of Marriage and Family* 72:440–59.

Burton, Linda M., Andrew Cherlin, Donna-Marie Winn, Angela Estacion, and Clara Holder-Taylor. 2009. The role of trust in low-income mothers' intimate unions. *Journal of Marriage and Family* 71:1107–24.

Bustamante, Arturo Vargas, Hai Fang, John A. Rizzo, and Alexander N. Ortega. 2009. Understanding observed and unobserved health care access and utilization disparities among U.S. Latino adults. *Medical Care Research and Review*. 66 (5): 561–77.

Buysse, Virginia, Dina C. Castro, Tracey West, and Martie L. Skinner. 2004. *Addressing the needs of Latino children: A national survey of state administrators of early childhood programs. Executive summary*. Chapel Hill: University of North Carolina, FPG Child Development Institute.

Caetano, Raul, and Frank Galvan. 2001. *Alcohol use and alcohol-related problems among Latinos in the United States*. San Francisco: Jossey-Bass.

Caldera, Yvonne M., Jacki Fitzpatrick, and Karen S. Wampler. 2002. Coparenting in intact Mexican American families: Mothers' and fathers' perceptions. In *Latino children and families in the United States: Current research and future directions*, edited by Josefina M. Contreras, Kathryn A. Kerns, and Angela M. Neal-Barnett, 107–31. Westport, CT: Praeger.

Callahan, S. Todd, Gerald B. Hickson, and William O. Cooper. 2006. Health care access of Hispanic young adults in the United States. *Journal of Adolescent Health* 39 (5): 627–33.

Camarillo, Albert M., and Frank Bonilla. 2001. Hispanics in a multicultural society: A new American Dilemma? In *America becoming: Racial trends and their consequences*, edited by Neil J. Smelser, William Julius Wilson, and Faith Mitchell, 103–34. Washington, DC: National Academy Press.

Camarota, Steven A. 2004. *Economy slowed, but immigration didn't—The foreign born population, 2000–2004.* Washington, DC: Center for Immigration Studies.

——. 2007. *Immigrants at mid-decade: A snapshot of America's foreign-born population in 2007.* Washington, DC: Center for Immigration Studies.

Caminero-Santangelo, Marta. 2007. *On Latinidad: U.S. Latino literature and the construction of ethnicity.* Gainesville: University Press of Florida.

Cammarota, Julio. 2004. The gendered and racialized pathways of Latina and Latino youth: Different struggles, different resistances in the urban context. *Anthropology and Education Quarterly* 35 (1): 53–74.

——. 2007. A map for social change: Latino students engage a praxis of ethnography. *Children, Youth and Environments* 17 (2): 341–53.

——. 2008. The cultural organizing of youth ethnographers: Formalizing a praxis-based pedagogy. *Anthropology and Education Quarterly* 31 (1): 45–58.

Canino, Glorisa, and Robert E. Roberts. 2001. Suicidal behavior among Latino youth. *Suicide and Life-Threatening Behavior* supplement volume 31:66–78.

Carrillo, J. Emilio, Alexander R. Green, and Joseph R. Betancourt. 1999. Cross-cultural primary care: A patient based approach. *Annals of Internal Medicine* 130 (10): 829–34.

Carrillo, J. Emilio, Fernando M. Treviño, Joseph R. Betancourt, and Alberto Coustasse. 2001. Latino access to health care: The role of insurance, managed care and institution. In *Health issues in the Latino community,* edited by Marilyn Aguirre-Molina, Carlos W. Molina, and Ruth E. Zambrana, 55–73. San Francisco: Jossey-Bass.

Cartagena, Juan. 2009. Lost votes, lost bodies, lost jobs: The effects of mass incarceration on Latino civic engagement. In *Behind bars: Latino/as and prison in the United States,* edited by Suzanne Oboler. 133–49. New York: Palgrave Macmillan.

Carter, Thomas P., and Roberto D. Segura. 1979. *Mexican Americans in society: A decade of change.* New York: College Entrance Examination Board.

Carter-Pokras, Olivia, and Lisa Bethune. 2009. Defining and measuring acculturation: A systematic review of public health studies with Hispanic populations in the United States. A commentary on Thomson and Hoffman-Goetz. *Social Science & Medicine (1982)* 69 (7): 992–95.

Carter-Pokras, Olivia, and Mariano Kanamori. 2010. Appendix: Latino Men's Health: An Overview. In *Social and Structural Factors Affecting the Health of Latino Males,* edited by Marilyn Aguirre-Molina, Luisa N. Borrell, and William Vega. New Brunswick: Rutgers University Press.

Carter-Pokras, Olivia, Ruth E. Zambrana, Carolyn F. Poppell, Laura A. Logie, and R. Guerrero-Preston. 2007. The environmental health of Latino children. *Journal of Pediatric Health Care* 21:307–14.

Cauce, Ana Mari, and Melanie Domench-Rodriguez. 2002. Latino families: Myths and realities. In *Latino children and families in the U.S.,* edited by Josefina M. Contreras, Kathryn A. Kerns, and Angela M. Neal-Barnett, 133–53. Westport, CT: Praeger.

Center on Budget and Policy Priorities (CBPP). 2002. *Improving TANF program outcomes for families with barriers to employment.* Washington, DC: CBPP. http://www.cbpp.org/files/1-22-02tanf3.pdf.

——. Centers for Disease Control and Prevention (CDC). 2004. Prevalence of cigarette use among 14 racial/ethnic populations—United States, 1999–2001. *Morbidity and Mortality Weekly Report* 53 (3): 49–52. http://www.cdc.gov/mmwr/PDF/wk/mm5303.pdf.

——. 2006. *Youth risk behavior surveillance—US, 2005.* Atlanta: U.S. Department of Health and Human Services.

——. 2007a. *HIV/AIDS surveillance report, 2005.* Vol. 17. Atlanta: U.S. Department of Health and Human Services, 1–46.

——. 2007b. Infant Mortality Statistics from the 2004 Period Linked Birth/Infant Death Data Set. *National Vital Statistics Reports* 55 (14): 1–32. http://www.sdhdidaho.org/psa/2007/may/nvsr55_14.pdf.

——. 2009. Cases of HIV infection and AIDS in the United States and dependent areas, by race/ethnicity, 2003–2007. *HIV/AIDS Surveillance Supplemental Report* 14 (2): 1–43.

Chandler, Kathryn, Christopher Chapman, Michael Rand, and Bruce Taylor. 1998. *Students' reports of school crime: 1989 and 1995* (National Center for Education Statistics), 98–241. Washington, DC: U.S. Departments of Education and Justice.

Chavez, Leo. 2001. *Covering immigration: Popular images and the politics of the nation.* Berkeley: University of California Press.

——. 2008. *The Latino threat: Constructing immigrants, citizens and the nation.* Stanford: Stanford University Press.

Children's Defense Fund (CDF). 2005. Child welfare poverty and families in crisis. In *State of America's Children.* Washington, DC: CDF.

Child Trends. 2006. Adolescent sexual relationships, contraceptive consistency, and pregnancy prevention approaches. In *Romance and sex in adolescence and emerging adulthood: Risks and opportunities, edited by* Jennifer. Manlove, Kerry Franzetta, Suzameryan Kristin, Kristin Moore, and Ann C. Crouter. Mahwah, NJ: Lawrence Erlbaum Associates, 181–212.

Chin, Marshal H., and Catherine A. Humikowskie. 2002. When is risk stratification by race or ethnicity justified in medical care? *Academic Medicine* 77 (3): 202–8.

Chun, Kevin M., Pamela B. Organista, and Gerardo Marín. 2003. *Acculturation: Advances in theory, measurement, and applied research.* Washington, DC: American Psychological Association.

Church II, Wesley T. 2006. From start to finish the duration of Hispanic children in out-of home placements. *Children and Youth Services Review* 28 (9): 1007–23.

Church II, Wesley T., Emma R. Gross, and Joshua Baldwin. 2005. Maybe ignorance is not always bliss: The disparate treatment of Hispanics within the child welfare system. *Children and Youth Services Review* 27 (12): 1279–92.

Clancy, Carolyn, and Francis Chesley. 2003. *AHRQ update: Strengthening the health services research to reduce racial and ethnic disparities in health care.* Rockville, MD: Health Services Research.

Clinton, William J. 1994. Welfare should be reformed. In *Welfare: Opposing viewpoints,* edited by Charles P. Cozic and Paul A. Winters, 22–28. San Diego: Greenhaven Press.

Close, M. M. 1983. Child welfare and people of color: Denial of equal access. *Social Work Research and Abstracts* 19 (4): 13–20.

Cofresi, Norma I. 1999. Gender roles in transition among professional Puerto Rican women. *Frontiers* 20 (1): 161–78.

Cohn, Divera. 2005. More Hispanics gain foothold in housing market. *Washington Post,* June 13.

Coleman-Miller, Beverly. 2000. A physician's perspective on minority health. *Health Care Financing and Review* 21 (4): 45–56.

Collins, Karen, Allyson Hall, and Charlotte Neuhaus. 1999. *U.S. minority health: A chart book.* New York: Commonwealth Fund.

Collins, Karen Scott, Cathy Schoen, Susan Joseph, et al. 1999. *Health concerns across a woman's lifespan.* New York: Commonwealth Fund.

Collins, Patricia Hill. 2000. *Black feminist thought: Knowledge, consciousness, and the politics of empowerment.* New York: Routledge.

Community Service Society. 2008. *Latino youths caught up in the juvenile system.* http://www.cssny.org/pubs/new_majority/2008_04_11.html.

Cooper, Lisa A., Debra Roter, Rachel Johnson, Daniel Ford, Donald Steinwachs, and Neil Powe. 2003. Patient-centered communication, ratings of care, and concordance of patient and physician race. *Annals of Internal Medicine* 139 (11): 907–15.

Cordoba, Rocio. 2007. Seeking solutions: The campaign for reproductive justice for Latinas in California. *Conscience* 28 (2): 21.

Cosentino de Cohen, Clemencia, Nicole Deterding, and Beatriz Chu Clewell. 2005. *Who's left behind: Immigrant children in high- and low-LEP schools.* Washington, DC: Urban Institute. http://www.urban.org/publications/411231.html.

Courtenay, Will H. 2000a. Constructions of masculinity and their influence on men's well being: A theory of gender and health. *Social Science and Medicine* 50 (10): 1385–1401.

——. 2000b. Engendering health: A social constructionist examination of men's health beliefs and behaviors. *Psychology of Men and Masculinity* 1 (1): 4–15.

——. 2001. Counseling men in medical settings. In *The new handbook of psychotherapy and counseling with men: A comprehensive guide to settings, problems, and treatment approaches,* edited by Gary R. Brooks and Glen E. Good, 1:59–91. San Francisco: Jossey-Bass.

Courtenay, Will H., and Richard P. Keeling. 2000. Men, gender, and health: Toward an interdisciplinary approach. *Journal of American College Health* 48 (6): 243–46.

Courtenay, Will H., Donald McCreary, and Joseph Merighi. 2002. Gender and ethnic differences in health beliefs and behaviors. *Journal of Health Psychology* 7 (3): 219–31.

Cox, Lisa A., Shibao Feng, Janet Canar, Maureen M. Ford, and Kenneth P. Tercyak, 2005. Social and behavioral correlates of cigarette smoking among mid-Atlantic Latino primary care patients. *Cancer Epidemiology Biomarkers and Prevention* 14:1976–80.

Crenshaw, Kimberle W. 2002. The first decade: Critical reflections, or "a foot in the closing door." Critical Race Studies. *UCLA Law Review* 49:1343–72.

Crespo, Carlos J., Catherine M. Loria, and Vicki L. Burt. 1996. Hypertension and other cardiovascular disease risk factors among Mexican Americans, Cuban Americans and Puerto Ricans from the Hispanic Health and Nutrition Examination Survey. *Public Health Reports* 111:7–10.

Crouter, Ann C., Kelly D. Davis, Kimberly Updegraff, Melissa Delgado, and Melissa Fortner. 2006. Mexican American fathers' occupational conditions: Links to family members' psychological adjustment. *Journal of Marriage and Family* 68:843–58.

Cruz, Arnaldo. 2002. *Queer globalizations: Citizenship and the afterlife of colonialism.* New York: New York University Press.

Cruz, Barbara. 2002. Don Juan and rebels under palm trees: Depictions of Latin American in U.S. history textbooks. *Critique of Anthropology* 22 (3): 323–42.

Cuellar, Israel, Elena Bastida, and Sara M. Braccio. 2004. Residency in the U.S., subjective well-being, and depression in an older Mexican origin sample. *Journal of Aging Health* 16 (4): 447–66.

Cuellar, Israel, Lorwen Harris, and Ricardo Jasso. 1980. An acculturation scale for Mexican Americans normal and clinical populations. *Hispanic Journal of Behavioral Sciences* 2:199–217.

Currie, Janet. 2006. The take-up of social benefits. In *Public Policy and the Income Distribution, edited by* Alan J. Auerback, David Card, and John M. Quigley, 80–148. New York: Russell Sage Foundation.

Dance, Lory J. 2009. Racial, ethnic, and gender disparities in early school leaving (dropping out). In *Emerging intersections race, class, and gender in theory, policy, and practice,* edited by Bonnie Thornton Dill and Ruth E. Zambrana. New Brunswick, NJ: Rutgers University Press.

Daponte, Beth O., Seth Sanders, and Lowell Taylor. 1999. Why do low-income households not use food stamps? Evidence from an experiment. *Journal of Human Resources* 34 (3): 612–28.

Darder, Antonia, Rodolfo Torres, and Henry Gutiérrez. 1997. *Latinos and Education: A Critical Reader.* New York: Routledge.

Darroch, Jacqueline E., and Suschela Singh. 1999. Why is teenage pregnancy declining? The roles of abstinence, sexual activity and contraceptive use. *Occasional Report.* New York: Alan Guttmacher Institute.

Davalos, Deana. B., Ernest Chavez, and Robert J. Guardiola. 2005. Effects of perceived parental school support and family communication on delinquent behaviors in Latinos and White non-Latinos. *Cultural Diversity and Ethnic Minority Psychology* 11 (1): 57–68.

Davalos, Karen Mary. 2008. Sin verguenza: Chicana feminist theorizing. *Feminist Studies* 34 (1/2): 151–97.

Dávila, Arlene A. 2001. *Latinos, Inc.: The marketing and making of a people*. Berkeley: University of California Press.

DeGaetano, Yvonne. 2007. The role of culture in engaging Latino parents' involvement in school. *Urban Education* 42 (2): 145–62.

de la Garza, Rodolfo. 2004. Latino Politics. *Annual Review of Political Science* 7:91–123.

de la Garza, Rodolfo, and Louis DeSipio. 2006. *New dimensions of Latino participation*. California: Tomas Rivera Policy Institute.

de la Garza, Rodolfo, Louis DeSipio, Chris F. Garcia, John Garcia, and Angelo Falcon. 1992. *Latino voices: Mexican, Puerto Rican, and Cuban perspectives on American politics*. Boulder, CO: Westview Press.

de la Torre, Adela. 1993. Hard choices and changing roles among Mexican migrant campesinas. In *Building with our hands: New directions in Chicana studies*, edited by Adela de la Torre and Beatríz M. Pesquera, 168–80. Berkeley: University of California Press.

de la Torre, Adela, and Beatríz M. Pesquera. 1993. Conclusion. In *Building with our hands: New directions in Chicana studies*, edited by Adela de la Torre and Beatríz M. Pesquera, 232–38. Berkeley: University of California Press.

Delgado, Ricardo, and Jean Stefancic. 2001. *Critical race theory: An introduction*. New York: New York University Press.

Delgado Bernal, Dolores. 2002. Critical race theory, Latino critical theory, and critical raced-gendered epistemologies: Recognizing students of color as holders and creators of knowledge. *Qualitative Inquiry* 8 (1): 105–26.

Delgado Bernal, Dolores, C. Alejandra Elenes, and Sofia Villenas 2006. *Chicana/Latina education in everyday life: Feminista perspectives on pedagogy and epistemology*. Albany, NY: State University of New York Press.

del Pinal, Jorge. 1996. Treatment of and counting of Latinos in the census. In *The Latino Encyclopedia,* edited by Rafael Chabrán and Richard Chabrán, 272–78. New York: Marshall Cavendish.

———. 2008. Demographic patterns: Age structure, fertility, mortality, and population growth. In *Latina/s in the United States*, edited by Havidán Rodriguez, Rogelio Sáenz, and Celia Menjívar, 57–72. New York: Springer.

Demuth, Stephen, and Susan L. Brown. 2004. Family structure, family processes, and adolescent delinquency: The significance of parental absence versus parental gender. *Journal of Research in Crime and Delinquency* 41 (1): 58–81.

DeNavas-Walt, Carmen, Bernadette D. Proctor, and Jessica C. Smith. 2007. *Income, poverty, and health insurance coverage in the United States: 2006*. Washington, DC: U.S. Census Bureau.

Denner, Jill, and Nora Dunbar. 2004. Negotiating femininity: Power and strategies of Mexican American girls. *Sex Roles* 50 (5/6): 301–14.

Denner, Jill, and Bianca L. Guzman. 2006. *Latina girls: Voices of adolescent strength in the United States*. New York: New York University Press.

Denner, Jill, Douglas Kirby, Karin Coyle, and Claire Brindis 2001. The protective role of social capital and cultural norms in Latino communities: A study of adolescent births. *Hispanic Journal of Behavioral Sciences* 23 (3): 3–21.

DeSipio, Louis. 2006. Latino Civic and Political Participation. In *Hispanics and the future of America*, edited by Marta Tienda and Faith Mitchell, 447–79. Washington, DC: National Academies Press.

Díaz, Rafael. 1998. *Latino gay men and HIV: Culture, sexuality, and risk behavior.* New York: Routledge.

Díaz, Rafael, Eduardo Morales, Edward Bein, Eugene Dilán, and Richard Rodríguez. 1999. Predictors of sexual risk in Latino gay/bisexual men. *Hispanic Journal of Behavioral Sciences* 21 (4): 480–501.

Díaz-Cotto, Juanita. 2009. Chicana(o) prisoners: Ethical and methodological considerations, collaborative research methods and case studies. In *Behind bars: Latino/as and prison in the United States,* edited by Suzanne Oboler, 239–61. New York: Palgrave Macmillan.

Diaz, Yamalis, and Ruth E. Zambrana. Forthcoming. Understanding contextual influences on parenting and child behavior in the assessment and treatment of ADHD in Latino children. In *Volume of Latina/o adolescent psychology and mental health,* vol. 1: *Early to middle childhood: Development and context,* edited by N. Cabrera, F. Villarruel, and H. Fitzgerald. Santa Barbara, CA: ABC-CLIO.

Dill, Bonnie T., and Ruth E. Zambrana. 2009. Critical thinking about inequality: An emerging lens. In *Emerging intersections: Race, class, and gender in theory, policy and practice,* edited by Bonnie T. Dill and Ruth E. Zambrana, 1–22. New Brunswick: Rutgers University Press.

Dinkes, Rachel, Emily Cataldi, and Wendy Lin-Kelly. 2007. *Indicators of School Crime and Safety: 2007* (NCES 2008-021/NCJ 219553). Washington, DC: National Center for Education Statistics, Institute of Education Sciences, U.S. Department of Education, and Bureau of Justice Statistics, Office of Justice Programs, U.S. Department of Justice.

Dixon, David, and Julia Gelatt. 2006. *Detailed characteristics of the South American born in the United States.* Washington, DC: Migration Policy Institute.

Donovan, Patricia. 1998. Falling teen pregnancy, birthrates: What's behind the declines? *Guttmacher Report on Public Policy* 1 (5). http://www.guttmacher.org/pubs/tgr/01/5/gr010506.html.

Dorrington, Claudia, Ruth E. Zambrana, and George Sabagh. 1989. Salvadorans in the United States: Immigrants and refugees. *California Sociologist* 12 (2): 137–70.

Douglas-Hall, Ayana, Michelle Chau, and Heather Koball. 2006 *Basic facts about low-income children: Birth to age 18.* Washington, DC: National Center for Children in Poverty. http://www.nccp.org/media/lic06b_text.pdf.

Dressler, William, Kathryn Oths, and Clarence Gravlee. 2005. Race and ethnicity in public health research: Models to explain health disparities. *Annual Review of Anthropology* 34:231–52.

Driscoll, Anne K. 1999. Risk of high school dropout among immigrant and native Hispanic youth. *International Migration Review* 33 (4): 857–75.

Duany, Jorge. 1998. Reconstructing racial identity: Ethnicity, color and class among Dominicans in the United States and Puerto Rico. *Latin American Perspectives* 25 (3): 147–72.

Duràn, Robert J. 2009. Legitmated oppression: Inner-City Mexican American experiences with police gang enforcement. *Journal of Contemporary Ethnography* 38:143–68.

Echazabal-Martinez, Lourdes. 1998. Mestizaje and the discourse of National/Cultural identity in Latin America, 1845–1959. *Latin American Perspectives* 25 (3): 21–42.

Eckstein, Susan E. 2009. *The immigrant divide: How Cuban Americans changed the U.S. and their homeland.* New York: Routledge.

Edelman, Marion Wright. 2009. Keeping children out of the pipeline to prison. Child Watch column. http://www.childrensdefense.org.

Ellen, Ingrid D., and Margery A. Turner. 1997. Does neighborhood matter? Assessing recent evidence. *Housing Policy Debate* 8:833–66.

Epstein, Jennifer A., Gilbert Botvin, and Tracy Diaz. 1998. Linguistic acculturation and gender effects on smoking among Hispanic youth. *Preventive Medicine* 27 (4): 583–89.

Epstein, Ronald M., and Edward M. Hundert. 2002. Defining and assessing professional competence. *JAMA* 287 (2): 226–35.

Erwin, Deborah O., Michelle Treviño, Frances G. Saad-Harfouche, Elisa M. Rodriguez, Elizabeth Gage, and Lina Jandorf. 2010. Contextualizing diversity and culture within cancer control interventions for Latinas: Changing interventions, not cultures. *Social Science & Medicine* 71:693–701.

Esbensen, Finn-Aage, and Donna P. Lynskey. 2001. Young gang members in a school survey. In *The Eurogang paradox: Street gangs and youth groups in the U.S. and Europe,* edited by Malcolm W. Klein, Hans-Jürgen Kerner, Cheryl L. Maxson, and Elmar G. M. Weitekamp. Amsterdam: Kluwer.

Espinosa, Gastón, Virgilio Elizondo, and Jesse Miranda, eds. 2005. *Latino religions and civic activism in the United States.* New York: Oxford University Press.

Evelyn, Jamilah. 2000. Research shows lag in Hispanic bachelor's attainment. *Black Issues in Higher Education* 17 (3): 1–16.

Excelencia in Education. 2005. *How Latino students pay for college: Patterns of financial aid (2003–04).* www.edexcelencia.org.

——. 2008. *Emerging Hispanic-serving institutions (HSIs): 2006–07.* HSI List. http://www.edexcelencia.org/research/emerging-hispanic-serving-institutions-list-2006–07.

Fairlie, Robert W., and Rebecca A. London. 2006. Getting connected: The expanding use of technology among Latina girls. In *Latina girls: Voices of adolescent strength in the United States,* edited by Jill Denner and Bianca L. Guzmán. New York: New York University Press.

Farkas, George. 1996. *Human capital or cultural capital? Ethnicity and poverty groups in an urban school district.* New York: A. De Gruyter.

——. 2003. Racial disparities and discrimination in education: What we know, how do we know it, and what do we need to know? *Teacher College Record* 105 (6): 1119–46.

Federal Interagency Forum on Child and Family Statistics (FIFCFS). 2007. *America's Children: Key National Indicators of Well-Being, 2007.* Washington, DC: FIFCFS.

——. 2009. *America's Children: Key National Indicators of Well-Being, 2009.* Washington, DC: FIFCFS.

Fernandez, M. Isabel, Tatiana Perrino, Scott Royal, and G. Stephen Bowen. 2002. To test or not to test: Are Hispanic men at highest risk for HIV getting tested? *AIDS Care* 14 (3): 375–84.

Fine, Michelle. 1991. *Framing dropouts: Notes on the politics of an urban public high school.* Albany: State University of New York Press.

Finkelstein, Barbara, Sara Pickert, Tracy Mahoney, and Douglas Barry. 1998. *Discovering culture in education: An approach to cultural education program evaluation.* Washington, DC: ERIC Clearinghouse on Assessment and Evaluation and Catholic University of America.

Flores, Elena, Susan G. Millstein, and Stephen L. Eyre. 1998. Sociocultural beliefs related to sex among Mexican American adolescents. *Hispanic Journal of Behavioral Sciences* 20 (1): 60–82.

Flores, Glenn, Elena Fuentes-Afflick, Olivia Carter-Pokras, et al. 2002. The Health of Latino children: Urgent priorities, unanswered questions, and a research agenda. *JAMA* 28 (1): 82–90.

Flores, Glenn, and Pauline Sheehan. 2001. Dealing with adolescent Latino patients. *American Family Physician.* http://www.aafp.org.

Flores, Glenn, and Luis Vega. 1998. Barriers to health care access for Latino children: A review. *Family Medicine* 30:196–205.

Flores, William, and Rina Benmayor. 1997. *Latino cultural citizenship: Claiming identity, space, and rights.* Boston: Beacon Press.

Flores, Yvette. 2006. La Salud: Latina adolescents constructing identities, negotiating health decisions. In *Latina girls: Voices of adolescent strength in the US,* edited by Jill Denner and Bianca L. Guzman, 199–211. New York: New York University Press.

Florsheim, Paul, Emi Sumida, Claire McCann, et al. 2003. The transition to parenthood Among Young African American and Latino couples: Relational predictors of risk for parental dysfunction. *Journal of Family Psychology* 17 (1): 65–79.

Foner, Nancy. 2005. *In a new land: A comparative view of immigration.* New York: New York University Press.

Foundation for Child Development. 2009. *How do families matter? Understanding how families strengthen their children's educational achievement.* Annual report. http://www.fcd-us.org/sites/default/files/FINAL%20How%20Do%20Parents%20Matter.pdf.

Franco, Jamie L., Laura Sabattini, and Faye Crosby. 2004. Anticipating work and family: Exploring the associations among gender-related ideologies, values, and behaviors in Latino and White families in the United States. *Journal of Social Issues* 60 (4): 755–66.

Franzini, Luisa, John Ribble, and Arlene Keddie. 2001. Understanding the Hispanic paradox. *Ethnicity and Disease* 11:496–518.

Frasure, Lorrie, and Linda Williams. 2009. Racial, ethnic, and gender disparities in political participation and civic engagement. In *Emerging intersections race, class, and gender in theory, policy, and practice,* edited by Bonnie T. Dill and Ruth E. Zambrana, 203–29. New Brunswick: Rutgers University Press.

Freedman, Rachel A., Katherine S. Virgo, Yulei He, Alexandre L. Pavluck, Eric P. Winer, et al. 2010. The association of race/ethnicity, insurance status, and socioeconomic factors with breast cancer care. *Cancer* n/a. doi: 10.1002/cncr.25542.

Fry, Richard 2002. *Latinos in higher education: Many enroll, too few graduate.* Washington, DC: Pew Hispanic Center.

——. 2005. *The high schools Hispanics attend: Size and other key characteristics.* Washington, DC: Pew Hispanic Center.

——. 2008a. *Latino settlement in the new century.* Washington, DC: Pew Hispanic Center.

——. 2008b. *The role of schools in the English language learner achievement gap.* Washington, DC: Pew Hispanic Center.

——. 2009. *College enrollment hits all time high, fueled by community college surge.* Washington, DC: Pew Hispanic Center.

——. 2010. *Hispanics, high school dropouts and the GED.* Washington, DC: Pew Hispanic Center.

Fry, Richard, and Felisa Gonzales. 2008. *One-in-five and growing fast: A profile of Hispanic public students.* Washington, DC: Pew Hispanic Center.

Fuentes-Afflick, Elena. 2006. Is limited access to care the new morbidity for Latino young adults? *Journal of Adolescent Health* 39:623–24.

Fuentes-Afflick, Elena, Nancy Hessol, Tamar Bauer, et al. 2006. Use of prenatal care by Hispanic women after welfare reform. *Obstetrics and Gynecology* 107 (1): 151–60.

Fuligni, Andrew J. 2007. *Contesting stereotypes and creating identities: Social categories, social identities, and education participation.* New York: Russell Sage.

Fuligni, Andrew J., and Christina Hardway. 2004. Preparing diverse adolescents for the transition to adulthood. *The Future of Children* 14 (2): 99–119.

Gaarder, Emily, and Joanne Belknap. 2002. Tenuous borders: Girls transferred to adult court. *Criminology* 40 (3): 481–517.

Gaarder, Emily, Nancy Rodriguez, and Marjorie S. Zatz. 2004. Criers, liars, and manipulators: Probation officers' views of girls. *Justice Quarterly* 21 (3): 547–78.

Galobardes, Bruce, Mary Shaw, Debbie Lawlo, et al. 2006. Indicators of socioeconomic position (part 2). *Journal of Epidemiology and Community Health* 60:95–101.

Gándara, Patricia. 1995. *Over the ivy walls: The educational mobility of low-income Chicanos.* New York: State University of New York Press.

——. 1999. Telling stories of success: Cultural capital and the educational mobility of Chicano students. *Latino Studies Journal* 10 (Winter): 38–54.

Gándara, Patricia, Gary Orfield and Catherine L. Horn, eds. 2006a. *Expanding opportunity in higher education: Leveraging Promise.* Albany, NY: State University of New York Press.

Gándara, Patricia, Barbara K. Keogh, and Barbara Yoshioka-Maxwell. 2006b. Predicting academic performance of Anglo and Mexican-American kindergarten children. *Psychology in the Schools* 17 (2): 174–77.

García, Eugene E. 2001. *Hispanic in the United States education: Raíces y alas.* Lanham, MD: Rowman and Littlefield.

Garcia, John. 2006. *Redefining America: Key findings from the 2006 Latino National Survey.* Washington, DC: Woodrow Wilson International Center for Scholars. http://www.wilsoncenter.org/index.cfm?fuseaction=events.event_summary&event_id=201793.

Garcia, Lorena. 2006. *Beyond the Latina virgin/whore dichotomy: Investigating Latina adolescent sexual subjectivity.* PhD diss., University of California, Santa Barbara.

García-Coll, Cynthia, Gontran Lamberty, Renee Jenkins, et al. 1996. An integrative model for the study of developmental competencies in minority children. *Child Development* 67 (5): 1891–1914.

Garrod, Andrew, Robert Kilkenny, and Christina Gómez, eds. 2007. *Mi voz, mi vida: Latino college students tell their life stories.* Ithaca, NY: Cornell University Press.

Garza, Hedda. 1993. Second-class academics: Chicano/Latino faculty in U.S. universities. In *Building a diverse faculty,* vol. 53, *New directions for teaching and learning,* edited by J. Gainen and R. Boice. San Francisco: Jossey-Bass.

Geiger, Jack. 2001. Racial stereotyping and medicine: The need for cultural competence. *Canadian Medical Association Journal* 164 (12): 1699–701.

Gellis, Les A., Kenneth Lichstein, Isabel Scariinci, et al. 2005. Socioeconomic status and insomnia. *Journal of Abnormal Psychology* 114 (1): 111–18.

Gershon, Sarah A., and Adrian D. Pantoja. 2008. Political orientations and Latino immigrant incorporation. In *Latinas/os in the United States: Changing the face of America,* edited by Havidán Rodriguez, Rogelio Sáenz, and Cecilia Menjivar, 340–51. New York: Springer.

Gerstle, Gary. 2001. *The American crucible: Race and nation in the twentieth century.* Princeton, NJ: Princeton University Press.

Giachello, Aida. 2001. The Reproductive Years: The Health of Latinas. In *Health Issues in the Latino Community,* edited by Mariyln Aguirre-Molina, Claudia.W. Molina, and Ruth E. Zambrana, 55–73. San Francisco: Jossey-Bass.

Giovannoni, Jeanne M., and Rosina M. Becerra. 1979. *Defining child abuse.* New York: Free Press.

Giddens, Anthony. 1993. *Sociology.* 2nd ed. Oxford: Polity Press.

Gilliam, Melissa L., Amy Berlin, Mike Kozloski, Maida Hernandez, and Maureen Grundy. 2007. Interpersonal and personal factors influencing sexual debut among Mexican-American young women in the United States. *Journal of Adolescent Health* 41 (5): 495–503.

Ginorio, Angela, and Michelle Huston. 2001. *Si se puede! Yes, we can: Latinas in school.* Washington, DC: American Association of University Women Educational Foundation.

Glenn, Evelyn Nakano. 2002. *Unequal freedom: How race and gender shaped American citizenship and labor.* Cambridge: Harvard University Press.

Glick, Jennifer E., and Jennifer Van Hook. 2002. Parents coresidence with adult children: Can immigration explain racial and ethnic variation? *Journal of Marriage and the Family* 64 (1): 240–53.

Gonzales, Felisa. 2008. *Hispanic Women in the United States, 2007.* Washington, DC: Pew Hispanic Center, http://pewhispanic.org/files/factsheets/42.pdf.

Gonzalez, Francisca. 2001. Haciendo que hacer—cultivating a Mestiza worldview and academic achievement: Braiding cultural knowledge into educational research, policy, practice. *International Journal of Qualitative Studies in Education* 14 (5): 641–56.

Gonzalez, Juan. 2000. *Harvest of empire: A history of Latinos in America*. New York: Penguin Books.

González, Manny J., and Danny González-Ramos, eds. 2005. *Mental health care for new Hispanic immigrants: Innovative approaches in contemporary clinical practice*. New York: Hadworth Press.

Gonzalez, Ray, ed. 1996. *Muy macho: Latino men confront their manhood*. New York: Doubleday.

Gonzalez-Ramos, Gladys, Luis H. Zayas, and Elaine V. Cohen. 1998. Child-rearing values of low-income, urban Puerto Rican mothers of preschool children. *Professional Psychology: Research & Practice* 29 (4): 377–82.

González-Lopez, Gloria. 2004. Fathering Latina sexualities: Mexican men and the virginity of their daughters. *Journal of Marriage and Family* 66:1118–30.

González-Lopez, Gloria, and Salvador Vidal-Ortiz. 2008. Latinas and Latinos, sexuality, and society: A critical sociological perspective. In *Latinas/os in the United States: Changing the face of America*, edited by Havidán Rodriguez, Rogelio Sáenz, and Cecilia Menjívar, 308–25. New York: Springer.

Goodyear, Rodney K., Michael D. Newcomb, and Russell D. Allison. 2000. Predictors of Latino men's paternity in teen pregnancy: Test of a meditational model of childhood experiences, gender role attitudes, and behaviors. *Journal of Counseling Psychology* 47 (1): 116–28.

Gordon, Rebecca. 2001. *Cruel and usual: How welfare "reform" punishes poor people*. Oakland, CA: Applied Research Center.

Gordon-Larsen, Penny, Melissa C. Nelson, Phil Page, and Barry M. Popkin. 2006. Inequality in the built environment underlies key health disparities in physical activity and obesity. *Pediatrics* 117:417–24.

Gorin, Sherri, and Julia E. Heck. 2005. Cancer screening among Latino subgroups in the United States. *Preventive Medicine* 40:515–26.

Gowan, Mary, and Melanie Trevino. 1998. An examination of gender differences in Mexican-American attitudes toward family and career roles. *Sex Roles* 38 (11/12): 1079–93.

Grewal, Inderpal. 2005. *Transnational America: Feminisms, diasporas, neoliberalisms*. Durham, NC: Duke University Press.

Griffin, Kimberly A., Walter R. Allen, Erin Kimura-Walsh, and Erica K. Yamamura. 2007. Those that left, those who stayed: Exploring the educational opportunities of high-achieving Black and Latina/o students at magnet and nonmagnet Los Angeles high schools (2001–2002). *Educational Studies* 42 (3): 229–47.

Guarnaccia, Peter J., Igda Martinez, and Henry Acosta. 2005. Mental health in the Hispanic immigrant community an overview. *Journal of Immigrant and Refugee Services* 3:21–46.

Gutiérrez, Elena. 2008. *Fertile matters: The politics of Mexican-origin women's reproduction*. Austin: University of Texas Press.

Guzmán, Betsy, and Eileen McConnell. 2002. The Hispanic population: 1990–2000 Growth and Change. *Population Research and Policy Review* 21 (1–2): 109–28.

Guzman, Bianca, Elise Arruda, and Aida L. Feri. 2006. Los papas, la familia, y la sexualidad. In *Latina girls: Voices of adolescent strength in the United States*, edited by Jill Denner and Bianca L. Guzman, 17–28. New York: New York University Press.

Guzman, Manolo 2006. *Gay hegemony/Latino homosexuality's*. New York: Routledge.

Habell-Pallán, Michelle, and Mary Romero. 2002. *Latino/a Popular Culture*. New York: New York University Press.

Handler, Joel F., and Yeheskel Hasenfeld. 1991. *Blame welfare, ignore poverty and inequality*. Cambridge, NY: Cambridge University Press.

Harden, Brenda. 2008. Inequities in infancy: Addressing the overrepresentation of African American infants in the child welfare system. *Zero to Three* 28 (6): 5–12.

Hardy-Fanta, Carol, Pei-te Lien, Diane Pinderhughes, and Christine M. Sierra. 2006. *The contours and context of descriptive representation.* London: Haworth Press.

Hardy-Fanta, Carol, and Christine M. Sierra, Pei-te Lien, Diane Pinderhughes, and Wartyna Davis. 2005. *Race, gender and descriptive representation: An exploratory view of multicultural elected leadership in the United States.* Paper presented at the annual meeting of American Political Science Association, Washington, DC, September 1–4.

Harknett, Kristen. 2001. Working and leaving welfare: Does race or ethnicity matter? *Social Service Review* 75 (3): 359–85.

Harper, Gary W., Audrey K. Bangi, Bernadette Sanchez, et al. 2006. Latina adolescent's sexual health: A participatory empowerment approach. In *Latina girls: Voices of adolescent strength in the United States,* edited by Jill Denner and Bianca Gúzman, 141–57. New York: New York University Press.

Harris, Marian S., and Mark E. Courtney. 2003. The interaction of race, ethnicity and family structure with respect to the timing of family reunification. *Children and Youth Service Review* 25:5–6.

Harris, Shannette M. 2004. The effect of health value and ethnicity on the relationship between hardiness and health behaviors. *Journal of Personality* 72 (2): 379–412.

Harvard Civil Rights Project. 2002. What works for the children? What we know and don't know about bilingual education. Harvard University. http://civilrightsproject.ucla.edu/research/k-12-education/language-minority-students/what-works-for-the-children-what-we-know-and-dont-know-about-bilingual-education/crp-what-works-for-children-2002.pdf.

Harwood, Robin L., Amy M. Miller, Vivian J. Carlson, and Birgit Leyedecker. 2002. Child-rearing beliefs and practices during feeding among middle-class Puerto-Rican and Anglo mother-infant pairs. In *Latino children and families in the United States: Current research and future directions,* edited by Josefina M. Contreras, Kathryn A. Kerns, and Angela M. Neal-Barnett, 133–53. Westport, CT: Praeger.

Hayes-Bautista, David E. 2002. The Latino health research agenda for the Twenty-First Century. In *Latinos remaking America,* edited by Marcelo Suarez-Orozco and Mariela Paez, 215–35. Berkeley: University of California Press.

Hedeen, Ashley N., and Emily White. 2001. Breast cancer size and stage in Hispanic American women, by birthplace: 1992–1995. *American Journal of Public Health* 91 (1): 122–25.

Hedrick, Tace. 2009. Queering the cosmic race: Esotericism, mestizaje, and sexuality in the work of Gabriela Mistral and Gloria Anzald a. *AZTLAN* 34 (2): 67–98.

Heine, James. 2008. La Voz: Mobilizing the Latino vote council on hemispheric affairs. http://www.coha.org/2008/10/la-voz-mobilizing-the-latino-vote-in-2008/.

Heitzeg, Nancy A. 2009. Education or incarceration: Zero tolerance policies and the school to prison pipeline. *Forum on Public Policy.* http://eric.ed.gov/PDFS/EJ870076.pdf.

Henderson, Debra, and Ann Tickamyer. 2009. The intersections of poverty discourses: Race, class, culture and gender. In *Emerging intersections: Race, class, and gender in theory, policy and practice,* edited by Bonnie Thornton Dill and Ruth E. Zambrana, 50–73. New Brunswick, NJ: Rutgers University Press.

Henry J. Kaiser Family Foundation. 2001. *Kaiser women's health survey.* Washington, DC. http://www.kff.org/womenshealth/20020507a-index.cfm.

Herek, Gregory M., and Milagritos Gonzalez-Rivera. 2006. Attitudes toward homosexuality among U.S. residents of Mexican descent. *Journals of Sex Research* 43 (2): 122–35.

Hernandez, Arelis. 2009. The re-education of a Pocha-Rican: How Latina/o studies Latinized me. In *Consejos: The undergraduate experiences of Latina/o students,* a special issue of the *Harvard Educational Review* 79 (4): 601–9.

Hernández, David Manuel. 2009. Pursuant to deportation: Latinos and immigrant detention. In *Behind bars: Latino/as and prison in the United States,* edited by Suzanne Oboler,
39–66. New York: Palgrave Macmillan.

Hernandez, Donald J. 2004. Demographic change and the life circumstances of immigrant
families. *The Future of Children, Special Issue on Children of Immigrants* 14 (2): 16–47.

Hernandez, Donald, Nancy Denton, and Suzanne Macartney. 2007. *Children in immigrant
families-the U.S. and 50 states: National origins, language, and early education.* Albany:
Child Trends and the Center for Social and Demographic Analysis.

Hidalgo, Nitza. 1998. Towards a new definition of Latino family research paradigm. *Qualitative Studies in Education* 11 (1): 103–20.

Hinton Hoytt, Eleanor H., Vincent Schiraldi, Brenda V. Smith, and Jason Ziedenberg.
2002a. *Pathways to Juvenile Detention Reform: Reducing Disparities in Juvenile Detention.* Baltimore, MD: Annie E. Casey Foundation.

———. 2002b. *Reducing racial disparities in juvenile detention.* Baltimore, MD: Annie E.
Casey Foundation.

Holzer, Henry J., and Michael A. Stoll. 2003. Employer demand for welfare recipients by
race. *Journal of Labor Economics,* 21 (1): 210–41.

Hondagneu-Sotelo, Pierrette. 1994. *Gendered transitions: Mexican experiences of immigration.* Los Angeles: University of California Press.

———, ed. 2003. *Gender and U.S. immigration contemporary trends.* Los Angeles: University
of California Press.

———. 2000. The international division of caring and cleaning work: Transnational connections or apartheid exclusions? In *Care Work: Gender, Labor and the Welfare State,* edited
by Madonna Harrington Myer. New York: Routledge.

Hondagneu-Sotelo, Pierrette, and Ernestine Avila. 1997. "I'm here, but I'm there": The
meanings of Latina transnational motherhood. *Gender and Society* 11 (5): 548–71.

Hoover-Dempsey, Kathleen V., and Howard M. Sandler. 1997. Why do parents become
involved in their children's education? *Review of Educational Research* 67 (2): 3–42.

Horno-Delgado, Asuncion, Nancy M. Scott, and N. M., Ortega, E. Nancy Sternback, eds.
1989. *Breaking boundaries: Latina writing and critical readings.* Amherst: University of
Massachusetts Press.

Horowitz, Roger, and Mark J. Miller. 1998. Immigration to Delaware: The changing face
of Georgetown, DE. *Migration World Magazine* 26:15–18.

House, James S., and David R. Williams. 2000. Understanding and reducing socioeconomic
and racial/ethnic disparities in health. In *Promoting health: Intervention strategies from
social and behavioral research,* edited by Brian D. Smedley and S. Leonard Syme, 81–124.
Washington, DC: National Academy Press.

Houston, Thomas, Isabel C. Scarinci, Sharina D. Person, et al. 2005. Patient smoking cessation advice by health care providers: The role of ethnicity, socioeconomic status, and
health. *American Journal of Public Health* 95 (6): 1056–61.

Hovey, James D., and Cheryl A. King. 1996. Acculturative stress, depression, and suicidal
ideation among immigrant and second-generation Latino adolescents. *Journal of the
American Academy of Child and Adolescent Psychiatry* 35 (9): 1183–92.

Humphreys, Jeffrey M. 2002. The multicultural economy 2002: Minority buying power in
the new century. *Georgia Business and Economy Conditions* 62 (2): 1–27.

Hunt, Geoffrey, Kathleen MacKenzie, and Karla Joe-Laidler. 2000. I'm calling my mom:
The meaning of family and kinship among homegirls. *Justice Quarterly* 17 (1): 1.

Hunt, Kelly, Roy Resendez, Ken Williams, and Steve Haffner, et al. 2003. All-cause and
cardiovascular mortality among Mexican American and non-Hispanic White older participants in the San Antonio Heart Study—evidence against the "Hispanic Paradox." *American Journal of Epidemiology* 158 (11): 1048–57.

Hunt, Kelly A., Avorkor Gaba, and Risa Lavizzo-Mourey. 2005. Racial and ethnic disparities and perceptions of health care: Does health plan type matter? *Health Services Research* 40 (2): 551–76.

Hunt, Linda M., Suzanne Schneider, and Brendon Comer. 2004. Should "acculturation" be a variable in health research? A critical review of research on US Hispanics. *Social Science and Medicine* 5 (5): 973–86.

Hurtado, Aida. 1995. Variations, combinations, and evolutions: Latino families in the United States. In *Understanding Latino Families, Scholarship, Policy, and Practice*, edited by Ruth E. Zambrana, 18–38. Thousand Oaks, CA: Sage.

——. 1996. *The color of privilege: Three blasphemies on race and feminism.* Ann Arbor: University of Michigan Press.

Hurtado, Sylvia. 2009. Foreword to *Consejos: The undergraduate experiences of Latina/o students,* a special issue of the *Harvard Educational Review* 79 (4). http://www.hepg.org/her/abstract/746.

Hyams, Melissa. 2006. La escuela: Young Latina women negotiating identities in school. In *Latina girls: Voices of adolescent strength in the United States,* edited by Jill Denner and Bianca L. Guzmán, 93–108. New York: New York University Press.

Institute of Medicine (IOM). 2001. *Envisioning the national health care quality report,* edited by Margarita P. Hurtado, Elaine K. Swift, and Janet M. Corrigan. Washington, DC: National Academy Press.

Israel, Barbara A., Stephanie Farquhar, Sherman James, Amy Schulz, and Edith Parker. 2002. The relationship between social support, stress and health among women on Detroit's east side. *Health Education and Behavior 29 (3)*: 342–60.

Jamieson, Amie C., Andrea Curry, and Gladys Martinez. 2001. School enrollment in the United States: Social and economic characteristics of students. Washington, DC: U.S. Census Bureau.

Jasso, Guillermia, Douglas Massey, Mark R. Rosenzweig, and James Smith. 2004. Immigrant health selectivity and acculturation. In *Critical Perspectives on Racial and Ethnic Differences in Health in Late Life,* edited by Norman B. Anderson, Rodolfo A. Bulatao, and Barney Cohen, 227–66. Washington, DC: National Academies Press.

Johnson, Allan G. 2000. *The Blackwell dictionary of sociology: A user's guide to sociological language.* Malden, MA: Blackwell.

Johnson, Kevin R. 1995. Civil rights and immigration: Challenges for the Latino community in the twenty-first century. *La Raza Law Journal* 8 (1): 42–90.

Johnson, Melissa A. 2000. How ethnic are U.S. ethnic media: The case of Latina magazines. *Mass Communication and Society* 3 (2/3): 229–48.

Jones-Correa, Michael. 2006. Redefining America: Key findings from the 2006 Latino national survey. http://www.wilsoncenter.org/index.cfm?fuseaction=events.event_summary&event_id=201793.

Jones-DeWeever, Avis, Bonnie T. Dill, and Sandford F. Schram. 2009. Racial, ethnic and gender disparities in the workforce, education and training under welfare reform. In *Emerging intersections: Race, class and gender in theory, policy and practice,* edited by Bonnie T. Dill and Ruth E. Zambrana, 150–79. New Jersey: Rutgers University Press.

Jonson-Reid, Melissa, and Richard P. Barth. 2000. From maltreatment report to juvenile incarceration: The role of child welfare services. *Child Abuse & Neglect* 24 (4): 505–20.

Juarez, Ana Maria, and Stella B. Kerl. 2003. What is the right (White) way to be sexual? Reconceptualizing Latina sexuality. *Aztlán: A Journal of Chicano Studies* 28 (1): 5–37.

Juniu, Susana. 2000. The impact of immigration: Leisure experience in the lives of South American Immigrants. *Journal of Leisure Research* 32 (3): 358–81.

Kaiser Commission on Medicaid Facts. 2007. *Medicaid and the uninsured: The Medicaid program at a glance.* Washington, DC: Kaiser Family Foundation.

Kaiser Family Foundation. 2009. *The uninsured: A primer.* Washington, DC: Kaiser Family Foundation.

Kann, Laura, Steve A. Kinchen, Barbara Williams, James Ross, Richard Lowry, et al. 2000. Youth Risk Behavior Surveillance—US, 1999. *Morbidity and Mortality Weekly Report* 49 (SS5): 1–96.

Kaplan, Celia P., Pamela Erickson, and Maria Juarez-Reyes. 2002. Acculturation, gender role orientation, and reproductive risk-taking behavior among Latina adolescent family planning clinics. *Journal of Adolescent Research* 17 (2): 103–21.

Kaplan, Elaine B., and Leslile Cole. 2003. I want to read stuff on boys: White, Latina, and Black girls reading *Seventeen* magazine and encountering adolescence. *Adolescence* 38 (149): 141–59.

Katz, Susan R. 1997. Presumed guilty: How schools criminalize Latino youth. *Social Justice* 24 (4): 77–95.

Kaufman, Philip, Martha Naomi Alt, and Christopher Chapman. 2004. *Dropout rates in the United States: 2001* (NCES 2005-046). U.S. Department of Education. National Center for Education Statistics. Washington, DC: U.S. Government Printing Office.

Kennedy, Bruce, Ichiro Kawachi, Roberta Glass, et al. 1998. Income distribution, socio-economic status, and self-rated health in the United States: Multilevel analysis. *BMJ* 317:917–21.

Kent, Mary, and Robert Lalasz. 2006. *In the news: Speaking English in the United States.* Population Reference Bureau. Washington, DC. http://www.prb.org/Articles/2006/IntheNewsSpeakingEnglishintheUnitedStates.aspx.

Kersey, Margaret, Join Geppert and Diane Cutts. 2007. Hunger in young children of Mexican immigrant families. *Public Health Nutrition* 10 (4): 390–95.

KewalRamani, Angelina, Lauren Gilbertson, Mary Ann Fox, and Stephen Provasnik. 2007. *Status and trends in the education of racial and ethnic minorities* (NCES 2007-039). National Center for Education Statistics, Institute of Education Sciences, U.S. Department of Education. Washington, DC: U.S. Government Printing Office.

Kim, Kwang, Mary Collins Hagedorn, Jennifer Williamson, and Christopher Chapman. 2004. *Participation in adult education and lifelong learning: 2000–01* (NCES 2004-050). National Center for Education Statistics, U.S. Department of Education. Washington, DC: U.S. Government Printing Office.

Kimbro, Rachel, Sharon Bzostek, Noreen Goldman, and German Rodríguez. 2003. Race, ethnicity, and the education gradient in health. *Health Affairs* 27 (2): 361–72.

Kirby, Douglas. 2001. Understanding what works and what doesn't in reducing adolescent sexual risk-taking. *Family Planning Perspectives* 33 (6): 276–81.

Kirby, Emily Hoban, and Kei Kawashima-Ginsberg. 2009. *The youth vote in 2008.* The Center for Research and Information on Civic Learning and Engagement. http://www.civic-youth.org.

Kochhar, Rakesh. 2003. *Jobs lost, jobs gained: The Latino experience in the recession and recovery.* Washington, DC: Pew Hispanic Center.

——. 2004. *The wealth of Hispanic households: 1996 to 2002.* Washington, DC: Pew Hispanic Center.

——. 2008. *Latino labor report, 2008: Construction reverses job growth for Latinos.* Washington, DC: Pew Hispanic Center.

Kochhar, Rakesh, Ana Gonzalez-Barrera, and Daniel Dockterman. 2009. *Through boom and bust: Minorities, immigrants and homeownership.* Washington, DC: Pew Hispanic Center.

Koniak-Griffin, Deborah N., Nancy Anderson, Mary-Lynn Brecht, et al. 2002. Public health care nursing for adolescent mothers: Impact on infant health and selected maternal outcomes at 1 year post birth. *Journal of Adolescent Health* 30 (1): 44–54.

Korenbrot, Carol, and Nancy Moss. 2000. Preconception, prenatal, perinatal, and postnatal influences on health. In *Promoting health: Intervention strategies from social and behav-*

*ioral research,* edited by Brian D. Smedley and S. Leonard Syme, 125–69. Washington DC: National Academies Press.

Korzeniewicz, Roberto P., and William C. Smith. 2000. Poverty, inequality, and growth in Latin America: Searching for the high road to globalization. *Latin American Research and Review* 35 (3): 7–54.

Kozol, Jonathan. 1991. *Savage inequalities: Children in America's schools.* New York: Crown.

Krieger, Nancy. 1999. Embodying inequality: A review of concepts, measures, and methods for studying health consequences of discrimination. *International Journal of Health Services* 29:295–352.

Krieger, Nancy, Dana Carney, Katie Lancaster, Pamela D. Waterman, Anna Kosheleva, and Mahzarin. 2010. Combining explicit and implicit measures of racial discrimination in health research. *American Journal of Public Health* 100 (8): 1485–92.

Krieger, Nancy, David R. Williams, and N. E. Moss. 1997. Measuring social class in U.S. public health research: Concepts, methodologies, and guidelines. *Annual Review of Public Health* 18:341–78.

Krivo, Lauren J., and Robert L. Kaufman. 2004. Racial and ethnic differences in home equity in the US. *Demography* 41 (3): 585–605.

Kumashiro, Kevin. 2008. *Against common sense: Teaching and learning toward social justice.* New York: Routledge.

Kurian, Anita, and Kathryn Cardarelli. 2007. Racial and ethnic differences in cardiovascular disease risk factors: A systematic review. *Ethnicity and Disease* 17 (1): 143–52.

La Fountain-Stokes, Lawrence. 2009. *Queer Ricans: Cultures and sexualities in the diaspora.* Minneapolis: University of Minnesota Press.

Landale, Nancy S., Ralph S. Oropesa, and Cristina Bradatan. 2006. Hispanic families in the United States: Family structure and process in era of family change. In *Hispanics and the Future of America,* 138. Washington, DC: National Academies Press.

Lansford, Jennifer E., Kirby Deater-Deckard, and March H. Bornstein, eds. 2007. *Immigrant families in contemporary society.* New York: Guilford Press.

Laó-Montes, Augustin, and Arlene Dávila. 2001. *Mambo montage: The Latinization of New York City.* New York: Columbia University Press.

Lareau, Annette. 2003. *Unequal childhoods: Class, race and family life.* Berkeley: University of California Press.

Lareau, Annette, and Erin McNamara Horvat. 1999. Moments of social inclusion and exclusion: Race, class, and cultural capital in family-school relationships. *Sociology of Education* 72 (1): 37–53.

Larraín, Jorge. 2000. *Identity and modernity in Latin America.* Malden, MA: Blackwell.

LatCrit. 2006. *Latina and Latino critical legal theory.* Storrs, CT: University of Connecticut. http://web2.uconn.edu/latcrit/index.php.

LaVeist, Thomas. 2005. *Minority populations and health: An introduction to health disparities in the U.S.* San Francisco: Jossey-Bass.

Lawson, Michael A. 2003. *School-family relations in context: Parent and teacher perceptions of parent involvement.* http://uex.sagepub.com.proxy-um.researchport.umd.edu/cgi/reprint/38/1/77.

Ledogar, Robert J., et al. 2000. Asthma and Latino cultures: Different prevalence reported among group sharing the same environment. *American Journal of Public Health* 90 (6): 929–35.

Lee, David J., Orlando Gomez-Marin, and Heidi M. Lee. 1997. Sociodemographic and educational correlates of hearing loss in Hispanic children. *Paediatric and Perinatal Epidemiology* 11 (3): 333–44.

Lee, Jongho. 2007. *Transnational engagement as a catalyst for Latino immigrants political involvement in the united states.* Paper presented at the annual meeting of the American Political Science Association, Chicago, IL, August 30.

Lee, Sunmin, Graham Colditz, G., Lisa Berkman, and Ichiro Kawachi. 2003. Caregiving and risk of coronary heart disease in U.S. women: A prospective study. *American Journal of Preventive Medicine* 24 (2): 113–19.

Lee, Valerie E., and David T. Burkam. 2002. *Inequality at the starting gate: Social background differences in achievement as children begin school.* Washington, DC: Economic Policy Institute. http://epicpolicy.org/files/Inequality%20at%20the%20Starting%20Gate.pdf.

Lesser, Janna, Jerry Tello, Deborah Koniak-Griffing, Barbara Kappos, and Moore Rhys. 2001. Young Latino fathers' perceptions of paternal role and risk for HIV/AIDS. *Hispanic Journal of Behavioral Sciences* 23 (3): 327–43.

Lewis, Oscar. 1959. *Five families: Mexican case studies in the culture of poverty.* New York: Basic Books.

———. 1965. *La vida: A Puerto Rican family in the culture of poverty.* New York: Random House.

Liberatos, Penny, Bruce G. Link, and Jennifer L. Kelsey. 1988. The measurement of social class in epidemiology. *Epidemiology Review* 10:87–121.

Lim, Jung-won. 2010. Linguistic and ethnic disparities in breast and cervical cancer screening and health risk behaviors among Latina and Asian American women. *Journal of Women's Health* 19 (6): 1097–107.

Lindsay, Ana C., Katarina M. Sussner, Mary L. Greaney, and Karen E. Peterson. 2009. Influence of social context on eating, physical activity, and sedentary behaviors of Latina mothers and their preschool-age children. *Health Education and Behavior* 36 (1): 81–96.

Livingston, Gretchen, Susan Minushkin and D'Vera Cohn, eds. 2008. *Hispanics and health insurance care in the United States. Access, information and knowledge.* Washington, DC: Pew Hispanic Center/Robert Wood Johnson Foundation.

Livingston, Gretchen, Kim Parker, and Susannah Fox. 2009. *Latinas online, 2006–2008: Narrowing the gap.* Washington, DC: Pew Hispanic Center.

Logie, Laura Ann. 2008. An intersectional gaze at Latinidad: Gender, nation and self-perceived health status. PhD diss., University of Maryland.

Long, Vonda O., and Estella A. Martinez. 1997. Masculinity, femininity and hispanic professional men's self-esteem and self-acceptance. *Journal of Psychology* 131 (5): 481–88.

Lopez, Iris. 2009. *Matters of choice: Puerto Rican's women's struggle for reproductive freedom.* New Jersey: Rutgers University Press.

Lopez, Mark H. 2003. Electoral engagement among Latinos. *Latino Research @ Notre Dame* 1 (2). http://latinostudies.nd.edu/pubs/pubs/LRNDv1n2.pdf.

———. 2009. *Latinos and education: Explaining the attainment gap.* Washington, DC: Pew Hispanic Center.

Lopez, Mark H., and Gretchen Livingston. 2009. *Hispanics and the new administration: Immigration slips as a top priority.* Washington, DC: Pew Hispanic Center.

Lopez, Mark H., and Paul Taylor. 2009. *Dissecting the 2008 electorate: Most diverse in U.S. History.* Washington, DC: Pew Hispanic Center. http://pewresearch.org/pubs/1209/racial-ethnic-voters-presidential-election.

Lopez, Nancy. 2002. Rewriting race and gender high school lessons: Second-generation Dominicans in New York City. *Teachers College Record* 104 (6): 1187–1203.

Loque, Ângela, and Helen M. Garcia. 2000. Hispanic American and African American women scholars. *Race, Gender and Class* 7 (3): 35–57.

Lumeng, Julie C., Danielle Appuglies, Harry J. Cabral, Robert H. Bradley, and Barry Zuckerman. 2006. Neighborhood safety and overweight status in children. *Archives of Pediatric Adolescent Medicine* 160:25–31.

Lynch, John, and George Kaplan. 2000. Socioeconomic position. In *Social epidemiology,* edited by Lisa F. Berkman and Ichiro Kawachi, 13–35. 1st ed. Oxford: Oxford University Press.

MacDonald, Victoria-Maria. 2001. Hispanics, Latinos, Chicano or other?: Deconstructing the relationships between historians and Hispanic-American educational history. *History of Educational Quarterly* 41 (3): 365–413.

——, ed. 2004. *Latino education in the United States: A narrated history from 1513–2000.* New York: Palgrave MacMillan.

Manning, Wendy D., and Nancy S. Landale. 1996. Racial and ethnic differences in the role of cohabitation in premarital childbearing. *Journal of Marriage & the Family* 58 (1): 63–77.

Marcano, Rosita. 1997. Gender, culture and language in school administration: Another glass ceiling for Hispanic females. *Advancing Women in Leadership Journal* 1 (1). http://www.advancingwomen.com/awl/spring97/awlv1_04.html.

Marchevsky, Alejandra, and Jean Theoharis. 2006. *Not working: Latina immigrants, low-wage jobs, and the failure of welfare reform.* New York: New York University Press.

Markides, Kyriakos S., and Karl Eschbach. 2005. Aging, migration and mortality: Current status of research on the Hispanic paradox. *Journal of Gerontology* 60 (2): 68–75.

Marlino, Deborah, and Fiona Wilson. 2006. Career expectations and goals of Latino adolescents: Results from a nationwide study. In *Latina girls: Voices of adolescent strength in the United States,* edited by Jill Denner and Bianca L. Guzman, 123–41. New York: New York University Press.

Marotta, Sylvia A., and Jorge G. Garcia. 2003. Latinos in the United States in 2000. *Hispanic Journal of Behavioral Sciences* 25 (1): 13–34.

Martinez, Dorie Gilbert. (1998). Mujer, Latina, lesbiana-Notes on the multidimensionality of economic and sociopolitical injustice. *Journal of Gay & Lesbian Social Services* 8 (3): 99–112.

Martinez, Ramiro. 2007. Incorporating Latinos and immigrants into policing research. *Criminology and Public Policy* 6 (1): 57–64.

Massey, Douglas S., Ruth E. Zambrana, and Sally Alonzo Bell. 1995. Contemporary issues in Latino families: Future directions for research, policy, and practice. In *Understanding Latino families,* edited by Ruth E. Zambrana, 190–93. Thousand Oaks, CA: Sage.

Mauer, Marc. 2007. Reducing incarceration to expand opportunity. In *All things being equal: Instigating opportunity in an inequitable time,* edited by Brian D. Smedley and Alan Jenkins, 96–127. New York: The New Press.

McConnell, Eileen D. 2008. U.S. Latinos/as and the "American dream": Diverse populations and unique challenges in housing. In *Latinos/as in the U.S.: Changing the Face of America,* edited by Havidán Rodriguez, Rogelio Sáenz, and Cecilia Menjívar, 87–100. New York: Springer.

McDermott, Peter, and Julia Rothenberg. 2000. Why urban parents resist involvement in their children's elementary education. *The Qualitative Report* 5 (3/4). http://www.nova.edu/ssss/QR/QR5-3/mcdermott.html.

McLoyd, Vonnie C., Ana Mari Cauce, David Takeuchi, and Leon Wilson. 2000. Marital processes and parental socialization in families of color: A decade review of research. *Journal of Marriage and the Family* 62 (4): 1070–93.

Merskin, Debra. 2007. Three faces of Eva: Perpetuation of the Hot-Latina stereotype in *Desperate Housewives. Howard Journal of Communications* 18 (2): 133–51.

Miller, Seymour, and Pamela Roby. 1970. *The future of inequality.* New York: Basic Books.

Milovanovic, Dragan, and Katheryn K. Russell-Brown. 2001. *Petit Apartheid in the U.S. criminal justice system: The dark figure of racism.* Durham: Carolina Academic Press.

Minushkin, Susan, and Mark H. Lopez. 2008. *The Hispanic vote in the 2008 democratic presidential primaries.* Washington, DC: Pew Hispanic Center.

Mirande, Alfred. 1997. Hombres y machos: Masculinity and Latino culture. *Journal of Men's Studies* 6 (3): 353.

Misra, Dawn. 2001. *Women's health data book: A profile of women's health in the United States.* 3rd ed. Washington, DC: Jacobs Institute of Women's Health.

Molina, Kristine. 2008. Women of color in higher education: Resistance and hegemonic academic culture. *Feminist Collections* 29 (1): 1–6.

Molina Guzmán, Isabel. 2006. Mediating Frida: Negotiating discourses of Latina/o authenticity in global media representations of ethnic identity. *Critical Studies in Media Communication* 23 (3): 232–51.

Molina Guzmán, Isabel, and Angharad N. Valdivia. 2004. Brain, brow, and booty: Latina iconicity in U.S. popular culture. *The Communication Review* 7:205–21.

Moore, Kristin A., Jennifer Manlove, and Kerry Franzetta. 2006. Facts at a glance. In *Child Trends*. Washington, DC. http://www.childtrends.org/Files//Child_Trends-2008_01_01_FG_Edition.pdf.

Moore, Philip, Nancy Adler, David Williams, and James Jackson. 2002. Socioeconomic status and health: The role of sleep. *Psychosomatic Medicine* 64:337–44.

Moraga, Cherríe. 2009. Queer Aztlan: The reformation of Chicano tribe. In *Latino/a thought: Culture, politics and society,* 2nd ed., edited by Francisco H. Vázquez. Maryland: Rowman & Littlefield.

Morín, José Luis. 2009. Latino/as and U.S. prisons: Trends and challenges. In *Behind bars: Latino/as and prison in the United States,* edited by Suzanne Oboler, 17–39. New York: Palgrave Macmillan.

Morland, Kimberly, Steve Wing, Ana Diez Roux, and Charles Poole. 2002. Neighborhood characteristics associated with the location of food stores and food service places. *American Journal of Preventive Medicine* 22 (1): 23–29.

Morris, Edward W. 2005. Tuck in that shirt! Race, class, gender, and discipline in an urban school. *Sociological Perspectives* 48 (1): 25–48.

Mosher, William D., Anjani Chandra, and Jo Jones. 2005. Sexual behavior and selected health measures: Men and women 15–44 years of age, United States, 2002. *Advance Data*. Atlanta, GA: Center for Disease Control and Prevention.

Moynihan, Daniel P. 1995. Welfare should not be turned over to the states. In *Welfare: Opposing viewpoints,* edited by Charles P. Cozic and Paul A. Winters, 182–185. San Diego: Greenhaven Press.

Mullings, Leith, and Alaka Wali. 2001. *Stress and resilience: The social context of reproduction in central Harlem.* New York: Academic/Plenum.

Murguia, Janet. 2008. *The Implications of immigration enforcement on America's children.* Washington, DC: National Council of La Raza.

Murray, Bruce. 2006. *Latino religion in the U.S.: Demographic shifts and trends.* http://www.nhclc.org/about/news/apr2006_4.html.

Nasser, Haya E. 2006. Analysis finds boom in Hispanics' home buying. *USA Today,* May 10. http://www.usatoday.com/news/nation/2006-05-10-hispanic-homeowners_x.htm.

National Alliance for Hispanic Health. 1999. *The state of Hispanic girls.* Washington, DC: National Alliance for Hispanic Health.

National Association of Latino Elected and Appointed Officials (NALEO). 2007. *A profile of Latino elected officials in the United States and their progress since 1996.* Los Angeles: NALEO Educational Fund. http://www.naleo.org.

National Center for Education Statistics (NCES). 1995. *The condition of education: The educational progress of Hispanic students* (NCES 95-767). Washington, DC: NCES, U.S. Department of Education.

——. 2001. *The condition of education 2001* (NCES 2001-072). Washington, DC: NCES, U.S. Department of Education.

——. 2003a. *Status and trends in the education of Hispanics* (NCES 2003-008), by Charmaine Llagas. Project Officer: Thomas D. Snyder. Washington, DC: NCES, U.S. Department of Education. http://nces.ed.gov/pubs2003/2003008.pdf.

——. 2003b. *The condition of education 2003* (NCES 2003-067). Washington, DC: NCES, U.S. Department of Education.

——. 2006. *The condition of education 2006* (NCES 2006-071). Washington, DC: NCES, U.S. Department of Education. http://nces.ed.gov/programs/coe/2007/section1/table.asp?tableID=662.

——. 2007. *Digest of education statistics, 2007*. Washington, DC: NCES, U.S. Department of Education.

——. 2009. *Percentage of high school dropouts, 1960–2008*. Washington, DC: NCES, U.S. Department of Education. http://nces.ed.gov/programs/digest/d09_108.asp.

——. 2010. *Digest of education statistics, 2009* (NCES 2010-013) Washington, DC: NCES, U.S. Department of Education.

National Center for Health Statistics (NCHS). 2002. *National Health Interview Survey Description*. Centers for Disease Control and Prevention, U.S. Department of Health and Human Services. Hyattsville, MD: NCHS. ftp://ftp.cdc.gov/pub/Health_Statistics/NCHS/Dataset_Documentation/NHIS/2000/srvydesc.pdf.

——. 2004. *Health, United States, 2004: With chartbook on trends in the health of Americans*. Hyattsville, MD: NCHS. http://www.cdc.gov/nchs/data/hus/hus04.pdf.

——. 2006. *Health, United States, 2006: With chartbook on trends in the health of Americans*. Hyattsville, MD: NCHS. http://www.cdc.gov/nchs/data/hus/hus06.pdf.

——. 2007. *Health, United States, 2007: With chartbook on trends in the health of Americans*. Hyattsville, MD: NCHS.

National Council of La Raza (NCLR) 1998. *Latino education: Status and prospects. State of Hispanic America*. Washington, DC: National Council of La Raza.

National Institute for Early Education Research. 2007. *The State of Preschool 2007*. New Brunswick, NJ: Rutgers Graduate School of Education/Pew Charitable Trusts.

National Parent-Teachers Association (PTA). 2010. *PTA's National Standards for Family-School Partnerships*. http://www.pta.org.

National Research Council. 2002. *Emerging issues in Hispanic health: Summary of a workshop*, edited by Joah G. Iannotta. Committee on Population. Division of Behavioral and Social Sciences and Education. Washington, DC: National Academies Press.

——. 2004. *Eliminating health disparities: Measurement and data needs*. Washington, DC: National Academies Press.

National Urban League. 2002. *Differences in TANF support service utilization: Is there adequate monitoring to ensure program quality?* June. New York: Institute for Opportunity and Equality.

National Women's Law Center and Mexican American Legal Defense and Educational Fund (NWLC and MALDEF). 2009. *Listening to Latinas: Barriers to high school graduation*. Washington, DC: National Women's Law Center.

Nesvig, Martin. 2001. The complicated terrain of Latin American homosexuality. *Hispanic American Historical Review* 81 (3/4): 689.

Newman, Katherine S., and Rebekah Peeples Massengill. 2006. The texture of hardship: Qualitative sociology of poverty, 1995–2005. *Annual Review of Sociology* 32:423–46.

Nielsen, Annie. 2000. Examining drinking patterns and problems among Hispanic groups: Results from a national survey. *Journal of Studies on Alcohol* 61:301–10.

Niemann, Yolanda Flores, Susan H. Armitage, Patricia Hart and Karen Weathermon, eds. 2002. *Chicana Leadership: The frontiers reader*. Lincoln, NE: University of Nebraska Press.

Niemann, Yolanda, Andrea Romero, and Consuelo Arbona, C. 2000. Effects of cultural orientation on the perception of conflict between relationship and educational goals for Mexican American college students. *Hispanic Journal of Behavioral Sciences* 2 (10), 46–63.

Nieto, Sonya. 2000. *Puerto Rican students in the U.S. schools*. Mahwah, NJ: Lawrence Erlbaum Associates.

Noguera, Pedro. 2003. *City schools and the American dream: Reclaiming the promise of public education*. New York: Teachers College Press.

Oboler, Suzanne, ed. 2006. *Latinos and citizenship: The dilemma of belonging.* New York: Palgrave Macmillan.

——, ed. 2009. *Behind bars: Latino/as and prison in the United States.* New York: Palgrave Macmillan.

O'Donnell, Kevin. 2008. *Parents' reports of the school readiness of young children from the National Household Education Surveys Program of 2007* (NCES 2008-051). Washington, DC: National Center for Education Statistics, U.S. Department of Education.

Office for Civil Rights. 2002. *Suspension and expulsion at–a–glance.* UCLA Institute for Democracy, Education, and Access. Los Angeles, CA. http://www.taalliance.org/con ferences/2008/materials/suspensionhandout.pdf.

Office of Minority Health. 2008. *Strategic framework for improving racial/ethnic minority health and eliminating racial/ethnic health disparities.* Washington DC: U.S. Department of Health and Human Services. http://www.omhrc.gov/npa/images/78/PrintFrame work.html.

Office of Research on Women's Health. 2002. *Women of color health data book.* Bethesda, MD: National Institutes of Health.

——. 2006. *Women of color health data book.* Bethesda, MD: National Institutes of Health. http://orwh.od.nih.gov/pubs/WomenofColor2006.pdf.

Ogden, Cynthia L., and Carolyn J. Tabak. 2005. Children and teens told by doctors that they were overweight—United States, 1999–2002. *MMWR* 54 (34): 848–49.

Olguín, Ben V. 2009. Toward a Pinta(o) human rights? New and old strategies for Chicana(o) research activism. In *Behind bars: Latino/as and prison in the United States,* edited by Suzanne Oboler, 261–81. New York: Palgrave Macmillan.

Oliver, Melvin L., and Thomas M. Shapiro. 1997. *Black wealth/white wealth: A new perspective on racial inequality.* New York: Routledge.

Oliver, Norman, Meredith Goodwin, Robin Gotler, Patrice Gregory, and Kurt Stange. 2001. Time use in clinical encounters: Are African-American patients treated differently? *Journal of the National Medical Association* 93 (10): 380–85.

Ong, Aihwa. 1999. *Flexible citizenship: The cultural logics of transnationality.* Durham: Duke University Press.

Ong, L. M., J. C. de Haes, A. M. Hoos, and F. B. Lammes. 1995. Doctor-patient communication: A review of the literature. *Social Science and Medicine* 40 (7): 903–18.

Organista, Kurt C. 2007. *Solving Latino psychosocial and health problems: Theory, research, and populations.* Hoboken, NJ: John J. Wiley and Sons.

Ortega, Robert M., Cindy Guillean, and Lourdes Gutierrez-Najera. 1996. *Latinos and child welfare/Latinos y el bienestar del nino voces de la comunidad.* Ann Arbor: University of Michigan, School of Social Work.

O'Sullivan, Lucia, and Henyo Meyer-Balhburg. 2003. African-American and Latina inner-city girls' reports of romantic and sexual development. *Journal of Social and Personal Relationships* 20 (2): 221–38.

O'Sullivan, Lucia, Henyo Meyer-Balhburg, and Beverly X. Watkins. 2001. Mother-daughter communication about sex among urban African American and Latino families. *Journal of Adolescent Research* 16 (3): 269–92.

Otero-Sabogol, Robert M., Fabio Sabogal, and Eliseo J. Perez-Stable. 1995. Psychosocial correlates of smoking among immigrant Latina adolescents. *Journal of the National Cancer Institute Monographs* 18:65–71.

Padilla, Amado M., and William Perez. 2003. Acculturation, social identity, and social cognition: A new perspective. *Hispanic Journal of Behavioral Sciences* 25:35–55.

Palacios, Joseph M. 2003. *Remaking the Latino family: Impact of social policy and religious institutions on the Latino family, 1965–2000.* Paper commissioned by the Pew Charitable Trust for the International Conference on the Family. Atlanta, GA: Emory University, May.

Palloni, Alberto, and Elizabeth Arias. 2004. Paradox lost: Explaining the Hispanic adult mortality advantage. *Demography* 41 (3): 385–415.

Parchman, Michael, and Sandra K. Burge. 2004. The patient-physician relationship, primary care attributes, and preventive services. *Family Medicine* 36 (1): 22–27.

Passel, Jeffrey S., Randy Capps, and Michael Fix. 2004. *Undocumented immigrants: Facts and figures.* Urban Institute Immigration Studies Program. http://www.urban.org/UploadedPDF/1000587_undoc_immigrants_facts.pdf.

Patel, Kushang V., Karl Eschbach, Laura A. Ray, and Kyriakos S. Markides. 2004. Evaluation of mortality data for older Mexican Americans: Implications for the Hispanic Paradox. *American Journal of Epidemiology* 159 (7): 707–15.

Perez, Debra, William M. Sribney, and Michael A. Rodríguez. 2009. Perceived discrimination and self-reported quality of care among Latinos in the United States. *Journal of General Internal Medicine* 24 (3): 548–54.

Perez, Emma. 2003. Queering the borderlands: The challenges of excavating the invisible and unheard. *Frontiers: A Journal of Women's Studies* 24 (2): 122–31.

Pérez, Gina M. 2004. *The near northwest side story: Migration, displacement, and Puerto Rican families.* Berkeley: University of California Press.

Pérez, Miguel A., Hilda Pinzon, and Reuben Garza. 1997. Latino families: Partners for for success in school settings. *Journal of School Health* 67 (5): 182–84.

Perez, William, and Amado Padilla. 2000. Cultural orientation across three generations of Hispanic adolescents. *Hispanic Journal of Behavioral Sciences* 22:390–98.

Perez-Stable, Eliseo J., Amelie Ramirez, Roberto Villareal, et al. 2001. Cigarette smoking behavior among U.S. Latino men and women from different countries of origin. *American Journal of Public Health* 91 (9): 1424–30.

Persons, Stow. 1987. *Ethnic studies at Chicago: 1905–45.* Urbana: University of Illinois Press.

Pesquera, Beatríz M. 1993. "In the beginning he wouldn't even lift a spoon": The division of household labor. In *Building with our hands: New directions in Chicana studies,* edited by Adela de la Torre and Beatríz M. Pesquera, 181–95. Berkeley: University of California Press.

Pew Hispanic Center. 2004. *Latino teens staying in high school: A challenge for all generations.* Fact Sheet, January. Washington, DC.

———. 2006. *Hispanics and the 2006 election.* Fact Sheet, October. Washington, DC.

———. 2007. *2007 national survey of Latinos: As illegal immigration issue heats up, Hispanics feel a chill.* Washington, DC.

———. 2008a. Pew Hispanic Center tabulations of 2000 Census (5% IPUMS) and 2006 American Community Survey (1%IPUMS). Washington, DC. http://pewhispanic.org/files/factsheets/foreignborn2006/foreignborn.pdf.

———. 2008b. *Statistical portrait of Hispanics in the U.S., 2006: Poverty by age, race and ethnicity.* Washington, DC.

———. 2008c. *Statistical portrait of foreign-born in the United States, 2006.* Washington, DC.

———. 2009a. *Cuban-Americans in the United States, 2007.* Washington, DC.

———. 2009b. *Statistical portrait fact sheets of 10 largest Hispanic subgroups.* Washington, DC. http://pewhispanic.org/data/profiles/.

———. 2009c. *Hispanics and the criminal justice system: Low confidence, high exposure.* April 7. Washington, DC.

———. 2009d. *Between two worlds: How Latinos come of age in America.* December 11. Washington, DC.

———. 2009e. *A Rising share: Hispanics and federal crime.* February 18. Washington, DC.

———. 2009f. *A statistical portrait of Hispanics in the United States, 2007.* Washington, DC. http://pewhispanic.org/files/factsheets/hispanics2007/Table-5.pdf.

Pew Hispanic Center/Kaiser Family Foundation. 2004a. *2002 National survey of Latinos: Bilingualism.* Menlo Park, CA: Kaiser Family Foundation/Washington, DC: Pew Hispanic Center.

———. 2004b. *The 2004 national survey of Latinos: Politics and civic participation.* Washington, DC. http://www.kff.org/kaiserpolls/upload/The-2004-National-Survey-of-Latinos-Politics-and-Civic-Participation-Summary-and-Chart-Pack.pdf.

Physicians for Human Rights. 2003. *The right to equal treatment: An action plan to end racial and ethnic disparities in clinical diagnosis and treatment in the United States.* September. Boston, MA. http://physiciansforhumanrights.org/library/documents/reports/report-rightequaltreat-2003.PDF.

Pippins, Jennifer R., Margarita Alegría, and Jennifer S. Haas. 2007. Association between language proficiency and the quality of primary care among a national sample of insured Latinos. *Medical Care* 45 (11): 1020–25.

Piven, Frances Fox, and Richard A. Cloward. 1977. *Poor people's movements: Why they succeed, how they fail.* New York: Pantheon Books.

———. 1982. *New class war: Reagan's attack on the welfare state and its consequences.* New York: Pantheon Books.

———. 1993. *Regulating the poor: The functions of public welfare.* New York: Pantheon Books.

Pleck, Joseph. H., Freya Sonenstein, and Leighton Ku. 2004. Adolescent boys heterosexual behavior. In *Adolescent boys: Exploring diverse cultures of boyhood,* edited by Niobe Way and Judy Chu, 256–70. New York: New York University Press.

Pon, Gordon. 2009. Cultural competency as new racism: An ontology of forgetting. *Journal of Progressive Human Services* 20:59–71.

Portes, Alejandro. 2000. The two meanings of social capital. *Sociological Forum* 15 (1): 1–11.

———. 2007. The new Latin nation: Immigration and the Hispanic population of the United States. *Du Bois Review* 4 (2): 271–301.

Portes, Alejandro, and Patricia Fernandez-Kelly. 2008. No margin for error: Educational and occupational achievement among disadvantaged children of immigrants. *Annals of the American Academy of Political and Social Science* 6 (20): 12–36.

Portes, Alejandro, Luis E. Guarnizo, and Patricia Landolt. 1999. The study of transnationalism: Pitfalls and promise of an emergent research field. *Ethnic and Racial Studies* 22 (2): 217–37.

Portes, Alejandro, and Rubén G. Rumbaut. 2001. *Legacies: The story of the immigrant second generation.* Berkeley: University of California Press.

———. 2006. *Immigrant America: A portrait.* Berkeley: University of California Press.

Powell, Lisa M., Christopher Auld, Frank Chaloupka, Patrick O'Malley, and Lloyd Johnston. 2007. Associations between access to foods and adolescent body mass index. *American Journal of Preventive Medicine* 33:S301–S307.

Powell, Lisa. M., Sandy Slater, Frank Chaloupka, and Deborah Harper. 2006. Availability of physical activity-related facilities and neighborhood demographic and socioeconomic characteristics: A national study. *American Journal of Public Health* 96:1676–80.

Preuhs, Robert R. 2007. Descriptive representation as a mechanism to mitigate policy backlash. *Political Research Quarterly* 60 (2): 277–92.

Quinn, Kevin. 2000. *Working without benefits: The health insurance crisis confronting Hispanic Americans.* New York: Commonwealth Fund.

Quiñones Rivera, Maritza. 2006. From Trigueñita to Afro-Puerto Rican: Intersections of the racialized, gendered, and sexualized body in Puerto Rico and the U.S. Mainland. *Meridians* 7 (1): 162–82.

Quiocho, Alice M. L., and Annette M. Daoud. 2006. Dispelling myths about Latino parent participation in schools. *Educational Forum* 70 (3): 255–67.

Raffaelli, Marcela, and Lenna Ontai. 2001. She's 16 years old and there's boys calling over to the house: An exploratory study of sexual socialization in Latino families. *Culture, Health, & Sexuality* 3:295–310.

———. 2004. Gender socialization in Latino/a families: Results from two retrospective studies. *Sex Roles* 50 (5–6): 287–99.

Ramirez, Amelie G., Lucina Suarez, Alfred McAlister, Roberto Villareal, Edward Trapido, Talavera Gregory A., Eliseo Pérez-Stable, Jose Martí. 2000a. Cervical cancer screening in regional Hispanic populations. *American Journal of Health Behavior* 24:181–92.

Ramirez, Amelie G., Gregory A. Talavera, Roberto Villareal, Lucina Suarez, Amelie McAlister, Edward Trapido, Eliseo Pérez-Stable, Jose Martí. 2000b. Breast cancer screening in regional Hispanic populations. *Health Education Research* 15:559–68.

Ramirez, Robert R. 2004. *We the people: Hispanics in the United States.* U.S. Department of Commerce. Washington, DC: U.S. Census Bureau 2000.

Ramirez, Robert R., and de la Cruz, G. Patricia. 2002. *The Hispanic population in the United States 2002* (Current Population Reports, P20-545). Washington, DC: U.S. Census Bureau.

Ramirez-Valles, Jesus, Marc A. Zimmerman and Michael D. Newcomb. 1998. Sexual risk behavior among youth: Modeling the influence of prosocial activities and socioeconomic factors. *Journal of Health and Social Behavior* 39 (3): 237–53.

Ramos-Gomez, Francisco, et al. 2005. Latino oral health: A research agenda towards eliminating health disparities. *Journal of American Dental Association* 136 (9): 1231–40.

Rangel, Carlos. 1977. *The Latin Americans: Their love-hate relationship with the United States.* New York: Harcourt Brace Jovanovich, 3–5.

Rathbun, Amy, and Sarah Grady. 2007. *The relationship of early home learning activities and infants' and toddlers' mental skills.* Paper presented at the annual meeting of the American Education Research Association (AERA), Chicago, IL, April 10.

Ready, Timothy J. 2006, June. *Hispanic Housing in the United States 2006.* Research report. Notre Dame, IN: University of Notre Dame, Institute for Latino Studies and Esperanza.

Reich, Jennifer. 2005. *Fixing families: Parents, power and the child welfare system.* New York: Routledge.

Repack, Terry A. 1997. New roles in a new landscape. In *Challenging fronteras: Structuring Latina and Latino lives in the U.S.*, edited by Mary Romero, Pierrette Hondagneu-Sotelo, and Vilma Ortiz, 247–64. New York: Routledge.

Reyes, Xaé Alicia. 2006. Cien porciento puertorriqueña (one hundred percent Puerto Rican): Latina high school students forge identity. In *Latina girls: Voices of adolescent strength in the United States,* edited by Jill Denner and Bianca L. Guzmán, 157–67. New York: New York University Press.

Rights Working Group (RWG). 2010. *Faces of racial profiling: A report from communities across America.* Washington, DC: RWG.

Riedel, Brant W., and Kenneth L. Lichstein. 2000. Insomnia and daytime functioning. *Sleep Medicine Reviews* 4:277–98.

Rios, Elsa A. 2005. Las olvidades/The forgotten ones: Latinas and the HIV/AIDS epidemic. New York: Hispanic Federation. http://www.hispanicfederation.org/images/pdf/publications/policy_brief/las_olvidadas-the_forgotten_ones_latinas_and_hivaids_epidemic.pdf.

Rios, Victor. M. 2006. The Hyper-Criminalization of Black and Latino Male youth in the era of mass incarceration. *Souls: A Critical Journal of Black Politics, Culture, and Society* 8 (2): 40–54.

———. 2009a. The consequences of the criminal justice pipeline on Black and Latino masculinity. *The ANNALS of the American Academy of Political and Social Science* 623:150–62.

———. 2009b. The racial politics of youth crime. In *Behind bars: Latino/as and prison in the United States,* edited by Suzanne Oboler, 97–113. New York: Palgrave Macmillan.

Rivadeneyra, Rocia, and Monique Ward. 2005. From *Ally McBeal* to *Sabado Gigante:* Contributions of television viewing to gender role attitudes of Latino Adolescents. *Journal of Adolescent Research* 20 (4): 453–75.

Rivera, Raquel. 2002. Hip Hop and New York Puerto Ricans. In *Latino/a Popular Culture,* edited by Michelle Habell-Pallán and Mary Romero, 127–147. New York: New York University Press.

Rivera, Wendy, and Ronald Gallimore. 2006. Latina adolescents' career goals: Resources for overcoming obstacles. In *Latina girls: Voices of adolescent strength in the United States,* edited by Jill Denner and Bianca L. Guzman, 109–23. New York: New York University Press.

Rodríguez, Antonio. 2007. Me against the wall. In *Mi voz, mi vida: Latino college students tell their life stories,* edited by Andrew Garrod, Robert Kilkenny, and Christina Gómez, 202–12. Ithaca, NY: Cornell University Press.

Rodriguez, Charles G. 1999. Education and Hispanic philanthropy: Family, sacrifice, and community. In *Hispanic Philanthropy,* edited by Lilya Wagner and Allan Figueroa Deck, 41–57. San Francisco: Jossey-Bass.

Rodríguez, Clara E. 2000. *Changing race: Latinos, the census, and the history of ethnicity in the United States.* New York: New York University Press.

——. 2004. *Heroes, lovers, and others: The story of Latinos in Hollywood.* New York: Oxford University Press.

Rodriguez, Juan M. 2003. *Queer Latinidad: Identity practices, discursive spaces.* New York: New York University Press.

Rodriguez, Luis. 1993. *Always running: La vida loca: Gang days in L.A.* New York: Touchstone.

Rodríguez, Michael A., Arturo Vargas Bustamante, and Alfonso Ang. 2009. Perceived quality of care, receipt of preventive care, and usual source of health care among undocumented and other Latinos. *Journal of General Internal Medicine* 24 (3): 508–13.

Rodriguez, Nestor. 2008. Theoretical and methodological issues of Latina/o research. In *Latinas/os in the United States,* edited by Havidán Rodriguez, Rogelio Sáenz, and Cecelia Menjívar, 3–15. New York: Springer.

Rodriguez-Trias, Helen, and Annette Ramirez de Arrellano. 1994. The health of children and youth. In *Latino health in the US: A growing challenge,* edited by Carlos Molina and Marilynn Aguirre-Molina. Austin: American Public Health Association.

Roemmich, James N., Leonard H. Epstein, Samina Raja, Li Yin, Jodie Robinson, and Dana Winiewica. 2006. Association of Access to parks and recreational facilities with the physical activity of young children. *Preventive Medicine* 43:437–41.

Rojas, Viviana. 2004. The gender of *Latinidad:* Latinas speak about Hispanic television. *The Communication Review* 7:125–53.

Rolón-Dow, Rosalie. 2005. Critical care: A color(full) analysis of care narratives in the schooling experiences of Puerto Rican girls. *American Educational Research Journal* 42 (1): 77–111.

Romero, Mary. 2002. *Maid in the U.S.A.* Routledge: New York.

——. 2006. Racial profiling and immigration law: Rounding up usual suspects in the Latino community. *Critical Sociology* 32 (2/3): 447–43.

Romo, Harriett D. 1998. Latina high school leaving: Some practical solutions. ERIC Digest (ERIC identifier ED423096). Charleston, WV: ERIC Clearinghouse on Rural Education and Small Schools.

Romo, Harriett, and Toni Falbo, eds. 1996. *Latino H.S. graduation: Defying the odds.* Austin: University of Texas Press.

Romo, Laura F., Eva S. Lefkowitz, Marian Sigman, and Terry K. Au. 2002. A longitudinal study of maternal messages about dating and sexuality and their influence on Latino adolescents. Journal of Adolescent Health 31 (1): 59–69.

Rosario, Margaret, Eric W. Scrimshaw, Joyce, Hunter. 2004. Ethnic/racial differences in coming-out process of lesbian, gay, and bisexual youths: A comparison of sexual identity development over time. *Culture Diverse Ethnic Minor Psychol* 10 (3): 215–28.

Rouse, Beatrice A. 1995. *Substance abuse and mental health statistics source book.* Washington, DC: Substance Abuse and Mental Health Services Administration.

Rudmin, Floyd W. 2003. Critical history of the acculturation psychology of assimilation, separation, integration, and marginalization. *Review of General Psychology* 7 (1): 3–37.

Ruiz, Vicki. 2002. Color coded: Reflections at the millennium. In *Decolonial voices: Chicana and Chicano cultural studies in the 21st century,* edited by Arturo J. Aldama and Naomi H. Quiñónez, 378–87. Bloomington: Indiana University Press.

Rumbaut, Rúben G. 2005. *A language graveyard? Immigration, generation, and linguistic acculturation in the United States.* Paper presented to the International Conference on The Integration of Immigrants: Language and Educational Achievement, Social Science Research Center, Berlin, June 30–July 1.

Rutledge, Everard O. 2001. The struggle for equality in healthcare continues. *Journal of Healthcare Management* 46 (5): 313–26.

Rutledge, Matthew S., and Catherine G. McLaughlin. 2008. Hispanics and health insurance coverage: The rising disparity. *Medical Care* 46 (10): 1086–92.

Ryan, Suzanne, Kerry Franzetta, and Jennifer Manlove. 2005. *Hispanic teen pregnancy and birth rates: Looking behind the numbers.* Child Trends Research Brief, Publication #2005-01. Washington, DC: Child Trends.

Sabagh, George, and Mehdi Bozorgmehr. 1996. Population change: Immigration and ethnic transformation. In *Ethnic Los Angeles,* edited by Roger Waldinger and Mehdi Bozorgmehr, 79–108. New York: Russell Sage Foundation.

Sabogal, Fabio, Gerardo Marín, Regina Otero-Sabogal, Barbara Vanoss Marín, and Eliseo J. Perez-Stable. 1987. Hispanic *familism* and acculturation: What changes and what doesn't? *Hispanic Journal of Behavioral Sciences* 9 (4): 397–412.

Saenz, Mario. 2002. *Latin America perspectives on globalizations: Ethics, politics, and alternative visions,* Lanham, MD: Rowman and Littlefield.

Sáenz, Rogeli. 2005. Latinos and the changing face of America. In *The American People Census 2000,* edited by Reynolds Farley and John Haaga, 352–79. New York: Russell Sage Foundation.

Sanchez-Johnsen, Lisa A. P., Bonnie J. Spring, Beth Kaplan Sommerfeld, and Marian L. Fitzgibbon. 2005. Weight control smoking in Latina and non-Latina white females. *Hispanic Health Care International* 3 (2): 95–101.

Sanders-Phillips, Kathy. 1996. Correlates of health promotion behaviors in low-income Black women and Latinas. *American Journal of Preventive Medicine* 12:450–58.

———. 2009. Racial discrimination: A continuum of violence exposure for children of color. *Clinical Child and Family Psychology Review* 12:174–95.

Sandoval, Chela. 2000. *Methodology of the oppressed.* Minneapolis: University of Minnesota Press.

Santiago, Anna M. 1995. Intergenerational and program-induced effects of welfare dependency: Evidence from National Longitudinal Survey of Youth. *Journal of Family and Economic Issues* 16 (2/3): 281–306.

Sarkisian, Natalie, Mariana Gerena, and Naomi Gerstel, N. 2006. Extended family ties among Mexicans, Puerto Ricans, and Whites: Superintegration or disintegration? *Family Relations* 55:331–44.

Satcher, David, and Rubens J. Pamies. 2006. *Multicultural medicine and health disparities.* New York: McGraw-Hill.

Savner, Steve. 2000. *Welfare reform and racial/ethnic minorities: The questions to ask.* Reprinted from *Poverty and Race* 9 (4): 3. http://www.prrac.org/full_text.php?text_id=73&item_id=1797&newsletter_id=51&header=Search%20Results.

Schaefer, Richard T. 2002. *Sociology: A brief introduction*. 4th ed. New York: McGraw-Hill.

Schaffner, Laurie. 2009. Caught in the net: Language and cultural resistance among Latina adolescents in juvenile detention. In *Behind bars: Latino/as and prison in the United States*, edited by Suzanne Oboler, 113–33. New York: Palgrave Macmillan.

Schoenborn, Charlotte A., Patricia F. Adams, Patricia M. Barnes, Jackline L. Vickerie, Jeannine S. Schiller. 2004. Health behaviors of adults: United States, 1999–2001. *Vital Health Stat* 219 (10): 1–79. Hyattsville, MD: National Center for Health Statistics.

Schulz, Amy J., Clarence C. Gravlee, David R. Williams, Barbara A. Israel, Graciela Mentz, and Zachary Rowe. 2006. Discrimination, symptoms of depression, and self-related health among African American women in Detroit. *American Journal of Public Health* 96:1265–70.

Schulz, Amy J., and Leith Mullings. 2006. *Gender, race, class, and health*. San Francisco: Jossey-Bass.

Sciarra, Danile T., and Joseph G. Ponterroto. 1998. Adolescent motherhood among low-income urban Hispanics: Familian considerations of mother-daughter dyads. *Qualitative Health Research* 8 (6): 751–63.

Scott, Gulnur, and Catherine Simile. 2005. Access to dental care among Hispanic or Latino subgroups: United States, 2000–03. *Advance Data from Vital and Health Statistics* 354. Hyattsville, MD: National Center for Health Statistics.

Sealander, Judith. 2003. *The failed century of the child*. New York: Cambridge University Press.

Segal, David R., and Mady Segal. 2004. America's military population. *Population Bulletin* 59:4.

Segura, Denise A. 1993. Slipping through the cracks: Dilemmas in Chicana education. In *Building with our hands: New directions in Chicana studies*, edited by Adela de la Torre and Beatríz M. Pesquera, 199–216. Berkeley: University of California Press.

Shaw, William S., Thomas L. Patterson, Shirley J. Semple, Joel E. Dimsdale, Michael G. Ziegler, and Igor Grant. 2003. Emotional expressiveness, hostility and blood pressure in a longitudinal cohort of Alzheimer caregivers. *Journal of Psychosomatic Research* 54 (4): 293–302.

Silliman, Jael, Marlene G. Fried, Loretta Ross, and Elena R. Gutierrez. 2004. *Undivided rights: Women of color organize for reproductive justice*. Boston: South End Press.

Simms, Mark D., Madelyn Freundlich, Ellen S. Battistelli, and Neal D. Kaufman. 1999. Delivering health and mental health care services to children in family foster care after welfare and health care reform. *Child Welfare* 78:166–83.

Singh, Gopal K., and Mohammad Siahpush. 2001. All-cause and cause-specific mortality of immigrants and native born in the United States. *American Journal of Public Health* 91 (3): 392–99.

Sinister Wisdom. 2008. *Latina Lesbians*. Issue #74. Berkeley, CA: Sinister Wisdom, Inc.

Skidmore, Thomas E., and Peter H. Smith 2005. *Modern Latin America*. 6th ed. Oxford: Oxford University Press.

Smedley, Brian, Adrienne Y. Stith, and Alan R. Nelson. 2003. *Unequal treatment: Confronting racial and ethnic disparities in health care*. Washington, DC: National Academy Press.

Snyder, Howard N., and Sickmund, Melissa. 2006. *Juvenile offenders and victims: 2006 national report*. Washington, DC: U.S. Department of Justice.

Social Science Research Council. 1954. Acculturation: An exploratory formulation. *American Anthropology* 56:973–1002.

Soja, Edward. 1996. *Los Angeles 1965–1992: From crisis-generated restructuring to restructuring generated crisis*. Berkeley: University of California Press.

Solorzano, Daniel G., and Dolores Delgado Bernal. 2001. Examining transformational resistance through a critical race and Latcrit theory framework: Chicana and Chicano students in an urban context. *Urban Education* 36:308–42.

Spivak, Gayatri. 1988. *In other worlds: Essays in cultural politics*. New York: Routledge.

Spradley, James. P. 1972. *Culture and cognition: Rules, maps and plans.* San Francisco: Chandler Press.

Stefancic, Jean. 1997. Latino and Latina critical theory: An annotated bibliography. *California Law Review* 85:1509–84.

Stewart, Anita L., and Anna M. Nápoles-Springer. 2003. Health-related quality of life assessments in diverse population groups in the United States. *Medical Care* 38 (9 Suppl. II): 102–24.

Stewart, Denice C. L., Alexander N. Ortega, David Dausey, and Robert Rosenheck. 2002. Oral health and use of dental services among Hispanics. *American Journal of Public Health* 62 (2): 84–91.

Stone, Rosalie A., Fernando Rivera, and Terceira Berdahl. 2004. Predictors of depression among non-Hispanic whites, Mexicans and Puerto Ricans: A look at race/ethnicity as a reflection of social relations. *Race and Society* 7 (2): 79–94.

Suarez, Elizabeth. 2007. *The changing face of Hispanics: Middle class and affluent.* http://www.avanzabusiness.com/ChangingFaceofHispanics.pdf.

Suarez-Orozco, Carola, and Desiree B. Qin Hillard. 2004. Immigrant boys' experiences in U.S. schools. In *Adolescent Boys: Exploring Diverse Cultures of Boyhood,* edited by Niobe Way and Judy Chu, 295–316. New York: New York University Press.

Suarez-Orozco, Carola, Irina L. G. Todorova, and Josephine Louie. 2002. Making up for lost time: The experience of separation and reunification among immigrant families. *Family Process* 41 (4): 625–43.

Suárez-Orozco, Marcelo. 2001. Globalization, immigration, and education: The research agenda. *Harvard Educational Review* 71 (3): 345–66.

Subervi-Veléz, Federico A., et al. 1994. Mass communication and Hispanics. In *Handbook of Hispanic cultures in the United States: Sociology,* edited by Felix Padilla, 304–57. Houston: Arte Publico Press.

Subervi, Federico A., Joseph Torres and Daniela Motalvo. 2005. Network Brownout 2005: The portrayal of Latinos and Latino issues in network television news, 2004, with a retrospect to 1995. National Association of Hispanic Journalists, Austin, TX, and Washington, DC.

Subramanian, S.V., Dolores Acevedo-Garcia, and Theresa L. Osypuk. 2005. Racial residential segregation and geographic heterogeneity in Black/White disparity in poor self-rated health in the US: A multilevel statistical analysis. *Social Science and Medicine* 60:1667–79.

Substance Abuse and Mental Health Services Administration (SAMHSA). 2002. *Illicit drug use among Hispanic females. The NHSDA Report.* Washington, DC: SAHSMA and Research Triangle Park, NC: RTI. http://oas.samhsa.gov/2k2/latinaDU/latinaDU.htm.

———. 2004. *Results from the 2003 National Survey on Drug Use and Health: National Findings.* Office of Applied Studies, NSDUH Series H–25, DHHS Publication No. SMA 04–3964. Rockville, MD.

Suleiman, Layla P. 2003. Beyond cultural competence: Language access and Latino civil rights. *Child Welfare* 82 (2): 185–200.

Suro, Roberto. 1998. *Strangers among us: How Latino immigration is transforming America.* New York: Knopf.

Suro, Roberto, Richard Fry, and Jeffrey Passel. 2005. *Hispanics and the 2004 elections.* Washington, DC: Pew Hispanic Center.

Suro, Roberto, and Audrey Singer. 2002. *Latino growth in metropolitan America: Changing patterns, new locations.* Brookings Institution, Survey Series; Census 2000.

Talavera, Gregory. 2002. Predictors of digital rectal examination in the US Latinos. *American Journal of Preventive Medicine* 22 (1): 36–41.

Taylor, Paul, and Richard Fry. 2007. *Hispanics and the 2008 election: A swing vote?* Washington, DC: Pew Hispanic Center.

Telles, Edward E., and Vilma Ortiz. 2008. Generations of exclusion: Mexican Americans, assimilation and race. New York: Russell Sage Foundation.

Tello, Jerry. 1998. *El hombre noble buscando balance:* The noble man searching for balance. In *Family violence and men of color: Healing the wounded male spirit,* edited by Ricardo Carillo and Jerry Tello, 35–60. New York: Springer.

Teranishi, Robert T., Walter R. Allen, and Daniel G. Solorzano. 2004. Opportunities at the crossroads: Racial inequality, school segration, and higher education in California. *Teachers College Record* 106 (11): 2224–47.

Teske, Raymond H. C., and Bardin H. Nelson. 1974. Acculturation and assimilation: A clarification. *American Ethnologist* 17:218–35.

Thomson, Gerald E., Faith Mitchell, and Monique B. Williams. 2006. *Examining the health disparities research plan of the national institutes of health: Unfinished business.* Committee on the Review and Assessment of the NIH's Strategic Research Plan and Budget to Reduce and Ultimately Eliminate Health Disparities Board on Health Sciences Policy. Washington, DC: National Academies Press.

Thornton, Arland. 2005. *Reading history sideways: The fallacy and enduring impact of the developmental paradigm on family life.* Chicago: University of Chicago Press.

Tienda, Marta, and Faith Mitchell. 2006. *Hispanics and the Future of America.* Washington, DC: National Academies Press.

Timberlake, Jeffrey M. 2007. Racial and ethnic inequality in the duration of children's exposures to neighborhood poverty and affluence. *Social Problems* 54 (3): 319–42.

Tolan, Patrick H., Deborah Gorman-Smith, and David B. Henry. 2003. The developmental ecology of urban males' youth violence. *Developmental Psychology* 39 (2): 274–91.

Toro-Morn, Maura I. 1995. Gender, class, family, and migration: Puerto Rican women in Chicago. *Gender and Society* 9 (6): 712–26.

———. 2008. Beyond gender dichotomies: Toward a new century of gendered scholarship in the Latino/a experience. In *Latinas/os in the United States: Changing the face of América,* edited by Havidán Rodríguez, Rogelio Sáenz, and Cecilia Menjívar, 277–93. New York: Springer.

Torres, Jose B. 1998. Masculinity and gender roles among Puerto Rican men: Machismo on the U.S. mainland. *American Journal of Orthopsychiatry* 68 (1): 16–26.

Trueba, Enrique (Henry) T. 1991. Linkages of macro-micro analytical levels. *Journal of Psychohistory* 18:457–68.

———. 1999. *Latinos Unidos from cultural diversity to the politics of solidarity.* Lanham, MD: Rowman and Littlefield.

———. 2002. Multiple ethnic, racial, and cultural identities in action: From marginalization to a new cultural capital in modern society. *Journal of Latinos and Education* 1 (1): 7–28.

Tschann, Jeanne M., Elena Flores, Lauri A. Pasch, and Barbara VanOss Marin. 2005. Emotional distress, alcohol use, and peer violence among Mexican-American and European-American adolescents. *Journal of Adolescent Health* 37:11–18.

Upchurch, Dawn M., Carol S. Aneshensel, Jyoti Mudgal and Clea Sucoff McNeely. 2001. Sociocultural contexts of time to first sex among Hispanic adolescents. *Journal of Marriage and Family* 63 (4): 1158–69.

Upchurch, Dawn M., Carol S. Aneshensel, Clea A. Sucoff, and Lené Levy-Storms 1999. Neighborhood and family contexts of adolescent sexual activity. *Journal of Marriage and Family* 61 (4): 920–33.

Urban Institute. 2002a. *Snapshots of America's families iii: Tracking change.* National Survey of American Families. Washington, DC: Urban Institute.

———. 2002b. *Discrimination in metropolitan housing markets: Phase 1.* Washington, DC: U.S. Department of Housing and Urban Development.

———. 2006a. *A decade of welfare reform:* Facts and figures. Assessing the New Federalism project. Washington, DC: Urban Institute.

———. 2006b. *Government work supports and low-income families: Facts and figures.* Assessing the New Federalism project. Washington, DC: Urban Institute.

U.S. Bureau of Labor Statistics. 2008. *The labor force in 2008: Race and Hispanic origin.* Washington, DC: U.S. Department of Labor.

U.S. Census Bureau. 2004a. Age by language spoken at home for the population 5 years and over, 2004. Table B16007. http://factfinder.census.gov/servlet/DTTable?_bm=y& state=dt&-context=dt&-ds_name=ACS_2004_EST_G00_&-mt_name=ACS_2004_ EST_G2000_B16007&-tree_id=304&-all_geo_types=Y&-_caller=geoselect&-geo_id= 01000US&-search_results=ALL&-format=&-_lang=en.

———. 2004b. American Community Survey, Selected Population Profiles. Table B02001. http://factfinder.census.gov/servlet/DTTable?_bm=y&-state=dt&-context=dt&-ds_ name=ACS_2004_EST_G00_&-mt_name=ACS_2004_EST_G2000_B02001&-tree_ id=304&-redoLog=true&-all_geo_types=Y&-_caller=geoselect&-geo_id=01000US& search_results=ALL&-format=&-_lang=en.

———. 2004c. Current Population Survey. *Historical Census of Housing Tables, Homeowner-ship by Race and Hispanic Origin, 2000.* Washington, DC: Ethnicity and Ancestry Statistics Branch, Population Division. http://www.census.gov/hhes/www/housing/census/his toric/ownershipbyrace.html.

———. 2004d. Current Population Survey, Annual Social and Economic Supplement, 2004. Washington, DC: Ethnicity and Ancestry Statistics Branch, Population Division. http:// www.census.gov/population/www/socdemo/foreign/ppl-176.html.

———. 2006. Current Housing Reports, Series H150/05, *American Housing Survey for the United States: 2005.* Washington, DC: U.S. Government Printing Office.

———. 2007. *The American Community—Asians: 2004.* American Community Survey Re-ports (February 2007). http://www.census.gov/prod/2007pubs/acs-05.pdf.

———. 2008. Current population reports, PPL-148; and earlier PPL and P-20 reports; and data published on the Internet. http://www.census.gov/population/www/socdemo/ school.html.

———. 2009. Hispanic Americans by the numbers. Fact sheet. Washington, DC. http:// www.infoplease.com/spot/hhmcensus1.html.

———. 2010. Race and Hispanic Origin of the Foreign-Born Population in the United States: 2007. http://www.census.gov/prod/2010pubs/acs-11.pdf.

U.S. Commission on Civil Rights. 2002. A new paradigm for welfare reform: The need for civil rights enforcement. A Statement by the U.S. Commission on Civil Rights. http:// www.usccr.gov/pubs/prwora/welfare.htm.

U.S. Department of Agriculture (USDA). 2007. *Characteristics of Food Stamp Households: Fiscal Year 2006* (Report No. FSP-07-CHAR), by Kari Wolkwitz. Project Officer, Jenny Genser. Alexandria, VA: USDA, Food and Nutrition Service. http://www.fns.usda.gov/ ora/menu/Published/snap/FILES/Participation/2006Characteristics.pdf.

U.S. Department of Commerce. 2009a. Census Bureau, Current Population Survey (CPS), October 1967 through October 2008, Washington, DC. http://nces.ed.gov/programs/ digest/d09/tables/dt09_108.asp.

U.S. Department of Commerce. 2009b. Census Bureau, *U.S. Census of Population: 1960,* vol. I, part 1; 1960 Census Monograph, *Education of the American Population,* by John K. Folger and Charles B. Nam; Current Population Reports, Series P-20, various years; and Current Population Survey (CPS), March 1970 through March 2009. http://nces. ed.gov/programs/digest/d09/tables/dt09_008.asp.

U.S. Department of Health and Human Services (USDHHS). 1996. *The personal respon-sibility and work opportunity reconciliation act of 1996.* Administration for Children and Families. Washington, DC.

———. 2000. Child abuse and sexual child abuse—substantiated fact sheet. Administration for Children & Families, Child Welfare Information Gateway. Washington, DC.

———. 2001a. *Mental health: Culture, race, ethnicity. A supplement to Mental Health: A Report of the Surgeon General.* Executive Summary. Rockville, MD: Substance Abuse and Mental Health Services Administration, Center for Mental Health Services.

———. 2001b. *Surgeon General's Report-Women and Smoking: Patterns of Tobacco Use Among Women and Girls.* Washington, DC.

———. 2006a. Temporary assistance for needy families program (TANF): Seventh annual report to congress. Administration for Children and Families, Office of Family Assistance. Washington, DC.

———. 2006b. Administration for Children & Families, Office of Family Assistance (OFA) TANF, Fact Sheet.

———. 2006c. Office of Family Assistance, Characteristics and Financial Circumstances-Fiscal Year 2006, Temporary Assistance for Needy Families-Active Cases, Percent Distribution of TANF Families by Ethnicity/ Race.

U.S. Department of Health and Human Services. 2009. Child Welfare Information Gateway. Adoption and Foster Care Analysis and Reporting System (AFCARS). http://www.childwelfare.gov/pubs/factsheets/foster.cfm.

U.S. Department of Housing and Urban Development (HUD). 1997. Office of Policy Development and Research, Special Variables Available from HUD's Database.

———. 2004. U.S. Housing Market Conditions, U.S. Department of Housing and Urban Development, February 2004.

———. 2008a. Resident Characteristics Report, All Voucher Funded Assistance, 2008.

———. 2008b. Resident Characteristics Report, Race/Ethnicity, National, Public Housing, 2008.

———. 2008c. Resident Characteristics Report, Race/Ethnicity, National, Section 8.

U.S. Department of Housing and Urban Development and U.S. Census Bureau. 2006. American Housing Survey for the United States: 2005.

U. S. Department of Justice (USDJ). 1997. *Survey of inmates in state and federal correctional facilities, 1997.* Bureau of Justice Statistics.

———. 2000. *Compendium of federal justice statistics.* Washington, DC: USDJ.

———. 2003a. *Compendium of federal justice statistics.* Washington, DC: USDJ.

———. 2003b. *Education and correctional populations.* Bureau of Justice Statistics Special Report. NCJ 195670.

———. 2004a. *Compendium of federal justice statistics.* Washington, DC: USDJ. http://bjs.ojp.usdoj.gov/content/pub/pdf/cfjs04.pdf.

———. 2004b. *Profile of jail inmates, 2002.* Bureau of Justice Statistics Special Report. NCJ 201932. http://bjs.ojp.usdoj.gov/content/pub/pdf/pji02.pdf.

———. 2006. *National youth gang survey: 1999–2001* (NCJ 209392). Washington, DC: Office of Justice Programs.

———. 2007. *Criminal offenders statistics.* Bureau of Justice Statistics.

———. 2010. *Highlights of the 2008 national youth gang survey.* Office of Juvenile Justice and Delinquency Prevention. NCJ 229249. Washington DC.

U.S. Department of Labor. 2006. *A profile of the working poor, 2004.* U.S. Bureau of Labor Statistics, report 994. http://www.bls.gov/cps/cpswp2004.pdf.

U.S. Equal Employment Opportunity Commission. 2006. *Occupational Employment in Private Industry by Race/Ethnic Group/Sex and by Industry, United States, 2006.* http://archive.eeoc.gov/stats/jobpat/2006/national.html.

United States Hispanic Leadership Institute. 1999. *The almanac of Latino politics.* Chicago, IL: United States Hispanic Leadership Institute.

U.S. Office of Management and Budget and Federal Agencies. 2003. Detailed information on the Food Stamp program assessment. Expectmore.gov, http://www.whitehouse.gov/omb/expectmore/detail/10001007.2003.html.

Vaden-Kiernan, Nancy, and John McManus. 2005. *Parent and family involvement in education: 2002–03* (NCES 2005-043). Washington, DC: National Center for Education Statistics, U.S. Department of Education.

Valenzuela, Angela. 1999. *Subtractive schooling: U.S. Mexican youth and the politics of caring.* New York: State University of New York.

Valle, Victor M., and Torres, Rodolfo D. 2000. *Latino metropolis.* Minneapolis: University of Minnesota Press.

VandenBos, Gary R. 2007. *APA dictionary of psychology.* Washington, DC: American Psychological Association.

van Ryn, Michelle. 2002. Research on the provider contribution to race/ethnicity disparities in medical care. *Medical Care* 40 (1): 140–51.

Van Velsor, Patricia, and Graciela Orozco. 2007. Involving low-income parents in the schools: Communitycentric stategies for school counselors. *Professional School Counseling* 11 (1): 17–24.

Vásquez, Manuel A., Chad E. Seales, and Marie Friedmann Marquardt. 2008. New Latino destinations. In *Latinas/os in the United States: Changing the face of America,* edited by Havidán Rodriguez, Rogelio Sáenz, and Cecilia Menjívar, 19–36. New York: Springer.

Vega, William A. 1995. The study of Latino families: A point of departure. In *Understanding Latino families,* edited by Ruth E. Zambrana, 3–17. Thousand Oaks, CA: Sage.

Vega, William, and Margarita Alegría. 2001. Latino mental health and treatment in the United States. In *Health Issues in the Latino Community.* San Francisco: Jossey-Bass.

Vega, William, Michael A. Rodriguez, and Alfonso Ang. 2010. Addressing stigma of depression in Latino primary care patients. *General Hospital Psychiatry* 32 (2): 182–91.

Vélez, William. 2008. The educational experiences of Latinos in the United States. In *Latinas/os in the United States: Changing the face of America,* edited by Havidán Rodriguez, Rogelio Sáenz, and Cecilia Menjívar, 129–49. New York: Springer.

Ventura, Stephanie, Joyce A. Martin, Sally Curtin, Fay Menacker, and Brady E. Hamilton. 2001. Births: Final data for 1999. *National Vital Statistics Reports* 49 (1). Hyattsville, MD: National Center for Health Statistics.

Ventura, Stephanie J., and Selma M. Taffel. 1985. Childbearing characteristics of U.S. and foreign-born Hispanic mothers. *Public Health Reports* 100 (6): 647–52.

Vermeire, Etienne, Hilary Hearnshaw, Paul Van Royen, and Joke Denekens. 2001. Patient adherence to treatment: Three decades of research. A comprehensive review. *Journal of Clinical Pharmacy and Therapeutics* 26 (5): 331.

Vigil, James D. 1988. *Barrio gangs: Street life and identity in southern California.* Austin: University of Texas Press.

Vigil Laden, Berta. 2001. Hispanic-Serving institutions: Myths and realities. *Peabody Journal of Education* 76 (1): 73–92.

Villanueva, Margaret A. 2002. Racialization and the Latina experience: Economic implications. *Feminist Economics* 8 (2): 145–61.

Villarruel, Francisco A., and Nancy E. Walker. 2002. *?Donde esta la justicia? A call to action on behalf of Latino and Latina youth in the U.S. justice system.* Building Blocks for Youth. Michigan State University: Institute for Children, Youth and Families.

Viruell-Fuentes, Edna A. 2007. Beyond acculturation: Immigration, discrimination, and health research among Mexicans in the United States. *Social Science and Medicine* 65:1524–35.

Waldinger, Roger. 2007. *Between here and there: How attached are Latino immigrants to their native country?* Washington, DC: Pew Hispanic Center.

Wang, Youfa, and Zang, Qi. 2006. Are American children and adolescents of low socioeconomic status at increased risk of obesity? Changes in the association between overweight and family income between 1971 and 2002. *American Journal of Clinical Nutrition* 84:707–16.

Wasserman, Melanie, Deborah Bender, and Shoou-Yih Daniel Lee. 2007. Use of preventive maternal and child health services by Latina women: A review of published intervention studies. *Medical Care Research and Review* 64 (4): 4–45.

Watkins-Hayes, Celeste. 2009. *The new welfare bureaucrat: Entanglements of race, class, and policy reform.* Chicago: University of Chicago Press.

Way, Niobe. 2004. Intimacy, desire, and distrust in the friendships of adolescent boys. In *Adolescent boys: Exploring diverse cultures of boyhood,* edited by Niobe Way and Judy Chu, 167–96. New York: New York University Press.

Weaver, Charles N. 2005. The changing image of Hispanic Americans. *Hispanic Journal of Behavioral Sciences* 27:337–54.

Weaver, Shannon E., Adriana Umana-Taylor, Jason D. Hans, and Sarah C. Malia. 2001. Challenges family scholars may face in studying family diversity. *Journal of Family Issues* 22 (7): 922–39.

Weber, Lynn. 2010. *Understanding race, class, gender and sexuality.* 2nd ed. Boston: McGraw Hill.

Weinick, Robin M., Elizabeth A. Jacobs, Lisa C. Stone, et al. 2004. Hispanic healthcare disparities: Challenging the myth of a monolithic Hispanic population. *Medical Care* 42 (4): 313–20.

Weir, Lori A., Debra Etelson, and Donald A. Brand. 2006. Parents' perceptions of neighborhood safety and children's physical activity. *Preventive Medicine* 43:212–17.

Weis, Lois, Craig Centrie, Juan Valentin-Juarbe, and Michelle Fine. 2002. Puerto Rican men and the struggle for place in the United States: An exploration of cultural citizenship, gender, and violence. *Men and Masculinities* 4 (3): 286–302.

Welch, Michael, Eric Price, and Nana Yankey. 2004. Youth violence and race in the media: The emergence of "wilding" as an invention of the press. *Race, Gender and Class* 11 (2): 36–58.

Wheary, Jennifer. 2006. *The future middle class: African Americans, Latinos and economic opportunity in the 21st century.* New York: Demos.

White House Initiative for Hispanic Educational Excellence (WHIHEE). 2003. President's advisory commission on educational excellence for Hispanic Americans. *From risk to opportunity: Fulfilling the educational needs of Hispanic Americans in the 21st century.* Washington, DC. http://www.yic.gov/paceea/finalreport.pdf.

Wight, Vanessa R., and Michelle Chau. 2009. *Basic facts about low-income children.* New York: National Center for Children in Poverty, Mailman School of Public Health.

Williams, David R. 1990. Socioeconomic differentials in health: A review and redirection. *Social Psychology Quarterly* 53 (2): 81–99.

Williams, David R., and Chiquita Collins. 1995. U.S. socioeconomic and racial differences in health: Patterns and explanations. *Annual Review of Sociology* 21:349–86.

Wingo, Phyllis A., Lynn A. Ries, Sherry L. Parker, and Clark W. Heath. 1998. Long-term cancer patient survival in the United States. *Cancer Epidemiology, Biomarkers and Prevention* 7 (4): 271–82.

Winthrop, Robert H. 1991. *Dictionary of concepts in cultural anthropology.* New York: Greenwood Press.

Wissow, Lawrence A., Debra Roter, Susan M. Larson, et al. 2003. Longitudinal care lessens differences in mothers' psychosocial talk to pediatricians attributable to ethnic and gender discordance. *Archives of Pediatrics and Adolescent Medicine* 157 (5): 419–24.

Wood, Daniel B. 2001. Latinos redefine what it means to be "manly." *Christian Science Monitor,* July 16.

Wordes, Madeline, and Sharon Jones. 1998. Trends in juvenile detention and steps toward reform. *Crime and Delinquency* 44 (4): 544–60.

Wyn, Roberta, Victoria Ojeda, Usha Ranji, and Alina Salganicoff. 2004. *Racial and ethnic disparities in women's health coverage and access to care: Findings from the 2001 Kaiser Women's Health Survey.* Menlo Park, CA: Kaiser Family Foundation.

Yarbro-Bejarano, Yvonne. 1999. Sexuality and Chicana/o studies: Toward a theoretical paradigm for the twenty-first century. *Cultural Studies* 13 (2): 335–45.

Ybarra, Lea. 1982. When wives work: The impact on the Chicano family. *Journal of the Marriage of the Family* 44 (1): 169–78.

Yin Daixin, Cyllene Morris, Mark Allen, Rosemary Cress, Janet Bates, and Lihua Liu. 2010. Does socioeconomic disparity in cancer incidence vary across racial/ethnic groups? *Cancer Causes Control* 21:1721–30.

Yosso, Tara, William Smith, Miguel Ceja, and Daniel Solórzano. 2009. Critical race theory, racial microaggressions, and campus racial climate for Latina/o undergraduates. In *Consejos: The undergraduate experiences of Latina/o students,* a special issue of the *Harvard Educational Review* 79 (4): 659–91.

Young, Terry, Paul E. Peppard, and Daniel J. Gottlieb. 2002. Epidemiology of obstructive sleep apnea: A population health perspective. *American Journal of Respiratory and Critical Care Medicine* 171 (66): 122–49.

Zalaquett, Carlos P. 2006. Study of successful Hispanic/Latino students. *Journal of Hispanic Higher Education* 5 (1): 35–47.

Zamboanga, Byron. 2005. Alcohol expectancies and drinking behaviors in Mexican American college students. *Addictive Behaviors* 30 (4): 673–84.

Zambrana, Ruth E. 1987. Toward understanding the educational trajectory and socialization of Latina women. In *The Broken web: The educational experience of Hispanic American women,* edited by Teresa McKenna and Flora Ida Ortiz, 61–77. Encino, CA: Tomás Rivera Center and Berkeley, CA: Floricanto Press.

Zambrana Ruth E., Carma Ayala, Olivia Carter-Pokras, Jasmin Minaya, and George A Mensah. 2007. Hypertension-related mortality among non-Hispanic white women and selected Hispanic subgroups of women aged 45 years and older—United States, 1995–1996 and 2001–2002. *Ethnicity and Disease* 17 (3): 434–40.

Zambrana, Ruth E., and Doris Capello. 2003. Promoting Latino child and family welfare: Strategies for strengthening the child welfare system. *Children and Youth Services Review* 25 (10): 755–80.

Zambrana, Ruth E., and Olivia Carter-Pokras. 2001. Health data issues for Hispanics: Implications for public health research. *Journal of Health Care for the Poor and Underserved* 12 (1): 20–34.

——. 2004a. Improving health insurance coverage for Latino children: A review of barriers, challenges, and state strategies. *Journal of the National Medical Association* 96 (4): 508–22.

——. 2004b. Latino health and behavior. In *Encyclopedia of Health and Behavior,* edited by Norman B. Anderson, 575–83. Thousand Oaks, CA: Sage.

——. 2010. Acculturation research in advancing science and practice in reducing health care disparities among Latina/os. *American Journal of Public Health* 100 (1): 18–23.

Zambrana, Ruth E., Llewellyn Cornelius, Stephanie Boykin, and Debbie Lopez Salas. 2004. Latinas and HIV/AIDS risk factors: Implications for harm reduction strategies. *American Journal of Public Health* 94 (7): 1152–58.

Zambrana, Ruth E., and Bonnie T. Dill. 2006. Disparities in Latina health: An intersectional analyses. In *Race, class, gender and health,* edited by Amy Schultz and Leith Mullings, 192–227. San Francisco: Jossey-Bass.

——. 2009. Conclusion: Future directions in knowledge building and sustaining institutional change. In *Emerging intersections, race, class and gender in theory, policy and practice,* edited by Bonnie Thornton Dill and Ruth E. Zambrana, 274–90. New Brunswick, NJ: Rutgers University Press.

Zambrana, Ruth E., Claudia Dorrington, and Sally Alonzo Bell. 1997. Mexican American women in higher education: A comparative study. *Race, Gender and Class* 4 (2): 127–49.

Zambrana, Ruth E., and Claudia Dorrington. 1998. Economic and social vulnerability of Latino children and families by subgroup: Implications for child welfare. *Child Welfare 77* (1): 5–27.

Zambrana, Ruth E., Kathleen Ell, Claudia Dorrington, Laura Wachsman, and Dee Hodge. 1994. The relationship between psychosocial status of immigrant Latino mothers and use of pediatric emergency services. *Health and Social Work* 19 (93): 93–102.

Zambrana, Ruth E., and Laura A. Logie. 2000. Latino child health: Need for inclusion in the U.S. national discourse. *American Journal of Public Health* 90 (12): 1827–33.

Zambrana, Ruth E., Nancy Breen, Sarah A. Fox, and Mary Lou Gutierrez-Mohamed, Mary Lou. 1999. Use of cancer screening practices by Hispanic women: Analyses by subgroup. *Preventive Medicine* 29:466–77.

Zambrana, Ruth E., and Victoria-Maria MacDonald. 2009. Staggered inequalities in access to higher education by gender, race, and ethnicity. In *Emerging intersections: Race, class, and gender in theory, policy and practice*, edited by Bonnie Thornton Dill and Ruth E. Zambrana, 73–101. New Brunswick, NJ: Rutgers University Press.

Zambrana, Ruth E., Wendy Mogel, and Susan C. M. Scrimshaw. 1987. Gender and level of training differences in obstetricians' attitudes toward patients in childbirth. *Women and Health* 12 (1): 5–24.

Zambrana, Ruth E., and Tamyka Morant. 2009. Latino immigrant children and inequality in access to early schooling programs. *Zero to Three* 29 (5): 46–53.

Zambrana, Ruth E., and Victor Silva-Palacios. 1989. Gender differences in stress among Mexican immigrant adolescents in Los Angeles, California. *Journal of Adolescent Research* 4 (4): 426–42.

Zambrana, Ruth E., and Irene M. Zoppi. 2002. Latina students: Translating cultural wealth into a social capital to improve academic success. *Social Work with Multicultural Youth* 11 (1/2): 33–53.

Zayas, Luis H., Rebecca J. Lester, Leopoldo J. Cabassa, and Lisa R. Fortuna. 2005. Why do so many Latina teens attempt suicide? A conceptual model for research. *American Journal of Orthopsychiatry* 75 (2): 275–87.

Zea, María C., Carol A. Reisen, and Rafael M. Díaz. 2003. Methodological issues in research on sexual behavior with Latino gay and bisexual men. *American Journal of Community Psychology* 31:281–91.

Zedlewski, Sheila R. 2003. Work and barriers to work among welfare recipients in 2002. *Snapshots of America's families III,* no. 3. Washington, DC: Urban Institute.

Zedlewski, Sheila R., and J. Holland. 2003. Work activities of current welfare recipients. *Snapshots of America's families III,* no. 4. Washington, DC: Urban Institute.

Zhu, Xuemei, and Chanam Lee. 2008. Walkability and safety around elementary schools economic and ethnic disparities. *American Journal of Preventive Medicine* 34:282–90.

Zuberi, Tukufu. 2001. *Thicker than blood: How racial statistics lie.* Minneapolis: University of Minnesota Press.

Zuberi, Tukufu, and Eduardo Bonilla-Silva. 2008. *White logic, white methods: Racism and methodology.* Lanham, MD: Rowman and Littlefield.

Zuñiga de Nuncio, María Luisa, M. H. Nader, M. Sawyer, et al. 2003. A prenatal intervention study to improve timeliness of immunization initiation in Latino infants. *Journal of Community Health* 28 (2): 151–65.

# Index

Note: Page numbers in *italics* indicate figures; those with a *t* indicate tables.